PSYCHOLOGY
of SUCCESS

Finding Meaning in Work and Life

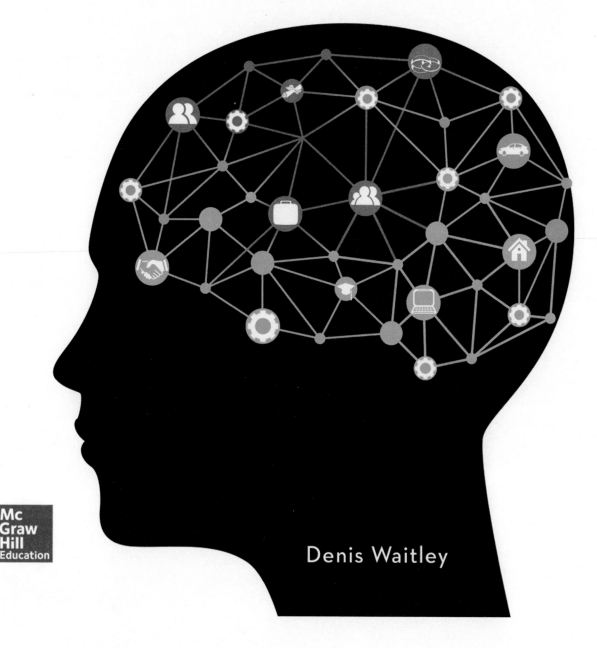

McGraw Hill Education

Denis Waitley

Psychology *of* Success

Psychology *of* Success

Finding Meaning in Work and Life

sixth edition

Denis Waitley, Ph.D.

Mc
Graw
Hill
Education

PSYCHOLOGY OF SUCCESS: FINDING MEANING IN WORK AND LIFE, SIXTH EDITION

Published by McGraw-Hill Education, 2 Penn Plaza, New York, NY 10121. Copyright © 2016 by McGraw-Hill Education. All rights reserved. Printed in the United States of America. Previous editions © 2010, 1990, and 1993. No part of this publication may be reproduced or distributed in any form or by any means, or stored in a database or retrieval system, without the prior written consent of McGraw-Hill Education, including, but not limited to, in any network or other electronic storage or transmission, or broadcast for distance learning.

Some ancillaries, including electronic and print components, may not be available to customers outside the United States.

This book is printed on acid-free paper.

1 2 3 4 5 6 7 8 9 0 RMN/RMN 1 0 9 8 7 6 5

ISBN 978-0-07-783633-7
MHID 0-07-783633-2

Senior Vice President, Products & Markets: *Kurt L. Strand*
Vice President, General Manager, Products & Markets: *Michael Ryan*
Vice President, Content Design & Delivery: *Kimberly Meriwether David*
Brand Manager: *Scott Davidson*
Product Developer: *Alaina Tucker*
Executive Marketing Manager: *Keari Green*
Marketing Specialist: *Lindsay Pawlik*
Director, Content Design & Delivery: *Terri Schiesl*
Content Production Manager: *Faye Schilling*
Content Project Managers: *Mary Jane Lampe, Judi David*
Buyer: *Jennifer Pickel*
Cover Designer: *Tara McDermott*
Content Licensing Specialists: *John Leland, Ann Marie Jannette*
Compositor: *Laserwords Private Limited*
Typeface: *12/15 TimesLTStd*
Printer: *R. R. Donnelley*

All credits appearing on page or at the end of the book are considered to be an extension of the copyright page.

www.mhhe.com

Brief Contents

About the Author

Denis Waitley is a world-renowned expert and motivational speaker on human performance and potential. Best known as the author/narrator of *The Psychology of Winning,* he has helped millions of people throughout the world in their quest for personal excellence. He is the author of several best-selling books, including *Seeds of Greatness, The Winner's Edge, Being the Best,* and *Empires of the Mind.* His newest book, *The Dragon and The Eagle,* compares the challenges facing both China and America in education and business as they attempt to survive and thrive together in a rapidly changing world.

Long recognized as an authority on high-level achievement, Dr. Waitley has counseled leaders in every field, from CEOs to Super Bowl champions. He has lent his understanding and expertise to American astronauts and POWs. Dr. Waitley has also served as Chairman of Psychology on the U.S. Olympic Committee's Sports Medicine Council, dedicated to the performance enhancement of Olympic athletes.

One of the country's most sought-after speakers, Denis Waitley was named Outstanding Platform Speaker of the Year by his peers and elected to the International Speakers' Hall of Fame. He is a graduate of the U.S. Naval Academy at Annapolis and holds a doctorate in human behavior. Dr. Waitley was a founding director of the National Association for Self-Esteem and has been a consultant to the President's Council on Vocational Education and the International Parenting Association.

Contents

CHAPTER 5   Positive Thinking   178

CHAPTER 6   Self-Discipline   220

CHAPTER 7   Self-Motivation   268

FIGURES Table of Figures

Introduction

Preface

Welcome to *Psychology of Success*. Success is a lifetime of personal fulfillment that comes from creating a sense of meaning in all aspects of life. To succeed in this way, students must take an active role in discovering and pursuing their personal definition of success, and use the psychological and fundamental strategies in this course to achieve their goals. This book introduces you to the fundamental psychological principles of success—principles applicable to everyone regardless of age, background, or specialty.

Unlike many psychology books, *Psychology of Success* doesn't take a one-size-fits-all approach. Instead, it asks you to take an active role in defining what is right for you as an individual. *Psychology of Success* calls on you to use self-awareness and critical thinking strategies to examine your dreams, values, interests, skills, needs, identity, self-esteem, and relationships. This will help you set and achieve goals that are in harmony with your personal vision of success.

Psychology of Success presents the principles of success in a logical order. First you will assess who you are and what special qualities you possess, which will help you develop self-awareness and clarify your goals. Next you will learn about the importance of self-esteem and positive thinking to a satisfying life. You'll also learn about self-discipline and self-motivation, which are the tools you'll need to keep yourself on track toward your goals. Once you have mastered these psychological tools, you'll learn the fundamentals of time and money management, communication, and positive relationships.

Because each chapter refers to concepts introduced in previous chapters, you'll derive maximum benefit from working through the book chapter by chapter. If your time is limited, however, you may choose to concentrate on the topics of greatest interest to you.

Features

The features of *Psychology of Success* are designed to help you understand and remember the psychological principles introduced in each chapter. They are also intended to provoke thought and discussion and to help you make the material relevant to your life.

Real-Life Success Story   Begin each chapter by reading the Real-Life Success Story, a vignette about an ordinary person struggling with the problems and challenges addressed in the chapter. Use the question following the story to put yourself in that person's shoes and take stock of what you already know about the topic of the coming chapter. At the end of the chapter, revisit the Real-Life Success Story and use the concepts you've learned to create a successful resolution to the character's situation.

Chapter Introduction and Learning Objectives   In each chapter, a short introduction previews the major topics that will be covered, and a list of objectives lays out the skills and information you can expect to have mastered after reading the text and completing the activities.

Opening Quote   The opening quote relates to the ideas discussed in the chapter and serves as food for thought. Take a moment to think about what the author of the quote is trying to say. Do you agree with the author? Why or why not?

Key Terms   Key terms appear in bold in the text and are defined in the margin for easy review. Key terms, along with italicized terms, are also defined in the Glossary.

Success Secret   Important lessons presented in the chapter are summarized in the Success Secret feature. These notes can be used to preview and review the chapter, as well as to remind yourself to apply these important principles of success in your daily life.

Applying Psychology

This feature focuses on thought-provoking issues such as culture and body image, impulse control, and the psychology of aging. It links one or more topics in the chapter to cutting-edge issues in psychology.

Professional Development

The Professional Development feature makes chapter concepts relevant to the world of work, providing information on topics such as job stress, problem solving, and résumé writing.

Internet Action

This technology feature discusses how to use computers, the Internet, and e-mail efficiently and effectively. It also illustrates the link between technology and psychology in areas such as artificial intelligence and online collaborative learning.

Activities

Each chapter has numerous activities that form an integral part of the material. The activities allow you to apply newly learned concepts to your own life through self-assessment, real-world observation, and critical thinking.

Personal Journals

Each chapter also has several Personal Journals, short notebook-style activities that let you pause to offer personal reflections on the material.

McGraw-Hill Connect®

Connect offers a number of powerful tools and features to make managing assignments easier, so faculty can spend more time teaching. With Connect, students can engage with their coursework anytime and anywhere, making the learning process more accessible and efficient. From Connect, instructors can also access chapter-by-chapter notes, test bank questions, a PowerPoint presentation, and additional resources. Student features include practice quizzes, assessment activities, links to related materials for research projects and helpful online tools, job hunting resources, and much more. References to specific Web site materials are provided throughout the text.

LearnSmart

Students want to make the best use of their study time. The LearnSmart adaptive self-study technology within Connect® provides students with a seamless combination of practice, assessment, and the remediation for every concept in the textbook. LearnSmart's intelligent software adapts to every student response and automatically delivers concepts that advance the student's understanding while reducing time devoted to the concepts already mastered. The result for every student is the fastest path of mastery of chapter concepts. LearnSmart:

- Adapts automatically to each student, so students spend less time on the topics they understand and practice more those they have yet to master.

- Provides continual reinforcement and remediation, but gives only as much guidance as students need.

- Integrates diagnostics as part of the learning experience.

Enables you to assess which concepts students have efficiently learned on their own, thus freeing class time for more applications and discussions.

Getting Started

Psychology of Success is a workbook as well as a textbook. Take notes, highlight important concepts, and flag passages that you want to explore further. Take time to do each Activity and Personal Journal thoroughly before moving on to the next—they will help you understand the material on a personal level. Don't worry, however, about finding the "right" answers—the only right answers are ones that are honest, true to yourself, and supported by reflection and critical thinking. When you complete *Psychology of Success,* you will have a valuable record of your goals and where you want the future to take you.

What's New

Chapter One—Psychology and Success

- Updated material on defining success
- NEW Professional Development Feature—Internal Career Motivation
- Updated material on Sense of Self
- NEW material on Individual Identity
- Updated material on Gender Roles
- NEW Internet Activities

Chapter Two—Self-Awareness

- NEW section on Natural Abilities
- Updated Professional Development Feature—Career Fulfillment
- NEW Internet Activity

Chapter Three—Goals and Obstacles

- NEW material on Goal Setting
- NEW material on Positive Self-Talk
- Updated material on digitizing goals
- NEW Applying Psychology Feature—Technology and Stress
- Updated Professional Development Feature—Job Stress
- NEW Internet Activity

Chapter Four—Self-Esteem

- NEW material on the Origins of Self-Esteem
- NEW material on Self-Expectancy
- NEW Professional Development Feature—Positive Image at Work
- NEW Internet Activities

Chapter Five—Positive Thinking

- NEW material on Why Positive Thinking Matters
- NEW section on Failure Avoidance
- NEW section on Learned Helplessness
- Updated material on Adopting Positive Habits
- NEW Professional Development Feature—Positive Thinking in Action at Work
- NEW Internet Action Feature—Building and Tracking Your Optimum Health Plan
- NEW Application Exercises
- NEW Internet Activity

Chapter Six—Self-Discipline

- NEW material on The Power of Persistence
- NEW material on Personal Control
- Updated Applying Psychology Feature
- NEW Internet Action Feature—Artificial Intelligence versus Human Intelligence
- Updated Professional Development Feature—Wanted: Problem Solvers
- NEW Application Activity
- NEW Internet Activities

Chapter Seven—Self-Motivation

- NEW Internet Action Feature—Staying Motivated with eLearning
- NEW Applying Psychology Feature—Six Types of Achievement Motivation

- Updated material on The Importance of Desire
- NEW Professional Development Feature— What Motivates Employees?
- Updated material on Rethinking Failure
- NEW Critical Thinking Activities
- NEW Application Activities
- NEW Internet Activities

Chapter Eight—Managing Your Resources

- NEW material on Taking Control of Your Time
- Updated Internet Action Feature—E-mail Efficiency and Effectiveness
- NEW Professional Development Feature— Investing in Your Future
- NEW Applying Psychology Feature—The "Mind" of Spending or Saving

- Updated Critical Thinking Activity
- NEW Application Activities
- NEW Internet Activities

Chapter Nine—Communication and Relationships

- Updated communications to reflect new digital landscape
- NEW Applying Psychology Feature— Emotional Intelligence
- NEW section on Listening and Leadership
- NEW Professional Development Feature— Your Cover Letter
- NEW Internet Action Feature—Managing Your Online Identity
- NEW Critical Thinking Activities
- NEW Application Activity
- NEW Internet Activities

Acknowledgment

McGraw-Hill would like to offer our sincerest gratitude and deepest appreciation to our valuable reviews whose feedback was instrumental in successfully compiling this text. We could not have done this without you! Thank you!

Jodie Peeler	Newberry College	jodie.peeler@newberry.edu
Michelle Conklin	El Paso Community College	mconkli1@epcc.edu
Mercedes Clay	Defiance College	mclay@defiance.edu
Elisabet Vizoso	Miami Dade College	evizoso@mdc.edu
Maleeka T. Love	Western Michigan University	maleeka.love@wmich.edu
Kristina Ehnert	Central Lakes College, Brainerd, MN	kehnert@clcmn.edu
Candace Weddle	Anderson University	cweddle@andersonuniversity.edu
Gina Floyd	Shorter University	gfloyd@shorter.edu
Susan Loughran	St. Edward's University	susanl@stedwards.edu
Laura Skinner	Wayne Community College	lsskinner@waynecc.edu
Jane Shipp	Tennessee College of Applied Technology Hartsville	jane.shipp@tcathartsville.edu
Amanda Mosley	York Technical College	amosley@yorktech.edu
Jean A. Wisuri	Cincinnati State Technical and Community College	jean.wisuri@cincinnatistate.edu
Terri Fields	Lake Land College	tfields@lakelandcollege.edu
Carol Scott	Texas Tech University	carol.scott@ttu.edu
Kim Long	Valencia College	klong@valenciacollege.edu
Dian Stair	Ivy Tech Community College	dstair@ivytech.edu
Dr. Brenda Tuberville	Rogers State University	btuberville@rsu.edu
Miriam Chirico	Eastern Connecticut State University	chiricom@easternct.edu
Carra Miskovich	RCC	cmmiskovich@randolph.edu
Sandy Lory-Snyder	Farmingdale State College	snydersb@farmingdale.edu
Eden Pearson	Des Moines Area Community College	efpearson@dmacc.edu
Gretchen Starks-Martin	College of St. Benedict/St. John's University	gmartin@csbsju.edu
Michael Kkuryla	Sunybroome Community College, (broome community college-suny)	kuryla_m@sunybroome.edu
Kimberly Schweiker	Lewis and Clark Community College	kschweiker@lc.edu
Lenice Abbott	Waubonsee Community College	labbott@waubonsee.edu
Linda Gannon	College of Southern Nevada	linda.gannon@csn.edu
Jennifer Scalzi-Pesola	American River College	scalzij@arc.losrios.edu
Donna Wood	Holmes Community College	dwood@holmescc.edu
Joseph Goss	Valparaiso University	joseph.goss@valpo.edu
DJ Mitten	Richard Bland College	dmitten@rbc.edu

Micki Nickla	Ivy Tech Community College	mnickla@ivytech.edu
Jon Arriola	Tyler Junior College	jarr5@tjc.edu
Julie Jack	Tennessee Wesleyan College	jjack@twcnet.edu
Ginny Davis	Tulsa Community College	ginny.davis@tulsacc.edu
Keith Klein	Ivy Tech - Bloomington, Indiana	kklein@ivytech.edu
Kathryn DiCorcia	Marist College	Kathryn.DiCorcia@Marist.edu
Ruth Williams	Southern Technical College	rwilliams@southerntech.edu
Stephen Coates-White	South Seattle College	stephen.coates-white@seattlecolleges.edu
Susan Silva	El Paso Community College	ssilva10@epcc.edu
Russell Kellogg	University of Colorado, Denver	russell.kellogg@ucdenver.edu
Valarie Robinson	University of North Florida	vrobinso@unf.edu
Vickie Brown	Daytona State College	brownv@daytonastate.edu
Linda Girouard	Brescia University	linda.girouard@brescia.edu
Dixie Elise Hickman	American InterContinental University, Atlanta	dhickman@aiuniv.edu
Paige Gordier	Lake Superior State University	pgordier@lssu.edu
Amy Oatis	University of the Ozarks	aoatis@ozarks.edu
Misty Joiner	Bainbridge State College	misty.joiner@bainbridge.edu
Frank Sladek	Kirkwood Community School	fsladek@kirkwood.edu
Barbara Putman	Southwestern Community College	bputman@southwesterncc.edu
Donna Musselman	Santa Fe College	Donna.musselman@sfcollege.edu
Faye Hamrac	Reid State Technical College	fhamrac@rstc.edu
M. Sheileen Godwin	King's College, Wilkes-Barre, PA	sheileengodwin@kings.edu
Anastasia Bollinger	GMC	abollinger@gmc.cc.ga.us
Kerry Fitts	Delgado Community College	kfitts@dcc.edu
Dennis Watts	Robeson Community College–Lumberton NC	dwatts@robeson.edu
Cindy Burgess	Dickinson State University	cindy.burgess@dickinsonstate.edu
Stephanie Foote	Kennesaw State University	sfoote@kennesaw.edu
Michelle Detering	Lansing Community College	Deteringm@gmail.com
Kevin Ploeger	University of Cincinnati	kevin.ploeger@uc.edu
Judi Walgenbach	Amundsen Educational Center	judi@aecak.org
D Mills	Salt Lake Community College	dmills5@brunmail.slcc.edu
Ruth Williams	Southern Technical College	rwilliams@southerntech.edu

Barbara Sherry	Northeastern Illinois University	B-Sherry@neiu.edu
Christi Boren	San Jacinto College	christi.boren@sjcd.edu
Nicki Michalski	Lamar University	nicki.michalski@lamar.edu
Pamela Moss	Midwestern State University	pam.moss@mwsu.edu
Walter Huber	Muskingum University	whuber@muskingum.edu
Pamela Bilton Beard	Houston Community College–Southwest	pamela.biltonbeard@hccs.edu
Laura Jean Bhadra	Northern Virginia Community College–Manassas	Lbhadra@nvcc.edu
Bonnie Kaczmarek	MSTC	bonnie.kaczmarek@mstc.edu
Jessica Hasson	CSUCI	jessica.hasson@csuci.edu
Julieta Garcia	MDC	Jgarci29@mdc.edu
Joan M. Valichnac	Northland Pioneer College	jvalichnac@npc.edu
Kitty Spires	Midlands Technical College	spiresk@midlandstech.edu
Catherine Griffith	Argosy University	thegriffithsok@aol.com
Keith Ramsdell	Lourdes University	keith.ramsdell@lourdes.edu
Juli Soden	El Camino College	jsoden@elcamino.edu
Elisa Velasquez	Sonoma State University	elisa.velasquez@sonoma.edu
Toni Woolfork-Barnes	Western Michigan University	toni.woolfork-barnes@wmich.edu
Katy Luallen	Butte College	Katyal74@yahoo.com
Paulette Clapp	Public	pegc133@yahoo.com
Cy Samuels	Palm Beach State College	samuelss@palmbeachstate.edu
Mark A. Dowell	Randolph Community College	madowell@randolph.edu
Kim Jameson	Oklahoma City Community College	kjameson@occc.edu
Gail Malone	South Plains College	gmalone@southplainscollege.edu
Patricia Riely	Moberly Area Community College	patricit@macc.edu
Cari Kenner	St. Cloud State University	cmkenner@stcloudstate.edu
Todd Butler	Jackson College	butlertodda@jccmi.edu
Sterling Wall	UWSP	swall@uwsp.edu
Valamere Mikler	University of Phoenix	vmikler@email.phoenix.edu
Valamere Mikler	Miami Dade College–Kendall Campus	vmikler@hotmail.com
Gretchen Wrobel	Bethel University	g-wrobel@bethel.edu
Darla Rocha	San Jacinto College	darla.rocha@sjcd.edu

LuAnn Walton	San Juan College	waltonl@sanjuancollege.edu
Gary R. Lewis	Southern Technical College Fort Myers	glewis@southerntech.edu
Deana Guido	Nash Community College	dguido@nashcc.edu
Christopher Lau	Hutchinson Community College	LauC@hutchcc.edu
Deborah Kindy	Sonoma State University	deb.kindy@sonoma.edu

"Am I Doing the Right Thing?"

Looking Ahead

Bill Santos, a freelance film production assistant in Los Angeles, was offered a full-time job as an assistant producer. Everyone congratulated him on the salary raise and more impressive title. Bill, however, wasn't completely happy about the prospect of the new job. The promotion would mean longer hours and more responsibility. Plus, now that he thought of it, he didn't even like the shows he had helped make. Why was he doing this?

Looking Within

Bill's dream had been to write for a living. Being a production assistant wasn't his dream job, but he

was good at it, and there were a lot of extra benefits. Recently, Bill had started writing for a start-up magazine. Although the pay was low, it reminded him why he had wanted to be a writer in the first place. If he took the new job he wouldn't be able to spend time writing. Bill knew it would be sensible to take the job, but he couldn't get enthusiastic about it.

What Do You Think? Do you think Bill would be more successful if he took the production job or if he spent more time writing? Why?

Psychology and Success

> " What lies behind us and what lies before us are small matters compared to what lies within us. "
>
> Ralph Waldo Emerson, Philosopher

introduction

The first step on the road to success is to define what success means to you. In Section 1.1 you'll clarify your vision of success and begin to think about how you can make it a reality. You'll also consider the personal qualities that will help you reach success and discover how studying psychology can help you understand yourself and your world. In Section 1.2 you'll begin thinking about your identity and self-image. You'll consider how you see yourself and what it means to be you.

learning objectives

After you complete this chapter, you should be able to:

- Define success.

- List several personal qualities that help people to be happy.

- Define psychology and cite its four major goals.

- Explain the relationship between thoughts, feelings, and actions.

- Define self, self-image, and identity.

- Describe the components of identity.

WHAT IS SUCCESS?

Success has a personal definition for each of us. About 95 percent of the human beings on earth are poor; the majority of them desperately poor.

Success to any member of such a family is to have some land to till, any job that pays, and a way to earn enough to provide nourishment for the children to grow in decent health into adulthood.

Success in our culture and in many of the industrialized nations is usually associated with material wealth and fame. The images of lifestyles of the rich and famous bombard our senses and we are seduced into equating skin-deep values with authentic fulfillment. A more meaningful definition of success was penned by Earl Nightingale—a 20th-century philosopher—in his classic audio recording *The Strangest Secret:* "Success is the progressive realization of a worthy ideal." It means that when we are working or moving toward something we want to accomplish, especially when that something brings us respect and dignity as members of the human race, we are succeeding. It has nothing to do with talent, IQ, age, gender, ethnicity, or birthright. It does not mean being a celebrity, icon, or tycoon.

So what is success? In this book, **success** means a lifetime of personal fulfillment. Personal fulfillment comes from creating a sense of meaning in your work and life. This kind of success is not given by anyone else and cannot be taken away by anyone else. It requires taking risks, overcoming challenges, and using your best resource—you—to its fullest potential.

Success is a journey, not a destination. Success is a process, not a status. You don't arrive at success. You engage in living successfully on a daily basis. It involves looking inward, considering what you value, and navigating the life path that is most meaningful for you. Begin to think about what success means to you in **Activity 1.** As you work through this text, you may wish to return to this exercise to clarify your vision of success.

Ingredients of Success

Lifelong success has several important ingredients, all of which you will learn about in this book. These ingredients, shown in Personal Journal 1.1 on page 9, are positive habits of thought and action that you can integrate into your life. The first important ingredient is self-awareness. Closely tied to self-awareness are self-direction, self-esteem, self-discipline, and self-motivation, which are the tools to keep you moving in the direction of your goals and dreams. Your attitude is an important ingredient of success, too; positive thinking can help you put things in perspective and make it

success Lifetime fulfillment that comes from creating a sense of meaning in your work and personal life.

success *secret*
Money and fame don't equal success.

ACTIVITY 1: What Success Means to You

A Take at least three or four minutes to brainstorm every word or phrase that comes to mind when you think of "success." Write these in the box below.

Success=

B Look at everything you wrote. What do these words or phrases tell you about your vision of success?

_____

_____

_____

_____

C Now put your definition of success down in writing.

To me, success means _____

_____

_____

_____

continued . . .

D Does your definition of success differ from the definition of success presented in this text? If so, how?

_____

_____

_____

_____

_____

_____

E Do you think you will become successful, according to your own definition of success? Why or why not?

_____

_____

_____

_____

_____

_____

F Describe two people you know who have achieved success the way you define it.

_____

_____

_____

_____

_____

_____

Internal Career Motivation

Knowledge of your attributes, abilities, interests, strengths, weaknesses, and traits is essential to becoming proactive in career choice and career change. It is important to draw a distinction between external and internal criteria in these crucial matters. The overwhelming majority of job-hunters and career-changers react to purely external pressures and circumstances—above all, to money. Their ideas about what careers pay well are likely to be outdated, since many of today's job descriptions didn't exist a decade ago; and even if you choose a career that *is* lucrative, but makes you miserable, you may well end up viewing "your work" as a necessary interruption between weekends.

Huge life decisions often turn on "starting salary and benefits" instead of on the homework to identify one's passions and talents. After money, the second external factor is ignorant advice, much of which is well-meaning but some of which is narrow-minded and prejudiced. The third external is family or social pressure: donning the old school tie to follow in Dad's or Mom's footsteps. The fourth is the perception of the job market as presented by nothing more substantial than recent advertisements or media spin. The fifth is leaving it all to luck.

Most people, locked in a strangely passive attitude, simply fall into their jobs, often with unsatisfactory results. We all must deal with external pressures and circumstances, but starting with them instead of the internal factors—our own minds and hearts—is a kind of mad reversal of priorities. Take the time to become fully engaged and honest with the exercises and assessments in this chapter. Look in the mirror, before you walk through that office door seeking your first or next job opportunity.

through the tough times. Finally, no real success is possible without positive relationships with others. Let's look at each of these key ingredients of success.

Self-Awareness

Self-awareness involves identifying and appreciating your individual values, personal qualities, skills, and interests. Without self-awareness, it's hard to figure out what you really want out of life. Successful people use self-awareness to build confidence in themselves and find the courage to go after their dreams. They also use self-awareness to understand their thoughts, feelings, and actions and to relate better to others.

success *secret*
Success is a journey, not a destination.

Self-Direction

Successful people set themselves apart from the rest by developing an important trait: self-direction. **Self-direction** is the ability to set a well-defined goal and work toward it. Successful people can tell you where they are going, what they plan to do along the way, and who will be sharing their adventure with them. They have a game plan for life. They set goals and get what they want. They direct themselves along the road to success.

self-direction The ability to set a well-defined goal and work toward it.

Self-Esteem

Self-esteem, a respect for oneself as a valuable, unique individual, is another foundation for success. Self-esteem helps people work toward their dreams and goals and keep going when other people criticize them or get in their way. It also helps them believe that they are worthy of success in the first place.

Positive Thinking

Everyone goes through good and bad experiences. Instead of dwelling on the bad ones, successful people learn to focus on future possibilities. They also use setbacks as opportunities to take stock and try again. Not every successful person is a born optimist, but successful people learn to use the power of positive thinking to propel themselves toward their goals.

Self-Discipline

Success doesn't just happen—it requires effort. No matter how well you plan, you'll need self-discipline to put your plans into action. Successful people take charge of their lives. They take responsibility when things go wrong, but they also take credit when things go well. They learn how to make necessary changes and break free of bad habits. Habits are replaced, over time, by consistent training and practice, requiring focused self-discipline. They also learn to think critically, to make good decisions, and to use these skills to manage their time and money.

Self-Motivation

To get and stay motivated, successful people set goals for themselves that are both challenging and inspiring. They focus on goals that have personal meaning for them, rather than goals that society or other people say they should have. They understand their needs and wants and are able to keep themselves moving forward despite their fears.

Positive Relationships

Healthy and diverse relationships are essential for a successful life. Even in a society like ours that values individual achievement, no one ever succeeds without the help, ideas, and emotional support of others. The happiest and most fulfilled people are usually those who make time for other people in their lives instead of focusing all their energy on piling up accomplishments.

Which of the ingredients of success do you already possess? Which do you need to develop? Record your thoughts in **Personal Journal 1.1.**

Who Is a Success?

Successful people get what they want out of life. They set and achieve goals that benefit others as well as themselves. They don't have to get lucky to succeed at life, and they don't have to gain success at the expense of others. They achieve success by taking the potential they were born with and have developed and using it toward a purpose that makes them feel worthwhile according to their own standards.

In our society, it is not always obvious who the truly successful people are. The media, for example, often glamorize people who have a great deal of money, fame, or power, but these people are not always the most successful. In fact, large amounts of money, fame, or power can sometimes lead to a feeling of aimlessness.

Just as we each have our own vision of success, we each have our own idea of who is successful. Who is successful in your eyes? Powerful

Personal Journal 1.1

Ingredients of Success

On the lines in each oval, write one way you think this action or quality could help you become the person you want to be.

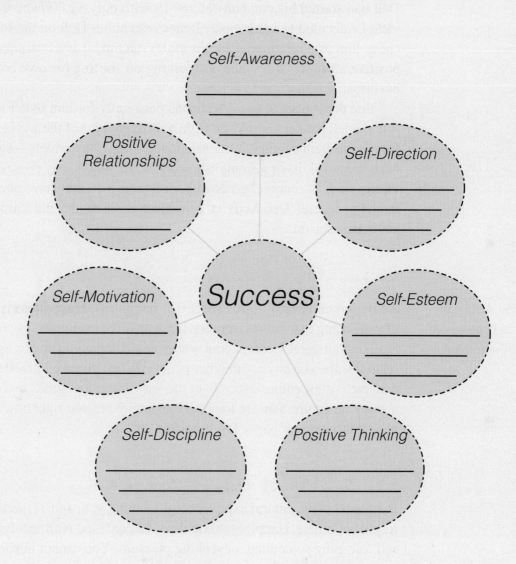

businesspeople? Movie stars? Nobel prize–winning scientists? Caring teachers? Dedicated craftspeople? Nurturing parents? To many of us, the most successful people are those who are special to us, such as a parent, relative, teacher, or friend. Often, we appreciate the successes of people who are close to us because they have made a difference in our lives and because we know how many obstacles they overcame to achieve their goals.

Role Models

If you think back to early childhood, you may remember having a role model. A **role model** is a person who has the qualities you would like to have.

Children need role models, but adults need them too. Our role models often represent what we would like to become as we get older. James, a student in information technology, takes inspiration from Michael Dell, founder and CEO of Dell Inc. When James learned that Dell had started his company at age 19 with only $1,000 and a good idea, he decided to learn more. James read about Dell on the Internet and chose him as a role model for his ethics, technical and business skill, and positive attitude. Now James is working on starting his own computer business.

You don't have to know someone personally for him or her to be your role model; the person may be from a different part of the world or even from a different century. Your role models may vary widely—some may have special skills or accomplishments, while others may possess personal virtues such as courage, generosity, or honor. You may have one role model or several. Use **Activity 2** to select a role model and learn more about that person.

Success and Happiness

An important benefit of true success is happiness. **Happiness** is a state of well-being that comes from having a positive evaluation of your life. It is an overall good feeling about who you are, what you are doing, and the relationships you have with other people. When you are interested in your daily activities, enthusiastic about the way things are going, and optimistic about your future, you are happy. How happy are you right now? Complete **Activity 3** on pages 15–16 to find out.

What Causes Happiness?

Happiness is the natural experience of winning your self-respect and the respect of others. Happiness should not be confused with indulging yourself, escaping something, or seeking pleasure. You cannot inhale, drink, or smoke happiness. You cannot buy it, wear it, drive it, swallow it, inject it, or travel to it. Happiness is not a result. It involves making the best out of whatever happens and remaining optimistic.

Did you know that outside factors, such as wealth, youth, physical health, marital status, physical attractiveness, educational level, and social status, have little effect on happiness? Corporate presidents who drive luxury cars are no happier, in general, than day laborers who take the bus. What if you woke up tomorrow looking like a movie star and with a winning lottery ticket in your pocket? You would probably be happier—but only for a while. In a year, life might not be so different for you after all. Studies show that a year or so after big changes like this, your happiness level is likely to

ACTIVITY 2: Your Role Model

A Select one person whom you admire and would like to imitate in some way. Research this person's life and fill out the profile below.

Role Model Profile

1. Name _____

2. Date and place of birth _____

3. Special accomplishments

   _____

   _____

   _____

4. Obstacle(s) he or she overcame

   _____

   _____

   _____

5. Ways he or she overcame these obstacle(s)

   _____

   _____

6. Special personal qualities

   _____

   _____

   _____

continued . . .

7. Ways he or she shows or showed these special qualities

_____

_____

_____

8. Ways he or she acquired these qualities

_____

_____

_____

9. Things you and your role model have in common (personal qualities, experiences, interests, challenges)

_____

_____

_____

_____

10. Areas in which you would like to become more like your role model

_____

_____

_____

_____

B Of all the people you could have chosen, why did you choose this person as your role model? What do you think your choice says about you?

_____

_____

_____

_____

_____

C Look at your answer to item 10 in your role model profile. What are some specific actions you could take to become more like your role model in these areas?

_____

_____

_____

_____

_____

_____

_____

_____

_____

_____

ACTIVITY 3: Self-Awareness Checklist

A Happiness seems to be a way of viewing ourselves and the world around us in terms of being part of the solution, rather than part of the problem. It is being aware of the limitations we place on ourselves and opening ourselves up to the potential around us for positive change. To determine your own level of self-awareness, place a check mark in the box you think describes how often you feel this way.

	ALWAYS	FREQUENTLY	SOMETIMES	RARELY	NEVER
I'm eager to learn.					
My work is exciting.					
I'm willing to listen with an open mind.					
I have new insights.					
I constantly network with people who have expertise in something I don't.					
I try to look at the world through the eyes of the other person.					
I focus on what I can control.					
When someone is talking to me, I really listen.					
I'm honest with myself and others.					
I've thought about my own strengths and weaknesses.					
I continually challenge my own assumptions.					
I recognize that others may think that I'm strange or odd in some ways.					
I adapt easily to the current environment and situation.					

B Hopefully, most of your check marks were in the FREQUENTLY box. It would be rare, indeed, for all check marks to land in the ALWAYS box. Each of us is unique, with different views about ourselves and the world. And no one is perfect. If some of your check marks were in the SOMETIMES box, what actions can you take to make your positive self-awareness more frequent in those areas?

_____

_____

_____

_____

C Do you feel that happiness is the result of what happens to you in life, or more how you deal with what happens to you? Why?

_____

_____

_____

_____

D What actions or events in your personal and professional do you feel have the greatest influence on your happiness?

_____

_____

_____

_____

E Two years from now do you think you will be happier than you are today? Why?

_____

_____

_____

_____

return to where it was the previous year. In other words, most people experience a fairly stable level of happiness despite life's ups and downs.

Does this mean that you can't raise your level of happiness? No. You can always seek out opportunities to create happiness, such as:

success *secret*
Create your own opportunities for happiness.

- creating a sense of purpose in your life
- building deep connections with others
- improving skills, learning, and being productive
- playing games and enjoying yourself
- getting to know yourself better
- striving to become more like people you admire
- actively looking forward to things in the future
- enjoying the beauty in your environment
- pursuing curiosity for its own sake

Happy people don't sit back waiting for happiness to appear. Instead, they create opportunities for happiness to enter their lives.

Positive Qualities   Another way to boost your happiness is to develop personal qualities that will help you enjoy life and cope with challenges. Psychologists who have researched success and happiness have found several of these qualities. Among the most important are:

- **Ability to love**—the ability to feel, express, and receive love, affection, warmth, and compassion and to act in a giving way
- **Vocation**—the ability to feel interest and excitement in something and to turn this into your life's work
- **Courage**—the ability to take risks and challenge yourself
- **Trust**—confidence in other people and their motives
- **Optimism**—hope that things will turn out for the best
- **Future-mindedness**—a focus on the possibilities of the future, rather than on the mistakes or disappointments of the past
- **Social skill**—the ability to understand others, get along with others, and build fulfilling relationships
- **Aesthetic sensibility**—the ability to appreciate and delight in the beauty of art, music, and nature
- **Work ethic**—commitment to honoring obligations, being dependable and responsible, getting things done, and being productive
- **Honesty**—thinking, speaking, and acting in a forthright way with yourself and others
- **Emotional awareness**—the ability to experience and express a wide range of emotions
- **Persistence**—the ability to persevere in the face of setbacks and adversity, to keep on track toward goals, and to handle stress
- **Forgiveness**—generosity of spirit, and the ability to avoid grudges and blame
- **Creative thinking**—the willingness to consider new beliefs and points of view and to try out new ways of thinking and doing

success *secret*
Try new ways of thinking and doing.

- **Spirituality**—the search for a greater good, purpose, or meaning to human existence
- **Self-esteem**—a positive feeling of your own value, which includes self-respect as well as respect for the rights, feelings, and wishes of others
- **Wisdom**—the ability to use your knowledge and experience to make sound decisions

Building these qualities will help you to be physically healthy, enjoy strong friendships and family relationships, derive satisfaction from a committed romantic relationship, be an effective and loving parent, find satisfaction in work, and feel good about yourself.

UNDERSTANDING PSYCHOLOGY

To have a clear vision of what you want out of life, you need to understand yourself first. Who am I? What are my wants and needs? Why do I think, feel, and act the way I do? These questions are at the beginning of the journey to success. These questions are also some of the important ones addressed by psychology. **Psychology** is the scientific study of human behavior. The word psychology comes from two Greek words: *psyche,* meaning "mind" or "self," and *logos,* meaning "science" or "study."

psychology The scientific study of human behavior.

The focus of psychology is human behavior. **Behavior** is anything we think, feel, or do, including:

behavior Anything that people think, feel, or do.

- acting
- reacting
- speaking
- perceiving
- sensing
- imagining
- wanting
- remembering
- sleeping
- dreaming

Psychologists learn about people by observing their behavior. Although psychologists cannot directly measure what people think or how they feel, they can observe their actions, listen to their words, and try to understand their experiences.

Why Study Psychology?

Psychology tackles basic questions about what it means to be human. Psychologists ask questions such as:

- Why and how are people different from one another?
- What needs do all people have in common?

VIRTUAL THERAPY

More and more psychologists are taking their services online. Many now offer consultations via e-mail, instant messaging, chat rooms, and even two-way videoconferencing. Online therapy is not appropriate for people dealing with serious crises, such as suicidal thoughts or mental illness. However, it can reach out to people who are geographically isolated, socially anxious, or physically disabled. People can also use the Internet to find virtual support groups, information on screening and treatment, and listings of counselors and psychologists in their area. But what's the downside to online mental health services? Critics say online therapy just doesn't work. Successful therapy is based on a human connection. Can two people really create a deep human bond on a computer screen? Critics also worry that people will fall victim to bogus therapists and that personal information is unsafe online.

Think About It

What do you see as the advantages and disadvantages of online therapy? Would you try it? Why or why not? Bring your ideas to class for a group discussion. To learn more about online psychotherapy, go to a search engine or go to one of the following websites:

http://www.psychology.info/
A site that explores aspects of online psychology and provides a list of resources

http://www.ismho.org
The home page of an organization that promotes the use of technology and the Internet in mental health treatment

http://locator.apa.org/
A Web page set up by the American Psychological Association to help individuals find a psychologist and read articles about mental health

http://www.metanoia.org/imhs/identity.htm
A Web service for checking the credentials of online therapists

---

- Where do emotions come from? What function do they serve?
- Where do attitudes come from? How do they change?
- What is the difference between the body and the mind?

By providing insights into questions like these, psychology helps us understand ourselves and others. Learning about psychologists' discoveries and theories, therefore, can help you better understand yourself and your world.

Goals of Psychology

Psychology has four major goals: to describe, predict, explain, and (in some cases) change human behavior.

Because human behavior is so complex, many psychologists focus on just one or two of these goals. For example, some psychologists focus on observing how people think and act in very specific situations. They then use their observations to create models of human thought and behavior in these situations. For example, psychologists who study marital relationships might investigate the factors that influence people's selection of a marriage partner or the ways marriage relationships tend to change over time.

Other psychologists are interested in describing how individuals and groups think and act in order to predict how they are likely to think and act in the future. For example, psychologists who study children may try to predict which children will be at risk for problems such as depression and low self-esteem.

Many psychologists focus on the fourth goal of psychology, changing human behavior. *Clinical psychologists,* for example, help people change the undesirable behaviors associated with psychological illness. A clinical psychologist who works with people who fear social situations might help these people confront their fear and take positive steps to overcome it. Clinical psychologists have that designation because they, like physicians, can aid their patients with prescription medicine.

Explaining Human Behavior

Why do people think, feel, and act the way they do? Until only a few centuries ago, people believed that human behavior was controlled by a soul that existed outside the body. In ancient times, people believed that psychological problems such as stress, anxiety, and depression were caused by evil spirits. Since psychology is concerned with observable behavior, today few psychologists focus on investigating the spiritual side of existence. Instead, most psychologists begin by trying to understand the biological basis of behavior.

Humans are biological beings, with a complex **nervous system** that regulates thoughts, feelings, and actions. The nervous system is a vast network of *neurons* (nerve cells) that carry messages to and from the brain. Neurons communicate with one another using chemical and electrical signals. They tell our glands and muscles what to do and relay signals to the brain from our sense organs. Millions of nerve impulses move throughout our bodies all the time, even when we are resting or sleeping.

nervous system
A system of nerve cells that regulates behavior by transmitting messages back and forth between the brain and the other parts of the body.

Consciousness   The nervous system is responsible for more than just monitoring our bodily functions. It is also responsible for *consciousness,* our awareness of the sensations, thoughts, and feelings we are experiencing at a given moment. Consciousness can take the form of extreme alertness, such as when we are taking a test or looking for a parking space on a crowded street. It can also take the form of reduced alertness, such as when we are daydreaming or driving a familiar route without having to think about what we are doing.

Conscious activities are controlled by the **conscious mind,** the part of the brain that controls the mental processes of which we are aware. The conscious mind collects information from our environment, stores it in our memory, and helps us make logical decisions. The conscious mind is not the whole story, however. We also have a **subconscious mind,** which stores the emotions and sensations that we are not quite aware of, the

conscious mind The part of the brain that controls the mental processes of which we are aware.

subconscious mind The part of the brain that controls the mental processes of which we are not actively aware.

feelings that are just under the surface. Our subconscious mind also helps us solve problems. Have you ever tried in vain to solve a difficult problem, only to have the solution pop into your head later when you were thinking about something else? This is the power of the subconscious mind. It came up with the solution while your conscious mind was busy with something else.

Thoughts, Feelings, and Actions

Do people act based on thoughts or on feelings? Do feelings cause thoughts, or do thoughts cause feelings? Actually, thoughts, feelings, and actions are all connected. Each influences the other in a continuous cycle.

Our thoughts about people, objects, events, and situations have a strong influence on our feelings about them. For example, if we believe that a certain event will turn out in our favor and it does not, we will probably experience a feeling of disappointment. On the other hand, if we believe that a certain event will not turn out in our favor and yet it does, we will probably experience a feeling of relief.

By the same token, our feelings about the world have a strong influence on our beliefs and thoughts about it. If we have positive thoughts and feelings about a certain situation, we will seek out that situation again. If we have negative thoughts and feelings about a situation, we will avoid that situation in the future.

The way we act also influences our thoughts and feelings. For example, acting responsibly at work makes us feel good about ourselves, while acting irresponsibly produces the opposite result.

Use **Personal Journal 1.2** to continue thinking about how your thoughts, feelings, and actions are related.

Cognition and Emotion

cognition Mental processing of information in any form.

What exactly are thoughts and feelings? Thought, known in psychology as **cognition,** refers to the functions of processing information. This information may be in the form of words, images, or sounds. We think every time we talk to ourselves, daydream, replay a scene from the past, hear a tune in our heads, or see a picture in our minds. Cognition includes activities such as:

- **Perceiving**—giving meaning to sensory information
- **Recognizing**—identifying whether you have, or have not, experienced a certain person, thing, idea, or situation before
- **Remembering**—storing and retrieving information
- **Reasoning**—using information to reach conclusions
- **Making decisions**—evaluating and choosing among various options or courses of action

Personal Journal 1.2

Your Thoughts, Feelings, and Actions

Think of a recent situation that provoked a strong emotion. In the circles below, write down how you thought, felt, and acted in that situation.

Situation:

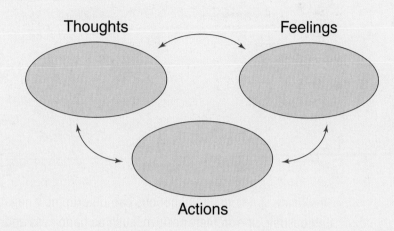

How did your thoughts, feelings, and actions influence each other?

- **Solving problems**—generating and evaluating ways to overcome obstacles that stand between you and your goals
- **Forming concepts**—grouping objects, events, or people based on shared characteristics
- **Visualizing**—creating detailed mental pictures of behaviors you want to carry out

Cognition is closely tied to emotion. **Emotion** refers to subjective feelings that are accompanied by physical and behavioral changes, such as facial expressions and gestures. Although there is no such thing as a "bad" or "good" emotion, some emotions are more pleasant than others. Joy, interest, and surprise, for example, are more pleasant than fear, anger, and guilt. In addition to being positive or negative, emotions can also be more or less intense, as shown in Figure 1.1 on page 22. For example, liking is a less intense emotion than love, which is less intense than passion. Emotions come from countless sources—sights, sounds, smells, memories, ideas, or interactions with others. In fact, we are always feeling something, even when we are washing the dishes or driving to work.

emotion A subjective feeling that is accompanied by physical and behavioral changes.

Positive emotions help us learn, solve problems, make decisions, relate to others, and relate to ourselves. Pleasant emotions include:

- **Joy**—a feeling of happiness following achievement of a goal
- **Love**—a feeling of affection, devotion, or attachment

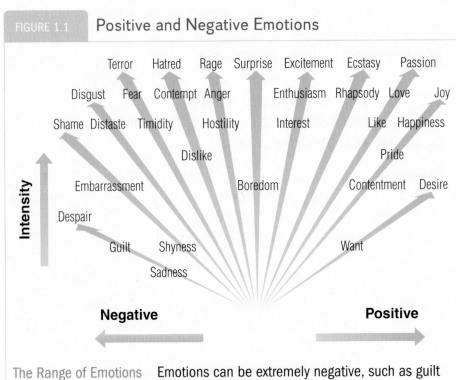

FIGURE 1.1 Positive and Negative Emotions

The Range of Emotions   Emotions can be extremely negative, such as guilt and despair, or extremely positive, such as happiness and joy. They can also be more neutral, such as boredom and surprise. *Describe an experience that provoked an intense feeling of joy.*

- **Interest**—a state of curiosity, concern, or attention
- **Pride**—a positive feeling about yourself that you experience when you achieve a personal success

Unlike positive emotions, negative emotions encourage us to focus our attention on the specific thing that is troubling us. If we feel fear, for example, we will focus all our energy on getting away from the object of that fear. Because negative emotions take up so much energy, they make it hard to do productive things such as learning or working toward our goals. Negative emotions include:

- **Embarrassment**—an unpleasant feeling about yourself that you experience when you believe that others have found a flaw in you
- **Guilt**—a negative feeling about yourself that you experience when you believe that your actions have harmed someone else
- **Shame**—a negative feeling about yourself that you experience following a personal failure
- **Despair**—an unpleasant feeling of hopelessness and defeat
- **Fear**—an unpleasant feeling of anxiety and anticipation of danger
- **Anger**—a strong feeling of displeasure, resentment, or hostility
- **Disgust**—a negative feeling of aversion or repulsion
- **Sadness**—a somber emotion of sorrow over a loss

success *secret*

Pay attention to what is happening inside you and why.

Being aware of the range of human emotions helps you understand what is happening inside you and why. Learn to occasionally stop and observe your thoughts, feelings, and actions the way a psychologist might. This will help you understand your behavior, which is the first step to making the positive changes that will lead you down the road to success.

✅ Self Check

1. What is a role model? (p. 10)
2. What are the benefits of studying psychology? (p. 17)
3. What is the nervous system? (p. 19)

Understanding Yourself

YOUR INNER SELF

self Your sense of being a unique, conscious being.

We are not born with a sense of **self.** It develops—as do many of our attitudes—over time, based on repeated inputs from our environment. The sum total of our past experiences—our successes and failures, our humiliations and triumphs, and the way we have interacted with those around us and who love us—gives us a subjective sense of the sort of person we are. But there is an important catch. All of our experiences are pieces of input that are colored by our *perceptions*, and, since our perceptions are not necessarily the same as reality, our sense of who we are may miss the mark by a wide margin. Unfortunately, once an idea becomes a belief, it becomes a "truth" as far as we are concerned.

Most of our understanding of the world is filtered through our understanding of self. We decide what is right and wrong, what is appealing and unappealing, what is pleasurable and painful based on the way we see ourselves and our relationship with the outside world. Having a firm sense of self helps us make plans and predictions. It gives us an emotional investment in what we are doing. It motivates us to achieve our goals and to improve ourselves. Having a firm sense of self also helps us build and maintain relationships with others.

Your Self-Image

self-image All the beliefs you have about yourself.

Each of us has a view of ourselves, known as our **self-image.** Our self-image is made up of all the beliefs we have about ourselves. Our self-image is very important—everything that we will ever do or try to do is based on the beliefs we hold about ourselves. Our self-image determines how we present ourselves to the world. It affects what we think we can accomplish professionally. It affects our choices in personal and professional relationships. If you have a positive self-image, you see yourself as someone worthy and capable of reaching goals and achieving success. You see yourself as someone who deserves happiness. A strong, positive self-image can be your greatest asset in going after what you want in life.

In addition to our overall self-image, we also have self-images in specific areas of our lives, such as school, work, and intimate relationships. If you believe that you are a successful student, for example, you have a strong academic self-image. Important areas in which we have self-images include:

success *secret*

A sense of self helps you understand the world and make plans and decisions.

* intellectual ability
* competence on the job, at school, and at sports
* creativity, sense of humor, and morality
* romantic appeal and physical appearance
* parental relationships and close friendships
* social acceptance/popularity

What is your self-image? Do you see yourself as creative, friendly, funny, and intelligent, or do you have a low view of yourself? Enter your thoughts in **Personal Journal 1.3** on page 26.

Building a Healthy Self-Image

A healthy self-image is positive but realistic. People with a realistic self-image aren't bothered by their weaknesses, however, because they know that their strengths outweigh them. Instead of worrying about the things they can't do well, they make the very best of all the things they can do well. Sarah, for example, knows that she is a whiz at math and computers but is a pretty ordinary artist. Emmett takes pride in being a good writer and musician, but knows that he tends to stumble when making oral presentations. They both have healthy, realistic self-images.

People with unrealistic, negative self-images, by contrast, overestimate their weaknesses and suffer from low self-esteem. (You'll learn more about the connection between self-image and self-esteem in Chapter 4.) People with unrealistic, positive self-images have high self-esteem, but they overestimate their strengths and don't put in the effort required to succeed. They also have trouble getting along with other people, because they usually seem hostile and arrogant.

Besides being realistic, a healthy self-image is also based on who you are right now. Who you are today does not limit who you will be next week, next month, or next year. Your potential, your interests, and your abilities are developing every day and will continue to develop. You are being influenced by the world around you, and you are influencing the world, too.

Complexity and Self-Image

A healthy self-image is also complex. Having a complex self-image means having a variety of positive ways of seeing yourself. People who have a complex self-image are less likely to suffer from psychological troubles such as stress, anxiety, and depression. When they suffer a setback or difficulty in one area of their lives, they can fall back on one of the many other positive roles they play in life. Ladonna, for example, has a complex self-image: She sees herself as a businesswoman, a mother, an artist, and an environmentalist. When things get tough at work, she has many other positive aspects of herself to take pride in. Jared, on the other hand, has a rather simple self-image: He sees himself mainly as an A student. When he occasionally does poorly on a test, he feels like a failure.

The key to a complex self-image is to strike a balance among the various important areas of your life, such as relationships, school, work and career, community, health, hobbies and leisure, and spirituality. When you devote time and energy to each important area of your life, you build a strong foundation for feeling good about yourself. How balanced is your life? Take a look in **Activity 4** on pages 27–29.

success *secret*
A healthy self-image is positive but realistic.

success *secret*
It's healthy to find balance in your life.

Personal Journal 1.3

How Do You See Yourself?

On the scales following each statement, circle one or more numbers between 1 and 10 according to how strongly you agree with it. The number 1 represents total disagreement, and the number 10 represents total agreement. You may select a single number or a range of numbers.

1. I have high intellectual ability.

   1   2   3   4   5   6   7   8   9   10

2. I am good at sports.

   1   2   3   4   5   6   7   8   9   10

3. I am creative.

   1   2   3   4   5   6   7   8   9   10

4. I have good relationships with my close friends.

   1   2   3   4   5   6   7   8   9   10

5. I have a good sense of humor.

   1   2   3   4   5   6   7   8   9   10

6. I am popular with others.

   1   2   3   4   5   6   7   8   9   10

7. I am competent on the job.

   1   2   3   4   5   6   7   8   9   10

8. I am competent at school.

   1   2   3   4   5   6   7   8   9   10

9. I am romantically appealing to others.

   1   2   3   4   5   6   7   8   9   10

10. I am physically attractive.

   1   2   3   4   5   6   7   8   9   10

11. I am a moral person.

   1   2   3   4   5   6   7   8   9   10

12. I have a good relationship with my parents.

   1   2   3   4   5   6   7   8   9   10

Identify the three areas to which you gave the highest ratings. What are you particularly proud of in these areas? Now look at the areas to which you gave low ratings. Is it possible that you are being overly critical of yourself?

ACTIVITY 4: Wheel of Life

A Read each of the statements below. Decide how true each statement is for you, then write in a number between 1 (not at all true) and 10 (totally true).

	Rating (1–10)
1. I go to movies, restaurants, etc., with friends.	
2. I spend time thinking about the meaning of life.	
3. I exercise regularly.	
4. I enjoy time with my romantic partner.	
5. I have goals for earning and spending money.	
6. I am satisfied with my career choice and my career progress so far.	
7. I am involved in community affairs.	
8. I enjoy reading books or magazines.	
9. I belong to a club or social group.	
10. I set time aside for meditation, prayer, worship, or other spiritual practice.	
11. I eat healthful foods.	
12. I write or call friends and family members from whom I am separated.	
13. I earn the income I want.	
14. I am involved in creative work on the job, at school, or elsewhere.	
15. I belong to a community association.	
16. I attend workshops or special courses to increase my knowledge or skills.	
17. I like to meet new people and socialize.	
18. I think about how I can make my life serve a greater purpose.	
19. I try to maintain a healthy weight.	
20. I have coworkers or fellow students who are also friends.	
21. I have a plan for saving money.	
22. I have reached some, but not all, of my professional goals.	
23. I volunteer for community or charitable projects.	
24. I watch or listen to educational programs.	

continued . . .

B Scoring: For each of the 24 items on the list, write the rating you gave it (1–10) on the line below.

Relationships	
Item 4	_____
Item 12	_____
Item 20	_____
Total	_____

Work and Career	
Item 6	_____
Item 14	_____
Item 22	_____
Total	_____

Community	
Item 7	_____
Item 15	_____
Item 23	_____
Total	_____

Learning and School	
Item 8	_____
Item 16	_____
Item 24	_____
Total	_____

Health and Fitness	
Item 3	_____
Item 11	_____
Item 19	_____
Total	_____

Hobbies and Leisure	
Item 1	_____
Item 9	_____
Item 17	_____
Total	_____

Spirituality	
Item 2	_____
Item 10	_____
Item 18	_____
Total	_____

Money	
Item 5	_____
Item 13	_____
Item 21	_____
Total	_____

C Record the total for each area on the wheel below by drawing a curved line in each section of the circle.

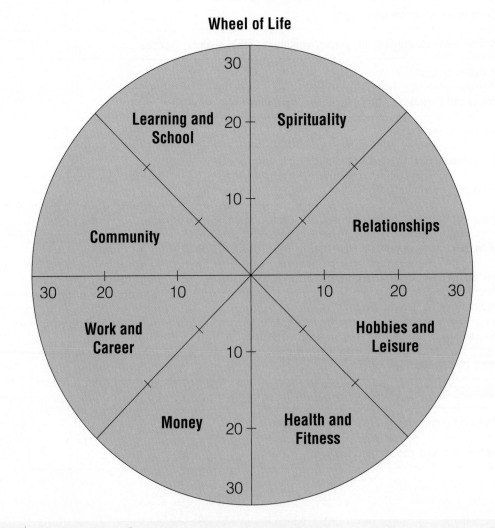

Wheel of Life

D   Ideally, your completed diagram should resemble a circle. However, most of us have different priorities at different stages of our lives. Were you surprised by your imbalance? Explain why or why not.

_____

_____

_____

_____

E   In which area(s) of your life do you want or need to spend more time? Explain.

_____

_____

_____

_____

F   Name specific things you could give up in one or two areas in order to make more time for the neglected area(s).

_____

_____

_____

_____

G   Are any of the eight life areas covered in this exercise particularly important to you? Explain.

_____

_____

_____

_____

YOU AND YOUR SOCIAL WORLD

If you wrote down a detailed description of your innermost self and then asked your best friend to write a description of you, how similar do you think the descriptions would be? What if you asked a sibling? A parent? What about a new acquaintance? Chances are, none of their descriptions would be very similar to yours. That's because no one sees you the way you see yourself. It's also because you probably act slightly differently with each of these people.

Have you noticed that people change their behavior depending on the social setting? Ginny, for example, is responsible and managerial at work, shy and quiet in the classroom, and sociable and outgoing with friends. Is she acting falsely in some situations? Is she unsure of who she is? Not necessarily. Ginny's behavior shows the power of social roles. A **social role** is a set of *norms* (standards of behavior) that define how we are supposed to behave in a social position or setting. Like Ginny, each of us is subject to many social roles: partner, friend, parent, citizen, son or daughter, student, employee.

social role A set of norms that define how you are supposed to behave in a given social position or setting.

We act according to social roles because we desire social acceptance. Sometimes this desire motivates us to act in ways that don't represent our true selves. Altering our behavior to make a good impression on others is known as **self-presentation.** Trina, for example, acts falsely modest after receiving a compliment because she is afraid of seeming stuck up.

self-presentation
Altering your behavior to make a good impression on others.

All of us use self-presentation, sometimes without being aware of it. We might act friendly and upbeat at a party to make a good impression, for example, even if we're feeling tired and grouchy inside. How do you behave around different people? Do you engage in self-presentation? Write your thoughts in **Activity 5.**

Identity

identity How you choose to define yourself to the world.

How we choose to define ourselves to the world makes up our **identity.** Our identity is our public self. An identity is complex and comes together, piece by piece, over a lifetime. Your identity can change over time as you encounter new people, places, ideas, and challenges.

Although each individual's identity is complex, most psychologists agree that it is made up of three major elements: individual identity, relational identity, and collective identity. Your identity takes shape over time as you integrate your individual, relational, and collective identities into a meaningful whole.

individual identity
The physical and psychological characteristics that distinguish you.

Individual Identity
Your **individual identity** is made up of the personal characteristics that distinguish you from other people. These characteristics are both physical, such as your appearance and possessions, and psychological, such as your personality and talents. Important components of individual identity are:

- name (given name, nicknames)
- age

ACTIVITY 5: Sides of Yourself

A On the figure below, write five adjectives to describe how you think, feel, or act when you are with each of the people named.

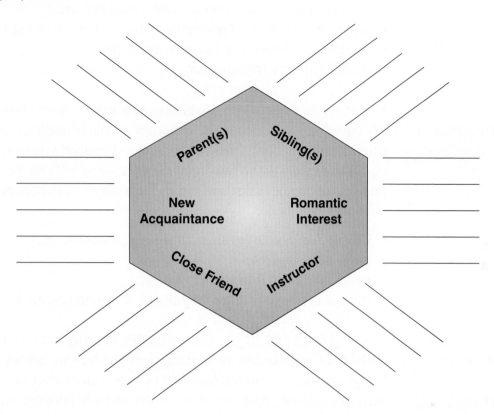

B Are you more "yourself" with one of the individuals on the figure, or do you think, feel, and act fairly consistently with all of them? Explain.

_____

_____

_____

C We all use self-presentation strategies from time to time. When do you use self-presentation? Explain.

_____

_____

_____

_____

- sex
- physical characteristics (tall, short, fit, red-haired, etc.)
- possessions (home, car, clothing, etc.)
- ways of interacting with others (shy, outgoing, nice, etc.)
- talents and personal qualities (intelligent, creative, athletic, etc.)
- likes and preferences (food, music, hobbies, etc.)
- emotions (happy, sad, moody, stable, excitable, etc.)
- beliefs and ideologies (environmentalist, conservative, etc.)
- intellectual interests (literature, science, etc.)
- artistic activities (painting, singing, dance, etc.)

relational identity
How you identify yourself in relation to important others.

Relational Identity

Relational identity refers to how we identify ourselves in relation to the important people in our lives, such as our parents, siblings, close friends, children, and romantic partner. These significant others are so important to our sense of self that we often take pride in their achievements as if they were our own. Important elements of relational identity are:

- kinship/family role (mother, father, son, daughter, etc.)
- romantic/sexual role
- professional role (boss, employee, etc.)
- friendship role (coworker, best friend, acquaintance, etc.)

collective identity
The sum of the social roles you play and the social groups to which you belong.

Collective Identity

Our **collective identity** is the sum of all the social roles we play and the social groups to which we belong. Human beings are social creatures, and each of us is a member of many groups, such as a cultural group, an ethnic group, and a religious group. Culture and ethnicity are particularly powerful influences on identity. Think about how different you would be today if you had grown up in another country or been born with a different ethnicity. Would you still be "you"?

Consider how the following elements of your collective identity make you who you are:

- race/ethnicity
- religion
- culture (European, Asian, etc.)
- social class or status (middle class, working class, etc.)
- occupation
- citizenship/territoriality (American, Californian, etc.)
- group membership (member of student orchestra, etc.)
- political affiliation (Democrat, Republican, Green, etc.)

Each of us values these aspects of identity differently. Some people, for example, may see their religion as a major component of who they are, while others may place much more importance on their profession.

What are the elements of your identity, and which ones are the most central to how you see yourself? **Activity 6** on page 34 will help you find out.

Culture and Identity

Culture has a powerful impact on identity. **Culture** consists of the behaviors, ideas, attitudes, and traditions shared by a large social group and transmitted from one generation to the next. Each culture has different values, ethics, beliefs, lifestyles, and standards of acceptable and unacceptable behavior, such as ways of dressing, expressing ourselves, and relating to others. Culture influences all aspects of life, from education to career to family.

culture The behaviors, ideas, attitudes, and traditions shared by a large social group and transmitted from one generation to the next.

Western cultures usually promote *individualism*. This means that people value individual goals over group goals and define their identity in terms of personal rather than group attributes. In individualist cultures, people place emphasis on competing with others and standing out from those around them. For that reason, people from countries such as the United States and Canada often value their individual identity over their collective or relational identity. Other values that are important to people in individualist cultures include:

- pleasure
- creativity and imagination
- a varied life filled with challenge, novelty, and change
- being daring, seeking adventure and risk
- freedom of thought and action
- independence, self-reliance, and choosing one's own goals

Unlike Western cultures, many Eastern cultures promote *collectivism*. This means that people value group goals over individual goals and define their identity in terms of group identifications rather than personal attributes. In collectivist Asian cultures, such as Japan, India, and China, for example, people value cooperation and harmonious interpersonal relationships more than being special or standing out from the crowd. Other values that are emphasized in collectivist cultures include:

- honoring and showing respect for parents and elders
- social order and stability in society
- national security and protection from enemies
- self-discipline and resisting temptation
- politeness, courtesy, and good manners
- obedience, fulfilling duties, and meeting obligations

Because of this emphasis on relationships and social order, people from collectivist cultures tend to value their relational and collective identities more than their individual identity.

ACTIVITY 6: Identity Profile

A Fill out the lines below for each aspect of your individual identity.

Individual Identity

My full name is _____

I am _____ years old

My sex is _____

Physical characteristics that distinguish me from other people are _____

_____

My most important possessions are _____

_____

When I am with other people, I usually act _____

_____

My special traits/talents include _____

_____

I like _____

I often feel the emotions of _____

I strongly believe in _____

_____

I am very interested in _____

_____

Relational Identity

I am the son/daughter of _____

I am the close friend of _____

I am the spouse/partner of _____

I am the mother/father of _____

Achievements or qualities of my close friends or relations that I am proud of include _____

_____

_____

_____

Collective Identity

My race or ethnicity is _____

My cultural background is _____

My religious beliefs are _____

By profession, I am (or will be) a(n) _____

I was born in _____

I live in _____

Social groups I belong to include _____

My political orientation is _____

B How well do you think the information above sums up your identity? Explain.

_____

_____

_____

_____

_____

C If someone who had never met you before was given this list, how well do you think that person would know you? Explain.

_____

_____

_____

_____

continued . . .

D Now consider how important each aspect of your identity is to you by filling out the following questionnaire. Assign each statement a number between 1 and 5, with 1 being not important at all to your sense of who you are and 5 being extremely important to your sense of who you are.

	Score (1–5)
1. My dreams and goals	
2. My closest friend(s)	
3. My relatives and close family	
4. My cognitions and emotions	
5. My life partner	
6. My race or ethnicity	
7. My self-image	
8. My occupation and economic status	
9. My religion	
10. My ethics and values	
11. My group of friends and acquaintances	
12. My sense of belonging to my community	

E **Scoring:** To determine your *individual identity* score, add up the number of points you assigned to items 1, 4, 7, and 10. To determine your *relational identity* score, add up the number of points you assigned to items 2, 3, 5, and 11. To determine your *collective identity* score, add up the number of points you assigned to items 6, 8, 9, and 12. What are your totals?

Individual Identity _____   Relational Identity _____   Collective Identity _____

Which component of your identity is most important to you? _____

F Which four or five individual aspects of your identity (from any of the three major components) do you value the most? Why?

_____

_____

_____

Gender and Identity

One particular aspect of culture—gender—has a particularly strong impact on our identity. *Gender* is the set of characteristics used to define male and female. Unlike *sex,* which is biological, gender is cultural. As children grow up and develop an identity, they are powerfully affected by gender roles. A **gender role** is a set of norms that define how males and females are supposed to behave.

gender role A set of norms that define how males and females are supposed to behave.

Gender roles vary widely from culture to culture. In Western societies, men have traditionally been expected to be assertive, independent, and competitive, while women have traditionally been expected to be helpful, expressive, and gentle. Gender roles like these are reinforced by the different ways that boys and girls are treated in school and at home. Girls, for example, are more likely to be punished for aggressive behavior than boys, because this kind of behavior is considered more appropriate for boys than for girls. Boys, on the other hand, are more likely to be punished for crying and to be told that "boys don't cry."

Even the toys given to girls and boys reinforce gender roles. Girls are often given dolls, dollhouses, and play makeup, while boys are often given toy trucks and trains, action figures, and even toy guns. A boy who is interested in dolls, or a girl who is interested in trucks, might face criticism and rejection from parents, teachers, and peers.

Gender roles are rapidly changing in the United States. More women graduate from high school than do men and our total workforce is nearly equally divided between men and women. There are more women enrolled in colleges than men and women have passed men in gaining advanced degrees as well as bachelor's degrees, part of a trend that is helping redefine who goes off to work and who stays home with the kids. About one of every five stay-at-home parents is a father. More than one-fourth of all businesses are owned by women and more than half of all new, small business are being created by women.

Unfortunately, even with great strides in our society to appreciate and reward competent employees whose skills, talents, and accomplishments meet or exceed expectations, **gender bias** (when someone is treated differently or unfairly due to one's gender) has not totally been wiped out. Women (and even men) may face a "maternal wall" bias, which assumes their commitment to family outweighs their commitment to career, and that the latter will suffer as a result. Or women who are perceived as "too assertive" may falsely be labeled as "too difficult" or "too ambitious," while their male counterparts may be rewarded for like behavior.

gender bias When one is treated differently or unfairly due to one's gender.

Also, most research indicates that women still earn less than men in the workplace, which in part can be attributed to gender bias. This is also due to the fact that women have often chosen lesser paying jobs within a career field. For example, a female math major is more likely to go into teaching, which has been a lower paying profession, than a male math major is. Also, women haven't been encouraged to negotiate for—but rather to accept—salaries or minimal pay increases, while men have been more inclined to negotiate (and be rewarded) higher rates. However, these are skills that anyone can learn and master.

success *secret*
Don't put limits on what you can become.

Defining Your Role

Many researchers suggest that it is healthiest to have a combination of both stereotypically masculine and stereotypically feminine qualities. People with a combination of traits can be forceful and logical when they need to, and emotional and sensitive when this is the best response. Women who possess traditionally masculine qualities such as logical reasoning, independence, and daring are better able to assert themselves in the workplace, for example, than women who are passive and submissive. Also, men who possess traditionally feminine qualities, such as gentleness, sensitivity, and compassion, are able to enjoy closer and more harmonious relationships than men who feel they must remain detached and unemotional.

We are all born with the capacity to feel and express the whole range of human thoughts and emotions. Viewing personal qualities as human, rather than as good or bad, strong or weak, or male or female, gives us the freedom to define our identities and our personal aspirations. As we will discuss later in this text, career selection should not hinge on your gender or cultural notions of "what is acceptable." It will be based on a number of personal factors, especially your interests and values.

Self Check

1. Define self-image. (p. 24)
2. What is a social role? (p. 30)
3. List the three components of identity. (p. 30)

Chapter 1 Review and Activities

Key Terms

success (p. 4)

self-direction (p. 7)

role model (p. 10)

happiness (p. 10)

psychology (p. 17)

behavior (p. 17)

nervous system (p. 19)

conscious mind (p. 19)

subconscious mind (p. 19)

cognition (p. 20)

emotion (p. 21)

self (p. 24)

self-image (p. 24)

social role (p. 30)

self-presentation (p. 30)

identity (p. 30)

individual identity (p. 30)

relational identity (p. 32)

collective identity (p. 32)

culture (p. 33)

gender role (p. 37)

gender bias (p. 37)

Summary by Learning Objectives

- **Define success.**   Success is lifetime fulfillment that comes from creating a sense of meaning in your work and personal life and from feeling satisfaction with yourself and your achievements.

- **List several personal qualities that help people to be happy.**   Personal qualities that foster a happy outlook on life include ability to love, vocation, courage, trust, optimism, future-mindedness, social skill, esthetic sensibility, work ethic, honesty, emotional awareness, persistence, forgiveness, creative thinking, spirituality, self-esteem, and wisdom.

- **Define psychology and cite its four major goals.**   Psychology is the scientific study of human behavior. Its four major goals are to describe, predict, explain, and (in some cases) change human behavior.

- **Explain the relationship between thoughts, feelings, and actions.**   Thoughts, feelings, and actions are all interrelated: each affects the other. Our beliefs about ourselves, for example, affect the way we feel about ourselves and the way we act.

- **Define self, self-image, and identity.**   Self is an individual's sense of being a unique, conscious being. Self-image is all the beliefs a person has about himself or herself. Identity is how a person chooses to define himself or herself to the world.

- **Describe the components of identity.**   Identity has three components: individual identity, relational identity, and collective identity. Individual identity is the physical and psychological characteristics that distinguish an individual. Relational identity is how an individual identifies himself or herself in relation to important others. Collective identity is the sum of the social roles an individual plays and the social groups to which he or she belongs.

Review and Activities

Review Questions

1. According to the text, what makes a person successful?

2. Explain the relationship between thoughts, feelings, and actions.

3. Why do negative emotions make it hard to learn or work toward a goal?

4. What is collectivism, and how is it different from individualism?

5. If you say, "I am Catholic," which part of your identity are you revealing?

6. Compare social roles with gender roles.

Critical Thinking

7. **Happiness** Many psychologists believe that each individual has a happiness "set point," a general level of happiness to which he or she usually returns. This suggests that some people are simply happier than others. If this is the case, do you think trying to become happier is worth the effort? Why or why not?

8. **Identity** Imagine that you had grown up in a different culture, either here or abroad. Do you think your identity would be the same as it is now—would you still be "you"? What if you had been adopted into a different family? Explain.

Application

9. **Gender Roles** Gender roles are reinforced through the toys given to girls and boys. Visit a local toy store or a local bookstore and look at the toys or books that are designed for boys and girls ages 6 through 12. (If you are unable to visit a toy or bookstore, visit the Web site of a large toy or book retailer.) Compare and contrast the girls' toys or books with the boys' toys or books. What percentage of the toys or books reinforce traditional gender roles?

10. **Life Balance** Survey two people about the balance in their life. Explain that you would like to interview them about the eight areas of their life shown in the Wheel of Life: relationships, learning and school, work and career, community, health, hobbies and leisure, money, and spirituality. Administer **Activity 4** to each interviewee. Add up each interviewee's score. Are your interviewees' lives in balance? Do they want more balance in their lives? Which of the eight areas of the Wheel of Life are most important to them? Compare and contrast their responses with your own.

Internet Activities

11. **Perspectives on Success**   Go to www.incomediary.com/50-great-thoughts-on-success which is a Web site that offers 10 definitions, quotes, formulas, misconceptions and principles concerning success. Select 2 from each of the 10 statements (in each of the 5 categories). Write them down. Then, write a one- to two-page summary on why your selections meant the most to you personally.

12. **Role Model Article**   In Activity 2, earlier in this chapter, you selected a role model who has had a positive impact on your life. Your instructor can provide the author's "Role Model" article for you to read. Pick a role model from history who inspires you and write a one-page description of why and how this individual influences you.

Real-Life Success Story	"Am I Doing the Right Thing?"

Look back at your response to the question in the Real-Life Success Story on page 2. Think about how you would answer the question now that you have completed the chapter.

Complete the Story   Write a paragraph continuing Bill's story, showing how he can use his own definition of success to help him decide on the right career path.

"What Do I Really Want?"

Searching for Work

Mariah Campione had worked for her family's fabric business for 12 years. She was officially the receptionist, but she had gradually taken on a variety of key responsibilities, from sales to accounting to staffing. Everything changed when Mariah's father fell ill. The family was forced to close the company and Mariah faced a difficult job search. After several months she was offered a temp-to-hire job as an office manager.

Searching Within

Mariah's family and friends encouraged her to take the new job, but Mariah doubted her ability to succeed. "I'm just a receptionist—what skills do I have?" Mariah remembered that a friend had offered her a telemarketing job, but she didn't know if that would interest her. She realized that she had never taken the time to think about who she was and what she wanted.

What Do You Think?   What could Mariah do to become more aware of her skills and interests?

Self-Awareness

> "Few people even scratch the surface, much less exhaust the contemplation of their own experience."
>
> Randolph Bourne, Essayist

introduction

Before you can get what you want out of life, you must know who you are and where you want to go. In this chapter, you'll gain self-knowledge through the process of self-awareness. In Section 2.1 you'll learn how self-awareness helps you find your direction. You'll look at your dreams for the future and define the values that will guide your choices. In Section 2.2 you'll look at several sides of yourself—your personality, your skills and intelligences, and your interests. You'll then put all this information together to consider the careers that might be right for you.

learning objectives

After you complete this chapter, you should be able to:

- Define self-awareness and cite its benefits.

- Explain the factors that influence people's values.

- Define personality and list the "big five" personality traits.

- Compare and contrast skills, knowledge, and interests.

- Explain how personality, skills, and interests relate to career choice.

DEVELOPING SELF-AWARENESS

Have you ever stopped to ask yourself what you want out of life? Whether you are heading in the right direction? To answer these important questions, you need to develop self-awareness. **Self-awareness** is the process of paying attention to yourself—your thoughts, feelings, attitudes, motivations, and actions. Self-awareness comes from stepping back and taking a good honest look at yourself and how you relate to the world around you.

Self-awareness has many benefits. It helps you identify what you are really feeling and thinking inside. It helps you act in accordance with your personal values, rather than be swayed by what other people say or do. It helps you appreciate your unique personality, skills, and interests. When you are self-aware, you can make the choices that are right for you.

The Importance of Self-Honesty

Self-awareness is important, but it can sometimes be so difficult. True self-awareness requires **self-honesty,** the ability to see your strengths and weaknesses clearly and realistically. Self-honesty is the foundation of self-knowledge. In order to improve yourself, it is important to be able to see yourself accurately, without being too harsh or too generous. Ask yourself, "Am I seeing myself as I really am? Am I overconfident, or am I selling myself short?" "Do my actions match my core values?" "Am I easily influenced by peers?"

Self-honesty requires effort. It involves telling the truth about yourself, both to yourself and to others. Telling the truth about yourself means admitting that you are human and therefore imperfect. Being honest can be challenging because it involves admitting to thoughts and feelings that we might dislike and that might not fit with our self-image. Self-honesty entails confronting aspects of your past and present that are unpleasant or even painful. It might even involve confronting painful feelings such as sadness, grief, anger, fear, shame, or guilt.

Benefits of Self-Honesty Fortunately, the benefits of self-honesty far outweigh the effort it requires. With self-honesty, you can see both what you have to offer and what you need to do to become the person you want to be. When you are honest with yourself, you are able to get in touch with your dreams, values, and interests. You are able to take pride in your progress because you know that you have set meaningful goals and invested the effort necessary to reach them. Who you are, what you think, and how you feel are all in harmony.

To become more self-honest, try to look at yourself like an astronomer viewing the universe through the lens of an orbiting telescope and discovering a new planet or star. An astronomer doesn't judge what he or

---

self-awareness The process of paying attention to yourself.

self-honesty The ability to see your strengths and weaknesses clearly.

success *secret*
Self-honesty helps you get in touch with your dreams, values, and interests.

she finds, but tries to understand it. In the same way, don't look for what "should" be—look for what is. Take inventory of everything you find— the precious treasures of current and future potential and joy, as well as the impacts of past events in your life that have shaped your beliefs. Each element is a vital part of what makes you unique. Use **Personal Journal 2.1** to start getting to know yourself.

Self-Consciousness

None of us is born self-aware; we learn to become more and more aware of ourselves as we grow into adolescence and adulthood. However, some

Personal Journal 2.1

How Well Do You Know Yourself?
Finish each of the following statements about yourself.

The person who knows me best is _____

One of my dreams in life is to _____

Three adjectives that describe me well are _____

What I like most about myself is _____

What I like least about myself is _____

I am good at _____

I am not very good at _____

I enjoy _____

I don't enjoy _____

Three careers that interest me are _____

My purpose in life is _____

Did you have trouble completing any of these statements, especially the last one? If so, you will benefit from taking a closer look at yourself and what you want out of life.

people do spend more time than others reflecting on themselves. The tendency to frequently reflect on oneself is known as **self-consciousness.**

Psychologists often distinguish between private self-consciousness and public self-consciousness. *Private self-consciousness* is the tendency to be aware of the private, inward aspects of yourself. *Public self-consciousness* is the tendency to be aware of the aspects of yourself that are on display in social situations. How self-conscious are you? Look at how you completed the first sentence in Personal Journal 2.1. Did you write "me," or does someone else know you better than you know yourself? Look at your levels of private and public self-consciousness by completing **Activity 7.**

Private Self-Consciousness
Private self-consciousness helps us understand ourselves. Privately self-conscious people usually have a realistic and complex self-image. They tend to reveal the private sides of themselves in intimate relationships, which strengthens human bonds and alleviates feelings of loneliness. They are also less likely to suffer from the physical ill effects of stress. (You'll learn more about stress in Chapter 3.) People who have a high level of private self-consciousness can fall victim to depression, however, because self-consciousness heightens the experience of negative emotions as well as positive ones.

Public Self-Consciousness
Like private self-consciousness, public self-consciousness has benefits. It helps us see how our behavior affects others, and it helps us adapt to our different social roles. A high level of public self-consciousness can be harmful, however, if it leads to anxiety in social situations. For example, some people become overly worried about how they look and what other people think of them.

Emotional Awareness

Another crucial part of self-awareness is emotional awareness. **Emotional awareness** is the process of recognizing, identifying, and accepting your emotions. It involves observing yourself, recognizing a feeling as it happens, and seeing the link between your thoughts, feelings, and actions. Being emotionally aware helps you handle your emotions in positive ways and use them to make good choices.

It is usually pretty easy to be emotionally aware when things are going well. If you get an A on an important exam, you will probably be aware of feeling happy, confident, proud, and capable. If you are enjoying a long-awaited vacation, you will probably delight in feelings of relaxation, freedom, and fulfillment.

It is much harder to be emotionally aware when things aren't going so well. In these situations, we may avoid looking at our emotions. In order to avoid facing painful feelings, we may tell ourselves that we don't care or don't feel anything. Other times, we may be aware that we are feeling *something,* but not know exactly what.

ACTIVITY 7: How Self-Conscious Are You?

A Read the statements below and indicate the extent to which each one is true for you by making a check mark in the appropriate column.

	Extremely Unlike Me	Somewhat Unlike Me	Neither Like Me Nor Unlike Me	Somewhat Like Me	Extremely Like Me
1. I'm always trying to figure myself out.					
2. I'm concerned about my style of doing things.					
3. Generally, I'm very aware of myself.					
4. I reflect about myself a lot.					
5. I'm concerned about the way I present myself.					
6. I'm often the subject of my own fantasies.					
7. I often scrutinize myself.					
8. I'm self-conscious about the way I look.					
9. I'm generally attentive to my inner feelings.					
10. I usually worry about making a good impression.					
11. I'm constantly examining my motives.					
12. One of the last things I do before I leave home is look in the mirror.					
13. I sometimes have the feeling that I'm off somewhere watching myself.					
14. I'm concerned about what other people think of me.					
15. I'm alert to changes in my mood.					
16. I'm usually aware of my appearance.					
17. I'm aware of the way my mind works when I work through a problem.					

Source: Adapted from A. Fenigstein, M. F. Scheier, and A. H. Buss, "Public and Private Self-Consciousness: Assessment and Theory," *Journal of Consulting and Clinical Psychology* 43 (1975): 522-527.

B **Scoring:** Give yourself four points for every Extremely Like Me, three points for every Somewhat Like Me, two points for every Neither Like Me Nor Unlike Me, one point for every Somewhat Unlike Me, and zero points for every Extremely Unlike Me. Add up the numbers you assigned yourself for all 17 statements. The higher the score, the higher your level of self-consciousness.

What is your total? _____

continued...

To determine your level of private self-consciousness, add up your responses to statements 1, 3, 4, 6, 7, 9, 11, 13, 15, and 17.

What is your total? _____

To determine your level of public self-consciousness, add up your responses to statements 2, 5, 8, 10, 12, 14, and 16.

What is your total? _____

C   The average score of people who have taken this test is 26 for private self-consciousness and 19 for public self-consciousness. How does your total compare to these averages? What does this tell you about yourself?

_____

_____

_____

_____

D   Would you like to become more self-conscious, less self-conscious, or remain about the same? Why?

_____

_____

_____

_____

E   How do you think you could enjoy the benefits of self-consciousness without falling prey to anxiety?

_____

_____

_____

_____

Identifying Your Emotions   As a first clue to identifying what emotions you are experiencing, pay attention to how your body feels. Tense? Relaxed? Excited? Agitated? Tired? Since emotions have a physical as well as a psychological component, being attuned to your body's reactions can help you identify your emotions.

As another clue to your emotional state, look at what occurred right before the emotion started. Did something happen? Did a certain thought go through your mind? After receiving criticism, for example, you might feel hurt or insulted. If you tripped and fell in front of someone you were trying to impress, you might feel embarrassed, silly, or inadequate. If you aren't sure of what situation led to the feeling, ask yourself where your feeling is directed. Are you feeling an emotion toward yourself, toward someone else, or toward no one in particular?

It also helps to look for the precise word to express the emotion you are experiencing. Let's say you are feeling "down" or "bad" but can't figure out exactly how. Ask yourself what adjective best expresses your current state. Are you feeling discouraged? Bitter? Lonely? Rejected? Developing a large vocabulary of feeling words can help you get in touch with your emotions. Figure 2.1 on page 50 lists a wide variety of feeling words that can help you pinpoint your emotions. Once you have found the right word, you may immediately feel a sense of empowerment. The simple act of naming your emotion lets you know what you're up against and how you might go about handling it. Identifying your feelings also helps you feel at peace with them.

success *secret*
Look for the exact word to express what you feel.

DEFINING YOUR DREAMS

Your dreams are a large component of who you are and what makes you special. A **dream** is an aspiration, a hope, or a vision of the future. Having dreams gives our lives meaning, helps us make choices, and helps us persevere in the face of obstacles or hardship. Living without a dream, by contrast, can leave us feeling adrift and unmotivated.

The most successful people are those who began with a dream. A dream is a powerful desire for you to hold on to and one day make a reality. Dreams give our lives purpose, a reason for existing. You, and only you, have the power to make your dream a reality. In order to make your dream a reality, you must have self-awareness and a strong desire to finish what you start.

dream   An aspiration, hope, or vision of the future that gives your life purpose.

The Importance of Purpose

Sometimes, having a purpose can mean the difference between life and death. Dr. Viktor Frankl was a psychiatrist in Vienna, Austria, in the 1930s and became a prisoner in Nazi prison camps during World War II. He experienced three years of horror at Dachau and Auschwitz, narrowly escaping the gas chamber and death several times. In his book *Man's*

success *secret*
Dreams give your life purpose.

FIGURE 2.1 Feeling Words

I Feel Comfortable

admired	delighted	inquisitive	satisfied
adored	devoted	intelligent	secure
amused	earnest	interested	self-accepting
appreciated	ecstatic	joyful	self-assured
attractive	effective	knowledgeable	sincere
brave	elated	loving	skillful
capable	encouraged	optimistic	tender
cheerful	excited	passionate	thrilled
competent	fascinated	pleased	useful
confident	flattered	proud	valued
contented	graceful	rambunctious	vindicated
courageous	grateful	resilient	warm
creative	heroic	resourceful	whole
curious	hopeful	respected	worthy
daring	important	romantic	zealous

I Feel Uncomfortable

afraid	devalued	incompetent	self-doubting
agitated	devastated	jealous	shaken
aloof	disappointed	jittery	silly
angry	discouraged	lonely	skeptical
anxious	embarrassed	lost	snubbed
ashamed	empty	mediocre	sorrowful
awkward	fearful	neglected	suspicious
betrayed	foolish	nervous	tense
burdened	frightened	out of control	terrified
cheated	guilty	panicky	ugly
clumsy	heartbroken	pessimistic	uptight
cranky	helpless	put down	useless
defensive	hostile	rejected	weary
dejected	humiliated	self-critical	worried
deserted	ignored	self-destructive	worthless

Emotional Awareness   To become more emotionally aware, practice asking yourself these three questions: How is my body feeling? What happened right before I started to experience this emotion? Can I put a specific name to this emotion? *Why would developing a vocabulary of feeling words help you become more aware of your emotions?*

Search for Meaning, Frankl used his experience and observations in the camps to write about human behavior under extreme conditions. Movies such as *Schindler's List, The Pianist,* and *The Book Thief* remind us of this human suffering. Seeing himself and others stripped of everything—their families, jobs, clothing, possessions, health, dignity—Frankl studied the behavior of the captives. He wrote down the facts without letting his emotions interfere. He noticed that the prisoners in the concentration camps, who faced the possibility of death every day, were able to survive starvation and torture if they felt they had a purpose for living. Those who felt they had no reason for staying alive died quickly and easily. Of the ones who lived through the death camps, nearly all had a fierce determination to see a loved one or do something important in their lives.

More than any other authority on human behavior, Frankl based his knowledge on firsthand experience. His observations are very different from Sigmund Freud's. Freud said that people may look different, but if they were all deprived of food, they would all behave the same. He felt they would all descend to their basic animal-like instincts.

When Frankl witnessed two people faced with the identical situation in a concentration camp, he saw one crumble and give up while the other stayed strong and hopeful. He saw that people react in very different ways to the same situation, depending on their inner drives and motivations. Many prisoners told Frankl that they no longer expected anything of life. Frankl pointed out that they had it backward. He said, "Life was expecting something of them. Life asks of every individual to discover what it should be." Purpose is what enables each of us to face difficult times and tragedies in our lives.

success *secret*
Life asks something of everyone.

What Should a Dream Be?

No dream is better than any other. No dream is too big to achieve, and no dream is too small to count. It doesn't matter what the contents of your dreams are, as long as they represent what you find meaningful and fulfilling. You might have dreams for your personal life, such as to raise a family or travel the world. You might dream of working with animals, or children, or plants. You might have dreams of recognition and accomplishment, such as to obtain a certain job or complete a certain degree. You might dream of living in a cottage in the countryside, or in a condominium high above New York City. You may have one guiding dream, or several dreams that add up to a picture of life satisfaction for you.

Knowing your dreams is a part of being self-aware. When you ask yourself what your dreams are, you are really asking: What do I want out of life?

success *secret*
A dream can be anything you want it to be.

Reclaiming Your Dreams
All children have dreams. As we grow up, however, our dreams often get lost, buried, or set aside. We become busy with the business of day-to-day existence. We begin to worry about what other people will think. Often, parents, relatives, and other significant adults in our lives damage our dreams by conveying messages of disapproval. Some parents want their children to follow in their footsteps. Other parents want their children to achieve things that they did not. For many of us, it is easier to go along with what other people want

success *secret*
Aim to satisfy yourself, not someone else.

than to figure out what we want for ourselves. But if you make plans to merely satisfy parents, partners, or peers, your success will make you feel empty—you will not be fulfilling your dream, but someone else's. That's why having and following your own dream is vital to achieving personal and career success.

If you are not sure what your dreams are, try thinking back to your early childhood, before you learned to criticize yourself or worry about what other people might think. What did you want to be when you grew up? What exciting vision did you have of the future? What subjects fascinated you? What did you want to accomplish before someone told you it was impossible, silly, or a bad idea? To begin getting in touch with your dreams, complete **Personal Journal 2.2.**

GETTING IN TOUCH WITH YOUR VALUES

values The beliefs and principles you choose to live by.

The next step in becoming more self-aware is exploring your values. **Values** are the beliefs and principles you choose to live by. Values include moral and religious beliefs, but they cover all other areas of your life, too. Your values help define who you are. They shape your attitudes and help you identify your priorities. If you have not defined your values, you will have difficulty laying out goals for the future.

ethics The principles you use to define acceptable behavior and decide what is right and wrong.

Values are closely intertwined with **ethics,** the principles you use to define acceptable behavior and decide what is right and wrong. However, there is no such thing as a "right" or "wrong" value. Your values reflect what matters to you as a unique individual.

Everyone has a different set of values. Author Rita Baltus tells the story of a missionary who had gone to a poverty-stricken nation to help people in need. Two tourists visiting the country saw the missionary cleaning a man who had leprosy, a disease that creates skin lesions. One tourist turned to the other and said, "I wouldn't do that for a million dollars." The missionary looked up and replied, "Neither would I." Clearly the missionary valued something other than money.

success *secret*
It's important to determine your own values.

Examining Your Values   Do you know which values are most important to you? Although everyone lives by different principles and beliefs, many people value at least some of the following:

- **Adventure**—exploring the world; seeking new experiences
- **Commitment**—dedicating yourself to a goal
- **Community**—feeling a connection to a neighborhood or group
- **Compassion**—having sympathy for suffering and working to reduce it
- **Competition**—testing yourself through rivalry and challenge
- **Courage**—taking risks; showing strength against fear, danger, and difficulty
- **Creativity**—experimenting; expressing yourself; trying new ideas
- **Environmentalism**—preserving the natural environment

Personal Journal 2.2

What Are Your Dreams?

Complete the following sentences. Write down your first thoughts without judging yourself.

I've always wanted to _____

_____

_____

If I were to receive an award, I would want it to be for _____

_____

_____

The things that make life worth living are _____

_____

_____

The best thing that could possibly happen to me is _____

_____

_____

If I were nearing the end of my life, I would regret not having _____

_____

_____

Look at what you wrote above. Do you see any common words, images, or subjects? Write down four or five dreams that you have right now. These dreams may be any size, take any amount of time, and belong to any area of your life, such as education, career, relationships, lifestyle, appearance, health, travel, or spirituality.

Applying **Psychology**

Lead by Example

When it comes to ethics on the job, management's actions definitely speak more loudly than words. According to research conducted by the Ethics Resource Center, employees are more likely to comply with standards of ethics if their managers clearly set a good example, keep promises and commitments, and openly support those who do the same. The research showed that these actions were much more effective than formal company training programs. In essence, employees want to see their managers "walk the talk."

According to the study, formal training of junior employees should focus on preparing them to handle specific situations of misconduct. Training for upper management should instruct them how to demonstrate to others their personal commitment to ethical standards. Obviously, these actions should be genuine—not phony or forced.

Most major companies have a written code of ethics that all employees are expected to adhere to (and in many cases must sign). These usually include the basics of employee behavior as well as specific issues related to the type of business (such as confidentiality).

Critical Thinking   If you were running a business, what are some of the important behaviors and values you might write into your "code of ethics"?

- **Fairness**—treating others in a just and impartial way
- **Financial security**—being free from worries about money
- **Fun**—enjoying yourself and having a good time in life
- **Generosity**—treating others in a giving way
- **Hard work**—giving your full effort on the job and at home
- **Health**—feeling fit; enjoying physical and mental well-being
- **Honesty**—thinking, speaking, and acting in a forthright way
- **Independence**—making your own decisions; having options
- **Integrity**—doing the right thing; acting ethically
- **Kindness**—behaving in a caring and helpful way toward others
- **Knowledge**—seeking truth and understanding
- **Learning**—pursuing education; growing as a person
- **Loyalty**—remaining faithful and devoted to a person or cause
- **Physical appearance**—looking attractive, groomed, and healthy
- **Power**—having influence over people and situations
- **Recognition**—receiving acknowledgement for your efforts
- **Relationships**—enjoying affection and belonging
- **Responsibility**—honoring obligations; being reliable
- **Security**—being free from anxiety; having your needs met
- **Social responsibility**—contributing to the welfare of society and to the solution of social problems
- **Solitude**—enjoying time alone for rest and renewal

- **Spirituality**—searching for a greater good, purpose, or meaning to human existence
- **Tolerance**—accepting other people, cultures, and ideas
- **Wealth**—having enough money to support an affluent lifestyle

Before you commit to a set of values, it's important to consider the factors that may influence your choice.

Like other aspects of ourselves, our values are greatly influenced by our family, religious beliefs, teachers, friends, and personal experiences. Our values are also influenced by the society in which we live. Values that are frequently promoted in democratic societies (such as the United States and Canada) include independence, freedom, responsibility, security, and tolerance. Sometimes, however, our society's values can be confusing. Although most of us are taught to respect hard work and generosity, for example, we are exposed to some media images that glamorize the idea of instant fame and riches.

We can also become confused about our values when we adopt other people's values as our own. Let's say your parents greatly value financial security, but you are willing to sacrifice financial security for adventure. Will you adopt your parents' values, perhaps following their career and lifestyle suggestions, or will you become your own person? Deep down, you may feel that your values are "wrong" and that your parents' values are "right." Remember, however, that values are personal beliefs about what is important, not absolutes of right and wrong. If you aren't sure whether or not you are really committed to a value, ask yourself:

- Did I choose this value, or did I copy it from someone else?
- Does this value make me feel good about myself?
- Will other people benefit if I act according to this value?
- Will something truly bad happen if I don't follow this value?
- Is this value flexible enough to allow me to pursue my needs and goals?

Now it's time to take a look at your values. Review the list of values above and on the previous pages, then complete **Activity 8.**

Your Values at Work

Values have a large influence on the choices we make in our lives. One of the most important of these choices is that of a career. If you value adventure, you can be sure you will be happier as a police officer or a flight attendant than as an accountant. If you value creativity, you will thrive in a job where you have the chance to express yourself and come up with new ideas. If you value knowledge, you might enjoy a career in teaching, research, science, or journalism.

Of course, no job can suit all of your values perfectly. One job might give you ample independence and adventure, for example, but offer little security. Another might reward you financially and creatively, but provide

success *secret*
Values are beliefs, not absolutes.

success *secret*
Values guide your choices in life.

ACTIVITY 8: Values Inventory

A Choose 10 values that matter the most to you. Choose from the values listed on pages 52, 54, and 55, or use another source if you feel that something is missing from that list. Write the name of each value in the left-hand column below.

Value	Ranking	Comments

B Now rank these values in order of their importance to you. In the ranking column, write in the numbers 1 (lowest) through 10 (highest) to represent each value's importance. In the Comments column at right, briefly explain why you rated each item as you did.

C Write down your top three values. For each one, explain why it is important to you and one way you use it, or plan to use it, to guide your choices in life.

#1 Value _____

_____

#2 Value _____

_____

#3 Value _____

_____

D Who or what do you think have been the greatest influences on your values? Explain.

_____

_____

_____

_____

_____

_____

_____

E What values do you feel are most important for your friends and romantic partners to have? Are they the same as your top-ranked values? Explain.

_____

_____

_____

_____

_____

_____

_____

F Think of an area of your life in which you are not following one of your values. For example, you may value honesty but be withholding important information from a friend or family member for some reason. Describe the situation and explain whether or not you feel you are doing the right thing.

_____

_____

_____

_____

_____

_____

_____

fewer opportunities than you would like to help others. That's why it is important to find a balance between fulfillment in work and fulfillment in life. That's also why it is important to decide which of your values you want to be foremost in your work.

Look at the 10 values you identified as most important in Activity 8. Which of these are most crucial to you in your work? Which would you be willing to sacrifice? For example, would you be willing to sacrifice some pay for a job that allows you to help others? Would you be willing to take a job that is high in independence even if it meant less time for family?

Also ask yourself how you could create more opportunities for yourself to express your values. What action could you take at work to better express your values? If you value solitude, could you schedule blocks of time when you could work alone and undisturbed? If you value learning, could you volunteer for a new project?

You can also create opportunities to express your values outside of work. If you value generosity, you might volunteer at a homeless shelter or deliver food to the needy. If you value relationships, you might make a start by reviving old friendships and strengthening your family bonds. Activities such as community service, independent study, artistic expression, and spiritual practice can all provide opportunities to express your values and fulfill your purpose in life.

success *secret*

Look for opportunities to express your values in a positive way.

Self Check

1. What is self-awareness? (p. 44)
2. Why is it important to have a dream? (p. 49)
3. What are values? (p. 52)

PERSONALITY AND INDIVIDUALITY

You should now know some important information about yourself—what you want out of life and what you value. Now it's time to look at the personal qualities and talents that make you unique.

There are over six billion people on our planet, but no two are alike. People are just as different from one another in their behavior, such as the way they react to situations or the kinds of emotions they tend to feel, as they are in their appearance, such as their hair color or body shape.

To make sense of the many ways in which people differ from one another, psychologists use the concept of personality. In everyday language, the word personality usually refers to a person's likability and popularity. In psychology, however, **personality** is the relatively stable pattern of behavior that distinguishes one person from all other people. In other words, a personality is an individual's pattern of emotions (feelings), cognitions (thoughts), and actions.

People's personalities can be described as collections of traits. A **trait** is a disposition to behave in a certain way regardless of the situation. For example, if optimism is one of your traits, you are likely to be optimistic in most situations. If friendliness is one of your traits, you are likely to be friendly to most people. Traits give consistency to our behavior. They make it possible for us to say that John is outgoing, or Gabriela is funny, or Joselyn is talkative.

Are some personality traits "better" than others? No, although some traits may help us succeed in a particular setting or profession. A sociable, talkative person would do better in a sales career, for example, than someone who is more reserved and quiet. An inquisitive, unconventional student might have trouble relating to a teacher who is closed-minded. Other traits, such as self-discipline, persistence, and self-motivation, are useful to everyone because they help us achieve our goals.

personality The relatively stable pattern of behavior that distinguishes you from all other people.

trait A disposition to behave in a certain way regardless of the situation.

Where Do Traits Come From?

Our traits are shaped by our genes, but also by our upbringing and experiences. Psychologists continue to debate which influence is more important, heredity ("nature") or environment ("nurture"). Evidence can be found for both sides. Identical twins, for example, tend to have similar personality traits whether they are raised together or apart. This suggests that we inherit a large portion of our personalities from our parents. Yet adopted children tend to share traits with their adoptive parents. This suggests the opposite conclusion—that the environment we grow up in has a decisive effect on our behavior. In short, heredity and environment both

success *secret*
Use your personality traits to help you succeed.

have an influence on our personality, but neither one controls the way we think, feel, or act.

Have you ever considered your personality traits? What do people tell you about your personality? What do you feel is true about you? Use the adjective checklist in **Activity 9** on pages 61–62 to construct a personality self-portrait.

How Many Traits Are There?

How many different personality traits are there? A hundred? A thousand? Nearly 150 traits were listed in **Activity 9.** You could probably come up with dozens of adjectives to describe your friends' personalities. Honest. Smart. Responsible. Lighthearted. Sensitive. Psychologists who examined *Webster's Dictionary* found 18,000 terms to describe people's personalities!

The "Big Five" Personality Traits

Which five traits did you pick to describe yourself in Activity 9? They are probably different from the five traits your classmates picked to describe themselves. But what if everyone could be described with the same five traits? Sound impossible? Recent research in personality has shown that people's personalities can, in fact, be fairly accurately described using only five traits. This model of personality uses the following "big five" personality traits:

- **Openness**—imaginativeness; openness to new people, ideas, and experiences
- **Conscientiousness**—self-discipline and desire to achieve

---

internet action

ONLINE PERSONALITY PROFILES

Do you like to spend your leisure time alone, or are you more at home in a crowd? Are you a risk-taker, or do you prefer to play it safe? Today dozens of Web sites offer personality tests that can help you answer these questions—and more. Online tests range from highly researched tools, such as the Keirsey Temperament Sorter, to light-hearted quizzes that interpret your personality based on your choice of color or dog breed. Taking a personality test can be an eye-opening experience. Which of these tests have real value? Some personality tests on the Web are backed by science, but most are really for entertainment, not serious self-exploration. How do you know which is which, especially when many Web sites don't make it clear? Trustworthy Web sites generally provide information on the psychological research behind their tests. You are

really the ultimate judge. If you think the results of an online test don't seem accurate, they probably aren't!

Think About It

Use the Internet to research personality tests. What kinds of tests exist? How do they differ from one another? Try a couple of the personality tests at the links below.

Big Five Personality Test
http://www.outofservice.com/bigfive/
Humanmetrics Jung Typology Test
http://www.humanmetrics.com/cgi-win/JTypes2.asp
Keirsey Temperament Sorter
http://keirsey.com
Three Sides of You Profiler
http://personal.ansir.com

ACTIVITY 9: Personality Self-Portrait

A   Consider all the personality traits listed below. Put a check mark in the box next to each trait that you feel describes you most or all of the time. (If you are unsure about the meaning of any word, consult a dictionary.) Remember that no trait is better than any other trait.

☐ abstract	☐ clever	☐ extroverted	☐ informal
☐ accurate	☐ competitive	☐ fair	☐ inquisitive
☐ active	☐ confident	☐ farsighted	☐ intelligent
☐ adaptable	☐ conscientious	☐ firm	☐ inventive
☐ adventurous	☐ conservative	☐ flexible	☐ kind
☐ affectionate	☐ considerate	☐ forceful	☐ lighthearted
☐ alert	☐ consistent	☐ forgiving	☐ likable
☐ ambitious	☐ cool	☐ forthright	☐ lively
☐ anxious	☐ cooperative	☐ friendly	☐ logical
☐ apprehensive	☐ courageous	☐ generous	☐ loving
☐ artistic	☐ creative	☐ gentle	☐ loyal
☐ assertive	☐ curious	☐ good-natured	☐ mature
☐ attractive	☐ deferent	☐ grounded	☐ methodical
☐ bold	☐ determined	☐ healthy	☐ modest
☐ broad-minded	☐ distant	☐ helpful	☐ motivated
☐ businesslike	☐ dominant	☐ hesitant	☐ neat
☐ calm	☐ down-to-earth	☐ honest	☐ open-minded
☐ capable	☐ eager	☐ hopeful	☐ optimistic
☐ careful	☐ easygoing	☐ humble	☐ organized
☐ caring	☐ efficient	☐ humorous	☐ original
☐ charming	☐ emotional	☐ imaginative	☐ outgoing
☐ cheerful	☐ energetic	☐ impulsive	☐ patient
☐ clear-thinking	☐ enthusiastic	☐ independent	☐ perfectionistic

continued...

☐ persevering	☐ resourceful	☐ sincere	☐ thoughtful
☐ pleasant	☐ responsible	☐ skeptical	☐ thrill-seeking
☐ polite	☐ rule-conscious	☐ sociable	☐ tolerant
☐ practical	☐ secure	☐ spontaneous	☐ tough
☐ private	☐ self-assured	☐ stable	☐ traditional
☐ quick	☐ self-confident	☐ steady	☐ trusting
☐ quiet	☐ self-disciplined	☐ strong	☐ trustworthy
☐ reactive	☐ self-reliant	☐ strong-minded	☐ understanding
☐ realistic	☐ sensible	☐ strong-willed	☐ vigilant
☐ rebellious	☐ sensitive	☐ supportive	☐ warm
☐ relaxed	☐ sentimental	☐ tactful	☐ wary
☐ reliable	☐ serious	☐ tenacious	☐ wistful
☐ reserved	☐ shy	☐ tense	☐ witty

B If you had to pick the five traits that describe you best, which would they be?

1. _____

2. _____

3. _____

4. _____

5. _____

C Of which one or two specific personality traits are you proudest? Why?

_____

_____

_____

_____

_____

_____

_____

D How is your personality different from the personalities of your family members? How is it similar? Explain.

_____

_____

_____

_____

_____

_____

_____

- **Extroversion**—assertiveness, sociability, and interest in excitement and activity
- **Agreeableness**—trustworthiness, warmth, and cooperativeness
- **Emotional stability**—resistance to negative emotions such as anxiety, anger, and depression

Each person shows each of these traits to a different degree. One person, for example, might show a very high degree of openness, another might show little or no openness, and a third might fall somewhere between these two extremes. These five traits have been tested in various countries, from China to Israel to Spain, with similar results.

Natural Aptitudes (Talents), Multiple Intelligences

Early in the 20th-century, Johnson O'Connor, a Harvard graduate in philosophy, realized that happy, productive, achieving, pace-setting leaders, professionals, craftsmen, and artists were generally engaged in work for which they had natural ability. This prompted O'Connor to devise a battery of tests for measuring innate ability—a battery still used by the Johnson O'Connor Research Foundation and, in a slightly modified form, by the Ball Foundation, both of which are non-profit, scientific research organizations in the United States. Landmark studies by Harvard's Dr. Howard Gardner confirmed O'Connor's discovery that intelligence is multiple and varied, not unitary and homogeneous—and that a variety of natural talents should be tested. Johnson O'Connor and his colleagues identified seventeen of these traits, and no doubt there are more.

The tests are broken down into categories:

Personality determines if a person is objective—best suited for working with others—or subjective and more suited for specialized individual work.

Graphoria identifies clerical ability and ability to deal with figures and symbols—abilities necessary for performing bookkeeping, editing, and secretarial tasks at high levels of speed and efficiency. Graphoria is usually also a good indicator of how well a person will do in school.

Ideaphoria measures creative imagination and the ability to express ideas, which is needed in fields such as sales, advertising, teaching, public relations, and journalism.

Structural visualization tests the ability to visualize solids and think in three dimensions. This aptitude, often possessed by concrete thinkers who do less well with abstract thinking, is critical for engineers, mechanics, and architects.

Inductive reasoning, which helps form logical conclusions from fragmented facts, is important for lawyers, researchers, diagnostic physicians, writers, and critics—all of whom must be able to move quickly from the particular to the general, perceiving patterns—and the big picture—from a collection of details.

Analytical reasoning is necessary for writers, editors, computer programmers, and others who must organize concepts and ideas into classifications and/or sequences.

Finger dexterity is needed for all forms of manual or mechanical work, including computing and word processing. Also important for creative arts such as sculpting and piano playing.

Tweezers dexterity is the skill in handling small tools with precision, which is vital for professions such as surgery, watchmaking, and assembling microchips. Surprisingly, there is little correlation between this skill and finger dexterity.

Observation, the ability to take careful notice, is tested by showing examinees a photograph of a number of objects, then asking them to identify the slight changes in ten more photos of the same objects. Valuable for artists and painters, keen powers of observation are especially useful for researchers and investigators of all kinds, as in the study of microscopic slides.

Design memory, the ability to remember designs of all kinds, is extremely helpful for everyone who works with plans or blueprints as well as in art.

Tonal memory is the ability to remember and reproduce sounds. *Pitch discrimination* differentiates musical tones. *Rhythm memory* measures rhythm timing.

Timbre discrimination measures the ability to distinguish sounds of the same pitch and volume.

Number memory, the ability to store many things in the mind at the same time, is useful in professions such as the law, medicine, and scholarship that require summoning quantities of facts and information on which to base judgments, diagnoses, or determinations.

Numerical reasoning, an aptitude for identifying relationships among sets of numbers, is most helpful in bookkeeping, accounting, computer programming, and actuarial work.

Silograms measure the ability to learn unfamiliar words and languages. Vital for translators, this skill is also important for speech teachers, language teachers, and persons doing written translation work.

Foresight is the ability to keep the mind on a distant goal and visualize paths and obstacles. Market research analysts, sales forecasters, political scientists, diplomats, politicians, and corporate leaders are among the many who need foresight.

Color perception, the ability to distinguish colors, is obviously essential for fashion designing, multimedia graphic artists, painting, interior decorating, and advertising—and for all professions and crafts involving art and layout functions.

Most people tested by the Johnson O'Connor and the Ball Foundations have three to five strong aptitudes; few have more than seven. In some of his earliest tests, Johnson O'Connor found a distinct correlation between vocabulary and career success. O'Connor consultants now stress the continuing importance of vocabulary. As we become more dependent on texting and tweeting on mobile devices as our communication methods of choice, vocabulary test scores have plummeted at the high school and college level in recent decades. Aptitudes, skills, and interests point which direction a person should go, and the vocabulary level helps predict how far a person probably will go in his or her chosen career. Another way to say this is that limited vocabulary and a lesser ability to communicate keep many people with excellent abilities of other kinds from developing them and profiting from them. The good news is that vocabulary, far more than any of the basic, natural aptitudes, can be improved with effort and discipline. Increased reading of both fiction and non-fiction works can be richly rewarding. Knowledge is gained, imagination is stimulated, and communication skills are enhanced.

Although the aptitude tests have been given to children as young as nine, they are probably most effective at age sixteen to eighteen, when high school students are making college or career choices. They are also important to anyone considering a career or industry shift. The earlier you can discover your natural gifts the better—but it's never too late. Identifying natural ability is also important for avoiding disappointment, frustration, and anger in career choices. One young son of a surgeon couldn't follow in his famous father's footsteps because he hesitated too much during simple surgical procedures. His father branded this as cowardice. In fact, it was a lack of tweezer dexterity. Structural visualization, another prerequisite for good surgeons, is not passed on from father to son, only from mother to son. Since daughters can inherit structural visualization from both parents, surgeons might better look more to their girls to carry on the family tradition.

It would be irresponsible to suggest that aptitude tests alone should determine career choice. Natural abilities, intelligences, acquired skills, interests, imitation of role models, youthful experience—all those factors are involved, together, of course, with circumstance. Our major decisions often hinge heavily on family considerations, particularly financial realities, at pivotal ages. Still, it's hard to be rational or wise about developing our lives without taking conscious steps to discover our natural abilities—and as early as possible. Even if we decide to pursue our gifts as hobbies and diversions, that promises less futility than if we ignore them entirely. Many of our frustrations lie deep within us. We can't explain them even to our loved ones; we can only say, "I don't know why I feel I'm wasting my life, but I do." Exhaustive testing demonstrates again and again that we all have talents. How much more satisfied and fulfilled we feel when we're able to express them creatively and regularly!

Another useful way to understand traits and abilities is to see them as ways of using intelligence. What does intelligence have to do with developing your innate talents into skills—isn't intelligence about having a high score on an IQ test? Not at all. In fact, IQ scores have almost no relationship to real-world intelligence. IQ tests measure verbal and mathematical ability, which you need to excel in traditional academic subjects. They don't measure your ability to choreograph a dance, navigate a ship, weave a basket, observe nature, or console an upset friend. All of these abilities represent intelligence, too. These different kinds of intelligence are known as *multiple intelligences.*

Researchers who study multiple intelligences define **intelligence** as a set of abilities that enables you to solve certain types of real-world problems. They have identified eight distinct kinds of intelligence:

intelligence A set of abilities that enables you to solve certain types of real-world problems.

- **Verbal/linguistic intelligence**—ability to use words and language, memorize information, and create imaginary worlds
- **Logical/mathematical intelligence**—ability in complex thinking and reasoning, using numbers, and recognizing abstract patterns
- **Visual/spatial intelligence**—ability to visualize objects and spatial dimensions and create mental images
- **Bodily/kinesthetic intelligence**—ability to understand and use the body and to control its motion in activities such as sports, dancing, acting, and crafts
- **Musical intelligence**—ability to recognize rhythms, beats, and sounds, remember melodies, and distinguish background sounds
- **Interpersonal intelligence**—ability in person-to-person communication, leadership, and conflict resolution
- **Intrapersonal intelligence**—ability to be self-aware and self-reflective, pursue interests, and set goals
- **Naturalistic intelligence**—ability to recognize patterns and make connections in nature, assemble collections, and identify plants and animals

success *secret*
Pinpointing your strongest intelligences helps you discover what you do best.

Each of us has all of these eight intelligences, but each of us is stronger in one or two particular intelligences than the others. Which intelligences are your greatest strengths? The self-assessment in **Activity 10** on page 72 will help you pinpoint your strongest intelligences.

FIGURE 2.2 Expanding Your Intelligences

Intelligence	Strategies
Verbal/Linguistic	• Join a book club or take a writing course. • Read anything and everything. • Use a new word in your conversation every day.
Logical/Mathematical	• Work on puzzles and brain teasers. • Visit a science center, planetarium, or aquarium. • Practice calculating problems in your head.
Visual/Spatial	• Work on jigsaw puzzles or visual puzzles. • Visit art museums and galleries. • Take a class in visual arts, such as photography.
Bodily/Kinesthetic	• Join a gym or a sports team. • Learn dance, yoga, t'ai chi, or martial arts. • Enroll in an aerobics or weight-training class.
Musical	• Attend concerts and musicals. • Take a class in music appreciation or performance. • Explore unfamiliar styles of music.
Interpersonal	• Join a volunteer or service group. • Learn about body language and communication. • Introduce yourself to new people often.
Intrapersonal	• Develop a meditative hobby, such as gardening. • Keep a journal of your thoughts and feelings. • Consult a counselor or therapist.
Naturalistic	• Explore the flora and fauna of your region. • Look for patterns in nature or architecture. • Start a collection of objects.

Learning + Practice = Progress Exploring new activities and meeting new people help you build your intelligences and discover new interests. *Select the intelligence you would most like to develop, and describe three specific actions you could take to do this.*

Developing Your Intelligences

You can strengthen your intelligences through learning and practice. To expand your interpersonal intelligence, for example, you might read a book about communication skills, then experiment with the strategies suggested in the book. To build your naturalistic intelligence, you might learn about plants and then try your hand at gardening. Strategies for developing all eight intelligences are listed in Figure 2.2.

EXPLORING YOUR SKILLS AND INTERESTS

Your personality and values are the foundation of who you are and where you will go in the future. They represent the core of who you are as a unique person. In addition to our personal qualities, however, each of us has a unique collection of skills that we can use to get where we want to go. A **skill** is the ability to do something specific as a result of learning and practice. Skills are often expressed as verbs, such as negotiating, speaking, memorizing, drawing, healing, photographing, or sewing.

Where do skills come from? No one is born knowing how to drive a car or do a crossword puzzle. Instead, skills are the result of knowledge combined with experience. **Knowledge** is an understanding of facts or principles in a particular subject area. For example, you might have knowledge of computers, Spanish, football, botany, cats, history, American literature, or interior design.

Knowledge alone is valuable, but it isn't a skill until it is combined with real-world experience. To perform surgery, you need more than knowledge of anatomy. You also need hands-on practice with a scalpel. So it is with any skill. To write well, for example, you need knowledge of grammar, style, and the subject you are writing about. You also need practice in organizing your ideas and expressing yourself clearly.

skill The ability to do something specific as a result of learning and practice.

knowledge An understanding of facts or principles in a particular subject area.

Types of Skills

There are two basic types of skills, *transferable skills* and *job-specific skills*. A job-specific skill is the ability to do a specific task or job. Setting a broken bone, using a table saw, and programming a computer are all job-specific skills. A transferable skill is an ability that you can use in a variety of tasks and jobs. Working with your hands, organizing information, writing, and making decisions are all transferable skills.

It's easy to think that job-specific skills are more important than transferable skills. After all, when you hire a plumber to fix your leaky toilet, you want someone who knows how to fix pipes. However, transferable skills are the foundation of specific skills. How would the plumber be able to solve plumbing problems if he or she wasn't too good at reasoning? How would he or she be able to run a business without skills in math and organizing information?

Building transferable skills helps you attain your goals, manage time and stress, and communicate well. From time to time, it is helpful to evaluate your skill strengths and weaknesses to see how far you have come and where you now want to go. If you aren't sure what your skills are, ask yourself these questions:

success *secret*
Transferable skills are the foundation of job-specific skills.

Copyright © 2016 The McGraw-Hill Companies

- What do I have experience doing?
- What areas of knowledge do I have?
- What projects have I completed at home, work, or school?
- What problems have I solved? What skills did that show?
- What do I enjoy doing? What kinds of skills does this require?

Consider the skills you currently have and examine those you want to develop in **Activity 11** on page 75.

Discovering Your Interests

Over the last pages, you have created a portrait of your skills and intelligences. Now you will complete the picture by looking at a closely related area—your interests. **Interests** are personal preferences for specific topics and activities. The better you know your interests, the easier it will be for you to plan your academic and career path.

What do you like and enjoy? If you're not sure what your interests are, it's never too late to begin your search. Get started by asking yourself the questions in **Personal Journal 2.3** on page 79.

As you consider your interests, think of all of them—don't omit any out of fear that they aren't important or special enough. It doesn't matter how many or how few people share a particular interest, as long as the interest is genuine. If you follow your interests, you will enjoy your work and hobbies more. People who ignore their interests often end up in careers they don't enjoy or care much about. Lynn, for example, enjoyed theater but decided to major in business because she thought that acting wasn't a "real" career. Gregg thought of his interest in carpentry as "just a hobby," and missed out on the chance to build it into an enjoyable and rewarding career.

Skills and Interests   Chances are, your interests and skills lie in the same areas. That's because people are usually skilled at the things they are interested in, and interested in the things they are skilled at. Why is this? For one thing, all of us are motivated to build skills at the things we like to do. Imagine two students in a piano class. One is interested in music and enjoys practicing. The other couldn't care less about music and does everything possible to avoid practicing. Which student is going to develop skill at playing the piano?

Another reason that skills and interests tend to go together is that having skill at something makes doing it more fun and interesting. If you have skill at playing soccer, for example, you're likely to be much more interested in the sport than someone who has no ability at the game. Look back at the multiple intelligences you identified in Activity 10. Notice that each section of the questionnaire asked you not only what you are good at but also what you like to do. If you have a high musical intelligence, for example, you probably enjoy music in addition to being good at it.

When you engage in activities you enjoy and are skilled at, you are more likely to experience what psychologists call flow. Flow is a state of exhilaration and intense productivity that occurs when you are absorbed in an activity that makes full use of your skills.

PUTTING IT ALL TOGETHER: SELF-AWARENESS AND WORK

Most of us will spend about 80,000 hours of our lives at work. The work we do, therefore, has an enormous impact on our success and happiness. Now that you know more about yourself, you can use this information to explore career fields that might be right for you. While friends, teachers, and family members often offer helpful suggestions for potential careers, you are ultimately in charge of making your own decisions. This is true whether you are a high school student or a longtime veteran of the working world. No matter where you are on your career path, you will benefit from considering the careers that would take full advantage of your skills and interests.

Why Work Matters

As a first step, it is worthwhile to stop and consider your ideas about work. What does work mean to you? A 9-to-5 job? A nameplate on a desk? When you have a positive attitude toward work, it becomes much more than this. Work brings many rewards, including:

- **Satisfaction**—We gain a sense of satisfaction and self-worth from a job well done. We also earn the respect and appreciation of others.
- **Relationships**—Work is a chance to meet and learn from other people who share our interests.
- **Meaning**—Through work, we can express our values, work toward our life goals, and fulfill our personal purpose in life.

With self-awareness and planning, work can help you expand your skills, express your values and interests, and challenge yourself to grow.

What if you find yourself in a job or career that's not right for you? Less than a generation ago, workers often stayed with a single company for life. Today, however, job mobility is the norm. In fact, the average American changes jobs six times by the age of thirty. While workers have less job security than they once did, they also have more freedom to explore different jobs and careers. Today it is common for people to switch jobs and even careers as they explore their interests and skills. If you change your mind, you haven't lost out. You've gained greater self-awareness and developed valuable transferable skills.

ACTIVITY 10: Discover Your Multiple Intelligences

A Put a check mark next to each statement that you feel accurately describes you. If you do not identify with a statement, leave it blank.

Section 1

_____ I like writing and reading almost anything.

_____ I enjoy public speaking.

_____ Foreign languages interest me.

_____ I enjoy word games.

_____ I am good at expressing myself in speech and writing.

_____ I like to keep a journal or write letters to friends.

Section 2

_____ I am quick to solve problems.

_____ I can easily remember formulas.

_____ Disorganized people frustrate me.

_____ I am good at finding and understanding patterns.

_____ I am able to follow complex lines of reasoning.

_____ I can perform quick calculations in my head.

Section 3

_____ I like to build, design, and create things.

_____ I have a good sense of direction and read maps easily.

_____ Rearranging a room is fun for me.

_____ I learn best by visualizing.

_____ I have a vivid imagination.

_____ I like music videos and multimedia art.

Section 4

_____ I can remember songs and rhymes easily.

_____ I like to make up tunes and melodies.

_____ I prefer musicals to dramatic plays.

_____ Musical instruments interest me.

_____ I notice rhythms and can easily pick up sounds.

_____ I have trouble studying if the television or radio is on.

Section 5

_____ I am good at sports and am physically coordinated.

_____ I like to demonstrate to others how to do something.

_____ I have trouble sitting still for a long time.

_____ I tend to use a lot of body language when I talk.

_____ I like to invent things, put things together, and take them apart.

_____ I live an active lifestyle.

Section 6

_____ I am good at listening and communicating with others.

_____ I am a good team player.

_____ I'd rather work in a group than by myself.

_____ I am sensitive to the moods and feelings of others.

_____ I am able to figure out the motives and intentions of others.

_____ I enjoy talk shows and interviews.

Section 7

_____ I am very curious.

_____ I am able to express my inner feelings.

_____ I tend to be quiet and self-reflective.

_____ I am very independent.

_____ I like to work alone and pursue my own interests.

_____ I am always asking questions.

Section 8

_____ I learn best by identifying and categorizing things.

_____ I like to collect items from nature and study them.

_____ I am good at picking up on subtleties.

_____ I notice patterns easily.

_____ I like being outdoors and observing nature.

_____ Environmental issues are important to me.

B Scoring: Add up the number of check marks you placed in each section.

Section 1 total _____ reflects your verbal/linguistic intelligence.

Section 2 total _____ reflects your logical/mathematical intelligence.

Section 3 total _____ reflects your visual/spatial intelligence.

Section 4 total _____ reflects your musical/rhythmic intelligence.

Section 5 total _____ reflects your bodily/kinesthetic intelligence.

Section 6 total _____ reflects your interpersonal intelligence.

Section 7 total _____ reflects your intrapersonal intelligence.

Section 8 total _____ reflects your naturalistic intelligence.

Which intelligence(s) are you strongest in?

continued...

C How do you use your strongest intelligence(s) at work or school? Give examples.

_____

_____

_____

_____

_____

_____

D Describe a situation in which you used your strongest intelligence(s) to solve a problem or accomplish a goal.

_____

_____

_____

_____

_____

_____

E Which one or two intelligences would you most like to develop further? Why?

_____

_____

_____

_____

_____

_____

_____

ACTIVITY 11: Skills Assessment

A You may think you don't have many transferable skills, but you may be surprised by how many you do have and exhibit every day. Think of anything and everything that you know how to do and write it down in 1. For example, are you good at speaking to children, friends, or groups of people? Repairing cars, machines, or tools? For help describing your skills, look at the words in 2 for examples of verbs. See 3 for examples of potential nouns to use.

1. **My skills:**

   Example: editing documents

   _____   _____
   _____   _____
   _____   _____
   _____   _____
   _____   _____
   _____   _____
   _____   _____
   _____   _____
   _____   _____
   _____   _____

2. **Verbs**

advising	deciding	finding	motivating	repairing
analyzing	describing	handling	negotiating	researching
assembling	designing	helping	organizing	selling
building	developing	identifying	performing	speaking (to)
calculating	drawing	inventing	persuading	teaching
coaching	editing	learning	planning	setting up
counseling	evaluating	listening (to)	reading	using
creating	expressing	managing	remembering	writing

3. **Nouns**

animals	equipment	individuals	numbers	tasks
art	events	information	objects	technology
books	experiments	languages	organizations	theater
cars	feelings	machines	plants	things
children	files	meetings	problems	time
computers	friends	money	projects	tools
concepts	groups of people	music	reports	words
documents	ideas	needs	sports	

continued...

B Look over all the skills you wrote down and select the three that you are proudest of. For each one, describe a situation in which you used that skill to accomplish something that mattered to you. For example, you may have helped someone, solved a difficult problem, or built or repaired something.

Skill #1 _____

_____

_____

_____

_____

Skill #2 _____

_____

_____

_____

_____

Skill #3 _____

_____

_____

_____

_____

C Now list three skills you would like to improve. For each one, think of some specific things you could do to improve it. (Remember that skills are a combination of knowledge and experience.)

Skill #1 _____

_____

_____

_____

_____

Skill #2 _____

_____

_____

_____

_____

Skill #3 _____

_____

_____

_____

_____

Myths About Work Many people see work as a daily grind—just a way to pay the bills. Consider the following common misconceptions about work and careers. Do any of them ring true for you?

1. By nature, work is unpleasant.
2. If I do what I enjoy, I won't make any money.
3. If I don't know what I want to do for the rest of my life, there must be something wrong with me.
4. I'm the only one who doesn't have a fixed occupational goal.
5. There is one, and only one, perfect career for me.
6. Somewhere, there is an expert or a test that will tell me exactly what I should do for the rest of my life.
7. A "real" job is 9 to 5, five days a week, working for someone else.
8. What I do at work defines who I am as a person.
9. Once I choose a career, I should stick with it no matter what.
10. You have to suffer to get ahead.

These myths spring from a negative attitude toward work. In reality, work can and should be something you enjoy. Your career is an important part of your identity, but it does not limit who you are as a person.

There are also many myths about the "right" way to pursue a career. In reality, each person's career path is different. Some people have very specific career goals from a young age, while others need time to explore career possibilities. There is no such thing as the one perfect career for you, either. You have a wide range of skills and interests, making it possible for you to thrive in a variety of careers. The key is to identify these careers, do research, and find out which path appeals to you the most right now.

Personality Types and Work

We've seen that skills and interests are closely related to one another and to career choice. Personality is an important part of the mix, too. People who have similar personalities are often interested and good at the same kinds of activities. Because of this, they often tend to enjoy and excel at similar kinds of careers.

How do you know which careers might be right for you? One way is to see what your values, personality, talents, skills, and interests have in common. According to career researcher John Holland, people's work personalities fall into six basic types. While everyone has some aspect of all the types, each individual tends to be strongest in one or two types. People who choose careers that match their dominant type are more enthusiastic

Personal Journal 2.3

Exploring Your Interests

What activities make you feel energized and alive? _____

_____

_____

_____

If you were at a library, bookstore, or newsstand, which subject area(s) would you enjoy browsing?

_____

_____

_____

What course(s) or subject(s) have you enjoyed the most in school? _____

_____

_____

_____

What subject(s) could you talk about endlessly? _____

_____

_____

_____

What were you enthusiastic about as a child? _____

_____

_____

_____

Now examine your answers. Does any subject, theme, or key word appear more than once? These are probably your strongest interests.

Career Fulfillment

There is an old saying, "Find a job you love and you will never work another day in your life." Finding a career that is fulfilling is one of our greatest achievements and pleasures. Most people spend approximately 25 percent of their entire adult lives working. If your job does not match your talents, skills, and interests, you are likely to experience physical and mental stress, as well as frustration and boredom. If finding the right career is so important, why do so many people stay in jobs they dislike? There are many reasons, including financial need, fear of change or unemployment, and a lack of aptitudes and skills that match their interests. Finding the best career requires self-awareness and self-knowledge. It is never too early, or too late, to assess your values, personality traits, innate talents, skills, and interests that lead to a career that will bring out the best in you. There are many careers that can provide you with personal satisfaction as well as financial stability.

Earlier in this chapter you learned about natural aptitudes (talents) and multiple intelligences. The non-profit Johnson O'Connor Foundation offers hands-on tests to discover nineteen natural talents. Select four of those aptitudes listed that you feel describe your major talents. Write the description of each talent and what possible career fields match those talents to your current skills and interests. For more resources on making career choices, ask your instructor to give you the additional Professional Development materials for this chapter, or try the Princeton Review Career Quiz here: http://www.princetonreview.com/cte/quiz/career_quiz1.asp.

about their work, are more comfortable in their work environment, and get along better with their coworkers. The six types are:

- **Realistic**—Realistic people are doers who prefer hands-on activities to activities involving words or relationships.
- **Investigative**—Investigative people are thinkers who like to investigate and solve problems.
- **Artistic**—Artistic people are creators who value self-expression and dislike structure.
- **Social**—Social people are helpers who value relationships more than intellectual or physical activity.
- **Enterprising**—Enterprising people are persuaders who enjoy using their verbal skills.
- **Conventional**—Conventional people are organizers who thrive in situations with rules and structure.

Can you tell which type is most "you"? **Activity 12** on pages 82–84 will help you evaluate your personality traits, skills, and interests and link them to a variety of career fields.

Next Steps   You have learned a lot about yourself in this chapter. Your self-awareness will continue to grow throughout your lifetime as you gain experience and knowledge. One way to learn more about yourself is simply to observe the world around you. What kinds of careers do you find interesting? What jobs do you want to know more about? Take every opportunity to ask questions and explore the many possibilities open to you.

Self Check

1. What are the "big five" personality traits? (p. 60)
2. What are the eight types of intelligence? (p. 67)
3. Once you have chosen a career should you stick with it no matter what? (p. 71)

ACTIVITY 12: Interest Survey

A In each of the following six categories, check the items that describe you.

REALISTIC

I am:	I can:	I enjoy:
☐ practical	☐ fix broken things	☐ tinkering with machines
☐ athletic	☐ figure out how things work	☐ working outdoors
☐ straightforward	☐ pitch a tent	☐ being physically active
☐ coordinated	☐ play a sport	☐ using my hands
☐ action-oriented	☐ read a blueprint	☐ building things
☐ honest	☐ work on cars	☐ working with animals

INVESTIGATIVE

I am:	I can:	I enjoy:
☐ inquisitive	☐ think abstractly	☐ exploring ideas
☐ intellectual	☐ solve math problems	☐ using computers
☐ scientific	☐ understand scientific theories	☐ working on my own
☐ observant	☐ do complex calculations	☐ performing experiments
☐ precise	☐ use a microscope	☐ reading scientific or technical magazines
☐ methodical	☐ analyze words and numbers	☐ testing theories

ARTISTIC

I am:	I can:	I enjoy:
☐ creative	☐ sketch, draw, paint	☐ attending concerts, plays, or exhibits
☐ intuitive	☐ play a musical instrument	☐ reading fiction, plays, or poetry
☐ original	☐ write stories, poetry, or music	☐ working on crafts
☐ emotional	☐ design fashions or interiors	☐ taking photographs
☐ independent	☐ sing, act, or dance	☐ expressing myself
☐ individualistic	☐ solve problems creatively	☐ thinking about ideas

Continue checking the items that describe you.

SOCIAL

I am:	I can:	I enjoy:
☐ friendly	☐ teach or train others	☐ working in groups
☐ helpful	☐ express myself clearly	☐ helping people with problems
☐ idealistic	☐ lead a group discussion	☐ participating in meetings
☐ generous	☐ mediate conflicts	☐ doing volunteer service
☐ trustworthy	☐ plan and supervise an activity	☐ working with young people
☐ understanding	☐ cooperate well with others	☐ nursing or giving first aid

ENTERPRISING

I am:	I can:	I enjoy:
☐ energetic	☐ change people's opinions	☐ making decisions affecting others
☐ assertive	☐ convince people to do things my way	☐ being elected to an office
☐ persistent	☐ sell things	☐ winning a leadership or sales award
☐ persuasive	☐ give talks or speeches	☐ starting my own political campaign
☐ enthusiastic	☐ organize activities and events	☐ meeting important people
☐ ambitious	☐ lead a group	☐ being in charge

CONVENTIONAL

I am:	I can:	I enjoy:
☐ responsible	☐ work well within a system	☐ following clearly defined procedures
☐ accurate	☐ do a lot of paperwork in a short time	☐ using a computer or calculator
☐ careful	☐ keep accurate records	☐ working with numbers
☐ reserved	☐ use a computer	☐ typing, organizing, or filing
☐ organized	☐ write business letters	☐ handling details
☐ efficient	☐ work with numbers	☐ succeeding in business

continued...

B **Scoring:** Add up the total number of items you checked in each of the six categories.

Realistic _____   Investigative _____   Artistic _____

Social _____   Enterprising _____   Conventional _____

C The following lists of career areas represent fields that people of each personality type often enjoy and excel in. Read the career areas that correspond to your first, second, and third-highest personality types.

R—construction, engineering, transportation, law enforcement, farming, mining, armed forces

I—science, medicine, dentistry, information technology, math, postsecondary education

A—music, dance, theater, design, fine art, architecture, photography, journalism, creative writing

S—education, religion, counseling, psychology, therapy, social work, child care

E—sales, management, business, law, politics, marketing, finance, urban planning, television or movie production, sports promotion

C—accounting, court reporting, financial analysis, banking, tax preparation, office management

Select one career area for your personality type that interests you but that you don't know very much about yet. How could you figure out whether it might be a good match for you?

_____

_____

_____

_____

_____

_____

_____

_____

Key Terms

self-awareness (p. 44)

self-honesty (p. 44)

self-consciousness (p. 46)

emotional awareness (p. 46)

dream (p. 49)

values (p. 52)

ethics (p. 52)

personality (p. 59)

trait (p. 59)

intelligence (p. 67)

skill (p. 69)

knowledge (p. 69)

interests (p. 70)

Summary by Learning Objectives

- **Define self-awareness and cite its benefits.** Self-awareness is about taking an honest look at yourself—your thoughts, feelings, attitudes, motivations, and actions. Self-awareness helps you identify what you are really feeling and thinking inside; it helps you act in accordance with your personal values, rather than be swayed by what other people say or do; and it helps you appreciate your unique personality, skills, and interests. When you are self-aware, you can make the choices that are right for you.

- **Explain the factors that influence people's values.** Your values reflect what is most important to you. Your values are greatly influenced by your family, religious beliefs, teachers, friends, and personal experiences, as well as by the values of the society in which you live.

- **Define personality and list the "big five" personality traits.** Personality is the relatively stable pattern of behavior that distinguishes one person from another. The "big five" personality traits are openness, conscientiousness, extroversion, agreeableness, and emotional stability.

- **Compare and contrast skills, knowledge, and interests.** Skills consist of the ability to do something specific as a result of learning and practice. Skills are the result of knowledge combined with experience. Knowledge is an understanding of facts and principles in a particular subject area. Interests are personal preferences for specific topics and activities. People's skills and interests often overlap.

- **Explain how personality, natural aptitudes, skills, and interests relate to career choice.** People who have similar personalities are often interested and good at the same types of activities. They therefore tend to enjoy and excel at similar careers. It is important to consider your personality type, innate talents, skills, and interests as you plan your career. When you are using your natural talents, developing them into skills, following your interests, and expressing your personality at work, you feel more satisfied with your life.

Review and Activities

Review Questions

1. What is the difference between private and public self-consciousness?

2. What are three questions you can ask yourself to help identify the emotions you are experiencing?

3. What influences people's choice of values?

4. How do people develop skills?

5. Compare and contrast intrapersonal intelligence and interpersonal intelligence.

6. What are the six personality types in John Holland's career theory?

Critical Thinking

7. **Self-Honesty**   Do you think that most people (or most people you know) are self-honest and self-aware? Why or why not? What do you think prevents people from becoming more self-honest and self-aware? Why?

8. **Value Conflict**   What do you do when values conflict? Imagine that you value generosity and spend a great deal of time and energy volunteering and giving to others. However, you also value financial security, which means that you need to work hard to support yourself and save money for your future. How might these two values come into conflict? How could you resolve this conflict in a way that benefits others as well as yourself?

Application

9. **Emotion Log**   Monitor your feelings by keeping a log with you for one week. Make a note each time you experience a moderate or strong emotion, and immediately answer these three questions about it: How does my body feel? What happened right before I started to experience this emotion? What specific name can I put to this emotion? At the end of the week, explain whether or not the log helped you to become more emotionally aware, and why.

10. **Personality Collage**   Using a large piece of paper, create a collage of pictures to represent your personality. The pictures can come from any source and can represent any person, thing, scene, or event that you feel represents your personality in some meaningful way. Prepare to present your collage to the class.

Internet Activities

11. **Personality Assessment**   Search online for a reputable Myers-Briggs Type Indicator and find an article about the Myers-Briggs Type Indicator and personality types. Your instructor may provide you with an article. What is your personality type? What are its characteristics? Take a quiz to determine your personality type, then write a page describing the personality type you were assigned and explaining whether or not you feel the quiz gave you accurate results.

12. **Talent and Interest Survey**   Go to www.jocrf.org and www.ballfoundation.org which are the Web sites for Johnson O'Connor Research Foundation and the Ball Foundation. After reviewing those sites, do you feel you have a better understanding of why self-awareness of your natural aptitudes is a first step? Are you confident that your talents, skills, and interests are aligned? Why or why not? You also should find a link to a Web site that lets you evaluate your interests and then match them to careers. Select three careers that relate to your interests and learn more about them. Write a brief description for each career, then rank the careers from most interesting to least interesting. Prepare to discuss your career selections in class.

Real-Life Success Story

"What Do I Really Want?"

Look back at your response to the question in the Real-Life Success Story on page 42. Think about how you would answer the question now that you have completed the chapter.

Complete the Story   Write a paragraph continuing Mariah's story, explaining some specific ways she can increase her self-awareness and take inventory of her skills and interests.

"Where Do I Go From Here?"

A New Direction

Trinh Hong was 25 years old and had been working for the past seven years as an assistant at a small accounting firm in San Francisco. Although she liked her job, she didn't see any chance for advancement. It seemed as if the past seven years had just flown by without much success. Trinh had never really thought about her goals for the future. Increasingly, however, she realized that she needed a direction.

New Goals, New Challenges

Trinh decided to go back to school to earn a degree in accounting. As she sat in her first class, though, she began to question her decision. How was she supposed to accomplish such a huge goal? Would she really be able to balance school and work? What if she didn't finish and then had to repay student loans on her current salary? Her heart began to beat faster, and her palms got sweaty. She asked herself whether she was in over her head.

What Do You Think?   What could Trinh do to make her long-term goal seem more attainable?

Goals and Obstacles

> " Whoever wants to reach a distant goal must take small steps. "
>
> Saul Bellow, Novelist

introduction

Setting goals is an important step toward achieving what you want out of life. Goals help you focus your effort on the things that are most important to you. In Section 3.1 you'll learn how to set attainable goals for yourself and how to break them down into small steps that you can begin working on right now. You'll also learn how to anticipate and overcome common obstacles to reaching your goals. In Section 3.2 you'll explore the causes and symptoms of stress and anger. By developing constructive strategies to deal with life's setbacks and frustrations, you'll be able to stay on track toward your goals.

learning objectives

After you complete this chapter, you should be able to:

- Explain the importance of setting goals.

- List the characteristics of well-set goals.

- Distinguish between short-term and long-term goals.

- Cite common obstacles to reaching your goals.

- Recognize the causes and symptoms of stress.

- Describe several strategies for relieving stress.

- Explain ways to deal with anger constructively.

WHAT ARE YOUR GOALS?

goal An outcome you want to achieve and toward which you direct your effort.

After completing Chapter 2, you should have a better idea of your dreams, values, personality traits, skills, and interests. Where do goals fit in? Goals are tools for translating dreams into reality. A **goal** represents an outcome that you want and toward which you direct your effort. A goal is a sign-post to the future, telling you which way to go. It translates your dreams into plans, and directs your abilities in the service of what you want most.

What kinds of goals are you committed to? Since we become what we think about most, we unconsciously move toward the achievement of the thoughts we have right now. Negative thoughts create negative goals; positive thoughts create positive goals.

You have the potential and the opportunity for success in your life. It can take just as much energy for an unfulfilling life as for a rewarding one. Many people lead unhappy, aimless lives, simply existing from day to day and year to year. You can set yourself free from this by actively deciding what to do with your life, by making goals happen.

Many people resist goal setting because they assume it leads to a formula-driven, highly uncreative life. Actually, the exact opposite is true. People who passively assume that everything will somehow work out in the end can hardly be termed creative. They're not creating their lives, they're just hoping that something good will happen to them somehow, and they'll arrive at some magical port of call on a fantasy island called "Someday I'll." Setting worthwhile goals is a much more imaginative approach. It's fashioning and molding the life of your choice.

Rather than being like a ship without a rudder, drifting until we end up on the rocks, we can discipline ourselves to decide where we want to go. We can chart a course and sail straight and far, reaching one port after another. We can accomplish more in just a few years than some people accomplish in a lifetime. We do this by setting and visualizing our goals. Think of a long ocean voyage halfway around the world. Even though the captain of the ship cannot *see* her destination for most of the journey, she knows what it is, where it is, and that she will reach it if she keeps following the right course.

success *secret*
Be proactive about your goals—only you can make them happen.

Setting Goals

For a goal to be vivid, meaningful, and have any real pulling power at all, it must be very specific. The human mind cannot focus and act upon nebulous, general thoughts. The more specific the input into your mind, the more detailed and defined the image creating the motivational force for achievement. One of the most highly regarded scientists who has studied goal-setting has been Professor Edwin Locke of the University of Maryland. In one study, he found that ninety-six percent of test subjects did better if they were given specific and challenging goals than if they were simply instructed to do their best. Numerous other studies have confirmed this.

It is very common today to try to motivate students and employees by telling them to do the best they can. The problem is that children and most adults really don't know what their best is and therefore don't have a good idea of what they're aiming for. A disturbing result discovered by these studies was that in society today, while most people are trying to "do their best," only about four percent of the population actually do perform near the top of their abilities. This is why it is so important to be motivated by your core passions—out of love and belief in what you are doing—and then to arm yourself with knowledge gained from other achievers showing what actions to take every step of the way. Reaching a goal can be likened to programing the GPS device in your car to reach a desired address. Put in the data from your starting point and your ultimate destination, and your mind becomes like a global positioning satellite; only it would be better labeled as a "goal positioning system."

Specific goals are much stronger because they are more thoroughly imagined and more tangible. Telling basketball players to concentrate on pulling in ten rebounds per game paints a much clearer target than telling them to go out on the court and do their best. The best coaches focus on developing and improving specific skills of their players for the special roles they will play as members of a winning team.

A well-set goal has five important characteristics: It is specific, measurable, achievable, realistic, and time-related (SMART), as shown in Figure 3.1. Let's look at each of these elements.

- **S—Specific** Is it clear what your plan of action should be to achieve this goal? Or is the goal so vague that you don't know how to get started?
- **M—Measurable** How will you know whether you've achieved your goal? Does the goal give you something concrete to measure—amount of money to be saved, number of books to be read, total miles to be jogged?
- **A—Achievable** Is it doable? Can you actually succeed at this goal, or are you dooming yourself to failure?

FIGURE 3.1 SMART Goals

Specific   Measurable   Achievable   Realistic   Time-Related

Look Before You Leap   The more time and thought you invest in formulating your goals, the more likely you'll be to achieve them. *Why do you think that many experts advise putting goals down in writing?*

- **R—Realistic** Is this goal possible and desirable given your values, skills, and interests? The way you act? Does it fit with your schedule and financial situation? Your personality? Your other goals?
- **T—Time-Related** Does the goal include a time frame for evaluating whether you have achieved it? Does it motivate you to get started right away, or is it off somewhere in the future?

Each of these SMART elements should be present for a goal to be well set. Let's say, for example, that your goal is to lose weight. This goal is achievable and probably realistic, but it isn't specific, measurable, or time-related. How much weight do you want to lose and in what amount of time? Instead try, "I will lose one pound a week for the next 15 weeks by watching my diet and walking for a half hour every day." This goal is specific, realistic, and time-related. It is certainly measurable—15 pounds over a 15-week period—and it is achievable because a reasonable target has been set. It is now a well-set goal.

A common mistake is to set goals in negative terms. Even though we have just illustrated that losing one pound per week for fifteen weeks meets the criteria as a SMART goal, it is more of an example of a sub-goal. Keep in mind that a goal should be a desired result. The real goal is to stabilize your body weight at a certain target weight and maintain that, not to dwell on the dominant thought of being overweight and needing to continually "lose weight." What is your ideal weight for a healthy body image? That's the ultimate goal.

For example, whether you are trying not to be late for appointments or not get so upset when things go wrong, you need to stay away from "negative," or "reverse" goal setting. The mind can't focus on the reverse of a concept, so the negative idea of trying to stop doing something destructive reinforces what's wrong. Even though you may be trying hard "not to be late," stating it in that way reminds you of the problem, not the solution. There will be specific examples of affirming your goals with positive self-talk in the next chapter.

For more practice at setting SMART goals, complete **Activity 13** on pages 93–94.

Short-Term and Long-Term Goals

Now let's look at the two main types of goals: short-term goals and long-term goals. A **short-term goal** has a short time frame for accomplishment. Short-term goals are the things you are working on today, tomorrow, next week. They are usually goals that can be accomplished in a year.

A **long-term goal** is a goal that is further in the future. Long-term goals represent things you want to accomplish in one, two, or several years. Long-term goals are the major targets in your life. Long-term goals often include things like continuing your education, buying a house, raising a family, or changing careers. Long-term goals can require a lot of patience, but they are worth it in the end. Ask yourself at the end of every day what you have done to bring yourself closer to your long-term goals. If you find that your day-to-day life is not bringing you closer to your long-term goals, it is probably time for a change.

short-term goal A goal with a specific plan of action to accomplish within the coming year.

long-term goal A goal you plan to achieve in the more distant future.

ACTIVITY 13: Setting SMART Goals

A Are the following SMART goals? If not, what is missing? Write S (specific), M (measurable), A (achievable), R (realistic), and/or T (time-related) in the middle column for each missing element. Write OK if all the SMART factors are present.

Goal	Missing Factor(s)?	SMART Goal
Example *Buy a used car for under $7,000.*	*S,T*	*Buy a reliable, 2-door used compact car for under $7,000 within six months.*
1. Complete my certificate or degree.		
2. Give more time or money to charity.		
3. Find out in next two weeks how to get financial aid.		
4. Pay off my credit cards by the end of this month.		
5. Eat healthfully three times a day.		
6. Work out in gym for an hour three times a week.		
7. Spend more time with my family and friends.		
8. Find something to do for fun.		
9. Read more.		
10. Join a volunteer program.		
11. Raise GPA to 3.8 by end of semester.		
12. Set aside $10 each week in a savings account.		
13. Get physical exam.		
14. Update my résumé.		
15. Watch less TV.		

B Using the right-hand column above, rewrite any flawed goals so that they are SMART goals.

continued...

C Think back to the dreams you formulated in Chapter 2. Translate each of your dreams into one or two SMART goals. If your dream is to travel, for example, your SMART goal might be to save $1,500 for a two-week trip to Europe next summer.

Goal	SMART Goal
1.	
2.	
3.	
4.	
5.	
6.	

D Will you be able to work on all of these goals at the same time? If so, explain how. If not, how will you choose which goals to work on first?

_____

_____

_____

_____

_____

It is easy to think of long-term goals as more important than short-term goals, but short-term and long-term goals are equally important. In fact, you can't achieve long-term goals without first achieving a series of short-term goals. For instance, let's say your long-term goal is to complete your degree in fine arts. Your short-term goals for the semester might be to maintain a B average, sketch for at least one hour each day, and improve your skill in a certain medium, such as acrylics or oils. Success at each of these short-term goals brings you one step closer to reaching your long-term goal.

Tying Your Goals Together

How do you make sure that your short-term goals will lead you to your long-term goals? The easiest way is to work backward in time, first formulating your long-term goals and then thinking of all the steps necessary to achieve each goal. Each step will represent a short-term goal. By always keeping your long-term goals in mind, you make sure that your daily, weekly, monthly, and yearly plans reflect the big picture in your life plan. For example, if your long-term goal is to become and remain healthy and physically fit, with a balanced diet and healthy weight, your short-term goal for the month might be to plan and begin a program of aerobic exercise. Your weekly plan might be to exercise for five days, and your daily plan might be to take a 30-minute walk at work or on campus. Your daily, weekly, and monthly goals then all relate directly to your larger life goal. Try this strategy in **Activity 14,** which is designed to help you break your goals down into doable steps.

Staying on Track

Once you have set your goals, make a commitment to reach them. Write your goals down and dwell on them morning and night as if you had already achieved them. Assemble support materials—news articles, books, tapes, pictures cut out of magazines—anything that can help you see your goals. Consider filling a collage or bulletin board with pictures that represent your goals. These might represent your dream career, satisfying relationships, or a series of landscapes that inspire you. Tell people in your life about your goals—it will inspire you to keep up your effort to achieve them. Review your goals with people who have accomplished what you want to and who are genuinely willing to help you. Ask your instructor or advisor for advice on pursuing your goals.

Put Them In Writing   Commit your goals to writing, whether on paper, laptop, tablet, or smart phone. Attorneys know the wisdom of a written contract. It requires that a commitment be put in very clear, concise terms, with all conditions, dollar amounts, responsibilities, and time frames carefully detailed. Make a contract with yourself, and you will enter into a successful relationship with yourself. Ideally, you should keep your goal journal or wallet-size cards in front of you for daily access, so you can review and add to them continually. Goals are not set in concrete and should be flexible enough to modify as you stair-step your way to achievement.

ACTIVITY 14: Generating Short-Term Goals

A List three long-term goals you'd like to accomplish in the next five years.

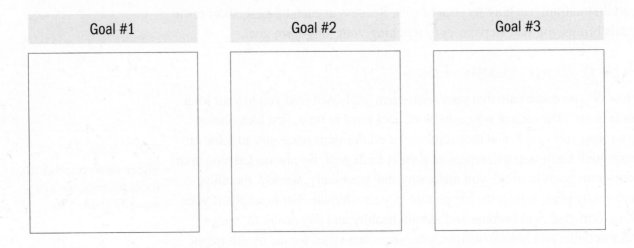

Goal #1	Goal #2	Goal #3

B Now list several smaller goals that you'll need to accomplish in order to reach these long-term goals. For example, if you want to buy a house, you'll need to look at houses in your price range, save money for a down payment, get information on qualifying for a mortgage, and so on. Write these goals in any order.

Short-Term Goals	Short-Term Goals	Short-Term Goals
_____	_____	_____
_____	_____	_____
_____	_____	_____
_____	_____	_____
_____	_____	_____
_____	_____	_____
_____	_____	_____
_____	_____	_____
_____	_____	_____

C Pick one of the long-term goals you listed on the previous page and examine your list of related short-term goals. Rewrite these short-term goals in the order that you'll need to complete them. For example, you'll need to save money before you begin looking at houses. Then assign each short-term goal a realistic time frame—today, tomorrow, this week, this month, this year, and so on.

1. _____

2. _____

3. _____

4. _____

5. _____

6. _____

7. _____

8. _____

9. _____

10. _____

D Choose one short-term goal that you could take action on immediately. Circle it. What can you do over the next 24 hours to accomplish (or begin to accomplish) this goal?

To accomplish one of my goals, I can _____

_____

_____

_____

E Now make a promise to yourself to take this action toward your goal.

To accomplish one of my goals, I will _____

_____

_____

_____

Signed (your name) _____

- Set a time for achieving your goal.
- Make sure your decision about your goal is right.
- Give your goal all your effort and never stop trying.
- Be a positive thinker.
- Once you have achieved one goal, go on to the next.

In addition to keeping a paper or electronic goal journal, many goal-setting coaches suggest writing each of your goals on a small card and carrying all your goals in your wallet. Every time you think of another goal, write it down on a card and add it to the others in your wallet. When you achieve one goal, remove the card. Take the cards out periodically—at least every week—and read them to remind yourself of the successes you are working toward.

Try this strategy yourself in **Personal Journal 3.1.** Write down four of the short-term goals you listed in Activity 14. Set a reasonable deadline for accomplishing each goal. Once you have filled out your goal cards, review them as often as possible to keep yourself motivated and to

Personal Journal 3.1

Goal Cards

Write down four goals that you want to achieve over the next few months. Review them as often as possible to keep yourself motivated and to remind yourself to stay focused. Photocopy them or cut them out and keep them in your wallet for reference.

Goal Card

I will _____

_____

I plan to accomplish this goal by
(time) _____

Goal Card

I will _____

_____

I plan to accomplish this goal by
(time) _____

Goal Card

I will _____

_____

I plan to accomplish this goal by
(time) _____

Goal Card

I will _____

_____

I plan to accomplish this goal by
(time) _____

remind yourself to stay focused. You can even photocopy them and keep them in your wallet.

Adjusting Goals as You Go

Remember that you have the freedom to adjust your goals as you go. Look over your goals periodically and reassess them. If one of them no longer inspires you, modify it. Changing your goals is normal. Your interests will change; your abilities will develop; and your potential will grow. Likewise, changes in technology, culture, and society will open doors to new possibilities. Don't be afraid to keep raising your personal stakes and keep reaching into the unknown.

Rapper Chuck D., says in his autobiography that when he started out as a college-radio disk jockey, he just wanted to release a record. Soon his group, Public Enemy, gained prominence on the airwaves and club scene, and he decided to add socially conscious lyrics and messages to his music. As his career developed, he developed new goals, including gaining exposure to non–hip hop audiences. U2 singer Bono publicly supported Chuck D., saying that although some people would criticize Public Enemy for daring to change, this shouldn't stop him from developing new and more ambitious goals. It is common for people to be criticized for making changes. Change, even if it is positive, is usually stressful, because it ushers in the unknown.

Not adjusting your goals as you gain experience and self-knowledge can stunt your growth. Some people know what they want out of life from the time they are very young, but most people need time to develop a direction. What you want out of life when you are 18 is often different from what you want when you're 30. A 50-year-old rarely has the same goals as a 20-year-old.

OVERCOMING OBSTACLES

Achieving goals is rewarding, but it isn't always smooth sailing. Obstacles often come along to roil the waters. An **obstacle** is any barrier that hinders us from achieving our goals. There are two main kinds of obstacles—internal and external. An *internal obstacle* is a barrier that comes from within ourselves or from within the goal itself—such as a goal that lacks all five SMART elements. An *external obstacle* is a barrier that a situation or another person puts in your path. Often, internal and external obstacles go hand in hand. For example, an external obstacle might be criticism or lack of support from people around you. This external obstacle can become an internal obstacle if you start to believe that your goal is wrong or stupid, or that you shouldn't reach for your goals if others don't approve.

What obstacles stand in the way of achieving your goals? Consider which of these common obstacles might apply to you and how you might overcome them.

obstacle Any barrier that prevents you from achieving your goals.

success *secret*
Choose your goals to please yourself, not others.

Trying to Please Someone Else

It is sometimes easy to confuse what we want for ourselves with what other people want from us. It is important to remember, however, that we must choose our goals to please ourselves, not others. No goal set for you by others will ever be sought with the same passion, effort, and time commitment as one you have set for yourself. Ask yourself whether the goal you are working toward really inspires *you*. Are you using valuable time and energy that you could be applying to a more motivating goal? Are you doing something just because you think you "should" be doing it? Are you building up resentment by trying to please someone else? If you try to please everyone, you are likely to please no one at all, including yourself. If you feel pressured by someone important in your life, such as a parent or partner, to strive toward a goal that doesn't inspire you, open the lines of communication. Tell the person that you respect his or her opinion but have the responsibility to yourself to do what is best for you.

Not Really Wanting It

Every goal requires effort. Is the satisfaction of achieving your goal worth the effort you'll need to apply? For example, let's say that your goal is to play competitive sports or to win a music competition. Are you willing to put in the intense training that will be necessary to achieve this end? Are you willing to give up other goals or opportunities to focus on this goal? More importantly, will you enjoy the process of working toward your goal? If not, ask yourself whether you really want this goal. If you don't want it, get rid of it and begin focusing on what you really do want.

Being a Perfectionist

perfectionism The belief that you are only worthwhile if you are perfect.

It's easy to get discouraged and give up when your efforts don't succeed immediately. If you often criticize yourself for failing to make progress, ask yourself whether you are a victim of perfectionism. **Perfectionism** means believing that you are only worthy as a person if you do everything perfectly. Perfectionists would rather give up on a goal than take the risk of failing to achieve it. Despite their lofty standards, perfectionists are usually less successful in life than nonperfectionists. Do you set unreasonable standards for yourself? Is your energy being drained by fear of failure? Do you interpret mistakes as evidence that you're just not good enough? If so, work to become more aware of your self-sabotaging thoughts. Try to see the situation from an outside point of view—if a good friend were in your place, would you consider him or her a "failure"? Celebrate reaching smaller goals that lead to the larger ones. Look at setbacks as lessons, not failures.

success *secret*

Don't hesitate to ask for support when you need it.

Trying to Go It Alone

Your goals are your own, but you can't accomplish them without moral and emotional support. Tell friends and loved ones about your goals and ask for advice and support when you need it. Seek out advisors, coaches, and role models who can offer tips and encouragement. Consider writing to someone you admire to ask for advice. Accept good-faith offers to assist you with your responsibilities so that you can focus on your goal. Enlist a friend as an exercise buddy to keep you to your exercise schedule. Also remember to give thanks to the people in your work and life who support and believe in you.

Resisting Change

Depending on how you look at it, change can be disruptive and threatening, or exhilarating and full of opportunity. Change is a fact of life, and resisting it can drain your energy. Many factors in life are outside your control, but if you concentrate on the big picture—your long-term goals—you'll be able to fine-tune your short-term goals as you go.

The key to turning unexpected change into opportunity is to learn the skill of adapting. **Adapting** means being flexible and open to change. Even if you stay in one neighborhood throughout your life, you will need to adapt to change—new technologies, new cultural phenomena, new people, and new personal interests, tastes, and goals.

adapting Being flexible to change.

What obstacles might you face as you make progress toward your goals? **Activity 15** will help you anticipate obstacles and find ways to overcome them *before* they sidetrack your efforts.

Opportunity Knocks   As you gain practice setting and achieving your goals, remember that sometimes obstacles are really opportunities in disguise. If you remain flexible and try new ways of thinking and doing, you'll often find that setbacks are sources of new ideas. Look at every side

internet action

SURFING THE DAY AWAY

When you are working toward your goals, it's easy to become sidetracked by time-wasters like excessive surfing of the Internet. It only takes a few clicks to go from completing a simple task, like checking your bank balance, to shopping online, participating in a chat room, or researching some offbeat topic, like bungee jumping. If you find yourself spending too much time online, ask yourself:

- Am I surfing to avoid a more difficult or unpleasant task?
- Am I surfing to avoid feelings of loneliness, stress, or anger?
- Do I make impulse purchases during my surfing sessions?

- Would I be a more effective student if I spent less time online?
- Is my Facebook, Twitter, and texting activity more tension-relieving or goal achieving?

Think About It

How do you think the Internet can be most useful? Least useful? What are some of the best Web sites you've visited? Some of the worst? Prepare your answers for a class discussion. For resources on using the Internet effectively, go to the links below: http://www.learnthenet.com/english/index.html
http://www.internet101.org
http://www.superpages.com/ilt/lessons/lesson104.html.

ACTIVITY 15: Anticipating Obstacles

A List three long-term goals you'd like to accomplish in the next five years. Use the goals you listed in Activity 14, or choose new ones.

Goal #1	Goal #2	Goal #3

B Consider what obstacles you are likely to face as you make progress toward these goals. Think of as many internal and external obstacles as you can to each goal. After you're done, circle the two obstacles that you believe will be the most difficult to overcome.

Possible Obstacles	Possible Obstacles	Possible Obstacles

C Now, working alone or with a classmate, brainstorm several ways that you could overcome these obstacles or keep them from getting in your way.

Obstacle #1 _____

_____

_____

_____

_____

_____

Obstacle #2 _____

_____

_____

_____

_____

_____

of a new situation before deciding that it really is an obstacle. This will help you find new ways to achieve your goals.

✅ Self Check

1. What is a goal? (p. 90)
2. What does SMART stand for? (p. 91)
3. What is one good way to make sure that your long-term and short-term goals are in synch? (p. 92)

STRESS AND STRESSORS

Focusing on your goals can at times become challenging, especially when you are sidetracked by obstacles. However, how you react and respond to life's setbacks—both big and small—is key to achieving your goals.

Stress is a natural part of life. **Stress** is a person's physical and psychological reaction to the demands in his or her life. Stress can be positive or negative. *Eustress,* or good stress, is the kind of pleasant, desirable stress you might feel when playing a sport or going on a date. *Distress,* or bad stress, is the kind of stress you might feel during an illness or a drastic life change.

Psychologist Albert Ellis believes that we cause distress for ourselves because we hold irrational beliefs. For example, we may become stressed when we see people whispering at a party because we irrationally assume that they are making fun of us. Ellis's ABC model, illustrated in Figure 3.2, shows how distress is the result of our beliefs about events rather than of the events themselves. An *activating event* (A) triggers people to form an irrational or negative belief (B) about it, which in turn shapes the *consequences* (C) of the event.

Stress is in the eye of the beholder. Each person has his or her own stressors. A **stressor** is anything that causes stress. Have you ever noticed how different people can react to the same event in different ways? You may feel excited about going on a long trip, while your friend might feel nervous and tense. Dr. Hans Selye, one of the first people to study stress, divides people into two categories: racehorses and turtles. A racehorse loves to run and will die from exhaustion if it is corralled or confined in a small space. A turtle will die from exhaustion if it is forced to run on a treadmill, moving too fast for its slow nature. We each have to find our own healthy stress level, somewhere between that of the racehorse and the turtle.

stress Your physical and psychological reaction to the demands in your life.

stressor Anything that causes stress.

success *secret*
It's normal to feel stress when faced with change.

FIGURE 3.2 The ABC Model

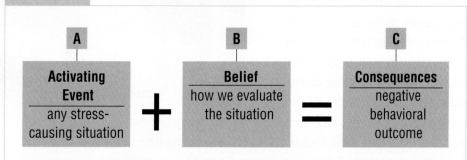

Taking Control   The ABC formula demonstrates how negative, irrational beliefs can create stress and lead to unwanted consequences. *How can becoming more aware of your personal stressors help you control stress?*

Whether you are a racehorse or a turtle, you are likely to feel stress when facing situations that require you to change old ways of doing or thinking. It is normal to experience stress when faced with:

- greater demands at school or work
- changes in family relationships
- new financial responsibilities
- changes in your social life
- exposure to new people, ideas, and situations
- uncertainty or shame about sexual identity
- internally generated demands, such as perfectionism, negative self-talk, or chronic worry and anxiety

Big changes usually bring on more stress than little ones, but a lot of small changes or challenges at one time can add up, too. It is normal to experience stress when faced with *hassles,* the small stressors of everyday life. Hassles include losing your car keys, getting a flat tire, and other everyday annoyances. Like major stressors, hassles can weaken the body's immune system. The good news is that small, positive events, known as *uplifts,* can have the opposite effect, boosting your body's defense mechanisms and protecting your health.

autonomic nervous system (ANS) The part of the nervous system that monitors and controls most involuntary functions, including heartbeat and sweating.

Symptoms of Stress

What happens when we experience stress? Stressors trigger a response from the **autonomic nervous system (ANS),** the part of the nervous system that sends impulses to the heart, muscles, and glands. The ANS controls a number of bodily functions, including heart and breathing rate and digestion.

Applying **Psychology**

Technology and Stress

Research from The University of Gothenburg in Switzerland has revealed that intensive use of mobile phones and computers can be linked to stress, sleep disorders, and depressive symptoms, especially in young people. Heavy mobile phone use is linked to an increase in sleeping problems in men and an increase in depressive symptoms in both men and women. "Regularly using a computer late at night is associated not only with sleep disorders, but also with stress and depressive symptoms in both men and

women," according to lead researcher Sara Thomée. A combination of both heavy computer use and heavy mobile use makes the association even stronger. "This means taking breaks, taking time to recover after intensive use, and putting limits on your availability," Thomée explains. Good advice: Don't surf the web, chat, text, and then try to sleep. Take a time-out, relax before bedtime, and don't be tethered to your phone, tablet, or laptop. Are you a techno-addict or are you in control?

Within the ANS, there are two subsystems, the *sympathetic nervous system* and the *parasympathetic nervous system.* In dangerous or stressful situations, the sympathetic nervous system speeds up your heartbeat and breathing rate and slows down the digestion of food. In relaxing situations, the parasympathetic nervous system slows your heartbeat and breathing rate and stimulates the digestion of food.

The ANS reacts to stressors by going through three physiological stages: alarm, resistance, and exhaustion. In the alarm stage, the body is confronted with a stressor and mobilizes to meet the threat. For example, suppose that you are lying in bed when you suddenly remember that you have a test tomorrow. Your ANS reacts with alarm.

In the resistance stage, the body works to resist the stressor, releasing adrenaline to give itself energy. The stressor may remain, but the symptoms that appeared in the alarm stage disappear. You get up, turn on the light, and start to make a plan of action.

In the exhaustion stage, which occurs after an extended period of stress, the body may not be able to resist stressors any longer. If the body reaches the exhaustion stage, the immune system is weakened, and the body becomes vulnerable to diseases, which Selye called diseases of adaptation. These can include ulcers, high blood pressure, coronary disease, and cancer.

How do you know if you are experiencing too much stress? People who are under a lot of stress become impatient, angry, and tired more quickly than they ordinarily would, and they experience physical symptoms, such as muscle tension, insomnia, and loss of appetite. To assess your own stress level, complete **Activity 16.**

success *secret*
Fatigue and irritability can be signs of stress overload.

Escape Responses

When faced with a stressful situation, it is tempting to indulge in an escape response rather than to confront the problem head-on. An **escape response** is a behavior, such as a thought or an action, that helps you get your mind off your troubles.

escape response A behavior that helps you get your mind off your troubles.

Some escape responses are positive. A *positive escape response* might be to go for a walk or talk with a friend. A positive escape response makes you feel better for a while, in a constructive way. You act in a way that does not harm you or add to the problem.

A *negative escape response,* by contrast, is an escape response that makes you feel better for a while, but actually increases your stress levels. Negative escape responses include overeating, drinking, and avoiding responsibilities. Extreme responses include alcoholism and drug abuse. A common negative escape response is **denial**—a way to reduce anxiety by ridding your mind of painful thoughts and feelings. When your troubles seem too difficult to manage, it is tempting to just forget about everything. Instead of fleeing your feelings, however, it is healthier to get in touch with them. It is normal to react to an unpleasant situation with stress, sadness, or anger. If you can, share your feelings with a trusted family member, friend, instructor, or advisor.

denial Refusing to face painful thoughts and feelings.

ACTIVITY 16: How Stressed Are You?

A For each statement, check whether it applies to you Never, Seldom, Sometimes, or Often.

	Never	Seldom	Sometimes	Often
1. I lose my appetite or eat when I am not hungry.				
2. My decisions tend to be hasty rather than planned; I change my mind frequently.				
3. The muscles of my neck, back, or stomach get tense.				
4. Thoughts and feelings about my problems run through my mind.				
5. I have a hard time getting to sleep; I wake up during the night or I feel tired in the morning.				
6. I feel the urge to cry to get away from my problems.				
7. I let anger build up and then explode.				
8. I have nervous habits.				
9. I feel tired, even when I have not been doing hard work.				
10. I have physical problems, such as headaches, intestinal disorders, or nausea.				
11. I cannot do what I or others expect because the expectations are unrealistic.				
12. I lose interest in physical intimacy.				
13. I get angry easily and quickly.				
14. I have bad dreams or nightmares.				
15. I worry a lot.				
16. I use coffee, tobacco, alcohol, and/or drugs.				
17. I feel uneasy, without any reason that I can name.				
18. When I talk, my words come out weak, fast, broken, or tense.				
19. I am short-tempered and testy or cross with people.				
20. Delays of any kind make me extremely impatient.				

B **Scoring:** Assign yourself one point for every time you checked Never; two points for every time you checked Seldom; three points for every time you checked Sometimes; and four points for every time you checked Often.

What is your total? _____

20–40 Low level of stress

41–60 Moderate level of stress

61–80 High level of stress

C Does your score reflect the level of stress you feel? Explain.

_____

_____

_____

_____

_____

D Change is a part of life, but it is also a cause of stress. What are some changes in your life right now that might be causing stress for you?

_____

_____

_____

_____

_____

_____

_____

Living with less stress does not mean that you will never feel anxious, worried, or tense. Everybody feels this way sometimes. To be successful, you need to balance the amount of tension in your life. Pay attention to your body and mind and learn to recognize your personal stressors. Once you know what situations cause you stress, you are one step closer to managing them and reacting to them with positive thoughts and actions.

Stress Management

In stressful or anger-causing situations, you have a lot more control than you might think. You may not have control over all the sources of your stress, but you can control your reaction to them. How? By developing **coping skills,** behaviors that help you deal with stress and other unpleasant situations.

coping skills Behaviors that help you deal with stress and other unpleasant situations.

Stress researchers have uncovered three core characteristics of people who cope with stress effectively. First, these people see problems not as catastrophes, but as challenges. Second, they have a sense of mission or purpose in life that helps them put setbacks in perspective. Third, they have a feeling of control over their lives.

No matter what your problems are, you can work on them in a way that is healthy and constructive. You can choose the method that best fits your personality and lifestyle.

Relaxation   A good way to deal with stress is through simple relaxation or *meditation.* Try sitting in a comfortable position in a quiet room. Focus your mind on a single calming word or phrase. Close your eyes; breathe deeply and slowly. "Breathe" from your stomach, not your chest. Feel your muscles relax. Assume this calm attitude for about 20 minutes. Make time for relaxation every day, and you'll feel better both mentally and physically.

Listening to music is another good way to relax. Slow music is more soothing than fast music, and instrumental music is more soothing than vocals. If you are very stressed, you may want to start with fast, loud music to match your mood and then gradually shift to more mellow sounds. Pick the musical genre of your choice, from classical to jazz to reggae to electronic, or try recordings of nature. Some people relax to the sound of the ocean's surf, rain or thunderstorms, or birds and insects in a meadow.

Watching nature can be even more relaxing than listening to nature. If you can't make it to a park, trail, lake, or beach, try sitting in front of a fireplace or fish tank and losing yourself in watching the movement.

Another way to reduce tension is to practice *progressive muscle relaxation,* the brief tightening and release of muscles throughout the body. Massage is another effective relaxation technique.

Exercise   Exercise can be a powerful stress reducer. Exercise includes walking, running, aerobics, *yoga,* and any other physical activity that helps you release tension. Exercise increases your heart rate and improves your circulation. Flexing muscles creates a massage effect and helps work out tension. Exercise also helps to burn off adrenaline in the bloodstream. Ideally, participate in some kind of cardiovascular fitness activity that requires exertion to the point of perspiration for 20 to 30 minutes five or more times a week. Steady, rhythmic aerobic activity is best, such as swimming, walking, jogging, or cycling.

Nutrition

Eat a regular, balanced diet that is high in fiber and low in saturated fat, and drink plenty of water daily. Take time to eat slowly and enjoy your meals. Minimize salt, sugar, caffeine, and alcohol intake. Respect your body and be cautious of fad diets, high-energy foods, and other quick-fix alternatives to good nutrition.

Sleep

Regularly get at least seven hours of complete rest. Develop a ritual or regular procedure in preparing for sleep. Read or reflect on peaceful thoughts or interesting ideas, then take them with you into sleep. Resolve arguments before going to sleep so that you do not lose sleep because of them. Take a break after intensive mobile phone or computer use before bedtime.

Mental Discipline

Practice a technique for developing concentration, clearing the mind of distracting or intrusive thoughts, and focusing your attention. These can be done in conjunction with physical relaxation techniques such as *meditation, biofeedback,* and *self-hypnosis.* Other techniques for developing concentration include martial arts, advanced yoga, *t'ai chi,* ballet, swimming, and other rhythmic activity.

professional **development**)))

Job Stress

Dealing with heavy workloads, impossible deadlines, competing priorities, and workplace politics contribute to stress on the job. Besides maintaining a healthy work/life balance, getting enough sleep, exercise, and nutrients, here are some important tips for overcoming stress during your workday. Here are 7 quick and easy activities you can incorporate on the job:

1. Breathe—Take 10 deep breaths to help you relax.
2. Stretch/Move—Stretch your body or take a quick walk down the hall.
3. Healthy Snack—Avoid caffeine and sugar, which spike your stress hormones.
4. Music Break—Listen to your favorite "calming" music on a break.
5. Visual Anchor—Have a favorite photo nearby to trigger positive emotions.
6. Specific Communication Times—Set aside certain times for inbound and outbound e-mails and phone calls.
7. See the Humor in Situations—Don't take challenges and setbacks too seriously.

What's Your Opinion?

What are some ways to achieve a balance between work and life? For more resources on stress management, go to http://health.discovery.com/centers/stress/stress.html or ask your instructor for additional links.

Self-Esteem Develop your self-esteem so that you can put setbacks in perspective. Feeling good about yourself helps you keep a positive attitude in the face of life's challenges. Find ways of appreciating and rewarding your personal qualities and efforts. Personal compliments on a job well done, positive self-talk, and reflecting on your accomplishments can boost your self-esteem. You'll learn more about these techniques in Chapter 4.

Relationships Establish a clear, confidential, reliable, and trustworthy network of people as a support network. They can provide direct, honest, and accurate feedback, as well as care and concern, encouragement and enthusiasm, and understanding and acceptance.

Time Management Based on your values and goals, set priorities and schedule your time to accomplish what you want and need to do. Build in protected time for relaxation training and meditation or reflection, family and social time, and slack time for unexpected events. Identify and reduce time wasters. Find out what events prevent you from making the time necessary to implement effective stress management techniques.

Mental Stimulation Keep learning! Read about and discuss ideas that excite you, preferably from a variety of fields. Use your creativity to view a problem from different perspectives, develop your intuition, and learn to redefine problems as opportunities. Also work on developing your environmental awareness. Look for beauty around you—in a sunrise or sunset, trees and flowers budding in the spring, leaves turning color in the fall, or the interesting curve of an arch. Take time to pay attention to the world around you.

Recreation Engage in hobbies, sports, and leisure time activities that provide a change of pace from your usual work. These should be refreshing or entertaining in themselves, not just more work. They may include photography, painting, languages, travel, gardening, inventing, woodworking, puzzles, music, or athletics.

Spirituality Reaffirm the values that underlie your daily living. Through meditation, prayer, contemplation, or reflection, consider the meaning of your life and work. Consider writing a journal entry at the end of the day to record your reflections. Read some of the great spiritual or philosophical literature from different cultures. Celebrate holidays and special events with true meaning.

Reality Check When stress hits, stop for a moment and try to step outside the situation. Ask yourself, "Am I overreacting?" How would you view the situation if it were happening to someone else? How do you think others might view your reaction? Ask yourself, "What is the worst thing that could happen?" Often you will realize that the situation isn't as bad as you first thought. This new, adjusted outlook might ease both your tension and your stress.

Laugh It Off   Keep your sense of humor. Remember that no one is perfect and that you probably learn more from your mistakes than from your successes. Look for the light side of your situation. If the situation doesn't seem to have a light side, read or watch something you find funny. Laughter affects the body in the same way that aerobic exercise does: It raises the blood pressure, increases heart rate, and tenses the muscles. Afterwards, a general relaxation takes place.

Clarity   Periodically review your dreams and goals and remind yourself why you are doing what you are doing. Seek commitment, challenge, and control in school and work. Set SMART goals and create step-by-step plans to reach them.

success *secret*
Remember to keep your sense of humor.

Obviously, no one can practice all of these techniques perfectly. The key to resisting stress is to practice healthy, positive thought patterns and to select coping strategies that work for you. First use **Personal Journal 3.2** to review the stress management techniques just discussed. Then turn to **Activity 17** begin taking action on the major stressors in your life.

COPING WITH ANGER

Uncontrolled stress is a major obstacle to achieving our goals—and so is uncontrolled anger. **Anger** is a strong feeling of displeasure, resentment, or hostility that results from frustration. Anger, one of the most basic

anger A strong feeling of displeasure, resentment, or hostility.

Personal Journal 3.2

Stress Management Techniques
The best stress management techniques for you are those that you will enjoy and be able to do consistently. Fill in the concept map below with the five stress relief strategies that you think would work best for you.

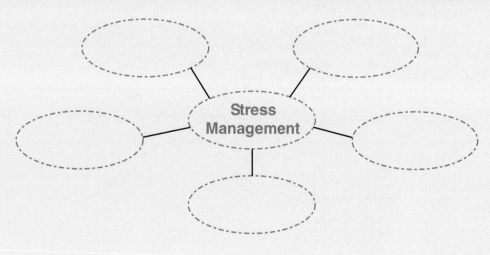

ACTIVITY 17: Personal Stressors and Relievers

A In the left-hand column, list situations in your life right now that are stressful. In the right-hand column, brainstorm several ways to relieve the stress. Working alone or with a classmate, list every constructive strategy that comes to mind, even if a given strategy might not be practical right now.

Stressor	Stress Relievers
Example *Too much homework, too little time.*	*I can get more sleep so I have more energy.* *I can do some homework on weekends.* *I can take the bus so I have more time to read.* *I can drop one of my classes.* *I can stop watching TV on Sunday night.* *I can do homework at the library, where it's quiet.*

Stressor	Stress Relievers
_____ _____ _____	*I can* _____ _____ _____
_____ _____	*I can* _____ _____
_____ _____	*I can* _____ _____
_____ _____	*I can* _____ _____

Stressor	Stress Relievers
_____	I can _____
_____	_____
_____	_____
_____	I can _____
_____	_____
_____	_____
_____	I can _____
_____	_____
_____	_____
_____	I can _____
_____	_____
_____	_____

B Draw a circle around the stressor that is bothering you most right now. Then look at the "I can" statements you wrote for this stressor. Write a promise to yourself:

To relieve some of my stress, by the end of this week I will _____

_____

_____

Signed (your name) _____

C Fill out the reminders in **Personal Journal 3.3** on the next page. Also remind yourself to come back to this page in a few days and write "I will" statements for the other stressors you listed.

Personal Journal 3.3

Stress Relief Reminders

Once you've identified strategies to reduce stress, remind yourself often to take action on them. Fill out the reminders below, then photocopy them or cut them out and post them where you will see them often.

To reduce the stress caused by _____

I will _____

- -

To reduce the stress caused by _____

I will _____

- -

To reduce the stress caused by _____

I will _____

human emotions, is a normal response to aggravating situations. Most of the time, though, anger doesn't really help us. It steals our energy and sidetracks us from achieving our goals. When we are angry, we feel helpless and even more frustrated.

You can't control every situation that causes you to feel angry. You can, however, control your anger and decide how you want to respond to a situation. When you start to feel angry, make a conscious effort to use your energy to come up with solutions to the problem that caused the anger.

Remember adrenaline? Anger is a trigger for your body to release both adrenaline and a stress hormone called *cortisol*. When these two hormones are working together in your body, your immune system becomes weakened and less able to fight off disease. Redford Williams, M.D., a Duke University internist, says, "Every time you get angry it hurts your health."

When your blood pressure jumps, heart rate quickens, and adrenaline pumps, strive to control your anger. Remember that not every annoying situation is a life-threatening struggle for survival. Instead of taking your anger out on other people, examine the source of your negative feelings and transform them into constructive words and actions.

success *secret*

Anger harms your physical and mental health.

When you feel angry or upset, you can also do something that will relieve your negative feelings in a healthy way, such as jogging around the block or listening to some soothing music. Self-awareness is an important part of the victory over anger. The more self-aware you are, the better you will be able to recognize the real causes of your anger and cope with the ups and downs of everyday life.

Responses to Anger

Anger is an emotion, not an action. However, people often express their anger through self-defeating actions: They yell, throw tantrums, even strike someone. After such an outburst, though, do they feel better? No. People who have frequent fits of rage usually feel bad about themselves. They are panicky and out of control, and the problems they are angry about still remain after they vent their rage.

People usually express anger in one of two ways. Sometimes we turn anger outward, and sometimes we turn it inward. Anger that we direct outward is often said to be "healthy" anger because we are openly expressing it. It is not healthy, however, if it does physical or mental harm. Outward anger often manifests itself as **aggression,** behavior intended to harm or injure a person (including you, the angry person) or an object. People who are aggressive harm both themselves and others. Aggressive people often express anger through:

aggression Behavior intended to harm or injure a person or object.

- yelling, name calling, or other verbal abuse
- physical abuse
- irrational demands
- controlling behavior
- criticism and judgment of others
- hostile disagreement with others
- revenge fantasies

Anger that is expressed inwardly seems safer. But is it? It can often do just as much long-term damage to our relationships and our physical and mental health. Inward anger often manifests itself as:

- sarcasm or cynicism
- avoidance or withdrawal
- the "silent treatment"
- annoyance
- pervasive distrust of others
- feelings of victimization
- jealousy or envy
- fatigue and anxiety
- depression

Anger that we keep inside can make us resent people. It can also make us resent ourselves, leading to guilt and depression.

Passive-Aggression   Anger that is repeatedly suppressed and directed inside can be dangerous. This suppressed anger can lead to **passive-aggression,** a way of dealing with emotional conflict or stressors by indirectly and unassertively expressing aggression toward others. Passive-aggression is a disguised form of aggression. It is a way of avoiding unpleasant feelings and events, such as anger and disagreement. Passive-aggressive people often:

passive-aggression
Indirect, disguised aggression
toward others.

- tell people what they want to hear, even if they have to lie to do so
- refuse to acknowledge their inner feelings
- fear letting their feelings show
- complain of being misunderstood or unappreciated
- blame failures or setbacks on others
- avoid conflict at all cost by giving in to others, and then secretly manipulate others to get their own way
- become angry but are afraid to show their anger, so quietly take revenge by undermining others
- put people down in a humorous-seeming way

Passive-aggression is based on unhealthy thoughts that make people feel afraid and victimized, yet also angry. These thoughts include:

- "I never win, so why try?"
- "Everyone else is more powerful than I am."
- "It's bad to get angry."
- "No one cares how I feel."
- "My problems are much worse than other people's."
- "I'm a loser and a failure."
- "What I feel is the opposite of what other people want me to feel."
- "I have to make sure people like and accept me."
- "People will never know I'm angry and that I disagree with them."
- "I'd rather lie than get into an argument with someone."

Most of us have felt these things at some time or another. Passive-aggressive people, however, think this way most or all of the time. To reduce these distressing and unhealthy thoughts, it is important to find the courage to express your emotions calmly and with reason, and to allow other people to do the same. Instead of seeing every situation as a win–lose situation, learn to accept and work toward compromises. Also work to make sure that your words and actions are consistent with your feelings.

Handling Anger Constructively

Instead of repressing anger, expressing it through aggression, or letting it emerge as passive-aggression, it is much healthier to use it to further your self-awareness. Dealing with anger constructively means understanding what causes it, staying calm, taking positive action, and using assertive communication to improve the situation.

success *secret*
Figure out what makes
you angry—and why.

Why Am I Angry?

The first step to conquering anger is to figure out what makes you angry—and why. According to Sandy Livingstone, author of *Dealing With Anger,* anger arises when we perceive that something might happen to:

- frighten us
- hurt us
- threaten us
- make us feel powerless

Often, the hurt or powerlessness we fear is not physical, but emotional. Take Sara's example: With a new baby, a part-time job, and night courses in management, Sara was having trouble keeping her stress level in check. Before the baby was born, she and her husband, Chuck, had agreed to share parenting duties equally. One evening Sara returned home to find that Chuck had neither bathed the baby nor made any preparations for dinner. Sara, who often became irritable when she was hungry and tired, suddenly exploded. Chuck became angry as well, saying that Sara was overreacting. This only made Sara angrier, because it made her feel emotionally powerless—Chuck was not taking her feelings seriously. Chuck's anger with Sara came from a fear of acknowledging that there might be problems in the relationship. For both of them, the constructive solution to this problem was to express their feelings and then work out a solution together.

Just as it is important to recognize your personal stressors, it is important to know your personal anger triggers. *Triggers* are the people, situations, or events that provoke anger. What are your anger triggers? Enter them in **Personal Journal 3.4.**

Stay Calm

When you feel yourself getting angry, focus on staying calm. For example, if after being put to bed, the two-year-old you are babysitting comes walking out to see you while you're studying, you might have several reactions. One might be to become angry and say, "That child never stays put!" In your anger, you might yell at the child and then remain so upset you can't concentrate on your studies. Another reaction might be to think, "We both need to relax. I'll take a break and read a soothing bedtime story so we can spend a little time together." After you've put the child back in bed, you are still calm and in control and can go back to your assignment.

The way you choose to think about a situation often determines your feelings about it. Instead of flying off the handle when faced with a frazzling situation, recognize that you are feeling angry and identify what you are angry about. If another person is involved, try to understand his or her point of view. Also try looking at the situation from outside, as a neutral observer. Is there another way of seeing the situation that might help you reduce your anger? Many situations can be a source of anger or stress because you see them in an unreal or exaggerated way. When you

success *secret*

Focus on staying calm.

Personal Journal 3.4

Anger Triggers

Which of these situations triggers your anger? Put a check mark next to the situations that cause you intense annoyance or anger.

I get angry when . . .

- ☐ Someone criticizes me.
- ☐ Someone does something better than I do.
- ☐ Someone looks better than I do.
- ☐ My partner looks at another man/woman.
- ☐ Things don't work out the way I planned.
- ☐ Someone doesn't listen to what I'm saying.
- ☐ My parents, friends, or partner tell me what to do.
- ☐ Someone questions my judgment.
- ☐ I have to wait in line.
- ☐ Someone cuts in front of me in line or in traffic.
- ☐ (Other—specify) _____
- ☐ (Other—specify) _____

Think about the situations you identified. How do you think they make you feel frightened, hurt, threatened, or powerless? Is this fright, hurt, threat, or powerlessness physical or psychological?

overreact to something, you are allowing yourself to be angry when anger isn't really necessary.

Take Positive Action   It is easy to think that other people are causing all of our problems. However, it is possible that the problem lies in the way we are looking at others. Instead of bottling up your anger and nurturing resentments against others, learn to express your feelings—calmly. Try to work out the current situation without bringing up past issues or other conflicts. Also ask yourself these questions:

- Am I trying to change or control others?
- Am I prejudiced against this person? Am I too judgmental?
- Am I expecting too much from other people?
- Do I want people to be more like me?

People often get angry because they think their situation is unfair. Things sometimes *are* unfair, and looking for fairness in every situation can be a fruitless search. It is important that we learn to accept things we cannot change. We can use our energy instead to change the things we can.

How can you put this idea into action? Let's say you have to study for an exam on Monday and your home is always noisy on the weekend. Look at the situation in a realistic, practical way. If it is unlikely that you can find a quiet corner of your home in which to study, make plans to study at the library. That is much easier than getting upset over the fact that your home is a lively, noisy one. You can choose not to create a stressful situation for yourself.

Try Assertiveness

Instead of resorting to aggression or passive-aggression, strive to develop assertiveness. **Assertiveness** is the ability to express your thoughts and feelings without violating the rights of others. It means recognizing that your thoughts and feelings are valid and that you have a right to express them. To be more assertive in your dealings with others, try the following:

- Deal with minor irritations before they become anger-triggering situations.
- Ask for help when you need it.
- Say "no" to unreasonable requests.
- Speak up if you are not being treated the way you want to be treated.
- Work toward a solution that benefits everyone involved.
- Be open to positive, constructive criticism and suggestions.
- Accept compliments with a simple "thank you," not by diminishing yourself.
- Use calm body language and maintain good eye contact.
- Practice active listening: showing a desire to listen, being attentive to the other person's words and body language, and reflecting back their words to let them know you have heard what they said.

As you learn to control your responses to anger, you will also be learning to control the frequency of your anger. For example, sometimes we feel angry because people criticize us or disagree with us. As we learn to slow down and take an inventory of our anger, we come to see that our anger is not caused by others' words—it is caused by our own silent fear that they may be correct. As we build a repertoire of healthy responses to anger, we build up our resilience and self-esteem, too.

success *secret*
Change what you can, and accept what you can't.

assertiveness
Standing up for your rights without threatening the self-esteem of the other person.

success *secret*
Your thoughts and feelings are valid, and you have a right to assert them.

Self Check

1. How does the body react to stress? (p. 106)
2. What is an escape response? (p. 107)
3. Define assertiveness. (p. 121)

Key Terms

goal (p. 90)

short-term goal (p. 92)

long-term goal (p. 92)

obstacle (p. 99)

perfectionism (p. 100)

adapting (p. 101)

stress (p. 105)

stressor (p. 105)

autonomic nervous system
(ANS) (p. 106)

escape response (p. 107)

denial (p. 107)

coping skills (p. 110)

anger (p. 113)

aggression (p. 117)

passive-aggression (p. 118)

assertiveness (p. 121)

Summary by Learning Objectives

- **Explain the importance of setting goals.**   Goals are tools for translating dreams into real-ity. Goals give our lives direction and channel our energy toward achieving success on our personal terms.

- **List the characteristics of well-set goals.**   Well-set goals have five characteristics, known by the acronym SMART: They are specific, measurable, achievable, realistic, and time-related.

- **Distinguish between short-term and long-term goals.**   Short-term goals can be accom-plished within a year. Long-term goals can be accomplished in a longer period of time. Short-term goals are stepping stones to long-term goals.

- **Cite common obstacles to reaching your goals.**   Common obstacles to reaching your goals include striving for someone else's goals; not being willing to put in the effort required; demanding perfection; lacking support; resisting change; and giving in to stress and anger.

- **Recognize the causes and symptoms of stress.**   Stress is caused by the demands of daily life, as well as by situations that require you to change old ways of doing or thinking. Symp-toms of stress include accelerated heartbeat and breathing rate. Symptoms of prolonged stress include muscle aches, a weakened immune system, and disease.

- **Describe several strategies for relieving stress.**   Powerful strategies for coping with stress include relaxation, exercise, a healthy diet and sleep schedule, a supportive network of relationships, mental exercises, hobbies, spirituality, humor, and focusing on the big picture in your life.

- **Explain ways to deal with anger constructively.**   To handle anger constructively, figure out what makes you angry, and why. When you feel yourself getting angry, try to stay calm and view the situation rationally. Express your thoughts and feelings, but also try to under-stand the other person's point of view.

Review and Activities

Review Questions

1. Explain this statement: "Goals are dreams with deadlines."

2. Why should goals be specific and measurable?

3. Give an example of a long-term goal and three related short-term goals.

4. When is stress positive? Give examples.

5. What is the difference between aggression and passive-aggression?

6. How can assertiveness help you cope with anger?

Critical Thinking

7. **Anger**   Consider this statement by Buddha: "Holding on to anger is like grasping a hot coal with the intent of throwing it at someone else; you are the one who gets burned." What do you think this statement means? Do you agree with it? Why or why not?

8. **Assertiveness**   Review the assertiveness tips presented in the chapter, then recall a situation in which you had, or still have, difficulty being assertive. Describe the situation and examine what feelings the situation created in you. Why did you find it difficult to be assertive? What will you do the next time you are in a similar situation to be more assertive?

Application

9. **Goal Survey**   Interview five friends or family members about their goals. Ask them to name their long-term goals and their related short-term goals. Why did they pick these goals? What deadline do they have for accomplishing the goals? What obstacles have they faced, and how have they overcome them? After you complete your interviews, write a one-page summary. What were your interviewees' goals? Were they SMART goals? How much thought had the interviewees given to their life direction? Did you learn anything that you can apply to your life?

10. **Stress Log**   Keep a "stress log" for one week. Monitor your stress level and write down the stressors (and hassles) in your life. Then pick a calm moment to evaluate your list. Are there any stressors or hassles to which you may have overreacted? How could you prepare yourself for these situations in the future in order to minimize your level of stress?

Internet Activities

11. **Online Goal Management**   Go to http://mygoals.com a Web site that lets you select and manage your goals online. Explore the pre-made "Goalplans" on the site and read more about ways to accomplish the goals that interest you. Write down several solutions suggested by the site to overcome common obstacles to your chosen goals. Which of these solutions are helpful for you? Would you be willing to pay the requested fee to use the site's services? Why or why not? Prepare notes for a class discussion.

12. **Anger Management Strategies**   Go to the Web site www.apa.org and click on the subject "Controlling anger before it controls you." Go through the strategies recommended for coping with anger and select those that you have used effectively to control your own anger. What method or methods have worked best for you? Are there others in the strategies mentioned that you feel can help you remain calm and even more in control? Write a one-page report on how you best deal with anger and how other techniques offered can help.

Real-Life Success Story	"Where Do I Go From Here?"

Look back at your response to the question in the Real-Life Success Story on page 88. Think about how you would answer the question now that you have completed the chapter.

Complete the Story   Write a paragraph continuing Trinh's story, showing how she can use goal-setting and stress management strategies to help her reach her goal.

"Do I Have What It Takes?"

A Step Forward

Paul DuPre had always loved animals. Although he had once dreamed of being a veterinarian, he gave up that dream in high school. His family could not afford to send him to college, and his grades weren't high enough to earn a scholarship. Neither of Paul's parents had gone to college, and they didn't believe that he should either. Paul, however, was able to earn enough money to enroll in a veterinary technician program.

A Step Backward

Paul worried that he didn't have the smarts to complete the program. His sister, Sarah, agreed.

She often made fun of him, saying that no amount of studying would make him any smarter. Why pay a school just to learn how to clean kennels? Paul was unsure of himself and overwhelmed with all the coursework. After getting low grades on two quizzes, he began to wonder if his sister was right. He thought he probably wasn't smart enough and shouldn't keep wasting his time.

What Do You Think?   What could Paul do to raise his self-esteem and do better in school?

Self-Esteem

> " Allow yourself to fail and you will be more likely to succeed. "
>
> Edward Deci, Psychologist

introduction

Self-esteem allows you to make the most of your potential. In Section 4.1 you'll learn what self-esteem is, where it comes from, and why it helps you achieve your goals. You'll also explore ways to build your confidence in your ability to attain your goals. In Section 4.2 you'll learn why self-acceptance is important to self-esteem and discover tactics to accept yourself and see the many qualities you already possess. You'll also learn how to handle negative criticism effectively without letting it erode your self-esteem.

learning objectives

After you complete this chapter, you should be able to:

- Define self-esteem and explain its importance.

- Describe how childhood experiences affect self-esteem.

- Define self-expectancy and explain two ways to boost it.

- Explain why self-acceptance is important for high self-esteem.

- Explain how to change negative self-talk into positive self-talk.

- Explain how to handle criticism well.

THE POWER OF SELF-ESTEEM

self-esteem Confidence in and respect for yourself.

Self-esteem is one of the most important basic qualities of a successful human being. **Self-esteem** is confidence in and respect for yourself. To *esteem* someone means to appreciate his or her value or worth. When you esteem yourself, therefore, you appreciate your value or worth as a person. You are confident in your ability to cope with life's challenges, and you believe that you are worthy of success and happiness. You don't need to be a top achiever or "Number 1" to have healthy self-esteem. You feel you have untapped potential and are eager to invest in and test that potential. This motivates you to work hard and succeed. People with healthy self-esteem can honestly say to themselves, "I really do like myself. I'm glad I'm me. I'd rather be me than anyone else living now or at any other time in history."

Healthy self-esteem is not the same as egotism, arrogance, conceitedness, narcissism, or a sense of superiority. In fact, people who demonstrate these traits are sometimes trying to cover up their low self-esteem. When you have healthy self-esteem, you appreciate your worth and importance, but you also realize that no one is any more or less worthy or important than you are.

People with low self-esteem, on the other hand, are afraid to take risks, are not confident of success, and are likely to view problems and setbacks as failures. This leads to a cycle of reduced effort, perceived failure, and lowered self-esteem.

Effects of High Self-Esteem

success *secret*
Self-esteem motivates you to work hard and succeed.

People with high self-esteem are confident. They know they are important, valuable individuals. They enjoy a deep-down, inside-the-skin feeling of their own worth, which frees them to achieve their goals for success and happiness. When you have high self-esteem, you are willing to take risks, are confident of success, and are able to use setbacks as motivation to redouble your efforts. Self-esteem lets you take pride in your accomplishments. This, in turn, energizes you to strive toward further successes.

High self-esteem has other benefits as well. When you enjoy high self-esteem, you can:

- accept your strengths and weaknesses
- express your true thoughts and feelings
- establish emotional connections to other people
- give and receive compliments
- give and receive affection
- try out new ideas and experiences
- express your creativity

- stand up for yourself
- handle stress and anger calmly
- see the future with optimism

Studies have shown that people with high self-esteem go after their goals. They are not roadblocked by people or circumstances. They tend to seek more challenging jobs that require them to work hard. They also have the confidence to pursue relationships with the people who interest them. People with high self-esteem don't let fear of rejection prevent them from reaching out to others.

High self-esteem can also help you make opportunities for yourself. Let's say you are interested in exploring a new career or major. Feeling good about yourself can encourage you to push ahead and take on the challenge of trying something new. Even if you decide it is not right for you, you are still secure in your sense of self-worth. You also know more about yourself and what you *do* like.

success *secret*
When you feel good about yourself, you have the confidence to try new things.

Effects of Low Self-Esteem

Many people suffer from low self-esteem. Low self-esteem creates a feeling that says, "I can't do anything." People with low self-esteem believe that they are worthless, that their lives have little meaning, and that they will always be unhappy. They lack confidence in their skills and have trouble acknowledging even their greatest accomplishments. This feeling of inferiority can lead to depression, anxiety, or social phobia.

People with low self-esteem are easily hurt by the words and actions of others. In fact, people with low self-esteem value others' opinions and judgments more than they value their own. When these judgments are negative, people with low self-esteem often become extremely hurt and upset. They feel undeserving, doubt their own abilities, and lower their opinion of themselves even further.

In addition, people with low self-esteem often:

- mistrust other people
- have difficulty developing intimate relationships
- fear mistakes and have trouble making decisions
- criticize themselves relentlessly, but have difficulty handling criticism from others
- anticipate problems, crises, and failure
- ignore their own needs
- give in to unreasonable requests
- dislike being the center of attention
- withhold their true thoughts and feelings from others
- live in fear of rejection and disapproval
- worry about being a burden on others
- feel they lack control of their lives
- miss out on the joy of life

People with low self-esteem expect themselves to fail; they see failure as an integral part of their lives. This breeds **anxiety,** a generalized feeling of worry and nervousness that does not have any specific cause. It's normal to feel some anxiety when coping with difficult situations. For example, people often feel anxious when they are lost in an unfamiliar city or when a family member is ill. This anxiety keeps them alert and helps them deal with the situation.

Anxiety is harmful, however, when it persists after the problem is resolved. When you suffer from anxiety, it becomes difficult to complete the necessary tasks to reach your goals, whether that is studying for a test, preparing for a job interview, or making a doctor's appointment. This lowers your self-esteem even further.

Origins of Self-Esteem

Where does self-esteem come from? Why do some people have more of it than others? Some people have a lot going for them from the start. An ancient Chinese proverb tells us, "A child's life is like a piece of paper on which every passerby leaves a mark." We cannot teach our children self-esteem. We can only help them discover it within themselves by adding positive marks and strokes on their slates. All positive motivation is rooted in self-esteem—the development of which, just as with other skills, takes practice. Think of self-esteem as a four-legged chair or table.

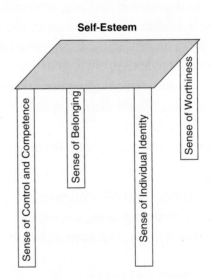

A Sense of Belonging

The first leg of self-esteem is a sense of belonging. We all have a deep-seated need to feel we're part of something larger than ourselves. This need, which psychologists call an affiliation drive, encompasses people, places, and possessions. Our instinct for belonging—for being wanted, accepted, enjoyed, and loved by close ones—is extremely powerful. It explains the bond of an extended family, friends, and teammates. It also

Now is a good time for you to measure your level of self-esteem. **Activity 18** is designed to do just that. This exercise is not a measure of your value as a human being, but an indicator of how much you value yourself. There is no such thing as a right or wrong answer, and no score is better or worse than any other.

Remember that no scale or inventory can reveal all the facts. Look at your results as possibilities for you to consider, not as the absolute truth. Use the results if they make sense to you and are helpful. If they don't, ignore them. Avoid making significant changes in your life based on your score; instead, use what you learn combined with appropriate professional support.

ACTIVITY 18: Test Your Self-Esteem

A For each item, circle the letter (a, b, or c) of the statement that best describes you.

1. a. I don't care if people say bad things about me. Sometimes, I even like it when someone is bothered by what I do or say.
    b. My feelings are hurt if someone disapproves of me or of what I do or say.
    c. When someone criticizes me, it increases my caring about or understanding of that person.

2. a. I feel I'm able to control what people do or how they feel. I seem to need that control.
    b. Too often, I feel out of control or powerless, or I feel manipulated.
    c. I am in control of myself. No one can control me, and I don't want to control anyone else.

3. a. I think of myself as being better than other people.
    b. I think of myself as being less important than other people.
    c. I'm no better or less important than anyone else.

4. a. How I look is very important to me. I always want to look my best and be in fashion.
    b. I don't care much about the way I look as long as I'm comfortable.
    c. How I look is important because it shows how I feel about myself. I keep myself in good shape.

5. a. I don't mind a good argument. It helps to clear the air and makes life more interesting.
    b. I dislike fighting or arguing, and I'll do whatever I possibly can to avoid it.
    c. I don't try to avoid arguments; they're all right with me. Still, I don't try to win them at the other person's expense.

6. a. I don't really care about helping other people. I easily turn down most requests for help.
    b. It's almost impossible for me to turn down a request for help.
    c. I help others but not if it means harming myself. I may turn people down when they ask for help.

7. a. I believe, or others tell me, that I'm a perfectionist. I'm not likely to be satisfied until things are done and done well.

continued...

b. Often, I don't care if everything gets done or how well it's done. It just isn't important to me.

c. Just about everything I do is done well. If not, I'm rarely bothered by it for very long.

8. a. I dislike making mistakes and avoid them whenever possible.

b. Too often, my life seems to be filled with mistakes. I don't seem to be able to avoid them for long.

c. I don't try to make mistakes, but when I do make them, I'm not bothered much or for very long.

9. a. I try not to ask for help. I feel I should be able to do without it.

b. I don't mind asking for help, but often I don't get the help I really need.

c. I usually know when I need help, and I'll ask for it until I get what I need.

10. a. I regularly criticize other people and situations. It makes me feel better to let out my feelings.

b. I was taught it isn't right to criticize, so I avoid criticism as much as I can.

c. I'm rarely critical. My mind simply doesn't work that way.

11. a. If someone disagrees with me, I think she or he has a different opinion. That's all right with me.

b. If someone challenges what I believe is true, I'm likely to assume I'm wrong.

c. If someone challenges what I believe is true, I usually think she or he is wrong, and I want to persuade her or him to think my way.

12. a. I'm comfortable with praise, but I don't require it to feel good about myself and what I do.

b. I need the recognition of praise for what I've accomplished.

c. I don't really care if I get praised or not. In fact, praise often makes me feel uncomfortable.

13. a. I don't usually pay attention to who does or doesn't like me or how many friends I have.

b. Few people like me. The ones who do like me are not people I care about.

c. Maintaining friendship is very important to me.

14. a. Material wealth or professional success comes to me as a result of living my life happily.

b. I don't much care about getting ahead in life. It would just mean having more to keep up with and worry about.

c. Getting ahead in life—achieving success or owning valuable things—is important to me, and I'm working hard for it.

15. a. I'm normally too busy enjoying or learning from what's going on to think or talk about past accomplishments.

b. I don't have much to be proud of. Even when I do, I keep it to myself because a person shouldn't brag.

c. I tell others about my successes and the good things that happen to me. I'm not shy about singing my own praises.

16. a. I'm entirely responsible for what happens in my life. Blaming other people or circumstances doesn't make any more sense than feeling bad about the past.

b. Many of the bad things that happen in my life are my fault. I tend to feel guilty about or regret such mistakes.

c. If something goes wrong, it usually isn't my fault. Other people or circumstances are more often to blame.

17. a. I have a positive sense of direction that comes more from my worth as a person than from the goals I set and attain.

b. My life lacks direction. I have trouble imagining my situation getting better.

c. I set goals and evaluate my progress in attaining them. When life gets tough, I think how good it will be someday.

18. a. I'm usually happy. When necessary, I speak up for myself without being harsh.

b. I'm usually reserved. I always try to be considerate, even if it means my needs go unmet. I don't like to confront people.

c. I'm outspoken and sometimes come across to others as aggressive. I have a manner that could be described as blunt or brusque.

19. a. People do what is in their interest whether it's fair or not. That's not wrong; it's just how people are.

b. Most people look out for themselves and do whatever they can get away with. It's not right, but it's how people are.

c. I have definite beliefs about what is and isn't fair. I'm upset when I am or other people are treated unfairly.

20. a. I know that what others say will not hurt me—only what I say can hurt me.

b. I try to be careful about what I say because I might hurt someone's feelings.

c. I try to be careful about what I say because someone else might use it to hurt me.

Source: Adapted from the Web site www.wellnessnet.com, version 2003. Copyright © 1990–2003 Richard Terry Lovelace, MSW, Ph.D. (www.wellnessnet.com). Reprinted by permission of the author. Originally published in SELF magazine and then by John Wiley & Sons, Inc., in *Stress Master*.

B **Scoring:** First, go back to number 11. Beginning with this item and continuing through number 20, change each A you circled to a C; change each C to an A. Now add up the total number of A's, B's, and C's you selected:

A's_____ B's_____ C's_____

Your number of C's reflects your level of self-esteem.

11 or more C's suggest that you honestly like yourself.

0–10 C's suggest that your self-esteem may need attention.

If you have low self-esteem (0–10 C answers), your number of A's and B's reflects the way you deal with this problem.

continued...

8 or more A's: You have an aggressive behavior pattern. You tend to be pushy, critical, arrogant, hostile, or perfectionistic. You may not realize that you have low self-esteem.

7 or more B's: You have a passive behavior pattern. You tend to be self-critical and to feel sad, hurt, or fearful. You rarely speak up for yourself.

Near equal number of A's and B's: You would benefit from working on your self-esteem, although you're neither very aggressive nor very passive.

C What does your score say about your level of self-esteem? Is it high or low?

_____

_____

_____

_____

_____

D If your self-esteem is low, do you show aggressive behavior, passive behavior, or a mix? Explain and give examples of your behavior.

_____

_____

_____

_____

_____

E Look back at the effects of high and low self-esteem described in the chapter. Which of the behaviors do you exhibit? Give examples.

_____

_____

_____

_____

_____

_____

explains why some adolescents join gangs. They want to belong, even if it's wrong.

Children should be proud of their family heritage in a home where they feel safe, loved, and welcome. Home also should be a place where children want to bring their friends, rather than a place they want to leave as soon as possible.

A Sense of Individual Identity

The second leg, which complements the sense of belonging, is a sense of individual identity. No human being is exactly like another, not even an identical twin. We are all unique combinations of talents and traits that never existed before and will never exist again in quite the same package. (This explains why most parents believe their children came from different planets!)

Children should be observed as they grow and play: Their learning styles, what they love to do in their free time, and discovery of their unique positive talents—so these can be nurtured into skills. Report cards don't necessarily measure talents. They often are a measure only of discipline, memory, and attention span, as well as the presence of an effective teacher.

A Sense of Worthiness

The third leg of self-esteem is a sense of worthiness, the feeling that I'm glad I'm me, with my genes and background, my body, my unique thoughts. Without our own approval, we have little to offer. If we don't feel worth loving, it's hard to believe that others love us; instead, we tend to see others as appraisers or judges of our value.

This is why children, especially, need to experience unconditional love and to learn to carefully separate the doer from the deed, and the performer from the performance. The message: "I love you no matter what happens, and I'm always there for you" is one of most important concepts in building a feeling of worthiness or intrinsic value in children. After every reprimand they need to know parents love them. Before they go to sleep at night, they need reassurance that, regardless of what happened that day, they are loved unconditionally.

A healthy sense of belonging, identity, and worthiness can only be rooted in intrinsic core values as opposed to outer, often material, motivation. Without them, we depend on others constantly to fill our leaking reserves of self-esteem—but also tend to suspect others of ulterior motives. Unable to accept or reject others' opinions for what they're worth, we are defensive about criticism and paranoid about praise—and no amount of praise can replace the missing qualities.

A healthy sense of belonging, identity, and worthiness is also essential to belief in your dreams. It is *most* essential during difficult times, when you have only a dream to hang on to.

A Sense of Control and Competence

There are many reasons why few individuals currently in high school and college believe they were born to win. The supportive extended family—in many cases, even the nuclear family—is disappearing. Role models are increasingly unhealthy. The commercial media bombards young senses ever more insistently with crime, violence, hedonism, and other unhealthy forms of escape. But whatever the explanation, constructive citizens and leaders in society cannot emerge and develop without the creative imagination that serves them like fuel—which is why the apprehension, frustration, and hesitation we frequently see and hear in many individuals is cause for concern. Without more emphasis on opportunity, rather than world problems, the future they imagine will help drive neither happiness nor success.

The chair's fourth leg is a sense of control and competence, which is self-efficacy, a functional belief in your ability to control what happens to you in a changing, uncertain world. A sense of worthiness may give you the emotional means to venture, but you need self-efficacy, the sense of competence and control, to believe you can succeed. That's why it is so important to assign responsibility for small tasks to children as early as possible so they can learn that their choices, efforts, and study habits result in consequences and successes. The more success they experience, the stronger their confidence grows—and the more responsibility they want to assume.

Children growing up, regardless of parents' income, should be given specific household chores and duties they can accomplish and be proud of. Each of us needs to learn that problems and setbacks are just temporary inconveniences and learning experiences. The idea that setbacks are not failures, but course corrections, needs to be constantly reinforced.

Armed with a view of failure as a learning experience, children can develop an early eagerness for new challenges and will be less afraid to try new skills. Although they appreciate compliments, they benefit most from their own belief that they are making a valuable contribution to life, according to their own internal standards. In an increasingly competitive global marketplace, each new, young member of the workforce simply must believe that he or she is a team leader, a self-empowered, quality individual who expresses that quality in excellent production and service. With increasing pressures on profit and the need to do more with fewer workers because of e-commerce and changing technology, it is essential that parents and business leaders help raise the value of their children's and employees' stock in themselves.

Obviously, none of us was raised in a perfect environment. Most parents rely on their own beliefs and experiences and pass those on to the next generation. Regardless of your early upbringing, it is important to know some of the fundamental roots of self-esteem, so that as you mature into leaders and parents, you can offer the most fertile growing ground for success and happiness in those who look to you for guidance.

Many children are encouraged by nurturing parents, outstanding teachers, coaches, and friends who gave them early feelings of self-esteem. This is probably the most important quality of a good parent or leader: giving positive encouragement to help others develop positive self-worth. Low self-esteem, on the other hand, is often a product of abusive or neglectful relationships, repeated rejection, family dysfunction, a physical or mental disability, or intense criticism from others. Self-esteem may also have a genetic component. Some people who are raised in an ideal environment with much praise and love may grow into insecure adults who are unhappy with their lives. Others, who grow up in the worst conditions, mature and find high self-esteem and success.

It is often said that success leads to high self-esteem, while failure leads to low self-esteem. This is not always the case, however. Many talented, accomplished people are plagued by feelings of worthlessness. Take Joan's example. Joan has an MBA and is a successful sales executive for a major record company. Even though she is well respected, highly accomplished, and highly paid, Joan feels insignificant and has low self-esteem. No matter what she achieves, she always falls short of her impossible standards.

While some people suffer from low self-esteem even though they seem to "have it all," many people of modest accomplishments feel great about themselves. Ron, for example, has been an administrative assistant at a computer manufacturer for five years. He doesn't have a fancy title or make a lot of money, but he feels great about what he contributes to his company. He enjoys his friends and family and has confidence about his future. Because he has healthy self-esteem, he feels good about himself and his accomplishments, no matter how big or small they may seem to others.

Conditional and Unconditional Regard   The foundations of self-esteem are laid in the first three or four years of life. When we are young children, we need to feel accepted and valued by our parents or other caregivers. Parental approval is extremely important to a child—parents represent safety and security, as well as physical and mental comfort to a developing mind. If our parents demonstrate love, nurturance, acceptance, encouragement, and support, we usually come to accept ourselves and develop positive self-esteem.

The *way* parents demonstrate love and acceptance also has an important influence on our developing self-esteem. Children and adolescents need to receive **unconditional positive regard**—love and acceptance regardless of their particular behavior. Children and adolescents who receive unconditional positive regard usually develop healthy self-esteem, as shown in Figure 4.1.

In some families, children do not receive unconditional positive regard. Instead, they are given the message that they must act in a certain way to earn acceptance and love. Some parents, for example, demand that their children earn perfect grades in school or excel in sports. These parents are giving their children **conditional positive regard**—love and acceptance

unconditional positive regard Love and acceptance of a person, particularly a child, regardless of his or her particular behavior.

conditional positive regard Love and acceptance of a person, particularly a child, on the condition that he or she behave in a certain way.

FIGURE 4.1   Childhood Origins of Self-Esteem

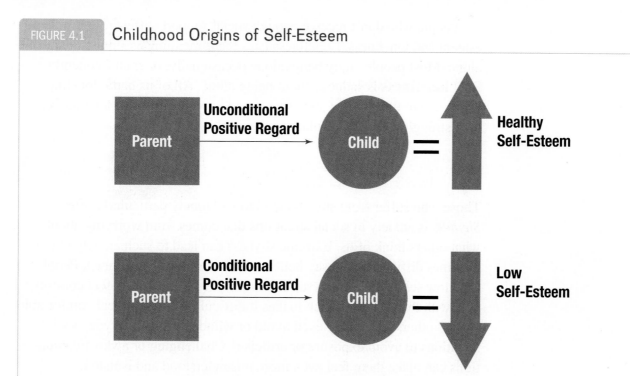

Positive Regard   Your self-esteem is developed and established early on in your life. Studies show that parents' style of child-rearing during the first three or four years greatly affects children's self-esteem. Besides parents, what other important adults might influence a child's self-esteem?

on the condition that they behave in a certain way. Children from such families generally develop low self-esteem. Instead of accepting themselves for who they are, they accept themselves only for what they do and how well they do it. They are satisfied with themselves only when they perform at a certain level. As adults, these people feel that their worth is dependent on specific achievements or outcomes, such as earning a certain salary, looking a certain way, or having certain possessions. If they fail to live up to their impossible standards, they feel bad about themselves.

Support and Loneliness

The need for acceptance and love does not disappear when we reach adulthood. No matter what our age, we all need to feel that we are noticed, appreciated, and valued in our social circle. All the words and actions from others that help us feel valued, cared for, and connected to a community are known as **social support.** Social support is a self-esteem boost.

Social support comes in two basic forms: *emotional support* and *instrumental support.* Emotional support is the giving of trust, empathy, caring, love, concern, and unconditional approval. Instrumental support is the giving of resources such as money, labor, time, advice, and information. A person who gives you emotional support will listen to your thoughts and feelings, encourage you, hug you, and remind you of your worth. A person who gives you instrumental support will help you out if you need advice, a job lead, a loan, a ride to the doctor, or another good turn.

social support Words and actions from other people that help you feel valued, cared for, and connected to a community.

People who don't receive enough social support suffer from low self-esteem and loneliness. Loneliness isn't the same thing as simply being alone. Most people enjoy being alone occasionally, or even frequently. Real **loneliness** is sadness about being alone. All of us battle loneliness from time to time. Many adolescents and young adults face loneliness as they struggle to find their place in the world.

Shyness and Self-Esteem

Those who suffer from shyness tend to feel lonely particularly often. *Shyness* is anxiety in social situations that comes from worrying about what others think of us. Extreme shyness can lead to such anxiety that it becomes difficult just to say hello to others or make eye contact. People with low self-esteem often suffer from shyness. They don't feel comfortable with themselves, which makes it difficult for them to feel comfortable around others. They may even avoid or withdraw from everyday social situations to avoid exposure or criticism. Challenging or awkward situations can make them feel even more misunderstood and isolated.

Both loneliness and shyness can be damaging to self-esteem. They are most damaging when you blame yourself for feeling lonely or socially anxious. If you lack confidence in your social skills, it becomes even harder for you to reach out. It is important to remind yourself that there are people who love and appreciate you. Use **Activity 19** on pages 141–142 to gauge your level of social support and loneliness. This will help you decide whether you need to expand your social support network.

success *secret*

Remind yourself that there are people who love and appreciate you.

*

Overcoming Loneliness   Overcoming loneliness requires building and strengthening your social support network. The first step is to reach out—instead of waiting for others to take an interest in you, show an active interest in them. For example, learn more about the interests or pastimes of a friend, acquaintance, or family member. Ask to participate in activities that interest you. Take the initiative in providing social support to others. If a fellow student is at home sick one day, for example, give him or her a copy of your notes.

Also consider using your time alone to explore your individual interests, perhaps joining a school group, neighborhood club, or volunteer project where you can build a sense of community. Also work on your communication and relationship skills, such as empathy and active listening; this will give you greater confidence in your ability to interact with others. If you have a large social network but still feel lonely often, examine the quality of your relationships. Do you maintain friendships or romantic relationships that do not feel nurturing? Do you still feel lonely when you are with your friends? If so, you may want to explore new friendships.

success *secret*

Supportive, nurturing relationships help guard against loneliness and low self-esteem.

*

ACTIVITY 19: Social Support and Self-Esteem

A For each statement, check whether it applies to you Never, Seldom, Sometimes, Often, or Always.

	Never	Seldom	Sometimes	Often	Always
1. I have someone to take me to the doctor if I need it.					
2. I have someone who listens to me.					
3. I have someone to share my most private worries with.					
4. I have someone who understands my feelings.					
5. I have someone who loves me and makes me feel wanted.					
6. I have someone to help with daily chores if I get sick.					
7. I have someone to hug me.					
8. I have someone to confide in.					
9. I have someone to relax with.					
10. I have someone to get together with for fun.					
11. I have someone to give me good advice about my problems.					
12. I have someone who understands and appreciates me.					

B **Scoring:** Assign yourself one point for every time you checked Never; two points for every time you checked Seldom; three points for every time you checked Sometimes; four points for every time you checked Often; and five points for every time you checked Always.

What is your total? _____

48–60 You enjoy a healthy level of social support.

31–47 You have only a moderate level of social support and may sometimes suffer from loneliness.

12–30 You lack adequate social support and probably suffer from loneliness.

C Describe how often you feel lonely, and what situations bring on the feeling.

_____

_____

_____

D Create a list of your social support network. In the first column, write the name of a person whom you can always or almost always rely on for support. In the second column, write the name of a person whom you can sometimes rely on for support.

I can always rely on:	I can sometimes rely on:
_____	_____
_____	_____
_____	_____
_____	_____
_____	_____
_____	_____
_____	_____
_____	_____

E Do you feel that you have emotional and instrumental support whenever you need it? If not, what could you do to build your social support network?

_____

_____

_____

_____

_____

YOUR SOCIAL NETWORK

The Internet provides unlimited opportunities to connect with people in your community and around the world who have similar interests. Whether you're into woodworking, researching your family tree, or dealing with an illness, there are message boards, chat rooms, and online forums for you to connect with others, ask for and offer advice, share ideas and tips, debate issues and topics, learn new techniques and skills, or simply share experiences, stories, and friendship.

There are obviously risks to interacting on the Internet. It's easy for a person to portray himself or herself as someone else and prey on you emotionally, financially, and sexually. You can also be at risk for identity theft if you make public your personal information. Thus, never post your address, phone number, birthdate, birthplace, or other specific information.

Popular social networking sites such as Facebook, Twitter, Instagram, and LinkedIn allow users to create and share profiles, which can be accessed by select members (or by anyone). These sites provide opportunities to keep in touch with family and friends and connect with people you otherwise may never meet. However, more and more employers are using these sites to research information on job candidates. Thus, never post embarrassing or inappropriate photos or comments—even to your selected members—as they may hurt your opportunities down the road.

Think About It

How might participating in an online chat room or forum help combat loneliness and build your social network?

To learn more about using the Internet to safely expand your social network, go to http://www.safesocialnetworking.com/ or ask your instructor for additional links.

Raising Your Self-Esteem

We've seen how important positive childhood experiences are to healthy self-esteem, but what if you are an adult with low self-esteem—can you do anything about it? Yes! The good news about self-esteem is that we can get more of it. No matter what kind of environment we come from or what genetic makeup we have, we can learn to value ourselves. Not everyone receives the gift of self-esteem from their parents. To attain success, many people have to earn their own esteem. As adults, regardless of our childhood experiences, we have the opportunity to create the positive self-esteem we wish to have.

Not all successful people grew up feeling good about themselves. Often, they had to learn to like themselves through practice. Author Daylle Deanna Schwartz, for example, struggled with low self-esteem from childhood into her adult life. When she started an independent record label, she often met with resistance from her male colleagues, who didn't believe a woman was suited to the competitive environment of the music industry. Schwartz had doubts about herself, too. Because of her determination to shatter industry stereotypes, however, her label became a great success. She began speaking at music industry seminars, and she launched another successful career as an author, helping people to boost their self-esteem. She learned to like herself by following her dreams and overcoming challenges.

success *secret*
No matter what your age, you can learn to value yourself.

SELF-EXPECTANCY AND SELF-ESTEEM

self-expectancy The belief that you are able to achieve what you want in life.

The way you are treated by your family, friends, and acquaintances has a large effect on your self-esteem. But the way you are treated by an even more important person—yourself—has an even greater effect. The things we say to ourselves have an enormous effect on our self-esteem. People with low self-esteem tell themselves, "I'm nobody, and I can't do anything." People with high self-esteem tell themselves, "I am somebody, and I can do whatever I put my mind to."

This self-confidence comes from a sense of self-expectancy. **Self-expectancy** is the belief that you are able to achieve what you want in life. It is the expectation that you will achieve your goals. Everyone tends to receive what he or she expects in the long run. You may or may not get what you deserve, but you will nearly always get what you expect. Whatever you spend the most energy thinking about is what will come to pass, whether it is something you fear or something you desire. People with low self-esteem expect to fail, be in financial peril, suffer poor health, and have troubled relationships; and this is usually what comes true for them. People with high self-esteem expect to succeed, have financial security, enjoy good health, and have happy relationships; and this is what usually comes true for them, too.

This is the power of self-expectancy. If you believe you will be successful at something, you probably will. If you believe you will fail, your mind is likely to trick you into failing.

Self-expectancy is not the same thing as skill or ability. Instead, it is your belief in what you can do with the skills and abilities you already have. In other words, it's not about what you really can accomplish but what you *think* you can accomplish. Our sense of self-expectancy influences which goals we select, how hard we try to reach these goals, and how we cope with obstacles along the way. If we believe we can achieve our goals, then we will be motivated to persevere in the face of difficulties. If, however, we believe that our goals are beyond our reach, we are likely to give up as soon as the going gets rough. Use **Personal Journal 4.1** to find out if you have a healthy sense of self-expectancy.

Building Your Self-Expectancy

Most of us have settled on a level of expectancy much lower than our potential and our innermost desires. It's as if we were waiting for someone to come along and confirm that we're worthy of greater challenges, when, in fact, no one can do that except ourselves.

There is a true story that illustrates this point nicely. It was a stormy night many years ago when an elderly couple entered the hotel lobby and asked for a room. "I'm very sorry," responded the night clerk. "We are completely full with a convention group. Normally, I would send you to another hotel that we use for our overflow in situations like this, but I couldn't imagine sending you out into the storm again. Why don't you

Personal Journal 4.1

Examine Your Self-Expectancy

Put a check mark in the box next to the statements with which you agree.

☐ I know I can accomplish my goals.

☐ When something unexpected comes my way, I find resourceful ways to handle it.

☐ I can solve almost any problem if I try hard enough.

☐ Stress and anger aren't a problem for me because I have good coping skills.

☐ I can handle whatever comes my way.

☐ If someone else can do something, then I can probably do it, too.

☐ If I don't succeed the first time, I try again.

☐ I am proud of what I can accomplish.

☐ I am capable of success.

The more statements you checked, the higher your self-expectancy. Look back at the long-term goals you set for yourself in Chapter 3. How confident are you that you will accomplish these particular goals? Explain.

stay in my room?" The young man offered this with a smile. "It may not be a luxury suite, but it's clean. I can finish up some bookkeeping here in the office since the night auditor won't be coming in."

The distinguished-looking man and woman seemed uncomfortable in inconveniencing the clerk, but they graciously accepted his offer. When the gentleman arrived to pay the bill in the morning, the clerk was still at his desk and said, "Oh, I live here full time so there's no charge for the room." The older man nodded and said, "You're the kind of person that every hotel owner dreams about having as an employee. Maybe someday I'll build a hotel for you." The hotel clerk was flattered, but the idea sounded so outrageous that he was sure the old man was joking.

A few years passed, and the hotel clerk was still at the same job. One day he received a registered letter from the elderly man. The letter expressed his vivid recollections of that stormy night, along with an invitation and a round-trip ticket for the clerk to visit him in New York. Arriving a few days later in Manhattan, the clerk met the gentleman at the corner of Fifth Avenue and Thirty-Fourth Street, where a magnificent new building stood.

"That," exclaimed the old man, "is the hotel I have built for you to run! The clerk was stunned. "What's the catch? Why me? Who are you anyway?"

"My name is William Waldorf-Astor, and there is no catch. You are the person I want." The hotel was the original Waldorf Astoria and the name of the young clerk who accepted the first managerial position was George C. Boldt.

There's a personal message in this true story for each of us. It's not that, if we're good people, a millionaire is going to come along and make all of our dreams come true, although that would be pretty cool. The message is in the form of a question: Why *should* a benefactor arrive to make us believe in our dreams? How is it that an outsider can see more potential in us than we can sometimes see in ourselves? By keeping a realistic eye on our expectations and where we are in relation to their achievement, we can succeed on our own without prompting from anyone else.

Self-expectancy comes from confidence in your ability to succeed and reach your goals. One excellent way to build this confidence is to take a good look at your past goals and successes. This helps remind you of how many skills and achievements you already have.

Are you worried that you don't have much to be proud of? This is a trick of your low self-esteem. If you have low self-esteem, you probably find it difficult to recognize your accomplishments. An **accomplishment** is anything that you have completed through effort, skill, or persistence. An accomplishment doesn't have to be something that was rewarded with a certificate or a trophy. No one else may even know of your biggest accomplishments. They may be significant to you alone. For example, learning to use a computer, recovering from an illness, going back to school, or rebounding from a personal loss are all accomplishments. The point is that you put in effort, demonstrated skill, and persisted to complete something that was important to you.

Creating Successful Experiences   Another excellent way to increase your self-expectancy is to set and accomplish a series of increasingly challenging goals. This gives you the feeling that you can do whatever you set out to do. As you set your goals, it's best to focus on a specific area where you can obtain measurable results. For example, let's say you are afraid of speaking in front of groups of people. Instead of setting a vague goal such as "develop public speaking skills," you might set a series of increasingly challenging SMART goals for yourself, such as:

1. Join in psychology class discussion once per week.
2. Join in psychology class discussion three times per week.
3. Join in psychology class discussion daily.
4. Participate in semester-end group presentation in psychology class.
5. Give a solo presentation at club meeting next quarter.
6. Give a speech at school meeting at the end of school year.

As you move from goal to goal, your confidence in your abilities will increase. Once you build self-expectancy in this one area of your life, you can move to another area and then another. Use **Activity 20** to take an

accomplishment

Anything completed through effort, skill, or persistence.

success *secret*

To boost your self-expectancy, work to accomplish a series of increasingly difficult goals.

ACTIVITY 20: Accomplishment Inventory

A Remember the times in your life, either recently or long ago, during which you felt a sense of satisfaction and accomplishment. Perhaps you helped someone, learned a skill, completed a project, or accomplished an important goal. Select four accomplishments. Briefly describe each one in a box below and explain why it is meaningful to you.

Accomplishment #1	Accomplishment #2

Accomplishment #3	Accomplishment #4

B Now write down the skills (such as developing software applications or creative writing) and personal qualities (such as determination or generosity) that these accomplishments demonstrate. If you aren't sure what to write, imagine that someone you like and admire had accomplished the same things you did. What skills and personal qualities would you see in that person?

Skills	Personal Qualities

continued...

C Now focus on the future. What skills would you like to develop over the coming years? For example, would you like to learn to play a musical instrument or a sport, design a Web site, speak another language, write poetry? List at least five skills you would like to acquire.

_____

_____

_____

_____

_____

_____

How confident are you in your ability to acquire these skills? Explain.

_____

_____

_____

D Pick one of the skills you listed above. Formulate a series of five or six increasingly challenging SMART goals that will help you acquire these skills.

Goal #1 _____

Goal #2 _____

Goal #3 _____

Goal #4 _____

Goal #5 _____

Goal #6 _____

E How confident are you that you can achieve the first goal on your list? What about the last goal on the list? Explain.

_____

_____

_____

inventory of your accomplishments and set yourself a series of goals that will lead to new successes.

Coping and Avoidance

As you build confidence in yourself and your skills, you will gain the courage to face tougher and tougher challenges. One of the biggest of life's challenges is coping with painful problems. **Coping** means facing up to threatening or uncomfortable situations. A threatening situation may be a problem in a relationship, a bad habit, a difficulty at work or school, or anything else that is unpleasant or painful. Any time we cope with something—regardless of the outcome—our self-esteem rises.

The opposite of coping is avoidance. **Avoidance** is an unwillingness to face uncomfortable situations or psychological realities. Whenever we avoid something we need to face, our self-esteem goes down. The longer we avoid it, the more damage it does to our self-esteem. Common avoidance behaviors include:

- self-criticism
- making jokes about the situation
- becoming obsessed with work to avoid thinking about the problem
- escaping through activities such as shopping, watching TV, or sleeping
- venting unpleasant feelings without taking action
- abusing alcohol or other drugs

Avoidance reduces short-term discomfort, but leaves you with the feeling that you are incapable of dealing with the situation. Do you ever feel powerless to resolve a difficult situation? Take a look at what you might be avoiding in **Personal Journal 4.2.**

Avoidance not only lowers self-esteem, but also turns small problems into big ones. Take Maia's example. Maia was struck by terror every time a credit card bill arrived in the mail. She immediately stuffed it in a drawer and told herself not to think about it. When bill collectors began calling, Maia stopped answering her phone and turned off her answering machine. The more Maia avoided paying her bills, however, the worse she felt about herself. Why was Maia so intent on avoiding this problem? As is often the case, it was to avoid a bigger underlying problem: She didn't want to face the fact that she was in debt and had out-of-control spending habits. When she finally found the courage to admit there was a problem, her self-esteem went up. This, in turn, gave her the confidence to begin coping with the loneliness that motivated her spending.

As this example shows, the first step in coping with a problem is to admit that it exists. Once you've done this, you can work step-by-step to improve the situation and build your self-expectancy.

coping Facing up to threatening situations.

avoidance An unwillingness to face uncomfortable situations or psychological realities.

success *secret*
When you face your problems head-on, your self-esteem grows.

Personal Journal 4.2

Learning to Cope

In the center below, briefly describe one specific, ongoing problem in your life that you often avoid. Close your eyes and relive a situation in which you avoided the problem. In the boxes on the left side of the diagram, write three adjectives that describe how you feel about yourself. Now close your eyes and picture yourself dealing confidently, fearlessly, and expertly with the problem. In the boxes on the right side of the diagram, write three adjectives that describe how you feel about yourself now.

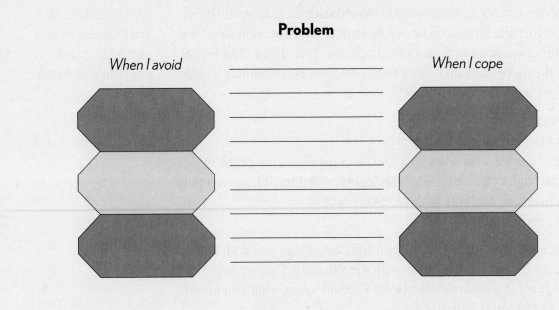

Problem

When I avoid   _____   *When I cope*

Compare the two sets of adjectives. Did the feeling of coping with the problem make you feel better about yourself? What is one action you could take today to start coping with this problem?

✓ Self Check

1. Why is self-esteem important for success? (pp. 128–129)
2. Define unconditional positive regard. (p. 138)
3. What does avoidance do to self-esteem? (p. 149)

Learning to Like Yourself

SELF-ACCEPTANCE AND SELF-ESTEEM

In the previous section, we looked at the origins of self-esteem and the role of self-expectancy in raising or lowering your self-esteem. Now we'll focus on self-acceptance. **Self-acceptance** means recognizing and accepting what is true about yourself. Self-acceptance allows you to stop criticizing yourself for falling short of your or other people's impossible standards. It allows you to discover and express who you really are inside. When you enjoy self-acceptance, you recognize that you are good enough just the way you are. So what if you still have areas you could improve? So what if you sometimes procrastinate or lose your temper or drive too fast? You are still worthy of respect, love, and success. That's why influential psychologist Alfred Adler called self-acceptance "the courage to be imperfect."

self-acceptance
Recognition and acceptance of what is true about yourself.

You, Flaws, and All

Your self-image mirrors your level of self-acceptance. When we have a healthy self-image, we see and accept both our strengths and weaknesses. When we have an unhealthy self-image, we focus too much on our weaknesses and end up rejecting ourselves.

The difference between people who accept themselves and people who reject themselves isn't the number of weaknesses they have, it's the way they look at them. People with a positive self-image realize that they have many more strengths than weaknesses. They accept the weaknesses they do have but choose not to be bothered by them. They know that they are a unique gift of creation, with skills and personal qualities in a combination that no one else has.

How healthy is your self-image? Look back at your responses to **Personal Journal 1.3** on page 26. (If you haven't completed this activity, now would be a good time to do so.) Did you give yourself mostly positive ratings or mostly negative ones? If you assigned yourself a five or less in three or more areas, you may have a negative self-image and low self-esteem. Also look at how wide a range of numbers you assigned yourself. Were you clear on your strengths and weaknesses, or did you circle a wide range of numbers? If you selected a wide range, you may need to work on your self-awareness.

How you feel about your "flaws" also has an impact on your self-esteem. If you feel shame or guilt about your weaknesses—even if you are proud of your strengths in other areas—your self-esteem will suffer. Take Gary's example. Gary knows he is an excellent student and worker and that he is popular with his classmates. However, he is ashamed about being overweight. This sense of shame poisons his entire self-image. When he thinks about himself, he can only focus on being overweight. To him, his successes seem insignificant by comparison.

success *secret*
Your skills and personal qualities are unlike anyone else's.

Ashleigh has a similar problem. She is confident about her appearance, athletic ability, and social skills but has nagging doubts about her intelligence. In fact, she often feels downright stupid. She lets her self-acceptance be weakened even more by comments from authority figures that she's "not using her brain" and "not living up to expectations."

Gary and Ashleigh are having difficulty separating their feelings from reality. Because they feel inadequate, they assume that everyone else must see them that way, too.

Mending a Negative Self-Image

If you have a negative self-image, how do you change it? First, you need to accept that it is distorted. This isn't always easy. Once our self-image is implanted in our brains, we see it as being completely true. We don't ask ourselves whether it is false. Unfortunately, if you have a negative self-image, the truth you feel about yourself is really a figment of your imagination. You see yourself as far less worthy than you really are. You may also believe that other people see you the same way as you do. In reality, though, no one is as cruel to you as you are to yourself.

If a negative self-image is holding you back, it's time to take a new look at yourself—objectively—and reassess your strengths and weaknesses. Having an accurate view of your strengths helps you set challenging goals, overcome obstacles, and take advantage of opportunities. Knowing your weaknesses helps you see that they aren't as bad as you thought. Look at them objectively: Are you really "ugly," or do you have a nose that you wish was a little smaller? Are you really a "slob," or do you just dislike doing housework?

professional **development**)))

Positive Image at Work/First Impressions Matter

First impressions are extremely important to job and career success. Therefore, your attire, grooming, and behavior impact how others perceive you. Every company has its own standards and policies for what is expected or considered acceptable in its employees. Studies show that job applicants who dress professionally and are well groomed are hired more often and perceived to be more competent.

Make sure you project a positive and professional self-image in your work environment, especially if you want to advance in your company and career. It's not about wearing "designer" clothing, it's about looking *your* best. Some companies offer mentoring programs, where "image-coaching" could be a valuable component. Seek out a mentor, colleague, peer, or someone you trust who can provide you with honest feedback and suggestions on how you can improve your professional image.

To learn more about the importance of first impressions and professional image, go to the following:
www.nwitimes.com/business/jobs-and-employment/
www.psychologytoday.com/blog.am-i-right/201302/thepower-first-impressions
www.uaex.edu/publications/pdf/4HFSFA301.pdf

Another benefit to knowing your weaknesses is that it helps you to pick activities and situations where your weaknesses won't be a problem. If you know you aren't particularly good at math, for example, you might decide to major in a field where this won't hold you back. If you are a night person who can't seem to make it to morning classes on time, you can choose classes that meet later in the day. When you know your weaknesses, you can find creative ways to work around them.

Take a Personal Inventory   Get to know your strengths—and weaknesses—by creating a personal inventory. A personal inventory is a list of your plusses and minuses in the key areas of your life, such as appearance, intimate relationships, social skills, school performance, work performance, and thinking skills. By putting all your strengths and weaknesses down on paper, you can get a better view of your strengths, as well as a more accurate and compassionate view of your flaws. Use **Activity 21** on pages 154–156 to create your own personal inventory. After completing the inventory, you should have a much fairer and more accurate assessment of yourself. Keep your self-inventory with you and go over it every day for a month, or more often if you're feeling low. Sometimes reading it out loud can increase its effectiveness. It is sometimes difficult to overcome patterns of negative self-thought, but using this new inventory will help you teach your mind to accept your flaws, affirm your positive qualities, and move on.

Accepting Your Physical Self   How did you describe your physical appearance in the last exercise? If you're like most people, you were extremely critical of many of your physical features. Unfortunately, it's almost impossible to have high self-esteem when we feel physically unattractive. In fact, studies have shown that how we feel about our physical appearance is the number-one indicator of our overall self-esteem. This is not surprising, because most of us are constantly bombarded with media images portraying physically "perfect" people. Trying to live up to these unrealistic images can lead to problems with **body image,** how you think and feel about your body and appearance. People with a poor body image see their bodies in distorted ways. Although they look just fine to others, they become convinced that they are unattractive.

body image How you think and feel about your body and appearance.

Studies have shown how important appearance is in life. When people are well groomed and dressed in clean clothes, they are treated better by their classmates and teachers. They feel attractive and therefore project a better image. Like it or not, we leave a lasting impression with our appearance.

Obviously, we cannot choose what looks we inherit from our parents. We can, however, choose how we take care of our health and appearance. We behave according to the way we *think* we look rather than the way we actually look. If we think we look good, then others will think the same. People who accept themselves are attractive to others. Their healthy self-esteem comes through from the inside out.

ACTIVITY 21: Personal Inventory

A In each box below, write down what you see as your good points and bad points in that area of your life. Include both things you like and don't like about how you look, act, think, or feel. Examples are provided.

Appearance	Romantic Relationships/Sexuality	Social Skills/Popularity
"I look good in black." *"My nose is too big."*	*"I have a great partner who respects my opinion."* *"I talk too much about my old girlfriend."*	*"I'm always asked first to head committees."* *"I never know what to say when I meet someone new."*

Thinking Skills/Intelligence	School	Work
"Every day I create a to-do list and stick to it." *"I can never seem to balance my checkbook."*	*"My history professor thinks I ask good questions."* *"I can never read my notes."*	*"I'm often asked to train new employees."* *"I'm always five minutes late to work."*

B Look over what you wrote about yourself, circling all the negative items. Rewrite each negative item according to the following rules:

- **Be objective.** Remove all negative, critical language. An entry like "ugly feet" could be changed to "larger feet than I would like."

- **Be accurate.** Don't exaggerate—stick to the facts. Instead of writing "terrible student," you might write "2.3 GPA."

- **Be specific.** Avoid extreme words like "always," "never," "totally." An entry like "always late to everything" might be changed to "often late to morning appointments."

- **Look for strengths.** Look for strengths that make up for your areas of weakness. An entry like "forgetful" might be changed to "often forgetful, although I have a great memory for faces."

Use the boxes below to rewrite your negatives according to these guidelines.

Appearance	Romantic Relationships/Sexuality	Social Skills/Popularity

Thinking Skills/Intelligence	School	Work

continued . . .

C   Now use your positives and rewritten negatives to write a letter or e-mail introducing and describing yourself to a person you have never met. You cannot enclose or attach a photograph, so you will have to use words to paint a picture of yourself, both physically and mentally. Write an honest description of yourself, but stress your strengths and be as realistic and specific as possible about your weaknesses.

Dear _____,

_____

_____

_____

_____

_____

_____

_____

_____

_____

_____

Sincerely,

_____

Applying **Psychology**

Culture and Body Image

We see them on magazine covers, on roadside billboards, and in television commercials: thin, beautiful people enjoying the good life. Are these real people? Not exactly. In North America, models are much taller and thinner than the average person. The average female model, for example, stands 5'10" and weighs 110 pounds, while the average woman is 5'4" and weighs 140 pounds. What about in other cultures? Tall and thin may be the ideal in the West, but most non-Western cultures have different ideas about beauty. Many traditional Asian-Pacific and African cultures, for example, equate a rounded physique with beauty. Today, however, this is changing. With greater exposure to Western media, more and more people in cultures across the world are dieting, falling victim to eating disorders, and striving to live up to an almost impossible ideal of beauty. Body image problems have a large impact on self-esteem, particularly among women. In one study, women who spent only three minutes looking at models in a fashion magazine felt depressed, guilty, and ashamed of their own bodies.

Critical Thinking   *How do you feel when you see media images portraying "perfect" people?*

Whether you are a man or a woman, accepting yourself means seeing advertising images for what they are: a select few people paid to be photographed under the best possible conditions. Instead of being your body's enemy, learn to think of yourself as its supporter. Appreciate not only how your body looks but also what it can do. Remind yourself that you are not just a body but a whole person—a spirit, soul, and mind contained in a physical body. Ask yourself how you want to spend your energy—pursuing the perfect body or enjoying family, friends, school, work, and life?

success *secret*

Think of yourself as your body's friend, not its enemy.

You're Okay   The better we can accept our human imperfections, the more we will accept and value ourselves. But what about self-improvement? Shouldn't we look for ways to fix our weaknesses? Only within reason. It's great to want to improve yourself, to be that special person you want to be. The real key to self-esteem, though, is to like and value yourself as you are *now*. You are valuable for who you are—not for what you have, how you look, or what you do. You can't change your genetics or go back in time and grow up in a different environment. Why beat yourself up about things you can't change? Accept yourself as you are at this moment with whatever weaknesses you have. Remember that the perfect human being has not yet been discovered. Accept and celebrate yourself as you are, flaws and all.

Kick the Comparing Habit

Another way to foster self-acceptance is to become aware of the way you compare yourself to other people. Many of us are addicted to **social comparison,** comparing our traits and accomplishments with those of other people.

social comparison

The practice of comparing your traits and accomplishments with those of others.

There are two types of social comparison: *downward comparison* and *upward comparison.* When we use downward comparison, we compare ourselves to people "below" us, such as fellow students who are earning lower grades or coworkers who have received fewer promotions. When we use upward comparison, we compare ourselves to people "above" us, such as students who are earning higher grades or coworkers who have been promoted above us. People who suffer from low self-esteem often use downward comparison to try to make themselves feel better. They tell themselves, "See, I'm not doing so badly. Look at him." Unfortunately, downward comparison only makes us feel better for a short time. Self-esteem comes from inside, not from knowing that someone else is struggling.

People with low self-esteem sometimes use upward comparison to make themselves feel worse—to reinforce their negative ideas about themselves. If we look at someone who is at the top of our field, for example, we might tell ourselves that we are unsuccessful and our accomplishments are insignificant. "Look how well she's doing! I'll never reach that level." This is equally unhealthy, because it means measuring your progress according to someone else's standards.

Everyone is interested in how they measure up to others, and everyone uses social comparison from time to time. Comparing ourselves to others too often, however, can damage our self-esteem. Do you use social comparison to evaluate yourself? Complete **Personal Journal 4.3** to find out if you have the comparing habit.

success *secret*

Measure your progress according to your goals, not someone else's.

Real or Ideal?

Comparing ourselves to other people and to media images can take a huge toll on our self-esteem. Comparing ourselves to our ideals can do the same thing. Each of us has an **ideal self,** a vision or idea of the kind of person we want or ought to be. Your ideal self is you without flaws—the perfect you. Everyone's ideal self, of course, is a fantasy. Mitch, a struggling actor, dreams of hitting it big in Hollywood. His ideal self is an Oscar-winning movie star who pulls in $20 million per film. Diane, a college student, dreams of winning the Nobel Prize in chemistry.

ideal self The person we want to be or feel we ought to be.

All of us have fantasies about our perfect lives and our perfect selves. The difference between our real and our ideal selves motivates us to keep improving ourselves. If our real and ideal selves are very different, however, it can erode our self-esteem, as shown in Figure 4.2. We may start to feel guilty or ashamed about who we are because we aren't who we think we ought to be.

possible selves The person or persons you might realistically become in the future.

Possible Selves   Instead of focusing on a fantasy about an ideal that no one can ever attain, it's healthier to think about what you really want to be and achieve. Think about your **possible selves,** the person(s) you think you might realistically become in the future.

Personal Journal 4.3

Social Comparison Log

Over the course of one full day, pay attention to how many times you compare yourself to other people. Make a note in the following log each time it happens. Describe the comparison you made and how it affected your self-esteem.

Comparison I Made	How It Made Me Feel About Myself

Now look at all the comparisons you made. Were most of these comparisons in a specific area (such as academic performance, appearance, or clothing)? Did your comparisons make you feel better or worse about yourself?

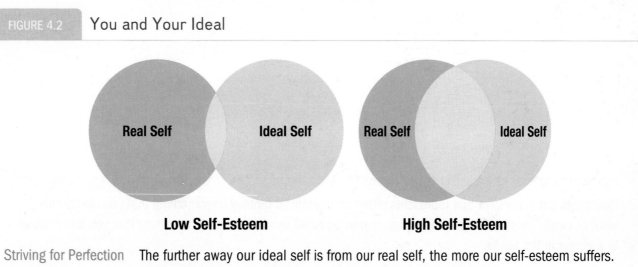

FIGURE 4.2 You and Your Ideal

Low Self-Esteem

High Self-Esteem

Striving for Perfection   The further away our ideal self is from our real self, the more our self-esteem suffers. *How can you control the gap between your real and ideal self?*

Our possible selves help guide our behavior by giving us positive images to inspire us. Mitch, the struggling actor, sees himself becoming a well-respected stage actor in local productions, or perhaps a character actor in films. These visions of himself aren't as glamorous as his dream of being a movie star, but it helps him to set specific goals. Diane, the college student, sees herself becoming a researcher at a pharmaceutical company. Instead of worrying about winning the Nobel Prize, she focuses on what she can do every day to get one step closer to her realistic goal.

To transform your ideal self into one or more possible selves, consider how many aspects of your ideal self are important to you. You might fantasize about being rich, for example, but do you need to be rich to be happy? Are you willing to put in the time and effort to make it happen? Do you really want this for yourself, or is this someone else's dream (society's, perhaps, or your parents' or friends')? Instead of wishing you had great riches, focus on working toward an attainable goal, such as achieving financial security.

Use **Personal Journal 4.4** to consider your ideal self and your possible selves. Then make a resolution: You will never criticize yourself for not having something that you don't really want anyway.

success *secret*
Remember the difference between fantasy and reality.

Personal Journal 4.4

Your Ideal Self

In the box below, write down how you would like to look, act, and feel and what you would like to be, achieve, and own in an ideal world. Don't edit yourself—write everything that comes to mind when you think of the perfect you.

The perfect me

Now cross out every item that represents either an unrealistic fantasy or something that you don't truly want or need. The remaining items make up your possible selves—the different selves that you can choose to become in the future.

USING POSITIVE SELF-TALK

So far, so good: You've taken a close look at yourself and made a commitment to accept yourself. This conscious commitment is important, but it's not the end of the journey. You now need to convince your subconscious mind that you are valuable and worthwhile.

You are constantly talking—either to others or to yourself. What you say to yourself about yourself, silently or out loud, is known as **self-talk.** When you have negative thoughts and feelings about yourself, they often come across in the form of negative self-talk. You may use negative self-talk and not even realize it.

self-talk What you say or think to yourself about yourself.

You can hurt your self-esteem with negative self-talk, but you can build your self-esteem with positive self-talk—giving yourself praise and encouragement. By changing the way you talk to yourself, you can change the way you feel about yourself, too.

Words have a powerful effect on our bodies as well as our minds. Thoughts can raise and lower body temperature, relax muscles and nerves, raise and lower pulse rate, and more. Self-talk is so powerful because it works on our subconscious mind, the part of our mind that stores many of the experiences, feelings, and thoughts that control our behavior. Many of the thoughts and attitudes that damage our self-esteem are subconscious ones. Positive self-talk works by turning these negative thoughts and attitudes into more positive ones.

Negative Self-Talk: Your Inner Critic

Unfortunately, many of us spend our days telling ourselves negative things: "I'm a loser." "I can't believe how lazy I am." "I blew it again." The critical voice that bombards you with constant negative self-talk is known as your **inner critic.** This inner critic might speak in your own voice or in the voice of someone from your past, such as a critical parent, sibling, or teacher. To develop self-esteem, you must drown out your inner critic with positive self-talk. This means telling yourself over and over again that you are a worthwhile, valuable person.

inner critic The critical voice that bombards you with constant negative self-talk.

Origin of the Critic
When we were growing up, many of us were made to feel bad about ourselves through repeated criticism. This early criticism has an extremely damaging effect. When children are given negative messages, they may conclude that they are fundamentally bad, or lazy, or ugly, or incompetent. This is especially common when parents send the message that the child, rather than the child's behavior, is bad. Often, a parent accompanies scolding with the withdrawal of love or attention. This sends the message, "I don't love you because you don't deserve it."

When we grow up, these internalized messages become the voice of our inner critic. When we berate ourselves for making a mistake, messages come sailing at us from the past: "I'm a screw-up. I can't handle anything." This self-critical voice can devastate our self-esteem.

label A simplistic statement that people use to define who they are.

Role of the Critic

Why do we allow ourselves to have these thoughts, even if we know they're not in our best interest? Ironically, we use our inner critic to protect us against the fear of rejection and failure. By telling ourselves that we are failures before anyone else has a chance to do the same, we feel that we are prepared for any attacks that may come. We may even use the critic to protect us from taking any action at all. By telling ourselves that we will fail, we have a handy excuse for not trying.

We also use the inner critic as a kind of psychological safeguard against uncertainty. When things go wrong, we feel an instinctive need for comfort and security. People with high self-esteem respond to that need by coping with problems directly, by finding solutions instead of worrying. They achieve a feeling of security by getting rid of the thing that is threatening it. As we saw, however, people with low self-esteem don't feel confident in their ability to cope. Instead, they rely on the inner critic. The critical self-talk originated from our parents, with whom we once associated the same comfort and security.

Labels

Labels are a particularly damaging form of self-talk. A **label** is a simplistic statement that we use to define who we are. As we are growing up, other people may give us labels such as "pretty" or "ugly," "smart" or "dumb," "popular" or "unpopular." These labels, formed early, often stay with us. The problem with labels is that they can be very limiting, and often are not even true. Labels tend to be negative. Yet people become so attached to the labels they have given themselves (or other people) that they can't let go of them. If you can't let go of labels, you can't begin to improve your self-esteem.

We undermine our own self-esteem by labeling ourselves and by accepting the labels that other people give to us. How often have you heard yourself or others say things like the following:

- "I look terrible no matter what I do."
- "I'm a lousy cook; I can't even boil an egg."
- "I can't dance."
- "I'm all thumbs."
- "I have no sense of humor."
- "I have a terrible memory."
- "I'm never on time."
- "I have bad luck."
- "I have no sense of style."

The more times we tell ourselves these negative things, the worse we feel about ourselves. Complete **Activity 22** on pages 164–165 to monitor your negative self-talk and convert your negative self-statements into positive ones.

Stop Those Thoughts!

Try to catch yourself whenever you engage in negative self-talk. Get in the habit of stopping your thoughts whenever you hear yourself thinking negatively. You can even tell your inner critic, "stop!" or "be quiet!" Some people see a specific image in their minds, such as a big red stop sign. Pause and really think about your attitude toward yourself. Are you beating up on yourself? Are you dwelling on the past? Are you blaming yourself for things that aren't your fault?

You may not be able to control everything that happens to you, but you can control the words you say to yourself. Changing negative self-talk isn't easy—it takes a conscious effort, applied over days, weeks, and even years. It takes discipline and dedication to boost your self-esteem from the inside out, but it's worth it.

success *secret*
Learn to stop the inner critic in its tracks.

Using Affirmations

Affirmations are positive self-statements that help you think of yourself in a positive, caring, and accepting way. Affirmations are a powerful tool for rejecting the labels we have accepted for ourselves and replacing them with new visions of ourselves as competent and worthy.

affirmation A positive self-statement that helps you think of yourself in a positive, caring, and accepting way.

One way to write affirmations is to take your negative self-statements and turn them into positive ones. Instead of telling yourself, "I'm always late," say, "I am becoming more and more organized and punctual" or "I have the power to be on time." Instead of saying, "I'm fat," say, "I am attractive and healthy" or "I have a strong, fit body."

Another way to write affirmations is to portray yourself as the successful person you want to be. Use language that is as specific and positive as possible.

- "I am a self-confident, compassionate person."
- "I can do whatever I set out to do."
- "I am a courageous, gentle, lovable person."
- "I am focused and persistent."
- "I am an attractive, loving person."
- "I am an intelligent and powerful person capable of attaining all of my goals."
- "I always do the best I can."
- "I am honest with myself and others."
- "I am a helpful, caring individual."
- "I create a positive environment for myself and those around me."
- "My vision of my future is clear and focused."
- "I have the strength to handle any situation."

success *secret*
Turn your negative self-statements into positive affirmations.

It might take a while for you to become comfortable using affirmations. The more you repeat them to yourself, however, the more these positive statements will feel right. You'll replace the habit of negative self-talk with a new habit of positive self-talk.

Focus on the Positive
When learning to use positive self-talk, remember that the subconscious mind doesn't react well to being told *not* to think or do something. We have all seen how a child, when told not to do something, suddenly develops an overwhelming urge to do it. Follow

ACTIVITY 22: Negative Self-Talk Log

A Monitor your self-talk throughout the course of an entire day. Try to catch at least 10 negative self-statements. Each time you hear yourself thinking something negative about yourself, note the following:

1. Time of day

2. Statement you made to yourself

3. How much of the statement was true, and how much was false

1. Time	2. Self-Statement	3. True or False
Example *6:45 AM*	*"I'm late again as usual. Why am I so lazy?"*	*"I sometimes leave late for work, but this doesn't mean I'm lazy."*

B Do you see a pattern to any of your negative self-talk? For example, did you criticize yourself repeatedly in one area, such as your appearance or intelligence? Explain.

C Pick out the three most painful and damaging self-statements you recorded in your log. Analyze their origins. Did you receive repeated criticism in this area in the past? When? Explain.

Negative Self-Statement: _____

_____

Possible Origin: _____

_____

Negative Self-Statement: _____

_____

Possible Origin: _____

_____

Negative Self-Statement: _____

_____

Possible Origin: _____

_____

D Now turn each of these negative self-statements into an affirmation. (See page 163 for guidelines.)

Affirmation: _____

_____

Affirmation: _____

_____

Affirmation: _____

_____

this same logic with your self-talk. Instead of saying, "I don't feel tired," say, "I feel rested and awake." Instead of saying, "I shouldn't use the car to travel short distances," tell yourself, "I will walk and ride my bike more." Make sure to focus on what you will do, not on what you won't do.

Concentrate on one good thought at a time. Instead of saying, "I can't" or "I wish," say:

- "I can."
- "Next time I'll get it right."
- "I have to take risks to get rewards."
- "I can learn from this mistake."
- "I will remain positive about this."
- "I look forward to . . ."
- "I'm feeling better about . . ."
- "Things will get better when I . . ."

These positive self-statements help us develop the coping skills we need to persevere and feel good about ourselves.

CRITICISM AND SELF-ESTEEM

criticism Any remark that contains a judgment, evaluation, or statement of fault.

All of us receive criticism from ourselves in the form of negative self-talk. From time to time, we receive criticism from others as well. **Criticism** is any remark that contains a judgment, evaluation, or statement of fault. People with low self-esteem are particularly vulnerable to criticism, especially when this criticism echoes the attacks of their inner critic.

For healthy self-esteem, we all need the love, support, and assistance of others. Encouragement from friends and family, instructors, coworkers, and fellow students can help to strengthen our self-esteem; but how do we continue to accept ourselves if we are criticized instead of loved and supported? We need to learn to ignore opinions that might hurt our self-esteem. For example, if your classmate makes a critical comment about your low test grade, does that make you a poor student? No! You are still the same hardworking student you were when you walked into the room. People's opinions don't change who you are. No matter what you do or say, or don't do or don't say, you will receive criticism at some point. Learn to respond to criticism effectively without allowing it to damage your self-esteem.

The key to handling criticism well is to realize that everyone sees a situation in his or her own unique way. Therefore, just because someone criticizes your appearance or driving or work habits doesn't mean that there is anything wrong with them. It's possible that you are dealing with a simple difference of opinion. It's also possible that your critic is motivated by personal difficulties. Perhaps he is having trouble accepting his own appearance. Maybe she is struggling with the very work habits for which she is criticizing you. Then again, perhaps your critic is simply in a bad mood and snapping at the first person to come by. Whatever the case, simply note that something other than you is motivating the person to be

success *secret*
Criticism often stems from a simple difference of opinion.

critical. This allows you to handle the situation more objectively, without letting it threaten your self-esteem. Once you take your self-esteem out of the equation, you are more open to receiving or rejecting a critic's message.

Destructive and Constructive Criticism

Not all criticism is created equal. Some criticism is constructive, designed to help us improve ourselves. Other criticism is destructive and can cripple our self-esteem.

What is the difference between the two kinds of criticism? *Destructive criticism* is often general, addressing your attitude or some aspect of yourself rather than focusing on specific behavior. It is also usually entirely negative, without any helpful suggestion about how to do things differently. Consider these examples:

- "The writing in this report is junk."
- "You're totally out of shape."
- "That color doesn't suit you at all."
- "You really screwed up on this project."
- "Your academic performance this term has been a real disappointment."

Constructive criticism, by contrast, addresses specific behavior and does not attack you as a person. It also usually makes mention of your positive points and offers helpful suggestions for improvement. Compare these constructive criticisms with the destructive ones above:

- "You did a great job researching this report. I think it would be even better if you used a more concise writing style."
- "I'm concerned about your health. What if we went speed-walking together a few times a week?"
- "That shirt looks great. I bet a blue one would look even better."
- "Let's talk about what we can do to make the next project work for both of us."
- "Let's think about how you can improve your grades next semester."

Which criticisms would you rather receive? Destructive criticism is delivered without empathy or compassion. It assumes that the person has done something wrong. Constructive criticism conveys caring and concern. It not only offers suggestions but also shows a willingness to help out with fixing the problem.

Handling Constructive Criticism

There are three major steps to handling positive, helpful criticism. First, listen. Make sure you understand exactly what is being said. If you don't, ask. It isn't easy to listen openly to criticism—even constructive criticism. However, it gets easier with practice. Second, restate the criticism. By summarizing the critic's message, you show that you are interested and not on the defensive. Third and finally, if the critic hasn't provided a suggestion, ask for suggestions on how to improve. Make a note of this information so you can use it to improve yourself. The three basic steps in handling constructive criticism are summarized in Figure 4.3.

Handling Destructive Criticism

Handling destructive criticism is more difficult. Destructive criticism can make us feel hurt, attacked, and defensive. There are many different ways of reacting to destructive criticism. Some are highly ineffective, however, because they invite further criticism. These faulty reaction styles are:

- **Aggressive style**—Aggressive reactors directly confront the critic, often with angry attacks similar to the ones they received.
  Critic: "You painted that? It looks like a three-year-old did it."
  You: "You just can't keep your mouth shut, can you?"
- **Passive style**—A passive reactor acknowledges that the criticism is true, then apologizes. Although this usually prevents further criticism, reacting passively is very damaging to your self-esteem.
  Critic: "You did a terrible job on this report."
  You: "You're right. I'm sorry I let you down."
- **Passive-aggressive style**—This style combines the worst of both the passive and the aggressive styles. Passive aggressors pretend to acknowledge the criticism, but later consciously or unconsciously get even with the critic somehow.
  Critic: "You look like you've put on weight."
  You: "I know. You're probably embarrassed to be seen in public with me." ("Accidentally" spills coffee on critic's shirt.)

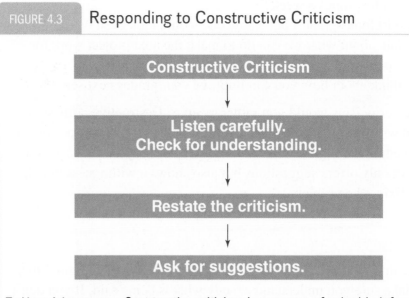

FIGURE 4.3   Responding to Constructive Criticism

Constructive Criticism

↓

Listen carefully.
Check for understanding.

↓

Restate the criticism.

↓

Ask for suggestions.

To Your Advantage   Constructive criticism is a source of valuable information. Asking for suggestions helps you find creative solutions to the problem behind the criticism. *If you were a manager, would you feel comfortable giving your employees constructive criticism? Why or why not?*

These response styles generate negative feelings and give the critic even more to criticize. A better way to handle destructive criticism is to acknowledge it and then put a stop to it in a rational, mature way. First, find something to acknowledge in the criticism, either a fact or a feeling that is motivating the critic. Second, assert yourself by correcting the part of the criticism that you believe to be mistaken, unfair, or insulting. Figure 4.4 on page 170 shows the process of handling criticism in a useful, self-esteem–boosting way.

- **Acknowledge facts.** Agree with the specific part of the criticism that you can honestly acknowledge to be true. This puts a stop to the criticism and saves your self-esteem.
  Critic: "You're so lazy. You spend all weekend watching TV."
  You: "You're right, I spend a lot of time watching TV on the weekends, but that doesn't mean I'm lazy."
- **Acknowledge feelings.** If you truly cannot find anything to agree with in the criticism, show the critic that you recognize the feelings that are motivating the criticism. This pacifies the critic and ends the criticism.
  Critic: "You're a slob. Just look at that sink overflowing with dishes."
  You: "I know you hate to leave dirty dishes in the sink. However, I like to let them pile up and then do them all at once."

By finding something—anything—to acknowledge in a piece of criticism, you let your critic know that he or she has been heard. By speaking up for yourself and refusing to be the victim of a personal attack, you boost your self-esteem.

Probing   What if the destructive criticism is vague and general? What if someone calls you lazy or overbearing? For general criticisms, a technique known as probing often has the best results. **Probing** involves asking the critic for specifics. Probing has the dual effect of reducing the argument down to more reasonable specifics, and disarming the critic with the notion that you are taking an interest in the criticism. Conversations involving probing might look like this:

probing Asking for specifics from a person who has given a general or vague criticism.

Critic: "I don't know how you get through life being so lazy."
You: "Can you give me an example of my laziness?"
Critic: "For one thing, you spend all weekend watching TV."
Critic: "You messed up all the files when you reorganized the office."
You: "How exactly did I mess up the files?"
Critic: "Nothing is in alphabetical order anymore."
Critic: "You're a slob."
You: "What makes you think of me as a slob?"
Critic: "Just look at that sink overflowing with dishes."

Continue probing until you have reduced the criticism from personal accusations to specific examples. Then you can evaluate whether the critic has anything useful to say.

Practice responding to constructive and destructive criticism in **Activity 23.**

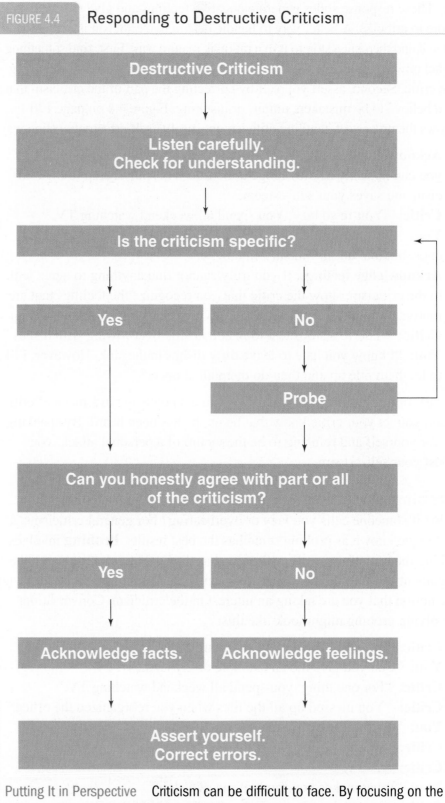

FIGURE 4.4 Responding to Destructive Criticism

Destructive Criticism

↓

Listen carefully.
Check for understanding.

↓

Is the criticism specific?

Yes — No

No → Probe

Can you honestly agree with part or all of the criticism?

Yes — No

Yes → Acknowledge facts.

No → Acknowledge feelings.

Assert yourself.
Correct errors.

Putting It in Perspective Criticism can be difficult to face. By focusing on the content of the message and using effective response techniques, however, you can diffuse criticism before it damages your self-esteem. *Do you think that some criticism doesn't deserve any response at all? Explain.*

ACTIVITY 23: Handling Criticism

A Practice responding to constructive criticism. Imagine that the people below are giving you accurate feedback. Write a response to each constructive criticism that 1. restates the criticism and 2. asks for specific suggestions for improvement.

Example

"Your writing is good, but you have used some terms incorrectly here."

Restate: <u>*Yes, vocabulary is my weak point.*</u>

Ask for suggestions: <u>*What are some ways I could work on this?*</u>

Instructor: "You always have interesting things to say in your homework. It's disappointing that you don't speak up more in class."

Restate: _____

Ask for suggestions: _____

Roommate: "I love the color you chose for the living room walls. It might be even better if the paint was a little more even."

Restate: _____

Ask for suggestions: _____

Boss: "I see how much effort you've put into this spreadsheet, but the small type makes it hard for me to read."

Restate: _____

Ask for suggestions: _____

Parent: "You forgot Michael's birthday last week, and his feelings were hurt. It's important to remember family occasions."

Restate: _____

Ask for suggestions: _____

continued...

B Now practice responding to destructive criticism by acknowledging facts or feelings. Imagine that you receive criticisms similar to those on the previous page, but that they are worded in a destructive way. Write a response to each destructive criticism that 1. acknowledges the facts and 2. asserts yourself by correcting the part of the criticism that is mistaken, unfair, or insulting.

Example

"You ruined your paper by using all these terms incorrectly."

Acknowledge: I see that I misused a few technical terms.

Assert yourself: However, I provided a lot of good information in this paper.

Instructor: "You never have anything to contribute in class."

Acknowledge: _____

Assert yourself: _____

Roommate: "You did a terrible job painting the living room walls."

Acknowledge: _____

Assert yourself: _____

Boss: "I practically need a microscope to read this spreadsheet. Please make it look like a professional did it."

Acknowledge: _____

Assert yourself: _____

Parent: "You forgot Michael's birthday again. I hope you're proud of yourself."

Acknowledge: _____

Assert yourself: _____

C Think back to the last time you received constructive criticism. How did you respond? Were you able to make use of the constructive criticism? Why or why not?

_____

_____

_____

_____

_____

D Now think back to the last time you received destructive criticism. Describe how it made you feel and how you responded.

_____

_____

_____

_____

E The next time you receive criticism, what can you say to yourself to keep your self-esteem from being hurt?

_____

_____

_____

_____

_____

_____

_____

_____

_____

Assertiveness and Self-Esteem

Handling criticism well requires assertiveness, the ability to stand up for your rights without threatening the self-esteem of the other person. People with low self-esteem often react to criticism passively or passive-aggressively. They hope they will avoid confrontation if they don't reveal their thoughts. They don't stand up for themselves, because they fear rejection and further criticism. It is true that others may dislike what you say or even dislike you. However, trying to achieve acceptance by withholding your real thoughts and feelings damages your self-esteem. It is better to risk rejection by showing your real self than to disrespect yourself by hiding your thoughts and feelings.

People with low self-esteem often let the fear of criticism and rejection stop them from asserting themselves in everyday situations. What happened the last time someone cut in front of you in line? Did you stand up for yourself and politely point out the end of the line, or did you stay silent to avoid a fuss? What about when you received a wrong order at a restaurant? Did you calmly call attention to the mix-up, or did you pretend everything was fine and eat it anyway?

Assertiveness can be difficult, because it involves showing your real self. It requires self-awareness, self-expectancy, and self-acceptance. Instead of silently tolerating words or actions that hurt you, you are standing up for your value as a human being. You are saying, "I have a right to exist and be treated with respect. My thoughts and feelings are just as important as everyone else's, and I deserve to have my voice heard." When you make assertiveness a habit, you increase others' esteem for you and your esteem for yourself.

success *secret*
You have the right to be treated with respect.

Self Check

1. Define self-acceptance. (p. 151)
2. What are the benefits of using positive self-talk? (p. 161)
3. Give an example of a constructive criticism and an example of a destructive criticism. (p. 167)

Chapter 4 Review and Activities

Key Terms

self-esteem (p. 128)

anxiety (p. 130)

unconditional positive regard (p. 138)

conditional positive regard (p. 138)

social support (p. 139)

loneliness (p. 140)

self-expectancy (p. 144)

accomplishment (p. 146)

coping (p. 149)

avoidance (p. 149)

self-acceptance (p. 151)

body image (p. 153)

social comparison (p. 157)

ideal self (p. 158)

possible selves (p. 158)

self-talk (p. 161)

inner critic (p. 161)

label (p. 162)

affirmation (p. 163)

criticism (p. 166)

probing (p. 169)

Summary by Learning Objectives

- **Define self-esteem and explain its importance.** Self-esteem is having confidence in and respect for yourself. When you esteem yourself, you are confident in your ability to cope with life's challenges, and you believe that you are worthy of success and happiness. This motivates you to work hard, succeed, try new things, take chances, and build positive relationships.

- **Describe how childhood experiences affect self-esteem.** The foundations of self-esteem are laid in the first three or four years of life. If our parents or other primary caregivers demonstrate love, nurturance, acceptance, encouragement, and support, we usually come to accept ourselves and develop positive self-esteem.

- **Define self-expectancy and explain two ways to boost it.** Self-expectancy is the belief that you are able to achieve what you want in life. One way to build this confidence is to take pride in your past successes. Another way is to set and accomplish a series of increasingly challenging goals.

- **Explain why self-acceptance is important for high self-esteem.** Self-acceptance means recognizing and accepting what is true about yourself. It allows you to stop criticizing yourself for falling short of your or other people's impossible standards. It allows you to discover and express who you really are inside. When you enjoy self-acceptance, you recognize that you are good enough just the way you are.

- **Explain how to change negative self-talk into positive self-talk.** To change negative self-talk into positive self-talk, stop your negative thoughts whenever they occur and replace them with affirmations.

- **Explain how to handle criticism well.** An effective way to handle constructive criticism is to restate the criticism and ask for suggestions. An effective way to handle destructive criticism is to acknowledge the truth of the criticism (if any) and assert yourself.

Review and Activities

Review Questions

1. Name five effects of high self-esteem and five effects of low self-esteem.

2. How do childhood experiences affect self-esteem?

3. Explain the statement: "You may or may not get what you deserve, but you will nearly always get what you expect."

4. What are some ways to change a negative self-image into a positive one?

5. Give an example of upward comparison and an example of downward comparison.

6. Explain the three steps in handling constructive criticism.

Critical Thinking

7. **Self-Acceptance and Avoidance**   For healthy self-esteem, it's important to know your weaknesses so that you can find creative ways to work around them. However, it's also important to cope with your problems rather than avoid them. Is this a contradiction? Why or why not?

8. **Criticism**   When someone is very critical of others, it is often said that the person has low self-esteem. Think of someone you know who often criticizes or makes fun of others. Do you think this person has low self-esteem? What do you think motivates him or her to criticize others? What relationship do you think exists between self-acceptance and acceptance of others?

Application

9. **Self-Esteem Journal**   Over the course of a week, keep a journal monitoring your level of self-esteem. Note the times you experience low self-esteem and high self-esteem. What situations make you feel good about yourself? Why? How can you create more of them? What situations damage your self-esteem? Why? How can you change this?

10. **Accomplishment and Self-Expectancy**   Interview two people. Ask them to describe the two accomplishments of which they are proudest; explain why they are proudest of these; and explain how confident they were beforehand in their ability to complete these accomplishments. Write up your findings, comparing and contrasting the interviewees' responses to the responses you gave in Activity 20. What did this experience teach you about accomplishment and self-expectancy?

Internet Activities

11. **Affirmations**   Your instructor may provide you with an article on "The Power of Self-Talk." Read the article. Write three "I am" affirmations using the guidelines in this article.

12. **Shyness and Self-Esteem**   Go to the following links:
    http://www.shyandfree.com
    http://www.shakeyourshyness.com
    http://www.shyness.com/encyclopedia.html
    These will provide you with information on shyness and its relationship to self-esteem. Ask yourself the following questions: Are there different types of shyness? How do you think shyness is related to self-esteem? Does shyness have positive aspects?

Real-Life Success Story

"Do I Have What It Takes?"

Look back at your response to the question in the Real-Life Success Story on page 126. Think about how you would answer the question now that you have completed the chapter.

Complete the Story   Write a paragraph continuing Paul's story, describing specific techniques he uses to overcome his negative self-talk and respond to his sister's destructive criticism.

"Will Things Go My Way?"

Hopes and Worries

Jessica Jimenez dreamed of a career in hotel management. On the morning of her interview for a clerk job at a luxury hotel, however, she woke up feeling nervous and unprepared. Jessica was bilingual, had great people skills, and had earned top grades in her hospitality program. Doing well in a job interview, however, was another story. Jessica reminded herself that she never did well when she was put on the spot. Why would today be any different?

A Self-Defeating Attitude

When Jessica arrived at the hotel for her interview, she noticed a coffee stain on her blouse and began to panic. "This interview is going to be a disaster," she thought. As she watched the hotel employees at work, she began to feel even more negative. "What's the point of this job? I'll never be able to keep up with the fast pace. The pay is lousy, and with my luck I'll never be promoted." By the time Jessica was called for the interview, she told herself she didn't even want the job anymore.

What Do You Think?　How was Jessica's negative attitude likely to stand in the way of her getting the job?

Positive Thinking

5 Chapter

> ❝ Whether you think you can or think you can't, either way you're right. ❞
>
> Henry Ford, automaker

introduction

In this chapter, you'll find out how to become a more positive thinker. In Section 5.1 you'll explore the habits associated with positive thinking and learn how your attitude can influence your mental and physical health. In Section 5.2 you'll learn why having positive expectations for yourself makes a huge difference in getting what you want out of life. You'll also investigate several types of negative thinking and learn techniques for transforming unpleasant thoughts and feelings into positive ones.

learning objectives

After you complete this chapter, you should be able to:

- Define positive thinking and cite its benefits.

- List six habits that can help you become a more positive thinker.

- Explain the link between positive thinking and good health.

- Describe how self-defeating attitudes create a vicious cycle.

- Define cognitive distortions and irrational beliefs and give an example of each.

- Summarize the ABCDE method for overcoming irrational beliefs.

Becoming a Positive Thinker

POSITIVE THINKING AND OPTIMISM

positive thinking
Focusing on what is good about yourself, other people, and the world around you.

optimism The tendency to expect the best possible outcome.

We've all heard of positive thinking, but what is it and why does it matter? **Positive thinking** means focusing on what is good about ourselves, other people, and the world around us. When we think positively about ourselves, we have the confidence to work toward our goals and overcome obstacles. When we think positively about others, we have the confidence to trust people and ask for what we need and want.

Positive thinking goes hand in hand with optimism. **Optimism** is the tendency to expect the best possible outcome. Optimists focus their energy on making their goals happen, rather than on bracing for the worst. Optimists don't fool themselves into thinking that the world is perfect and that everything always goes perfectly. Instead, optimists simply choose to focus on what's going right.

Why Positive Thinking Matters

Positive thinking helps you enjoy work, school, friends, family, and free time. Positive thinking gives you the drive to work hard to make good things happen. Positive thinking does not promise success, but there is no success without it. To attain success, you should actively expect success in all parts of your life.

success *secret*
Positive thinking gives you the drive to make good things happen for yourself.

Feeling positive or optimistic is a trait of virtually all successful people. The best leaders, for example, are able to inspire positive feelings in the people they lead. They possess energy and a vision of the future that inspires a positive outlook in those around them. Think of how Martin Luther King, Jr., mobilized millions with his "I have a dream" speech, which painted an inspiring picture of a better future. His optimistic vision made him a great leader.

One of the most desirable attitudes of a prospective employee, leader, or manager is an ability to see challenges as opportunities and setbacks as temporary inconveniences. This positive attitude also welcomes change as friendly, and is not upset by surprises, even negative surprises. How we approach challenges and problems is a crucial aspect of our decision-making process, whether in business or in our personal lives.

In the 1920s, when Ernest Hemingway was working hard to perfect his craft, he lost a suitcase containing all his manuscripts—many stories he'd laboriously polished to jewel-like perfection—which he'd been planning to publish as a book. The devastated Hemingway couldn't conceive of redoing his work. He could think only of the months he'd devoted to his arduous writing—and for nothing, he was now convinced. But when he lamented his loss to the poet Ezra Pound, Pound called it a stroke of good luck. Pound assured Hemingway that when he rewrote the stories, he would forget the weak parts; only the best material would reappear.

Instead of framing the event in disappointment, Pound cast it in the light of opportunity. Hemingway did rewrite the stories—and the rest, as they say, is history: He became one of the major figures in American literature.

Cartoonist Cathy Guisewite has her mother to thank for teaching her the importance of positive thinking. "When my mother first suggested I submit some scribbles to a syndicate, I told her I knew nothing about comic strips. Mom said, 'So what? You'll learn.' When I pointed out that I didn't know how to draw, she said, 'So what? You'll learn.'" Without that encouragement and confidence, Guisewite might never have turned those scribbles into the popular comic strip *Cathy* which was syndicated in more than 1400 newspapers and collected into more than 20 books, along with several national TV specials. The comic strip endured for 34 years as a national favorite.

Like Guisewite, when we worry that we don't know how or might fail, we can tell ourselves, "So what? Other people have tried it before and made bigger fools of themselves. Other people have started out with nothing and built their success brick by brick. Other people have overcome bigger hurdles and still survived. Other people have failed, picked themselves up, and done it again. I can do the same thing."

Thinking and Attitude

Positive thinking is really an attitude toward life. An **attitude** is a belief or opinion that predisposes us to act in a certain way. Attitudes have a powerful effect on the way we see the world. Although you may not realize it, you have attitudes about practically everything. You have attitudes

attitude A belief or opinion that predisposes you to act in a certain way.

Applying **Psychology**

Aging with an Attitude

One hundred years ago, most North Americans died by age 48. Today most of us can expect to live to about 78. Instead of welcoming the prospect of a longer life, however, more and more people are worrying about growing old. Aging is a natural process, so why do we fear it? In our youth-obsessed culture, growing older is associated with social isolation and physical and mental decline rather than with growth, wisdom, and freedom. Antique furniture and classic cars may be all the rage, but people in their 60s, 70s, and beyond are often seen as dependent, disabled, and unattractive. In an attempt to stay young, consumers spend billions of dollars every year on anti-aging weapons such as plastic surgery and pricey beauty creams. The real key to successful aging, however, is a positive attitude. Researchers have uncovered evidence that people who have a positive view of aging age better and live longer than those who fear it. According to their findings, a healthy attitude toward aging has a more positive effect on health than exercising, lowering cholesterol, or even quitting smoking. Positive thinking reduces stress on the heart and arteries, and motivates people to stay mentally and physically fit. In one study, people who had a positive attitude toward aging lived seven and a half years longer on average than those with a negative attitude toward aging.

Critical Thinking   *Make a list of ten things you fear about getting older, and why.*

toward particular individuals (including yourself) and toward people who are a certain age or do a certain job. You have attitudes toward particular objects, such as smartphones, music, cars, and clothing, as well as toward ideas about the environment, education, and careers.

Positive and Negative Attitudes   Attitudes can be positive, negative, or both, combining both positive and negative elements. For example, depending on your experience, you might believe that doctors are intelligent and noble, or that they are impersonal and condescending, or that they show all of these features. You might believe that welfare is a good program because it helps needy people, or that it is unfair because it promotes dependency and uses taxpayers' money, or that it has both plusses and minuses.

There's nothing wrong with having negative attitudes about some things. People who have mostly negative attitudes, however, have trouble feeling good or taking positive actions. People with positive attitudes embrace life. They make a conscious effort to think positive thoughts and take positive actions.

We've seen that the way we think influences the way we feel and act. Positive thoughts are the foundation of positive feelings and positive actions. By thinking positive thoughts, we inspire ourselves to have positive feelings and take positive actions, as shown in Figure 5.1.

Negative Thinking and Pessimism   Now let's contrast positive thinking with negative thinking. **Negative thinking** means focusing

negative thinking
Focusing on the flaws and problems in yourself, other people, and the world around you.

| FIGURE 5.1 | The Power of Positive Thoughts |

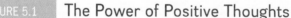
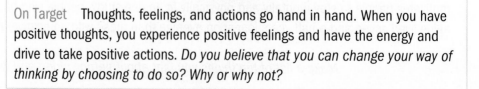

On Target   Thoughts, feelings, and actions go hand in hand. When you have positive thoughts, you experience positive feelings and have the energy and drive to take positive actions. *Do you believe that you can change your way of thinking by choosing to do so? Why or why not?*

on the flaws and problems in ourselves, other people, and the world around us. Negative thinking dampens our mood and blocks us from taking risks, making changes, and expressing our real selves. Negative thinking can also make us unpleasant to be around. When we think negatively, we often spend more time complaining and blaming others than we do taking action to solve our problems.

Negative thinking goes hand in hand with pessimism. **Pessimism** is the tendency to expect the worst possible outcome. Pessimists find signs of failure and disaster everywhere they go. Pessimists are often motivated by intense fear of failure, loss, or rejection. They hope to protect themselves from disappointment by constantly preparing themselves for the worst. Novelist Thomas Hardy once wrote, "pessimism is the only view of life in which you can never be disappointed." Pessimists expect nothing from themselves and nothing from others, and that's what they usually get.

pessimism The tendency to expect the worst possible outcome.

Failure Avoidance

In organizations, institutions, and environments in which criticism, pessimism, cynicism, and motivation by fear prevail, a condition develops that we see all too often in business and the professions. Fear of failure leads to avoiding failure at all costs. The trouble with failure avoidance is that it's simultaneously avoidance of success, which depends on taking risks. Innovation and creativity are impossible when employees are afraid because they're penalized for failure.

Early experience usually teaches that failure is to be avoided at all costs. This begins in childhood, when we encounter the first "No!" It grows like a weed when we are criticized by our parents and other family members, by our teachers, and by our peers. It leads to associating ourselves with our mistakes, to a self-image of clumsiness and awkwardness. Our world of put-downs does little to relieve this—a world in which the media magnifies problems and celebrity status, but where entrepreneurial success is often viewed as the product of manipulative selfishness. Many people seek security from that noise by going along quietly with the system, not rocking the boat. Despite biographies, documentaries, and other programs about rags-to-riches success and courageous public service, most people, unable to imagine it for themselves, develop a habit of looking back at past problems—which is failure reinforcement—and of imagining similar performances in the future, which is failure forecasting. They either set their sights too high, reinforcing their fears and ensuring failure, or low enough to avoid failure with a sure thing. Their inner dialogue usually falls within the two extremes. "Stand by. Things are going too well, something will spoil it." Or, "I knew this was too good to be true. With my luck, it was bound to go sour."

Fear of failure can become a built-in motivation. Leaders like to succeed and feel good about themselves; fearful people, focused on failure avoidance so as not to feel worse about themselves, refuse to try. External factors can also boost fear of failure. If, for example, half a division must be laid off, factory or office workers who have long performed well may be seized by the diminishing, damaging fear.

A large division of a well-known American company manufacturing integrated circuit boards in competition with the Japanese called an employee productivity meeting. The huge facility's general manager mounted the stage and gave his two thousand workers what he thought was a parting motivational message. "What we must have from all of you is a 17 percent increase in quality production in six months, or we're faced with closing down the plant. Have a good weekend."

His words had the predictable effect. The leaders and optimists increased their performance by about 20 percent. But many pessimists found more secure jobs and quit within weeks—and the plant did shut down after about six months. This was more confirmation that genuine leaders focus on the benefits of success, while those chiefly motivated by fear concentrate on failure's painful consequences. Some bosses and managers argue that employees motivated by fear work as hard or even harder than those with positive motivations. They are deluding themselves. Fear motivation, though still practiced in some companies and cultures, is as obsolete as the concept of declaring "Firings will continue, until morale improves." Anxiety about failure doesn't merely diminish performance. It also stifles the motivation to succeed in the first place.

Learned Helplessness

Learned helplessness is a belief that we're at the mercy of external forces and no longer in control of what is happening to us. Behaviorists emphasize that this feeling is indeed learned. Martin Seligman, a psychologist at the University of Pennsylvania and author of the best-selling *Learned Optimism,* has made a very detailed study of learned helplessness—and confirms it's a trait we acquire, not inherit at birth. Although we are born with specific personality traits, we learn to be optimists or pessimists by the way we handle obstacles and setbacks. There's a saying: "It's not what happens to you that counts. It's how you take it and what you make of it." This distinction between negative and positive attitudes is referred to by psychologists as "explanatory style." More specifically, a person's explanatory style is the way he or she understands and explains the bad things that happen in life.

Dr. Seligman found specific evidence for the practical effects of explanatory style in a study of collegiate swimmers. At the outset of the study, the athletes were given a psychological test to determine their levels of optimism and pessimism. Following the test, they were timed in some practice laps, but when the times were told to the swimmers, they were deliberately reported as being a second or two slower than they actually were. Since one second can mean the difference between winning or coming in last in a competition, all the athletes took the disappointing news very seriously. But they also responded in very different ways. When the pessimists were timed again, they were consistently slower than their usual performances. It was as if they somehow felt they had to confirm the negative results they'd received earlier. The optimistic athletes, however, either maintained the level of their times or in some cases got even faster. When general optimism about life is internalized, it leads to very tangible, positive results.

Take a moment to look at your thinking. Are you a positive or negative thinker? **Activity 24** on pages 187–188 is designed to help you assess your thinking style and begin making positive improvements. As always, strive to be honest as you complete the exercise. Go with your first instinct; don't be false to yourself in an attempt to find the "right" answer. Being a negative thinker doesn't make you a bad person. Negative thinking is a habit that drains your energy and makes you feel bad about yourself, but like any habit it can be changed.

ADOPTING POSITIVE HABITS

No matter how positive or negative your thoughts are right now, you can become a more positive thinker. Sound too good to be true? It's not. Over decades of study, psychologists have discovered that people can significantly improve their lives by consciously *choosing* to think positively. Everyone can cultivate habits of thought and action that help them think positively. Habits are like submarines. They run silent and deep. Most of what we do on a daily basis is habitual. We seldom even realize we are engaging in subconscious reflexes. Habits are more easily replaced than broken. That is why it is so important to focus on practicing new positive thoughts and actions on a daily basis. It takes time and effort to override unhealthy habit patterns that have been ingrained since childhood. Six important positive habits of thought and action are described below.

Look for the Good

It's easy to take the good things for granted and dwell on the bad things. It's important to make an active effort to look for the good in events, situations, and people, including yourself. If things look 100 percent terrible, you are sure to have overlooked something. Sometimes you may have to look hard, but your search is always rewarded. Are you taking a class you find boring? Look for one positive thing about it. Soon you will find another and another.

Cultivate the habit of gratitude for everything you have and are working toward. Give yourself time each evening to look for the good in the day's events. Did you accomplish a goal at work? Did someone give you a kind word? Did you enjoy playing with your cat?

Work alone, with a friend, or with a family member to provide mutual encouragement and suggestions. Make sure to use positive language and to focus on what went right, rather than on what didn't go wrong. Instead of saying, "I didn't get in a car accident," for example, say, "I stayed healthy and safe." Use the space in **Personal Journal 5.1** on page 186 to write down three things that you are grateful for in your life, three good things

success *secret*
Look for things to be grateful for.

Personal Journal 5.1

Focusing on the Good

Develop the habit of looking for the good by taking stock of each day's positive events. What do you feel good about today?

Today I'm grateful for:

1. _____
2. _____
3. _____

Three good things that happened to me today:

1. _____
2. _____
3. _____

Three good things that I have to look forward to in the future:

1. _____
2. _____
3. _____

that happened to you over the course of the day, and three good things that you have to look forward to in the future.

Choose Your Words

Analyze your language. How often do you use negative words such as *can't, won't, impossible,* or *horrible?* How often do you exaggerate the terrible consequences of events? Our words influence our thoughts and our moods. Make a note of negative expressions you may overuse and train yourself to replace the negative words with positive ones. Also make a habit of speaking positively to other people. Give thanks, appreciation, and praise to the people who are kind to you. Giving a compliment or a kind word generates goodwill and makes you feel good about yourself, too.

success *secret*

Use positive words and choose positive friends.

ACTIVITY 24: Are You a Positive Thinker?

A Read each statement below. For each one, decide whether you Agree Totally, Agree Slightly, Disagree Slightly, or Disagree Totally.

	Agree Totally	Agree Slightly	Disagree Slightly	Disagree Totally
1. People who have a positive attitude are kidding themselves.				
2. You can try to change your way of thinking, but it won't work.				
3. I often worry about the same problems again and again.				
4. Many of my problems are actually someone else's fault.				
5. Criticizing other people helps to keep them on their toes.				
6. Let's face it: Every opportunity has at least one hidden difficulty.				
7. I often complain about people and situations that are getting me down.				
8. Before I help other people, I make sure they're not using me.				
9. My friends are mostly positive thinkers.				
10. I compliment others often and express my appreciation for them.				
11. Most of my comments to other people are positive.				
12. I rarely criticize myself.				
13. When I talk to myself, I use encouraging, helpful words.				
14. Good things usually happen to me.				
15. I always look for the good in people and situations.				
16. I have a genuine interest in other people.				

B **Scoring:** For statements 1 through 8, give yourself 0 points for Agree Totally, 1 point for Agree Slightly, 2 points for Disagree Slightly, and 3 points for Disagree Totally.

Total for this section: _____

For statements 9 through 16, give yourself 3 points for Agree Totally, 2 points for Agree Slightly, 1 point for Disagree Slightly, and 0 points for Disagree Totally.

Total for this section: _____

Add the two scores: _____

41–48 You think positively almost all the time; you're on the right track.

31–40 You think positively most of the time, but you will benefit from making a more consistent effort to think positively.

17–30 You have a mix of positive and negative attitudes. You need to pay attention to your negative thoughts and work hard to replace them with positive ones.

0–16 You think negatively almost all of the time. You need to adopt new habits of thinking.

continued...

C Are you a positive thinker or a negative thinker? Explain.

_____

_____

_____

_____

_____

_____

_____

D All of us tend to think more positively about some things than about others. Which events, situations, people, or aspects of yourself do you think positively about? Which do you think negatively about? Why?

_____

_____

_____

_____

_____

_____

_____

Surround Yourself with Positive People

The enthusiasm of optimistic people is contagious; you can "catch" a healthy attitude by being around someone who is upbeat. The people with whom we associate have a big impact on our attitude. At work and school, seek the company of positive-minded people who enjoy sharing ideas, helping others, and taking constructive action. Choose not to spend your time with people who make a habit of complaining, gossiping, whining, criticizing, or blaming others.

Accept, Don't Judge

Be on the lookout for one of the most common negative habits: judgmentalism. **Judgmentalism** is the habit of condemning people or things because they are not the way you think they should be. Judgments are easy to make, but they are hurtful. Have you ever shared your feelings with someone only to be told, "you're overreacting" or "you brought this on yourself"? Have you ever received a harsh and critical comment for no apparent reason? If so, you know how painful judgmentalism can be.

When you find yourself about to make a judgmental comment, stop and examine what is going on inside you. Are you jumping to negative conclusions without all the facts? Are you spending more time finding fault than looking for the good? Are you judging others to make yourself feel (falsely) superior? People who find fault with others usually find fault with themselves, too. It's painful to be judged. Try not to do it to others or yourself. Instead, strive to accept the world and other people as they are without comparing them to an unfair ideal.

judgmentalism The habit of condemning people or things because they are not the way you think they should be.

Limit Complaints

There is nothing wrong with occasional complaining. A **complaint** is simply the sharing of distress, discomfort, or worry with another person. Sharing feelings and frustrations can help you deepen friendships and cope with the stresses of everyday life. However, complaining can easily become a habit. Some people use the complaining habit to get sympathy and attention or to reinforce a "poor me" image.

There is a fine line between complaining and blaming. Are you taking responsibility for your situation, or are you blaming someone else for your feelings? When you speak poorly of others, you're likely to feel poorly about yourself, too.

Remember, too, that every minute you spend complaining is a minute that you aren't working on a solution. Consider keeping a "complaint log" in which you note every time you complain and for how long. Set a time limit for your complaints—perhaps three or four minutes. When the time is up, resolve to stop complaining and start acting.

We saw in Chapter 4 that coping actively with your problems is a big boost to your self-esteem. In a similar way, taking action on problems can boost your positive outlook on life. Instead of grumbling that no one is

complaint The sharing of distress, discomfort, or worry with another person.

success *secret*
Taking constructive action feels better than complaining.

doing anything, for example, ask yourself, "What can I do?" Even the act of writing down possible solutions to difficult problems can relieve some of the distress that caused the complaints in the first place.

Don't Worry

Worry is a major barrier to positive thinking. **Worry** is distress and anxiety caused by contemplating worst-case scenarios. How can you focus on the positive when you are always bracing for the worst?

It's natural to have worries about serious problems such as crime, ill health, or paying bills. Common subjects of worry include:

- money
- health
- school
- career and job security
- relationships and children
- crime, terrorism, and war

No matter what you have to worry about, however, frequent worry harms your health by keeping you focused on the negative side of life. Consider these myths and realities about worry:

professional **development**)))

Positive Thinking in Action at Work

Being a positive thinker not only benefits your own productivity at work, it can also impact your work environment. The more positive you are, the more positive those around you will feel and then behave. A positive attitude is contagious! Whether you're an employee, team member, or manager, you always have the ability to improve your workplace, and the responsibility starts with you!

Here are some strategies for maintaining a positive attitude at work, and creating a positive environment for others:

- Find enjoyment in your work, no matter how tedious, boring, or stressful it may be.
- See the value you bring to your job, and understand how your role contributes to the overall mission and vision of the company.
- View work problems as opportunities to challenge yourself, focusing on improvement ideas, and solutions.
- Foster positive peer camaraderie by being a good team player, sharing ideas with others, and offering praise and encouragement whenever possible.
- Learn as much as you can about your job, company, and field to stay motivated.
- See the value you bring to your job, and understand how your role contributes to the overall mission and vision of the company.

What's Your Opinion?

Brainstorm a list of actions you could take to help create a more positive environment at your workplace or school. To explore the topic of positive thinking in the work environment further, visit http://career.careesma .in/8-tips-to-make-a-positive-work-environment or ask your instructor for additional links.

Myth: "Worrying helps me prepare for action."

Reality: Worrying drains your energy.

Myth: "Worrying helps me deal with my problems."

Reality: Worrying is a substitute for dealing with your problems.

Myth: "The more I worry about something, the less likely it is to happen."

Reality: This is known as *magical thinking*. Thoughts don't influence what happens—actions do.

Myth: "Worrying means I care."

Reality: Caring and worrying are not the same.

Often, people worry because they feel they need to do *something* about a problem but aren't sure what. You can always do something about a problem. Get the facts. Ask for advice or help. Brainstorm ideas with a friend. When faced with worry, try these strategies:

- **Focus on solutions, not worst-case scenarios.** This helps you feel that you can deal with whatever happens.
- **Cope, don't avoid. Take action!** Facing the situation head-on not only helps make things right, but also boosts your self-esteem.
- **Share your worries.** Get another perspective. Research shows that worry gets worse when you do it alone.
- **If you really can't do anything about the situation, try to let the worry go.** Make a conscious decision not to worry. This is difficult at first but gets easier with practice.
- **Drown out the worry with positive affirmations.** Tell yourself, "I am capable of handling whatever comes my way" or "I accept that some things are out of my control."
- **Channel your nervous energy into physical activity.** Try exercise, gardening, dance, yoga, housecleaning, or sports.

Some experts recommend writing each of your worries down on a small slip of paper and stashing them in a worry jar or box. This process helps you separate yourself from your worries. (Make your own worry slips at the end of **Activity 25** on pages 192–193.) Take the slips out of the jar once a week and read them, and you will probably find that your worries don't seem as bad as they did at first. Instead of putting your worry slips in a jar or box, you can shred them and recycle them to indicate that you are letting go of them.

Get Realistic   Above all, the key to banishing worry is to stop thinking of worst-case scenarios and learn to think in terms of realistic outcomes. Imagine that you want to ask someone out on a date, but you worry that the person will say no. Your worries deepen even further when you imagine the worst possible outcome: The person rejects and humiliates you in front of everyone. Although this worst-case scenario is unlikely to occur, the possibility that it might happen can't stop you from worrying about it. Unfortunately, worrying about things that *might* happen prevents you from taking important risks, making you miserable as the opportunities slip away.

ACTIVITY 25: Banishing Worry

A Describe the biggest worry you have right now.

_____

_____

_____

_____

B Describe the worst-case scenario. What would happen if all of your worst fears came true in this situation?

_____

_____

_____

_____

C How likely is it that the worst-case scenario will come true?

_____

_____

_____

_____

D What is the most likely *realistic* outcome?

_____

_____

_____

E Write down six things you are worried about right now. When you're done, photocopy or cut out these worry slips and place them in your own personal worry jar or box.

<table>
<tr><td>WORRY #1</td></tr>
</table>

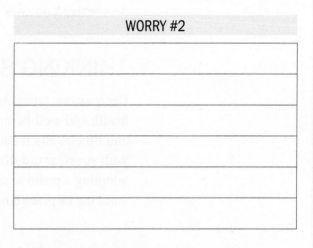

<table>
<tr><td>WORRY #2</td></tr>
</table>

<table>
<tr><td>WORRY #3</td></tr>
</table>

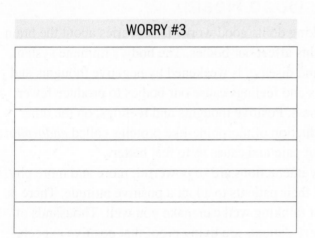

<table>
<tr><td>WORRY #4</td></tr>
</table>

<table>
<tr><td>WORRY #5</td></tr>
</table>

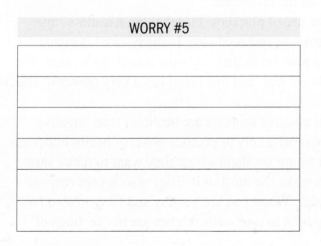

<table>
<tr><td>WORRY #6</td></tr>
</table>

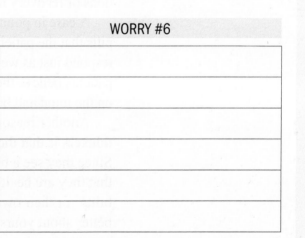

success *secret*

Worrying prevents you from taking risks.

✳

Instead of being overwhelmed by worries, learn to distinguish between worst-case scenarios and realistic, probable outcomes. Let's say that you have asked someone out on a date and are now planning your outing together. Immediately you find yourself bracing for the worst possible outcome—your date can't stand you, everything goes wrong, and you both have a terrible time. Stop yourself and ask how realistic this scenario is. Sure, it *might* happen, but how probable is it? Not very. Instead, think about a realistic outcome. If you pick a fun activity, you will probably have a good time and enjoy getting to know one another, even if you decide that you aren't meant to be a couple.

THINKING STYLE AND HEALTH

Because our thoughts are so powerful, they have a big influence on our health and well-being. Negative thinking makes us vulnerable to stress and illness, and it shortens our life span. Positive thinking helps us cope with stress, avoid illness, and live longer. Studies have even shown that adopting a positive attitude can add more years to your life than quitting smoking or practicing regular physical exercise.

Good Attitude, Good Health

How does positive thinking do its good work? Discoveries about the brain may explain how thoughts affect our bodies. The body's immune system, which fights infection and disease, is weakened by negative thoughts and feelings. These thoughts and feelings cause our bodies to produce fewer *antibodies* that fight illness. Positive thoughts and feelings, on the other hand, stimulate the production of morphine-like proteins called *endorphins* that reduce the feeling of pain and cause us to feel better.

Because mind–body interactions are so powerful, more and more physicians are encouraging their patients to adopt a positive attitude. There is increasing evidence that thinking well can make you well. Thousands of former open-heart surgery patients are living proof that positive expectations of recovery make all the difference.

A case in point is the use of placebos. Placebos are harmless sugar pills that the patient is told are real medicine. In many cases, patients respond just as well to a placebo as they do to the actual medication. The patients believe the pills are real, and that belief has a very powerful effect on the mind and body.

Another reason that positive thinkers are healthier than negative thinkers is that they are more likely to practice positive health behaviors. Since they see a bright future for themselves, they want to make sure that they are healthy to make the most of it. They also accept responsibility for their own health. When you are healthy and fit, you also feel better about yourself, which in turn leads to even greater feelings of optimism.

success *secret*

Thinking well can make you well.

✳

Negative Thinking and Mental Health

Positive thinking can make us mentally and physically healthy, while negative thinking can delay healing and cause us to neglect our health. But negative thinking also does more—it damages our psychological health by providing an invitation to depression. **Depression** is an illness characterized by profound feelings of sadness, hopelessness, and helplessness. Depression affects 20 million people each year in the United States and Canada.

Although the causes of depression are complex and not fully understood, psychologists believe that negative thinking makes people more vulnerable to the disease. In studies involving college students before and after exams, for example, researchers found that students who had a pessimistic attitude and received a failing grade ended up feeling depressed. In a study of prison inmates, people who had the most negative attitudes became the most depressed about their imprisonment. Of course, no one wants to fail an exam or go to prison. The difference is that optimistic people are able to bounce back from negative experiences. They have normal feelings of disappointment, sadness, or frustration, but they find ways to make the best of the situation and make plans to improve their lives. When pessimistic people suffer setbacks, on the other hand, they feel like failures, lose hope for the future, and simply give up. To screen yourself for symptoms of depression, complete **Personal Journal 5.2.**

depression An illness characterized by profound feelings of sadness, hopelessness, and helplessness.

Getting Healthy

An important part of positive thinking, as well as self-esteem, is caring enough about yourself to make healthy choices. Our bodies are machines whose performance depends on good health. We must each treat our body as our one and only transportation vehicle for life. We must care for it with the fuel of good nutrition, activity, and health care. We can't trade in our bodies for new models.

Your attitude toward your health makes a big difference: The more responsibility you take for your well-being, the more motivated you will be to treat yourself right. Don't try to nag yourself into changing; you'll resent the inner critic and rebel. Instead, see a healthy lifestyle as something positive you can do for yourself. **Activity 26** will help you examine your health attitude.

success *secret*
Following a healthy lifestyle is one of the most positive things you can do for yourself.

Eat Right A healthy diet is essential to good health. Following a healthy diet means not only eating nutritious foods, but also limiting foods that can have negative effects, particularly foods high in fat, sugar, and salt. The most healthful foods are whole grains, fruits, vegetables, nonfat dairy products, and lean protein sources, such as white meat, chicken, fish, and tofu. Avoid caffeine, alcohol, and other drugs, which sap your energy and can become addictive. Consider these tips as well:

success *secret*
Eat for health and energy.

- Don't eat for emotional reasons. Eat when you are hungry, eat slowly, and stop when you are beginning to feel full.

Personal Journal 5.2

Depression Self-Check

Negative thinking is not only a cause of depression but also one of its symptoms. Do you think negatively? Are you worried that this might be a symptom of depression? Put a check mark next to each statement that is true for you most or all of the time.

- ☐ I feel low in energy, or slowed down.
- ☐ I blame myself for things.
- ☐ I have poor appetite, or I overeat.
- ☐ I sleep too little or too much.
- ☐ I feel hopeless about the future.
- ☐ I feel down, or blue.
- ☐ I don't have much interest in anything.
- ☐ I feel like a pretty worthless person.
- ☐ I have thoughts of suicide.
- ☐ I have difficulty concentrating, remembering things, or making decisions.

If you have experienced five or more of these symptoms for two weeks or more, you may be suffering from depression; you should contact your doctor or mental health professional immediately.

- Take time out for meals—don't eat while doing something else.
- Shop with a list—you'll buy more nutritious foods.
- Try a variety of foods to make it easier to eat healthfully.
- Learn to read and understand nutrition labels.

Above all, cultivate a positive attitude toward food. Enjoy eating and make food choices for health and energy.

Get Moving   Exercise is just as important as good eating to a healthy lifestyle. Even in moderate amounts, exercise gives you more energy and boosts your mood. Regular exercise also lowers the risk of major diseases such as heart disease and diabetes.

Make sure to get both types of exercise—aerobic and anaerobic exercise. *Aerobic exercise* is sustained, rhythmic physical activity that strengthens the heart and lungs, lowers cholesterol and blood pressure, and relieves stress. It includes activities such as basketball, brisk walking, and swimming. *Anaerobic exercise* is higher intensity exercise that strengthens

BUILDING AND TRACKING YOUR OPTIMUM HEALTH PLAN

Since there are many internet Web sites providing us with the latest information and recommendations on how to adopt a healthy lifestyle, there also continues to be an explosion of apps designed to ensure we get results! Covering the areas of fitness and strength, tracking and analytics, food and nutrition, weight management, and even the mind and brain, these apps can offer us the support we need to reach our wellness goals . . . and most of them are free!

MyFitnessPal, a popular calorie tracker, boasts of a substantial food database with more than three million foods, allowing you to keep tabs on your daily nutritional eating habits. Fitocracy provides its users with a powerful social community of fitness enthusiasts, including fitness coaches and nutrition experts. You can enter strength training and cardio and nutrition challenges to gain points and track your progress toward your ultimate goal of optimal health. Argus is an app that tracks "everything," and produces detailed charts with numerous bio-feedback data points to achieve your health goals and boost your overall wellbeing. You are able to uncover important personal health habit trends that you didn't realize existed. The app, Carrot, even serves as your personal "motivational" coach, spouting out negative quips when you don't reach your goals, and sharing new workout tips for every pound you drop.

In today's world, there are numerous support tools at your fingertips. Of course, it's still up to you to eat the right foods and stay physically active. Combined with a positive mental attitude, your excuses for not living a healthy lifestyle should fall by the wayside.

To view a more detailed description of some of the top Health and Fitness apps, go to http://greatist.com/fitness/best-health-fitness-apps. Conduct your own internet searches on a regular basis to ensure you are obtaining the most current information.

---

muscles and involves short bursts of intense exertion. Anaerobic exercise includes push-ups, stomach crunches, pull-ups, and weight training. Aim for a healthy attitude toward exercise. Try these strategies:

- Try to be physically active for at least 20 minutes each day.
- Vary your activities so you don't get bored.
- Don't overdo it. Take time to warm up, cool down, and stretch.
- Set SMART exercise goals for yourself. If you get off track, just start again.
- Motivate yourself by learning about health and fitness.
- Exercise for strength and energy, not to look a certain way.

Choose to look at exercise as fun time, not as a chore. Do what you like to do—if you hate going to the gym, for example, try dancing, yoga, hiking, or gardening. Be creative—even housework can get your heart pumping. The better you feel physically, the better you'll feel emotionally, too.

> **success** *secret*
> Look at exercise as a fun time for you, not as a chore.

✔ Self Check

1. Define positive thinking and negative thinking. (pp. 180–182)
2. Why is it a good idea to avoid being judgmental? (p. 189)
3. Describe the two main types of exercise. (p. 196)

ACTIVITY 26: What's Your Health Attitude?

A Read each statement below. For each one, decide whether you Agree Totally, Agree Slightly, Disagree Slightly, or Disagree Totally.

	Agree Totally	Agree Slightly	Disagree Slightly	Disagree Totally
Section 1				
1. Good health and good life habits (i.e., regular physical activity, healthy diet, stress management) are interrelated.				
2. Committing the effort to change my habits is how I would get better from an illness or disease.				
3. If I get sick, it's usually because I have not maintained a healthy diet.				
4. Recovering from an illness or disease is due to my efforts, not my physicians'.				
5. Taking personal responsibility for my health is essential to avoiding illness.				
Section 2				
6. Having a competent physician is the key to improving my health and recovering from illness.				
7. I believe that what my physician says about my health is always correct.				
8. I rely on my physician to take care of me so I do not get sick.				
9. The right medication is essential to improving and maintaining my health.				
10. There are toxins in the air that we can't do anything about.				
Section 3				
11. What happens to me in life is due to fate and luck.				
12. I consider myself lucky if I avoid getting sick.				
13. If I get sick, it was meant to happen.				
14. If I get the flu, I must have picked it up from someone else during the day.				
15. Dying from an illness is fate, because no one really has control over getting sick.				

Source: Modified from Phillip C. McGraw, *The Self Matters Companion* (New York: The Free Press, 2002).

B **Scoring:** Score each section separately. For each section, give yourself 8 points for every statement you checked Agree Totally, 4 points for every statement you checked Agree Slightly, 2 points for every statement you checked Disagree Slightly, and 1 point for every statement you checked Disagree Totally.

Total for Section 1: _____

Total for Section 2: _____

Total for Section 3: _____

Section 1 measures how much you think that your health depends on your own behavior. The higher your score, the more responsibility you take for your own health. If you scored 33 or above, you understand and act on the fact that most major health issues can be influenced by what you do or don't do. You have retained power over your health choices.

Section 2 measures how much you think your health depends on external sources, such as medicine and the actions of doctors. The higher your score, the less active you are about managing your health. If you scored 22 or above on this section, you are highly dependent on powers outside yourself, whether they are people or things. You are probably too passive about your health management.

Section 3 measures how much you think your health is a matter of chance. The higher your score, the less in control you feel of your own health. If you scored 26 or above on this section, you consider yourself at the mercy of random factors, which probably makes you very passive about the management of your health.

C Do you have an active, positive attitude or a passive, negative attitude toward taking care of your health? Explain and give examples.

_____

_____

_____

_____

_____

_____

_____

D Why is it more positive to believe that you have the power to get and stay healthy than to believe that doctors and medicines have the power to make you healthy?

_____

_____

continued...

E Think back to the last time you were sick. Did you "make an effort to get well"? Explain.

_____

_____

_____

_____

F List five things you can do to have a healthier lifestyle and improve your physical health.

Example

I can make time for breakfast at home instead of grabbing something from the vending machine.

1. _____

   _____

2. _____

   _____

3. _____

   _____

4. _____

   _____

5. _____

   _____

OVERCOMING SELF-DEFEATING ATTITUDES

As we move through life, all of us experience ups and downs. It's not hard to think positively during the ups—but what about the downs? It can be tough to think positively when we are facing a tough challenge or a bitter disappointment. However, these are the times when we need the power of positive thinking the most.

Negative thinkers usually have negative attitudes toward themselves. A negative attitude about ourselves that dooms us to failure is known as a **self-defeating attitude.** People with a negative self-image develop a self-defeating attitude in which they see themselves failing before they even try. They reinforce this self-defeating attitude through negative self-talk: "I'll probably flunk this test" or "I know I won't be invited to go out with everyone after work."

self-defeating attitude A negative attitude about yourself that dooms you to failure.

The Power of Attitude

Self-defeating attitudes make it hard to succeed. The student who sees herself as a "D" student will often receive that grade. Why should she put in any effort to improve? She thinks she'll never get a better grade. Self-defeating attitudes can make it hard to succeed socially, too. The new employee who has an image of himself as unpopular may find it hard to make friends. Why should he try? He doesn't think there is anything he can do to change his circumstances. Unfortunately, this type of negative thinking can invite rejection. We have all noticed people at a social gathering who look uncomfortable, self-conscious, or maybe a little hostile. Why would anyone want to approach such people? Even though they may want to attract people, they really are driving everyone away. Negative thinkers need to encourage themselves to put on friendly smiles and introduce themselves to others.

Like all types of negative thinking, self-defeating attitudes seem logical enough on the surface. Consider the following example. A teacher once conducted an experiment on the students in her class, with their parents' consent. The teacher told the class that scientists had found that people with blue eyes have greater natural learning abilities than people with brown eyes. She then divided the class into two groups, those with blue eyes and those with brown eyes. She had them wear signs that said "blue eyes" or "brown eyes." After a week, the grades of the brown-eyed students fell significantly, while the grades of the blue-eyed students improved. The teacher then made a startling announcement to the class. She had made a mistake: Brown-eyed students are actually smarter than blue-eyed students. Up went the grades of the brown-eyed students, and down went the grades of the blue-eyed students. The students'

success *secret*
Self-defeating attitudes trick you into believing you can't succeed.

performance depended less on their abilities than on their attitudes toward themselves. Self-defeating attitudes seem logical on the surface, but they are based on negative, distorted perceptions of ourselves and the world.

A Vicious Cycle

How do self-defeating attitudes do their damage? Let's say you are convinced that you are no good at sports. This belief leads you to avoid athletic activities for fear of looking incompetent. The less you practice sports, however, the fewer opportunities you have to improve your athletic skills. When you do participate in sports, you are so worried about your performance that you can't concentrate on the game, fumbling and stumbling as you miss key plays. Finally, you give up, convinced more than ever that you can't play sports. Self-defeating attitudes like this one create a **vicious cycle,** a chain of events in which one negative event causes another negative event. The self-defeating attitude leads to self-defeating behavior. The self-defeating behavior leads to a negative outcome. The negative outcome strengthens the self-defeating attitude. This cycle is shown in Figure 5.2.

vicious cycle A chain of events in which one negative event causes another negative event.

As an example, let's say you are assigned to coordinate a big project at work. You immediately adopt a self-defeating attitude, telling yourself, "No one will help me on this project." This self-defeating attitude leads to self-defeating behavior: You don't ask anyone for help, and you even turn down offers of help. What is the outcome? No one helps. This negative outcome reinforces your self-defeating attitude: "See, I knew I couldn't count on anyone." As another example, let's say you want to ask a friend

FIGURE 5.2   Self-Defeating Attitudes: A Vicious Cycle

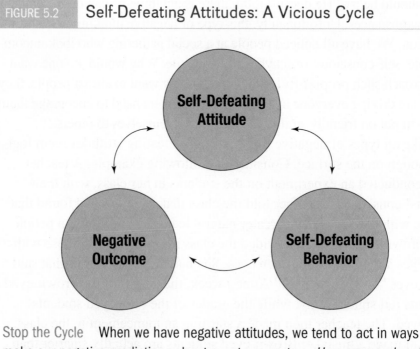

Stop the Cycle   When we have negative attitudes, we tend to act in ways that make our negative predictions about events come true. *How can you break this vicious cycle?*

out on a date. Your self-defeating attitude, however, causes you to tell yourself, "Someone like that would never go out with me." Self-defeating behavior follows: You never ask your friend to go out with you. The predictable outcome? Your friend never goes out with you.

Changing Your Attitude

We can overcome self-defeating attitudes in the same way that we can overcome the inner critic that destroys our self-esteem—through self-awareness and positive self-talk. The first step is to realize what our self-defeating attitudes are doing to us. The second step is to replace our negative attitudes with positive self-statements.

Consider the following example: You have agreed to go to a big end-of-semester party. Instead of looking forward to it, though, you tell yourself, "I'm going to have a terrible time." You have what seems like pretty good reasons for this self-defeating attitude—you have had a terrible time at parties in the past because you aren't confident in your social skills. However, you need to realize that your attitude is making it impossible for you to have fun and meet new people. If you let this self-defeating attitude go unchallenged, you really will have a terrible time at the party.

What should you do now? You need to make an effort to replace your negative self-talk with positive self-talk. Every time you hear yourself thinking, "I'm going to have a terrible time," immediately say to yourself, "I'm going to have a great time at this party." Make an effort to stop dwelling on everything that could go wrong and to start focusing on ways you could have a good time.

All of us have self-defeating attitudes from time to time, especially when facing a situation that we are afraid we won't be able to handle well. The key is to recognize the self-defeating attitudes and stop them in their tracks before they lead to a vicious cycle. Get up close and personal with your own self-defeating attitudes in **Activity 27.**

success *secret*
Learn to recognize your self-defeating attitudes and turn them around with positive self-talk.

RECOGNIZING DISTORTED THOUGHTS

We've seen that self-defeating attitudes undermine our expectations and trick us into failing and feeling bad about ourselves. Now let's take a look at a variety of distorted ways of thinking, known as cognitive distortions, that get in the way of positive thinking. A **cognitive distortion** is a self-critical, illogical pattern of thought. Cognitive distortions are often described as automatic thoughts because they occur to us automatically, before we think a situation through. Consider the following statements, which contain cognitive distortions:

cognitive distortion
A self-critical, illogical pattern of thought.

- "I didn't get an A on that exam. I'm a failure."
- "Four people I invited to my party didn't come. I feel like such a loser!"
- "My girlfriend broke up with me. Well, there goes my last chance at happiness."

ACTIVITY 27: Challenging Self-Defeating Attitudes

A In numbers 1 through 3 below, imagine what self-defeating behavior would likely result from the self-defeating attitude described, and what negative outcome would result from this self-defeating behavior. In numbers 4 through 6, construct similar scenarios using self-defeating attitudes that you have experienced in your own life.

1. **Self-Defeating Attitude:** <u>"I'm no good at making friends."</u>

   Self-Defeating Behavior: <u>"I don't say hello to anyone in class because I don't know what to say after that."</u>

   Negative Outcome: <u>"I didn't meet any new friends in class."</u>

2. **Self-Defeating Attitude:** <u>"I'm going to make a fool of myself at this dance class."</u>

   Self-Defeating Behavior: _____

   _____

   Negative Outcome: _____

3. **Self-Defeating Attitude:** <u>"This date is going to be a disaster."</u>

   Self-Defeating Behavior: _____

   _____

   Negative Outcome: _____

4. **Self-Defeating Attitude:** _____

   Self-Defeating Behavior: _____

   _____

   Negative Outcome: _____

5. **Self-Defeating Attitude:** _____

   Self-Defeating Behavior: _____

   _____

   Negative Outcome: _____

6. **Self-Defeating Attitude:** _____

   Self-Defeating Behavior: _____

   _____

   Negative Outcome: _____

B Now use positive self-talk to turn around these self-defeating attitudes. Think of three positive self-statements that you could use to drown out these self-defeating attitudes and replace them with more positive ones. Then think of the positive behaviors and outcomes that would result from the new positive attitudes. (For numbers 4 through 6, use the self-defeating attitudes you described on the previous page.)

1. **Self-Defeating Attitude:** _"I'm no good at making friends."_

   Positive Self-Talk: _"I may be shy, but my instructors tell me I ask intelligent questions. I'll think of 4 or 5 good questions that will help start the conversation."_

   Positive Behavior: _"After class, I asked the student next to me if she works part-time too and what course topics she thought were difficult."_

   Positive Outcome: _"I found out we both have Mondays off and we set a time to meet for coffee and go over notes together."_

   _____

2. **Self-Defeating Attitude:** _"I'm going to make a fool of myself at this dance class."_

   Positive Self-Talk: _____

   _____

   _____

   _____

   _____

   Positive Behavior: _____

   _____

   Positive Outcome: _____

   _____

continued...

3. **Self-Defeating Attitude:** <u>"This date is going to be a disaster."</u> _____

   Positive Self-Talk: _____

   _____

   _____

   Positive Behavior: _____

   _____

   Positive Outcome: _____

   _____

4. **Self-Defeating Attitude:** _____

   Positive Self-Talk: _____

   _____

   _____

   _____

   Positive Behavior: _____

   _____

   Positive Outcome: _____

   _____

5. **Self-Defeating Attitude:** _____

   Positive Self-Talk: _____

   _____

   _____

   _____

Positive Behavior: _____

_____

Positive Outcome: _____

_____

6. **Self-Defeating Attitude:** _____

Positive Self-Talk: _____

_____

_____

Positive Behavior: _____

_____

Positive Outcome: _____

_____

C Look over the positive self-statements you wrote above and on the previous page. Pick your three favorite statements and copy them below in large handwriting.

1. _____

_____

2. _____

_____

3. _____

_____

Read these three statements out loud. Whenever you find yourself thinking negatively, return to this page and read these statements out loud again. You may even want to photocopy them or cut them out and carry them with you.

These statements are obviously distorted and exaggerated. Where is it written that not getting an A makes you a failure? Why are you a loser because four people couldn't make it to your party? Who says your happiness is controlled by a single person?

The way we look at the problems and obstacles in our lives has a powerful effect on our happiness and our potential for success. How do you react to life's frustrations and disappointments? Do you blame yourself, blame other people, or decide that life is out to get you? Or do you chalk it up to circumstance and hope for better luck next time?

Psychologist Aaron Beck, a founder of *cognitive therapy,* identified several types of cognitive distortions that people use to make themselves miserable. As you read about the following types of cognitive distortions, consider whether any of them might apply to you.

All-or-Nothing Thinking

All-or-nothing thinking causes you to view issues as black and white, with no shades of gray in between. For example, Elesha sees people as law-abiding citizens or crooks. When she discovers that a coworker registers her car at her mother's address to save money on insurance, she views her coworker as a criminal.

overgeneralizing

Drawing broad negative conclusions based on limited evidence.

Overgeneralizing

Overgeneralizing is drawing broad negative conclusions based on limited evidence. If one bad thing happens, you conclude that only bad things will happen to you for the rest of your life. Overgeneralizers get a lot of mileage out of the words *always* and *never.* Jason's girlfriend breaks up with him to date someone else. On the basis of this one event, Jason assumes that every woman he dates will leave him.

Filtering

Filtering is a mental habit of blocking positive inputs and focusing on negative ones. When you filter, you focus so intensely on the negative that it takes over your entire field of vision. Your good qualities don't count; your achievements mean nothing. Jamaal walks away depressed from a meeting with his instructor because of one small criticism, even though he received many compliments. Keiko, an A student, gets a D in a difficult science class. She immediately forgets her string of successes and tells herself she is a terrible student.

Helpless Thinking

Helpless thinking is the irrational belief that your life is not under your own control—that someone else is pulling the strings. Diane leaves projects unfinished, lets bills go unpaid, and allows relationships to fizzle because she feels that nothing she does will make any difference anyway. As we discovered earlier in this chapter, helpless thinking is "learned," and can be changed into "learned optimism" over time.

Self-Blame

Self-blame is the habit of blaming everything on yourself, regardless of the real cause. Self-blamers apologize whenever something goes wrong. Sheila, an executive assistant, apologizes profusely when her boss's plane is delayed due to fog. She is convinced that she is to blame somehow for the bad weather.

Personalizing

Personalizing is assuming that everything has to do with you somehow. Personalizing is sometimes known as egocentric (self-centered) thinking. Leslie hears a group of students laughing and assumes they are laughing at the way she looks. In fact, they were laughing at a harmless joke. Jahi receives a group e-mail from his boss asking people to limit their personal phone calls. He immediately assumes that his boss is angry at him personally and that the message is really intended just for him.

Mind Reading

Mind reading means assuming that other people think the same way you do: When you think bad thoughts about yourself, you assume that everyone else is doing the same. Dwight assumes that his girlfriend is constantly angry with him because she often comes home from work in a bad mood. The fact is, his girlfriend is unhappy with her job.

Emotional Reasoning

Emotional reasoning involves assuming that your negative emotions reflect the way things really are: You feel it, so it must be true. Jorge asks a friend out on a date, and she declines. Jorge feels rejected and unattractive, so he concludes that he is an unattractive reject.

Catastrophizing

Catastrophizing means dramatically exaggerating the negative consequences of any minor event. Catastrophizers don't just worry about real problems—they also worry about imaginary problems. Catastrophizers are constantly worrying, "What if. . .?" Onida's instructor tells her that she can raise her grade by expanding her research paper. Onida immediately catastrophizes, worrying, "What if I make the paper worse? What if I fail the class?"

Do any of these ways of thinking sound familiar? They are closely related, and if you have done one of them, you have probably done the others at one time or another, too. They all have one important thing in common: a pessimistic outlook that transforms the frustrations and disappointments of everyday life into earth-shattering disasters.

Irrational Beliefs

Why do people think in distorted, negative ways? According to Albert Ellis, founder of *rational emotive behavior therapy (REBT),* each of us has a variety of underlying ideas and assumptions that interfere with our thinking. Ellis calls these distorted, self-destructive assumptions **irrational beliefs.** Irrational beliefs are harsh rules about how the world should work and how we and other people should act. Like most rules, they are rigid and absolute, containing words such as *always, never, totally, must,* and *have to.* Ellis identified several common irrational beliefs, including:

- I must succeed at everything.
- I must be loved by everyone.
- If _____ doesn't love me, I'm worthless.
- I should never make mistakes.
- I should be kind, generous, competent, and loving at all times.
- I should worry about every bad thing that could possibly happen.
- I should be very upset about other people's problems.
- I should always put other people's needs first.
- I can't do anything about my feelings.
- I can't do anything about my bad habits—they're stronger than me.
- My past is the cause of all my problems.
- If I don't get what I want, it's terrible, and I can't stand it.
- If people do something I don't like, they must be punished.
- I should never feel angry, anxious, inadequate, jealous, or vulnerable.
- If I'm alone, then I have to feel miserable and unfulfilled.
- People should be the way I expect them to be.

According to Ellis, these irrational beliefs all boil down to three faulty assumptions:

1. I must do well. (If I don't, I'm worthless.)

2. You must treat me well. (If you don't, you must be punished.)

3. The world must be easy. (If it isn't, it's intolerable.)

These beliefs are irrational because they have no basis in fact. They are based on the way we think things ought to be, not the way things really are. Why must I always do well? Why must everyone treat me the way I want? Why should life be easy all the time?

Irrational beliefs get in the way of attaining our goals, and they produce conflict with others. They lead to negative thought patterns and to negative emotional reactions such as guilt, anger, and sadness. Take Annike's example. Her husband Jaime has told her he wants a divorce. Annike is in emotional pain. However, she makes the situation even more painful for herself through irrational beliefs: "Jaime left me, so every man will leave me." "Jaime doesn't love me, so no man will ever love me." "Jaime abandoned me, so I deserve to be abandoned." "Jaime doesn't love me, so I'm worthless."

To make these irrational beliefs more rational, we need to learn to say, "I would like," "It would be nice if," or "I would rather" instead of, "I must" or, "I should." For example, consider the irrational belief, "I must be loved by everyone." This belief is setting you up for failure and emotional pain. It is healtheir to tell yourself, "Sure, it would be nice to be loved by everyone, but that just isn't possible or realistic. I can't realistically expect everyone to love me. After all, no one can please everyone all the time." Try rewriting your irrational beliefs in a similar way in **Personal Journal 5.3.**

Personal Journal 5.3

From Irrational to Rational

Reread the list of irrational beliefs on page 210. Choose four that resonate with you, then rewrite them to be more realistic. Remember to remove all extreme words such as *must, should, can't, have to, never,* and *always.*

Irrational Belief:

_____

Rational Belief:

_____

Irrational Belief:

_____

Rational Belief:

_____

Irrational Belief:

_____

Rational Belief:

_____

Irrational Belief:

_____

Rational Belief:

_____

CHANGING YOUR NEGATIVE THOUGHTS

As we saw in Chapter 3, much of our distress is caused by the way we view events, not by the events themselves. Ellis's theory, known as the ABC model, describes how negative consequences such as stress, unhappiness, guilt, and anger result from a combination of an event and our belief about the event:

- **A**—activating event
- **B**—belief
- **C**—consequences

To see how the ABC model works, imagine the following situation. You spend two weeks preparing for a big oral report in your biology class. On the day of the presentation, however, nothing goes right. You're nervous; you forget some of your notes; and the class isn't paying attention. When you get your evaluation, you find that you've received a full grade lower than you had hoped. This is **A,** the *activating event.* Now comes **B,** your *irrational belief.* Deep down, you believe that you have to do everything perfectly; if you don't, you're a failure. You tell yourself, "I'm a zero. I might as well forget about a career in science." What are the *consequences,* **C?** You feel depressed and worthless. Perhaps you even drop the class or change majors.

Learning Your ABCDEs

To keep negative consequences from getting in our way, we need to change our irrational beliefs. We can change our beliefs by adding two more steps, D and E, to the ABC model:

- **D**—Dispute
- **E**—Exchange

ABCDE method An approach to coping with negative thoughts and feelings by disputing irrational beliefs.

This revised model, known as the **ABCDE method** and depicted in Figure 5.3, describes how we can alter our irrational beliefs and produce better, more positive emotional and behavioral consequences for ourselves.

D stands for **dispute.** To dispute our irrational beliefs means to confront them with the facts of the situation. We must remain vigilant about negative thoughts and, when they occur, dispute them vigorously. When you have a negative, irrational, exaggerated thought, ask yourself:

dispute To confront irrational beliefs with the reality of the situation.

- Why? Who says so?
- Where is it written that this is true?
- Am I jumping to conclusions?
- Am I exaggerating?
- Am I demanding the impossible?
- What evidence is there for this thought?
- Is it really as bad as it seems?
- Is there another explanation that would work as well or better?
- What if the worst happens—so what?
- What other interpretations are possible?
- Do I have all the facts?
- Am I looking at things all in extremes?

FIGURE 5.3   The ABCDE Method

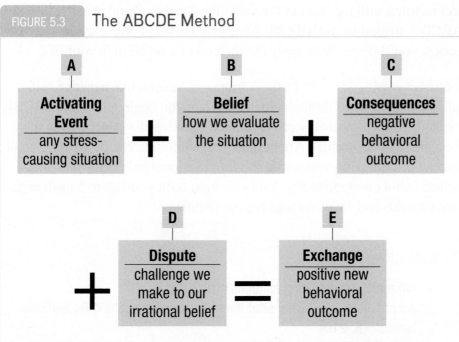

Turning Beliefs Around   Once we are aware of the irrational beliefs that are distorting our thinking and making us unhappy, we can use effective disputes to create healthier, more positive outcomes for ourselves. *What are some questions you can ask yourself to help dispute an irrational belief?*

- Am I taking one example and assuming it is a pattern?
- Am I focusing on the negative and ignoring the positive?
- Am I exaggerating the negative consequences of the situation?
- Am I assuming that something is going to happen because I'm afraid it will?
- Am I using emotional words that trigger negative feelings?
- Is this thought producing feelings I want to have?

To be an effective disputer, try to separate your emotional reaction from the reality of the situation. Are you really being objective? For instance, in the example on page 212, when you begin having negative thoughts about your biology presentation, you can stop yourself and think, "OK, wait. I'm exaggerating. Does getting a so-so grade on one oral report mean I'm a total failure? No. I'm also ignoring the positive. I almost forgot that the instructor said she enjoyed having me in the class." This dispute is based on rational thinking and evidence.

The fifth and last element of the ABCDE method is **E,** *exchange.* Exchange stands for the new, positive outcome that you want to substitute, or exchange, for the negative one. In this case, **E** means forgiving yourself and focusing on the future. Now you can tell yourself, "No one's perfect. I'll make a point of being more organized next time."

The ABCDE method is easy to use in your daily life. When you find yourself jumping to distorted negative conclusions, stop and consider what irrational beliefs might be motivating them. Dispute the negative thoughts

success *secret*
Separate your emotional reaction from the reality of your situation.

and feelings with the facts of the situation. Try your hand at using the ABCDE method in **Activity 28.** After tackling some hypothetical scenarios, you'll be ready to apply the method to a problem in your life.

Practice Makes Perfect Irrational beliefs, like negative self-talk, can be changed through practice. When you begin to use the ABCDE method, you will probably catch yourself thinking the same irrational thoughts. This is normal. After all, negative thinking can be a strong habit. Instead of criticizing yourself for having irrational beliefs, dispute the beliefs calmly and rationally. You will soon train yourself to banish negative thoughts and focus on positive possibilities.

Self Check

1. What are self-defeating attitudes? (p. 201)
2. According to Albert Ellis, what three faulty assumptions drive irrational beliefs? (p. 210)
3. What does ABCDE stand for? (p. 212)

ACTIVITY 28: Disputing Negative Thoughts

A Consider the following situations. Given the activating events and the beliefs that follow, identify the likely negative consequences (thoughts, feelings, and actions).

1. **Activating Event:** Your boss snaps at you when you ask how he's doing.

   Belief: "He must be unhappy with my work."

   Consequences: "I'm sure I'm going to get a bad review next week. Instead of working late on this project tonight I should probably start updating my résumé."

   Dispute: "All my reports have been thorough and on time and our sales are on target. I must have just walked by at a bad time."

   Exchange: "I'll stay focused on my work and continue with the project goals I've set."

2. **Activating Event:** A friend throws a party, but she doesn't invite you.

   Belief: "I guess I'm not cool enough for her."

   Consequences: _____

   Dispute: _____

   Exchange: _____

3. **Activating Event:** You and your best friend have planned to meet for lunch, but she fails to show up.

   Belief: "It's totally unfair of her to stand me up."

   Consequences: _____

   Dispute: _____

   Exchange: _____

continued...

4. **Activating Event:** You don't get a new job you were hoping for.

   Belief: "I'm a failure."

   Consequences: _____

   _____

   Dispute: _____

   _____

   _____

   Exchange: _____

   _____

5. **Activating Event:** You're looking forward to a relaxing weekend, when a friend asks you to spend the next two days helping him move into a new apartment.

   Belief: "I should always put other people's needs first."

   Consequences: _____

   _____

   Dispute: _____

   _____

   _____

   Exchange: _____

   _____

B Use the following space to record one of your own experiences with the ABCDE method. What upsetting event, A, led you to have a negative, distorted thought, B, and what were the consequences, C? Fill in disputes, D, you made to your negative beliefs and describe the positive outcome that you exchanged, E, for the old one. If you didn't think of an effective dispute at the time the event occurred, think of one now and describe what might have happened differently if you had used this dispute at the time.

A: _____

_____

B: _____

_____

C: _____

_____

D: _____

_____

E: _____

_____

Chapter 5 Review and Activities

Key Terms

positive thinking (p. 180)

optimism (p. 180)

attitude (p. 181)

negative thinking (p. 182)

pessimism (p. 183)

judgmentalism (p. 189)

complaint (p. 189)

worry (p. 190)

depression (p. 195)

self-defeating attitude (p. 201)

vicious cycle (p. 202)

cognitive distortion (p. 203)

overgeneralizing (p. 208)

personalizing (p. 209)

catastrophizing (p. 209)

irrational belief (p. 209)

ABCDE method (p. 212)

dispute (p. 212)

Summary by Learning Objectives

- **Define positive thinking and cite its benefits.** Positive thinking means focusing on what is good about ourselves, other people, and the world around us. Positive thinking can help you achieve your goals, overcome obstacles, boost your mood, improve your relationships, and maintain a healthy lifestyle.

- **List six habits that can help you become a more positive thinker.** Six positive habits that can help boost your positive attitude toward life are: 1. look for the good; 2. choose positive words; 3. surround yourself with positive people; 4. accept people and things for what they are; 5. limit complaints; 6. focus on realistic outcomes.

- **Explain the link between positive thinking and good health.** Positive thinking speeds healing and motivates you to eat right, exercise, and adopt a healthy lifestyle. Feeling fit and healthy, in turn, helps you think positively.

- **Describe how self-defeating attitudes create a vicious cycle.** Self-defeating attitudes create a vicious cycle by leading to self-defeating behaviors, which in turn lead to negative outcomes. These negative outcomes "prove" that the self-defeating attitude was correct, which causes the cycle to repeat itself again and again.

- **Define cognitive distortions and irrational beliefs and give an example of each.** Cognitive distortions are self-critical, illogical patterns of thought that people use to make themselves miserable. One common cognitive distortion is catastrophizing, dramatically exaggerating the negative consequences of any minor event. Irrational beliefs are distorted, self-destructive assumptions such as "I should never make mistakes."

- **Summarize the ABCDE method for overcoming irrational beliefs.** In the ABCDE method, **A** stands for the activating event that triggers **B**, an irrational belief. **C** stands for the negative consequences of the belief. **D** stands for dispute, which means analyzing the logic of the irrational belief. **D** leads to **E**, exchange, a more desirable outcome.

Review and Activities

Review Questions

1. Why does having positive expectations of success help you attain it?

2. What is the relationship between negative thinking and depression?

3. Name three healthy eating habits and three healthy exercise habits.

4. Give an example of a self-defeating attitude and the vicious cycle it creates.

5. Which cognitive distortion involves the false belief that you are not in control of your life?

6. Explain how to dispute irrational beliefs.

Critical Thinking

7. **Worry** William James, a pioneering 19th-century psychologist, once said this: "If you believe that feeling bad or worrying long enough will change a past or future event, you are residing on another planet with a different reality system." Explain what this statement means and whether you agree with it. Could worrying ever change a future event? Why or why not?

8. **Optimism and Academic Success** A study was conducted on a large group of college freshmen in Pennsylvania to investigate the relationship between optimism and academic performance. The results? The optimistic students dramatically outperformed the pessimistic students. They even outperformed pessimistic students who had much higher standardized test scores and high school GPAs. What do the results of this study show? Why do you think optimism would be so closely linked to success in college?

Application

9. **Negative and Positive News** The majority of news programs begin their broadcast with the most negative stories of the day to create "shock appeal" for viewers and audience ratings for their sponsors. Watch 30 minutes of your daily local or national news. Note each of the stories covered (such as crimes, political, world, celebrity news). How many of the stories are negative? How many are positive? Why do you think negative stories capture viewers' attention? What stories were you attracted to most, and why?

10. **Spreading Positive Energy** Whether you're feeling positive or not, making an effort to engage others in a positive manner, if only for a brief encounter, will do wonders to boost your mood, and most likely, theirs. Practice this experiment for one day: *Try interacting with everyone you meet with a positive greeting, statement, or even just a smile.* Whether it's a grocery store cashier or someone you pass on the street, try offering up something positive: eye contact, a smile, a greeting (hello, how are you today?), a compliment (I really like your shirt), or just an observation (great weather today, isn't it?). Describe what you did and how people responded to you. How did it make them feel? Did it boost your positive attitude?

Internet Activities

11. **Optimist's Creed**   Read "The Optimist's Creed"
    1. Be so strong that nothing can disturb your peace of mind.
    2. Talk health, happiness, and prosperity to everyone you meet.
    3. Make your friends feel there is something good in them.
    4. Look at the sunny side of everything and make your optimism come true.
    5. Think only of the best, work only for the best, and expect only the best.
    6. Be just as enthusiastic about the success of others as you are about your own.
    7. Forget the mistakes of the past and move on to the greater achievements of the future.
    8. Wear a cheerful face at al/ times and give everyone you meet a smile.
    9. Give so much time to the improvement of yourself that you have no time to criticize others.
    10. Be too large to worry, too noble for anger, too strong for fear, and too happy to look for trouble.

    For each of the ten points in the creed, write down an action you could take to incorporate it into your life. Then write an eleventh point of your own choosing that could be added to the creed.

12. **This I Believe**   Go to http://thisibelieve.org/ and read or listen to some of the essays. Write a This I Believe of your own and share it with a classmate. See below for an example.

    (personal creed of an unknown community college freshman woman, age 19) I believe in myself. I believe that all people have the equal right to become all they are willing and able to become. I believe that I am as good as anyone in the world. Although I may never be on the cover of *Time* magazine, I still have time to make a really positive difference in my life. I believe that although I may not be the best looking in the group, I'll always be looking my best in every group. I believe in this and the next generation, and believe we'll build a better nation. I believe good health means more that wealth. I believe in caring and sharing, rather than comparing. I believe of all the people I see, still I'd rather be me.

Real-Life Success Story

"Will Things Go My Way?"

Review your answer to the question in the Real-Life Success Story on page 178. Think about how you would answer the question now that you have completed the chapter.

Complete the Story   Pretend that you are a friend of Jessica's and are waiting with her for her interviewer to arrive. Write a dialogue between Jessica and yourself in which you explain why her self-defeating attitude will lead to a vicious cycle. Also give her tips to use positive self-talk to turn her attitude around.

"Should I Make a Change?"

Big Dreams, Big Fears

Jeannette Slawson, a legal secretary, found herself thumbing through her local university's catalog of prelaw courses. She had thought many times about becoming a lawyer, but it always seemed like an impossible dream. She would have to complete several prelaw courses even before going to three years of law school—four years if she took night classes. She wondered if she really had the self-discipline to see her plans through. She pictured herself handling the tough schedule for a year or two, then dropping out.

Big Changes

Deep down, Jeannette knew that no one was stopping her from changing but herself. For every obstacle she could imagine, she could think of a workable solution; but every time she thought about taking action, she became nervous. She didn't hate her job, and she had a comfortable routine. It was easier to accept her life as it was than to force herself to make a change.

What Do You Think? Should Jeannette follow through on her plan to become a lawyer? Why or why not?

Self-Discipline

6 Chapter

> " Not everything that is faced can be changed, but nothing can be changed until it is faced. "
>
> James Baldwin, Author

introduction

This chapter introduces self-discipline—what it is, why it's important, and how to practice it. In Section 6.1 you'll explore the benefits of self-discipline and learn about the key concepts of self-determination and persistence. You'll also learn how to control your impulses by considering the long-term consequences of your actions. Then you'll look at how self-discipline can help you make difficult changes, including changing bad habits into better ones. In Section 6.2 you'll learn about self-disciplined thinking by exploring the elements of critical thinking and learning how to make logical, step-by-step decisions.

learning objectives

After you complete this chapter, you should be able to:

- Define self-discipline and cite its benefits.

- Explain how to control impulses.

- Describe the process of replacing bad habits with good ones.

- Define critical thinking and list its seven standards.

- List the steps in the decision-making process.

WHAT IS SELF-DISCIPLINE?

self-discipline The process of teaching yourself to do what is necessary to reach your goals, without becoming sidetracked by bad habits.

No matter how motivated you are, how many skills you have, and how self-confident you are, you will need self-discipline to achieve your goals. **Self-discipline** is the process of teaching yourself to do what is necessary to reach your goals, without becoming sidetracked by bad habits. Self-discipline can be hard, but it's worth it. It gives you a feeling of self-expectancy and control over your life.

In earlier chapters, you considered what you want out of life and how your goals can help you get there. To achieve your goals, you need to keep yourself on track and move forward. Self-discipline helps you do this by strengthening your ability to:

- control your destiny
- persist in the face of setbacks
- weigh the long-term consequences of your actions
- make positive changes
- break bad habits
- think critically
- make effective decisions

Self-discipline helps you in countless areas of your life. You rely on self-discipline to stick to your study schedule when you would rather go to the movies, to push yourself away from the table instead of eating a second piece of pie, and to get up when the alarm rings in the morning.

success *secret*

All successful people rely on self-discipline.

All successful people rely on self-discipline. A time comes when the small daily gains that come from being disciplined add up to extraordinary success. Take rock musician Suzanne Vega. She started out playing in coffeehouses and developing a small following. Then she made her own mailing list and sent out flyers to advertise her shows. She kept a notebook recording the details of every show: the songs she sang, what the audience response was, even how she did her hair. Each time she performed, she tried to outdo herself, to make her music better. Her self-discipline helped her achieve her goal of becoming an outstanding songwriter and performer.

Elements of Self-Discipline

The word *discipline* comes from the Latin verb meaning "to teach." To build strong self-discipline, we teach ourselves to act in positive ways, even when we are tired, bored, frustrated, or feeling down. This requires two key abilities, as shown in Figure 6.1:

- **Persistence**—Persistence allows you to put in effort, again and again, until you reach your goal. You need persistence to keep going instead of giving up.

FIGURE 6.1 Ingredients of Self-Discipline

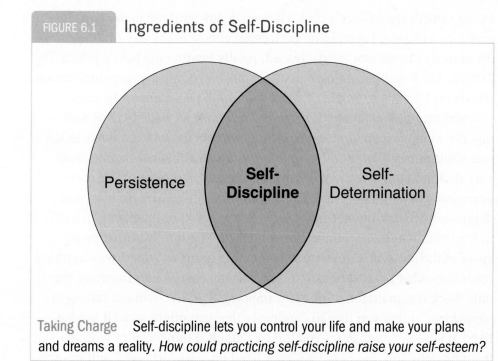

Persistence | Self-Discipline | Self-Determination

Taking Charge   Self-discipline lets you control your life and make your plans and dreams a reality. *How could practicing self-discipline raise your self-esteem?*

- **Self-determination**—With self-determination, you are the master of your life. Instead of sitting back and waiting for something to happen, you take action.

Both of these elements are equally important. Without persistence, you can't rely on yourself to see your plans through and do what it takes to succeed. Without self-determination, you can't take control of your decisions and actions.

The Power of Persistence

The first half of self-discipline is **persistence**—the ability to go on despite opposition, setbacks, and occasional doubts. Persistence is a never-say-die attitude—a determination to succeed.

persistence The ability to go on despite opposition, setbacks, and occasional doubts.

History is full of people who have used persistence to make it against all the odds. Helen Keller (1880–1968) was blind and deaf from infancy, yet with the help of a dedicated teacher, she learned to speak and read. A determined teacher in France, Louis Braille (1809–1852), blind from age three, invented a system in 1829 to help sightless people read. Millions of people still use the Braille system today.

Author James Michener once said, "Character consists of what you do on the third and fourth tries." In other words, keep working toward your goal even if you don't have success on the first or second try. Don't give up.

Comedian Jay Leno didn't succeed on his first try. Told early on that he had a face that would "scare children," Leno didn't give up on his dream of becoming a professional comedian. When a college admissions officer told Leno he wasn't college material, Leno didn't give up either.

He sat outside the officer's desk 12 hours a day until the man agreed to give him a chance. Later, Leno performed almost every day of the year on the comedy circuit to improve his act, finally landing the host's job on *The Tonight Show* and becoming one of the most recognizable personalities on television. "I'm an example of success through persistence," he says.

Another great example of persistence against all odds is JK Rowling, the wealthiest and most successful author in the world, thanks to her incredible *Harry Potter* collection. Did you know that her parents were very disappointed that she was born female and that most of her early years through adulthood were filled with fears, insecurity, failure, and depression? She wrote her first *Harry Potter* book, in longhand, in a café in Scotland, while on welfare. She remarked, "Failure was a stripping away of the inessential. I stopped pretending to myself that I was anything other than what I was. I began to direct all my energy into finishing the only work that mattered to me. It is impossible to live without failing at something, unless you live so cautiously that you might as well not have lived at all—in which case, you fail by default. I think you're working and learning until you die. I can, with my hand on my heart, say I will never write for any reason other than I burningly wanted to write the book." Imagine what persistence could do for you in **Personal Journal 6.1.**

Self-Determination

self-determination

Determining the path your life travels.

The second part of self-discipline is **self-determination.** Self-determination means determining the path your life travels.

Some people believe that fate, luck, or some other force outside their control shapes the outcome of their lives. People who feel that life is determined by chance circumstances or by being in the right place at the right time are more likely to doubt and fear their future than people who know they are in control. People who feel that they do not control what happens to them believe they are victims of circumstance. They simply float along wherever the current of life takes them.

No matter who you are, you are in charge of where you are right now and where you go from here. Ask yourself, "Am I steering my own ship, or am I a victim of fate?" Are you doing things in life because you want to do them or because you feel they have been forced upon you? If you allow yourself to be pressured into doing things that you would rather not do, you may be giving up control of your life to other people.

responsibility The ability to make independent, proactive decisions and to accept the consequences of those choices.

Taking Responsibility   People who are in control of their lives display **responsibility,** the ability to make independent, proactive decisions and to accept the consequences of those choices.

We are given a set of characteristics at birth, but we make the decisions that determine our success in life. We have to ask ourselves who we are and how we got where we are. The 18th-century French writer Voltaire compared life to a game of cards. Each player is dealt a certain hand. This

Personal Journal 6.1

Going Against the Odds

Imagine that your dream is to write and publish a novel about your life. Listed in the left-hand box below are some obstacles that you might face. Think of one way that you could use persistence to overcome each obstacle.

Obstacle	To overcome this obstacle:
Not enough free time for writing	
Don't know how to start novel	
Life isn't interesting enough	
Writer's block	
Accidentally delete first five chapters from computer	
Rejected by publisher	
Rejected by publisher again	
Other:	

How could you use persistence to overcome obstacles standing between you and your dream?

hand is the genetics and environment that are given to us. We as players, however, are responsible for how we play that hand, what to keep and what to toss out. We make the decisions that determine our success in life. We decide how to shape our lives.

In his book *Taking Responsibility: Self-Reliance and the Accountable Life,* Nathaniel Branden speaks of responsibility as "the practice of making oneself the cause of the effects one wants, as contrasted with a policy of hoping or demanding that someone else do something while one's own contribution is to wait and suffer." Are you waiting, perhaps without even realizing it, for someone to "do something"? Make that person be you!

Although many things in life are beyond anyone's control, you do have a great deal of control—more than most of us are willing to acknowledge—over many circumstances and conditions.

- You can control what you do with most of your free time during the day and evening. Instead of watching other people making money enjoying their professions on prime time TV, turn off the TV and your online devices and start living in Prime Time. Read, interact with family, go out to ethnic restaurants, attend artistic and artisan shows. Get up from the chair and explore the great outdoors!

- You can control how much energy you exert and effort you give to each task you undertake. Prioritize your projects. Balance personal and professional goals. Finish what you start. Learn what times of day your energy levels are the highest. Do important work during those peak periods.

- You can control your thoughts and imagination, and channel them. Limit your TV news viewing to events immediately impacting your personal and professional life. Avoid violent entertainment. Read more inspirational biographies of people who have overcome enormous obstacles to become successful.

- You can control your attitude. Hang out and network with optimists on a regular basis.

- You can control your tongue. You can choose to remain silent or choose to speak. If you choose to speak, you can choose your words, body language, and tone of voice. When you meet someone new, ask more questions and don't try to impress him or her with your exploits. The less you try to impress, the more impressive you will be. Say to yourself, "I'll make them glad they talked to me." And hope that they will be thinking, "I like me best when I'm with you."

- You can control your choice of role models. The best role model is not necessarily the celebrity or expert. It is more likely someone you can get to know personally and closely—preferably someone with a background or career path similar to yours; someone who has been where you are now. For personal role models and mentors, seek those who have not only achieved external success but whose whole lives, including their personal conduct, merit emulation. Career success can rarely be separated from character; one facet of a person's life invariably affects the other facets.

- You can control your commitments, the things you absolutely promise yourself and others that you'll do. Don't over commit; in that way you won't have to make excuses when deadlines are missed. Break your commitments into stair-step priorities and goals, ones that are reasonably easy to hit and easy to correct if missed.

- You can control the causes to which you give your time and emotion. Focus more on positive programs with socially redeeming benefits. Instead of a protestor, become a producer and protector.
- You can control your memberships. Congregate with people having similar goals or those who are overcoming similar challenges with knowledge, attitude, skills, and habits.
- You can control your concerns and worries. Find a relaxation and exercise program that helps you release tension. A quiet place, a garden, the sea, and soft music can do wonders for the soul. So can interaction with wildlife, as well as interaction with domestic animals.
- You can control your response to difficult times and people. One of the best ways to overcome depression is to become active in helping other people in need.

Do you feel in control of your life? Do you see yourself as responsible for your success, or are you sitting on the sidelines of your life? To test your attitude, complete **Activity 29** on page 228.

CONTROLLING IMPULSES

One excellent way to increase your self-discipline is to learn and practice impulse control. An **impulse** is a sudden wish or feeling that can lead to unplanned and unwise actions.

We all do things on impulse. We might buy a magazine, go to the movies, or take a day trip just because we suddenly feel like it. Acting on impulse once in a while is relatively harmless. When impulses guide our behavior too often, however, we lose the ability to plan for the future. If we get in the habit of following our impulses, we can even do self-destructive things that we will regret later. Take Richard's example. Stressed and overworked, Richard got annoyed with his boss one day and quit his job on impulse. Unfortunately, it took Richard several months to find a new job. He lost the good recommendation of his former employer and had to sell some of his belongings to make ends meet.

Even if we don't make such big mistakes, acting on impulse can cost us. It can cause us to spend too much money, waste time, overeat, overreact, and do other things that are not good for us or others, such as:

- yelling
- making comments we wish we could take back later
- drinking alcohol or smoking
- disregarding obligations and letting people down
- driving dangerously

Poor impulse control contributes to major problems such as gambling, drug addiction, and compulsive spending.

impulse A sudden wish or feeling that can lead to unplanned and unwise actions.

ACTIVITY 29: Do You Control Your Life?

A Indicate with a check mark whether you Agree or Disagree with each statement below.

	Agree	Disagree
1. Success is a matter of hard work.		
2. My life seems like a series of random events.		
3. Marriage is pretty much a gamble for most people.		
4. Persistence and hard work usually lead to success.		
5. If I don't get something I want, that means it's just not meant to be.		
6. Many tests are so unfair that studying is practically useless.		
7. Successful leaders are the ones who work hard.		
8. It's hard to know whether anyone really likes you.		
9. People either respect you or they don't.		
10. Voters are ultimately responsible for bad government.		
11. Success at work is a matter of knowing the right people.		
12. If I don't succeed on a task, I tend to give up.		

B **Scoring:** Assign yourself one point for each of the following statements that you *agreed* with: 2, 3, 5, 6, 8, 9, 11, and 12. Also, assign yourself one point for each of the following statements that you *disagreed* with: 1, 4, 7, and 10. The higher your score, the stronger your belief that outside forces control your life. The lower your score, the stronger your belief that you control your life.

What is your total? _____

1–4 You feel in control of your life, and you are willing to work hard for success.

5–8 You feel that some things are under your control but not others. You will benefit from developing a more positive, can-do attitude toward your life.

9–12 You don't feel in control of your life or your success, and you probably give up easily. You need to analyze your self-defeating attitudes and replace them with more positive ones.

C What are some specific steps you can take to feel more in control of your life?

_____

_____

_____

Applying **Psychology**

A Little Guilt Can Be Good for You

Considering 59 percent of Americans have credit card debt, chances are impulse buying has played a major role. According to a survey conducted by the Consumer Federation of America, 37 percent of respondents cited impulse buying—making purchases that aren't preplanned—as a major obstacle to saving money. Think of how many times you've gone into Wal-Mart or Target for a few items—and come out with a full cart. And think of how many online shopping carts you've filled on Amazon.com, eBay.com, or on any of the 30 million e-commerce sites.

After the "rush" you may feel from your had-to-have purchase is gone, now comes the credit card bill to pay for the unplanned items, and often anxiety over figuring out how to pay for it all. Research indicates that how you cope with a poor spending experience can determine how you shop in the future. According to a study conducted by the University of Guelph, feeling some guilt after an impulse purchase may actually cause you to take positive steps the next time, such as cutting back on other expenses, refraining from window shopping and mall trekking, and creating a shopping list before heading out or logging in. Thus, you've learned from your mistake and are taking steps to avoid doing it again.

However, those who experience shame (negative feelings related to self-worth) from impulse purchases may end up digging a deeper hole for themselves by hiding their purchases from others, ignoring credit card bills, and becoming defensive and isolated. If this is your reaction, you should seek help to determine if there are underlying emotional reasons for your impulse buying and how you can work to overcome them.

Critical Thinking   *How does one's self-esteem play a role in impulse shopping or how one copes after an impulse purchase?*

Thinking Long Term

Acting on impulse is appealing because it offers instant gratification (reward). Buying that new outfit or cutting off an inconsiderate driver in traffic is a lot more satisfying than saving money for college or driving quietly and politely. That's why impulses can be so hard to resist—they're tempting! Unfortunately, when the credit card payment is due or when we find ourselves in a traffic accident, we wish we could go back in time and do things differently. How do we stop this from happening? Instead of living day to day or moment to moment, we need to examine how our choices will affect our long-term goals.

To do this, we need to think about **consequences,** the logical effects of our actions. Consequences can be negative or positive, short-term or long-term. *Short-term consequences,* the immediate results of an action, are usually fairly obvious and easy to predict. *Long-term consequences,* the further off results of an action, aren't always obvious or easy to predict, but they can be major. They can have a big impact on your ability to reach your goals.

consequences The logical effects of an action.

Small Choices, Big Results   It's easy to trick yourself
into believing that small, impulsive actions don't have any long-term

consequences. But over time, the small things add up. Spending those few extra minutes reviewing class notes before an exam or passing up that second handful of potato chips can make the difference between achieving and not achieving a goal.

Delaying gratification doesn't mean punishing yourself. Instead, it means choosing a later, bigger reward over a more immediate, smaller one. Focusing on the bigger reward—your goal—helps you put things in perspective.

When you feel an impulse coming on, stop yourself, think, and make a measured decision:

1. **Stop.** Realize that you are about to act impulsively.
2. **Think.** What will I gain in the short term by acting on this impulse? What will I lose in the long term by acting on this impulse?
3. **Decide.** Given the short-term and long-term consequences, is it worth it?

success *secret*

Before you act on impulse, stop, think, and decide.

Let's say you are studying for a test when a friend calls with a tempting invitation to go to that movie you have been wanting to see. Before you say yes, stop and ask yourself what you are about to do. This gives you a moment to think. What are the short-term consequences of going out to the movie? You're sure to have fun, and you haven't seen your friend in a while. Maybe this movie is just the study break you need. (When you are really tempted to do something, it's amazing how many good excuses you can think up!) Before you rush for the door, however, ask yourself about the long-term consequences. Since you won't have as much time to study, your grade in this course may suffer. If your grade suffers, you might not get that scholarship you are counting on. The reality is that there just isn't room in your life tonight for an outing. Looking at the long-term consequences of your actions helps you pick the path that is best for you.

Of course, controlling your impulses doesn't mean eliminating fun from your life. Instead of a movie, a half-hour study break might give you a chance to relax while still being productive. Use long-term thinking to tackle one of your impulses in **Personal Journal 6.2.**

EMBRACING CHANGE

success *secret*

Self-improvement requires the willingness to change.

Impulse control, like any other kind of self-improvement, requires a willingness to change. In fact, being open to changing negative things about yourself and your life circumstances is the first step toward improving them. Change is easier if we start small, identifying small improvements we would like to make and working on them one by one. As we prove to ourselves that we can make constructive plans and stick to them, we gain the confidence and self-discipline to make bigger and better changes.

Personal Journal 6.2

Thinking Long Term

It's important to look at the consequences of your actions. Select one impulse, such as spending, eating, or cutting people off in traffic, that is a problem for you.

Impulse: _____

_____

1. *What are the satisfying or pleasurable short-term consequences of giving in to this impulse?*

_____

_____

2. *What are the possible negative long-term consequences for you, your goals, or the people you care about?*

_____

_____

3. *Do the positive short-term consequences outweigh the negative long-term consequences? Explain.*

_____

_____

How can you remind yourself to use the stop-think-decide approach the next time you are facing a situation like this?

Do You Resist Change?

Change isn't easy, especially when it involves controlling impulses, replacing bad habits, taking risks, or altering our ways of thinking. Change can also be scary. As we saw in Chapter 3, change is a major cause of stress. Most of us fear change because of the uncertainty involved. Some people have trouble changing because they fear that they will make the wrong choices or expose themselves to failure and ridicule. They may know they have the potential to control their own lives, but they do not take a firm stand or risk breaking out of the mold. They have not persuaded themselves that they should be in control of their choices and decisions. People who think this way have difficulty setting goals, reaching their goals, and fulfilling their ambitions.

Sometimes people resist change so strongly that they literally put their lives in danger. Consider the following story. Members of a village were dying of an unknown cause. Scientists went to the village and discovered that an insect living inside the clay walls of the villagers' homes was biting, poisoning, and killing them. The scientists told the villagers that they should consider killing the insects, tearing down the homes and building new ones, or moving to a new location. The villagers said they would not move; they would stay in their deadly, insect-infested homes and take their chances. They continued to die off one by one. The villagers were so used to their way of life that they preferred to die than to make a change. They hoped that something would come along to save them, but nothing came.

Like the villagers, most of us will put up with practically anything to avoid changing. Even if we aren't satisfied with our lives, it's easier to do things the old way than to take a chance on something better. Take a look at some changes you might make in **Activity 30.** By planning for change ahead of time rather than having it forced on you in a moment of crisis, you can take greater control of your life.

success *secret*
It takes courage to try something new.

What's Holding You Back?

Often, when we think of changes we'd like to make in our lives, it's easy to find a reason to put them off. "I really would," we tell ourselves, "but now isn't a good time. . . I'm tired. . . I don't have enough time. . . I don't have the money."

If you find yourself making excuses, use positive self-talk to help get yourself going. Remind yourself how much better you will feel once you take action. Think about the specific benefits of making the change. If you're "too tired," just do a little bit before you go to bed. Too busy? You'll be amazed how much you can get done in only 10 minutes a day. Overwhelmed by the whole idea? You only need to take one action to get started and make yourself feel better.

success *secret*
Your self-esteem rises when you make positive changes.

Hidden Resistance
Sometimes what holds us back from making positive changes isn't fatigue or laziness but a hidden psychological resistance to change. Often we are unwilling to change because we do not want to give up the rewards we get from staying the way we are. What hidden rewards could there be in not making positive changes? One reward is that you don't have to face your problems or stressors and admit that they are real. Another reward is that you don't have to take action, risk failure, or make an effort.

ACTIVITY 30: Making Positive Changes

A On the lines below, list three changes you would like to make in each area of your life. List only changes that you think you can really make. (Some changes may be desirable but not possible right now. Omit such changes from your list.) Your changes can be small or big, short term or long term.

Example

School: class attendance, commuting, study/homework, etc.

Attend all class meetings unless a real emergency arises.

Leave for class 10 minutes earlier to plan for possible traffic jams.

Set aside one extra hour a week to review my class notes.

1. School: class attendance, commuting, study/homework, etc.

   _____

   _____

   _____

2. Household: housekeeping, shopping, meal planning and preparation, money management, etc.

   _____

   _____

   _____

3. Relationships: friendships, parenting, family ties, romantic relationships, etc.

   _____

   _____

   _____

4. Job: commuting, gaining new knowledge or skills, relating to supervisor and coworkers, etc.

   _____

   _____

   _____

continued...

5. Leisure: hobbies, reading, blogging, television, Internet, sporting events, concerts, etc.

_____

_____

_____

6. Personal fitness: exercise, hygiene/grooming, eating, sleeping, etc.

_____

_____

_____

7. Community: volunteer work, political campaigns, religious participation, neighborhood events, etc.

_____

_____

_____

B Review all your possible changes. Select the three that you believe would make the biggest difference in your life. Copy them below.

1. _____

2. _____

3. _____

C What is one specific thing you can do to get started on these important changes?

_____

_____

D When will you do this? Schedule a specific day and time for this week.

Day: _____   Time: _____

Signed (your name): _____

You may also get comfort from staying the way you are. If you are stuck in a job you dislike, for example, it might be easier to remain in that job and think of yourself as a victim than to make the effort to improve your circumstances. What hidden rewards are you getting from not changing? **Activity 31** on page 236 is designed to help you think about your hidden resistance to change. Try to be honest with yourself without being self-critical.

CONQUERING BAD HABITS

Self-discipline is an important tool for making any kind of important change. Nowhere is self-discipline more necessary than in making one of the hardest changes of all—changing a bad habit. A **habit** is a behavior that has become automatic through repetition. If we give in to a certain impulse often enough, for example, we may soon find that this behavior has become a habit. A habit can also be an attitude, a way of looking at things that soon becomes second nature. Habits start off weak but soon grow strong, so strong that we hardly even notice them anymore. For this reason, habits can be very difficult to break.

Just about everything in life is a choice. You don't have to work, go to school, eat, or even get up in the morning. You decide to do things because they are good for you. Often, we are victims of habit: We do things only because we have been doing them. As children, we look to adults to give us cues for behavior. When we mature and become adults, we must make decisions and be responsible for ourselves.

Habits can have negative consequences. They can make us feel bad about ourselves. They can hurt other people and get in the way of close relationships. They can even damage our physical and emotional health. Common habits in this category include cigarette smoking, drinking too much coffee or alcohol, procrastinating, being late, overspending, overeating, and gossiping.

All of us have indulged in these behaviors at some time or another. Overeating at Thanksgiving isn't a problem, but eating a family-size bag of potato chips for a snack is. Drinking coffee with your morning muffin isn't a problem, but drinking coffee all day to stay awake is.

How do you know whether bad habits are causing you problems? Ask yourself whether any of your habits:

- make you unhappy or feel bad about yourself
- drain your energy or stand in the way of your goals
- get you into trouble at work or school
- hurt or seriously inconvenience others

When a habit causes you to do any of these things, it's time to change. Lasting change doesn't happen overnight. Changing habits involves three major steps:

Step 1: Wanting to change the habit

Step 2: Understanding the habit

Step 3: Replacing the bad habit with a good habit

Let's go through each of these steps.

habit A behavior that has become automatic through repetition.

success *secret*
Almost everything in life is a choice.

success *secret*
When your habits have negative consequences, it's time to change them.

ACTIVITY 31: Overcoming Resistance to Change

A Think of one life change that you would like to make but that you have been avoiding. This change may be from any area of your life, such as career, education, relationships, spirituality, hobbies, health, and so on. What is that change?

_____

_____

_____

_____

_____

B Why do you think you have been avoiding making this change? Think about the risks that would be involved in making this change. For example, would you be risking failure or rejection or making a wrong decision? Would you be giving up your self-image as a victim?

_____

_____

_____

_____

_____

_____

C Do you ever pretend to yourself that you don't need to change and that things are just fine the way they are? Explain.

_____

_____

_____

_____

_____

_____

D Now think about the drawbacks of staying the way you are and the benefits of changing.

Drawbacks of Staying the Same	Benefits of Changing

Which benefit is most important to you and why?

_____

_____

_____

_____

E Describe the specific actions you would need to take to make this change. Which of them would be most difficult for you?

_____

_____

_____

_____

Step 1: Wanting to Change

Before you can break a bad habit, you must want to change from within, not because of someone else's criticism or advice. You must commit to changing and accept that lasting change takes time and effort.

By studying people who are trying to kick bad health habits, such as drinking or smoking, psychologists have identified three mental stages that people go through before they even begin to take action.

These three stages are the precontemplation stage, the contemplation stage, and the preparation stage. In the precontemplation stage, you still have no intention of changing. You may not even see a need to change since you may not recognize the negative effects of a behavior. In the contemplation stage, you begin thinking about changing a behavior. In this stage, you evaluate the pros and cons of a certain habit and explore the different ways you could make a change. In the preparation stage, you edge closer to making serious efforts to change. This is the stage you are in if you have attempted to change before but did not have all the necessary skills to successfully carry it through.

As you can see, it takes time and mental effort to commit to change. Think about the little things in your life that may be affected by your habit change, and resolve in advance not to beat yourself up if you relapse. Ask for advice from someone who has made a similar change, and talk with the people close to you about how they can help you.

Step 2: Understanding the Habit

Step 2 is to know your bad habit. To change any behavior, you first need to understand it. What reward do you get from it? When, where, and with whom does it occur? Why has it become a habit? Ask yourself:

- When do I give in to my bad habit?
- Where do I give in to my bad habit?
- Who is present when I give in to my bad habit?
- How do I feel just before I give in to my bad habit?
- How do I feel just after I give in to my bad habit?

The first three questions help you understand the circumstances in which the habit occurs. For example, you might find yourself gossiping while in the company of certain friends, smoking at the same time every afternoon, or drinking sugary sodas during a certain class.

The last two questions help you understand why you fall into your habit. What feelings drive you to eat that pint of rocky road ice cream? Stress, anger, self-doubt, or boredom? What reward do you get from having that cigarette? Relaxation, satisfaction, or a break from work?

It is important to pinpoint the emotions that are feeding your habit. We are most vulnerable to bad habits when we are troubled by painful or unpleasant emotions. We use our old behavior patterns to comfort us and take our minds off the unpleasant feeling. Take a good look at your worst habit in **Activity 32** on page 240.

Step 3: Replacing the Habit

Now that you know your habit and why it occurs, you can take action. Step 3 involves replacing the bad habit with a positive habit. Replacing a bad habit is easier than simply getting rid of it altogether. Habits are a natural reaction to certain situations, stressors, and emotions. Therefore, you need to find a new, healthy way to release the emotions and nervous energy that are driving your habit. Let's say you want to break the habit of eating chocolate bars to keep yourself going in the late afternoon. The habit is bad for your health, and all that sugar and caffeine makes you dead tired by early evening. You're more likely to break your habit successfully if you switch to a healthy snack, such as vegetables or fruit, than if you simply try to ignore your habit.

Once you choose a replacement for your old ways of thinking and acting, you'll need to repeat the new habit many, many times. Because we've repeated our bad habits so many times, we have to repeat our attempts to break them many times, too. Your bad habits may be quite stubborn, but you can be more so. It's often helpful to use a chart, as in **Personal Journal 6.3** on page 242, to record your progress. This helps you figure out when and where you tend to relapse. Seeing results on paper also boosts your confidence by reminding you of all the times you've already succeeded at resisting the old habit.

Relapse Is Normal   It's normal to revert to a bad habit, especially when we think we've almost beaten it. Suppose you try ten times to break a bad habit, and not until the tenth attempt do you succeed. Does that mean you failed nine times? Does it mean you had no self-discipline? No, it means that with each attempt, your goal got closer and your self-discipline got stronger until you beat the habit. As Mark Twain once said, "Habit is not to be flung out of the window, but coaxed downstairs a step at a time."

Once you successfully replace a habit, you need to maintain it, working continuously to practice your new, positive behavior. You need to develop your new skills and prevent yourself from falling back into your old habits. This effort can last a lifetime.

Use Positive Self-Talk   As you work to change a habit, make sure to support yourself with positive self-talk. Many familiar bad habits—procrastinating, smoking, overeating, oversleeping, and being late—can all be helped with positive self-talk. Positive self-talk helps you paint a new picture of yourself acting in a positive way, creating a new habit pattern to replace the old one.

As you learned in Chapter 4, self-talk has a powerful effect on your subconscious mind. To become more self-disciplined, you need to replace

success *secret*
Are your habits stubborn? Be *more* stubborn!

success *secret*
Use positive self-talk to create a mental image of the new you.

ACTIVITY 32: Getting to Know Your Bad Habits

A What do you see as your worst habit? In other words, what habit is interfering with your life the most right now?

_____

_____

_____

B What negative effects is this habit having on your life? Why?

_____

_____

_____

C What negative effects is this habit having on people you care about? Worry, irritation, hurt feelings? If you aren't sure, ask.

_____

_____

_____

D Spend a few days carefully observing the circumstances surrounding the habit you want to change. Then answer the following questions.

1. When does the habit most often occur (in the morning, on the weekend, etc.)? How often does it occur?

_____

_____

2. Where does the habit occur (at home, at school, in the car, etc.)?

_____

_____

3. When or where is it easier to not give in?

_____

_____

4. Who is usually present when this habit occurs (a certain acquaintance, family members, strangers, peers, etc.)?

_____

_____

5. What unpleasant feelings do you experience just before you give in to your bad habit?

_____

_____

6. What emotional relief or reward do you get from the bad habit?

_____

_____

E Look for a pattern to your habit. What times, places, people, and emotions are associated with your habit? How do they interact with one another?

_____

_____

_____

_____

_____

F What are some more positive ways you could deal with the unpleasant or painful feelings that are behind your habit?

_____

_____

_____

_____

_____

Personal Journal 6.3

Habit Change Chart

Use this chart to track your progress as you substitute a good habit for a bad one.

+   Carried out new habit

0   Carried out neither old nor new habit

—   Carried out old habit

SELF-DISCIPLINE CHART								
Instead of . . . I will . . .	M	T	W	Th	F	Sa	Su	Description of Experience
Example *Instead of drinking sugary soda, I will drink water.*	+	+	0	—	+	+	0	*At first I felt deprived without my usual sugar "fix." When I relapsed, I felt guilty but realized that the sugar high from the soda actually made me feel tired later.*

the information you have already stored in your subconscious mind with new thoughts. By constantly repeating these new thoughts through positive self-talk, you will cause them to take root in your subconscious. The result is a new, positive habit, goal, or self-image.

If you try to change something about yourself only at the conscious level, using willpower, the change usually will be only temporary. Let's say you have been a pack-a-day smoker for many years and decide to give it up. You tell your conscious mind that you are quitting smoking. Then your subconscious mind remembers all the times you have tried to quit in the past and whispers to you that you will fall back into the habit one day soon.

To use self-talk to change a habit, you need to persuade your subconscious mind that the change has already taken place. Instead of saying, "I will stop smoking," say, "I am a nonsmoker." Instead of saying, "I will stop being late," say, "I arrive on time." By thinking of yourself as someone who is on time or a nonsmoker, you will start to see yourself this way. If you say that you will start being on time in the future, you are implying that you are still being late. As long as you see yourself in the present moment as having a bad habit, you will continue to act as if you do.

For habit change, positive self-talk can begin with single sentences:

- I arrive on time for all my classes.
- I am proud of myself for arriving on time.
- Being on time shows respect for the instructor and for the rest of the class.
- Arriving on time shows that I am a responsible person.

The more you use positive self-talk, the more your new self-image and new behavior will become part of you. Soon you will have really kicked the bad habit and replaced it with something more positive.

✅ Self Check

1. Define self-discipline. (p. 222)
2. Why is persistence important? (p. 223)
3. What are the three steps to changing bad habits? (p. 235)

LEARNING TO THINK CRITICALLY

Self-discipline helps us accomplish what we need to do in order to succeed, but it also helps us to do something more—to think.

Our thinking determines much of what we do. Yet few of us stop to consider how we think. Do we think logically, questioning the world around us and coming to our own conclusions? Or do we passively accept what parents, teachers, friends, politicians, advertisers, and "experts" tell us?

Active, self-reflective thinking is known as **critical thinking.** It involves both skills and the self-discipline to consistently apply those skills. Critical thinking requires asking questions and searching for answers. Critical thinkers are able to think objectively about their own and others' opinions. They can look at an issue from all sides before coming to a conclusion. Critical thinkers demand evidence before they believe something that someone else says is true. They are not satisfied with looking at the surface of things. Critical thinkers ask, "Is this true? Is this important? Is this fair?" Passive thinkers ask, "Is this going to be on the test?"

critical thinking
Active, self-reflective thinking.

Benefits of Critical Thinking

Critical thinking is necessary for making important decisions that will affect your life: deciding on a major, choosing or changing a career, going back to school, getting married, having children. As a critical thinker, you need to understand the problem or issue at hand, look at all the different angles, consider the various options, and arrive at the best possible decision.

As a critical thinker, you are also a problem solver. This means that you know how to use tools to reach the best possible solution to any problem. In Chapter 3, you looked at how to overcome obstacles and reach your goals. Critical thinking is essential to overcoming obstacles. It helps you clarify the problem and come up with creative solutions.

In addition to helping with decision making and problem solving, critical thinking helps you develop many other skills and personal qualities that are central to success, including self-awareness, self-honesty, self-motivation, open-mindedness, and empathy.

success *secret*
Critical thinking helps you solve problems and overcome obstacles.

Are You a Critical Thinker?

Critical thinking doesn't come easily. By nature, humans are often irrational. We often view and react to events in a self-serving way, without bothering to think things through. We have a tendency to believe that our ideas, our ways of doing things, and the groups we belong to are better than other people's. For example, many of us are raised to look down on the ways of other families or cultures, such as their child-rearing practices or their religious beliefs. Studies have even shown that we prefer the letter

ARTIFICIAL INTELLIGENCE VERSUS HUMAN INTELLIGENCE

Will there come a day when computers surpass human intelligence? Many believe it's not a question of "if," but "when." With the rapid advancements in artificial intelligence (AI), computers are already taking over jobs meant for humans. Robots have replaced factory workers, surgeons, pilots, and astronauts, as they tend to work faster, don't get easily fatigued, and have exceptional job-task accuracy. Oxford researchers are concluding that 45 percent of U.S. occupations will be at risk for computerization within 20 years. Some experts believe that by the end of the century, intelligent robots may actually "overtake" humans.

IBM's super computer, "Watson," beat out the world's best contestants on the quiz show, "Jeopardy." The Pentagon's mad-science research arm, "Darpa," is looking into humanoid robots capable of working in disaster areas too dangerous for humans, while Momentum Machines is boasting about a robotic burger flipper.

Human beings are able to solve problems by using fast, intuitive judgments, can think unexpectedly when faced with peculiar situations, can think of original ideas, and can plan about the future and foresee potential outcomes of this plan. The psychology field expands human intelligence to include social and emotional components as well. Whether computers and robots can be programmed to match or exceed the sophistication, flexibility, and creativity of the human mind remains to be seen.

Think About It

In what ways will society benefit from computers that are able to think like humans? What are some possible negative repercussions? Why do you think it is important to continue to develop your own critical thinking skills? To learn more about artificial intelligence, go to http://www.livescience.com/29379-intelligent-robots-will-overtake-humans.html or conduct your own search using the keywords "artificial intelligence."

---

our names begin with to other letters of the alphabet! This kind of self-centered thinking is a major obstacle to critical thinking. Do you let laziness and self-centeredness get in the way of your thinking? Complete **Activity 33** to evaluate your critical thinking skills.

Standards of Critical Thinking

Critical thinking is a learned skill; no one is born a critical thinker. The key to thinking critically is to hold yourself to high standards. The Foundation for Critical Thinking specifies seven important standards for excellent critical thinking:

1. Clarity
2. Precision
3. Accuracy
4. Relevance
5. Depth
6. Breadth
7. Logic

Whenever we think, speak, or write, we should try to follow each of these standards.

ACTIVITY 33: How Critical Is Your Thinking?

A Read each statement below. For each one, decide whether you Disagree Totally, Disagree Slightly, Agree Slightly, or Agree Totally.

	Disagree Totally	Disagree Slightly	Agree Slightly	Agree Totally
1. When making an important decision, I am willing to take my time.				
2. I don't feel the need to be right about everything.				
3. I examine my own beliefs as critically as I examine the beliefs of others.				
4. I am more concerned with being fair and accurate than with appearing to be fair and accurate.				
5. I am willing to criticize a popular belief if it is the right thing to do.				
6. When I don't know something, I don't mind admitting it.				
7. I make sure that my beliefs are based on factual evidence.				
8. When I learn material in school, I really try to make sense of it instead of just memorizing it.				
9. I would say that my point of view is a combination of truth and error.				
10. It's more important to be fair and accurate than to be loyal to someone.				
11. I make sure I fully understand something before I judge it.				
12. Just because something is my point of view doesn't mean it's the absolute truth.				
13. I see things in shades of gray rather than in black and white.				
14. I give consideration to facts that contradict my beliefs.				
15. When I encounter a generalization, I immediately look for exceptions.				
16. Before I accept someone's point of view, I evaluate how well they are in a position to know what they are talking about.				
17. I would rather find a solution that benefits everyone than get my own way.				
18. I demand evidence before I will believe something.				
19. I'm willing to try any good idea, even if it's unpopular.				
20. I know exactly why I believe or don't believe certain things.				
21. Before I accept a fact as evidence for a certain statement, I make sure that the fact is relevant to the issue.				
22. An idea can "feel right" but still be wrong.				

B **Scoring:** Give yourself 3 points for every Agree Totally, 2 points for every Agree Slightly, 1 point for every Disagree Slightly, and 0 points for every Disagree Totally.

What is your total? _____

57–66   You are already an accomplished critical thinker. Look back at the statements with which you didn't agree fully and think about how you could integrate them into your thinking.

45–56   You have critical thinking skills, but you are probably too quick to make judgments without thinking things through. Slow down and take time to think systematically.

23–44   You understand some of the basics of critical thinking. You will benefit from investing more time and effort to analyze others' thinking and your own.

0–22   You tend to accept things at face value without questioning. You probably don't analyze your beliefs and have been more concerned with fitting in than with finding the truth.

C All the statements in the questionnaire on the previous page represent habits and attitudes of critical thinkers. Reread the questionnaire and pick the six habits that you believe are most important to fair, impartial, logical thinking. Rewrite them in the format shown below. Then, below each statement, describe how you can apply this habit or attitude in your life.

Example

Critical thinkers make sure they fully understand something before they judge it.

Application: *Instead of criticizing every comment I hear in class, I will give all comments fair consideration.*

1. *Critical thinkers* _____

_____

Application: _____

2. *Critical thinkers* _____

_____

Application: _____

_____

continued...

3. *Critical thinkers* _____

_____

Application: _____

4. *Critical thinkers* _____

_____

Application: _____

_____

5. *Critical thinkers* _____

_____

Application: _____

6. *Critical thinkers* _____

_____

Application: _____

_____

D Look at the different applications you wrote above. What kinds of global changes do you need to make to be a more critical thinker?

_____

_____

_____

_____

_____

_____

1. Clarity

Clarity is the foundation of critical thinking. A thought or statement is clear if it is plainly worded and easily understood. When a thought or statement is muddled and unclear, it is impossible to know whether it is true or false, fact or opinion. Do you think and communicate clearly? Or do you use complicated language to appear more intelligent and sophisticated? Consider the difference between these clear and unclear statements:

Unclear: Students need to indicate which classes on the sign-up sheet they would like to take due to the fact that the December 13 deadline is approaching.

Why It's Unclear: This sentence is too wordy and long-winded. It makes a simple statement into a complicated mess. Economize your thoughts; be direct.

Clear: Students need to sign up for classes before December 13.

Unclear: Many items are discounted up to 50 percent and more.

Why It's Unclear: This statement is deliberately misleading: We don't know which items are discounted, and we don't know whether the discounts are less or more than 50 percent. "Many" could be 20, 200, or 2,000.

Clear: All men's clothing is discounted 25 to 55 percent.

2. Precision

Precision means exactness. Being precise is the opposite of being vague and general. Vague and general statements are sometimes true, but they usually don't say very much. Ask yourself:

precision Exactness.

- Is this statement specific enough to be meaningful?
- Do I need more detail here?

Imprecise: Too much TV makes kids more violent.

Why It's Imprecise: This statement does not specify what kinds of programs make children more violent.

Precise: Children who are exposed to gratuitous violence on TV are more inclined to become aggressive.

Imprecise: Smoking is harmful.

Why It's Imprecise: This statement is true but doesn't provide any useful or memorable specifics.

Precise: Smoking is the number-one preventable cause of death in the United States.

3. Accuracy

Accuracy means factual truth. A statement is accurate if it is supported by facts. A statement is inaccurate if it is an error, a

accuracy Factual truth.

guess, or an opinion pretending to be a fact. If something is based on fact, it can be checked and verified. Ask yourself:

- Is this really true?
- Is it possible to check whether this is true? (If not, the statement is probably not accurate.)
- What is this based on?
- How reliable is the source of this information?

success *secret*

Learn to distinguish facts from opinions.

Inaccurate: Lupita Nyong'o is the most beautiful person in the world.

Why It's Inaccurate: Beauty is subjective, so it's impossible to prove or disprove this statement.

Accurate: In 2014, editors of *People* magazine chose Oscar winner, Lupita Nyong'o, for the cover of their "most beautiful people" issue.

Inaccurate: Our universe started with the "Big Bang."

Why It's Inaccurate: This is a theory, not a fact. It is impossible to check and verify the creation of the universe.

Accurate: No one is really sure how the universe began, but most scientists support the "Big Bang" theory.

4. Relevance
A fact or idea is relevant if it has a direct connection to the subject being discussed. A fact or idea is irrelevant if it has nothing to do with the subject. Ask yourself:

- Is this connected to the issue?
- Is this being introduced to change the subject, criticize others, or shift the blame?

success *secret*

Learn to separate the relevant from the irrelevant.

Irrelevant: Martin is getting a divorce, so he wouldn't be a good choice for vice president.

Why It's Irrelevant: Martin's personal life doesn't have anything to do with his work performance.

Relevant: Martin shows a lack of focus at work, so he wouldn't be a good choice for vice president.

Irrelevant: Juanita once was a vegetarian and shouldn't be elected president of the local meat packers council.

Why It's Irrelevant: Juanita's prior eating habits have nothing to do with the duties she would perform as council president.

Relevant: Juanita does not have a full grasp of her responsibilities as council president and evades direct questions about her previous employment. She should not be elected to the council.

5. Depth
A thought has *depth* if it digs below the surface to consider the substance of the issue. A shallow argument only scratches the surface, while a deep argument examines all sides of the issue. Ask yourself:

- Am I just skimming over the problem?
- Am I going along with what someone else says without thinking things through?
- Is this issue more complex than it seems?

Shallow: Building more prisons will solve our drug problem.

Why It's Shallow: This is a superficial solution to a difficult problem.

Deep: Building more prisons will allow more drug dealers to be imprisoned, but it won't address the causes of drug addiction.

Shallow: This smartphone is the latest model, so it must be the best.

Why It's Shallow: Just because something is the newest doesn't mean it's the best.

Deep: This CD player has lots of new features, but it doesn't have better sound quality than older models.

6. Breadth

Breadth is the degree to which a statement considers other arguments and points of view. To think broadly, you need to detect and analyze the biases that affect other people's judgments, as well as your own. Ask yourself:

- Is there another way to look at this?
- How are my own experiences and values coloring my thinking?
- Am I seeing things from a narrow point of view?
- How would this look from a different point of view?

Narrow: Environmentalists think owls are more important than people.

Why It's Narrow: This statement deliberately distorts environmentalists' point of view. Job losses occur when land formerly used for logging becomes protected habitat for endangered species. This doesn't mean that environmentalists are anti-human.

Broad: Environmentalists want to preserve wildlife habitat by reducing logging on public lands.

Narrow: I don't know why people like Mike's guitar playing—it's terrible.

Why It's Narrow: This statement assumes that there is only one correct point of view on Mike's guitar playing.

Broad: Mike's guitar playing appeals to jazz fans, but it doesn't appeal to me.

> **success** *secret*
> Remember that your point of view is only one of many.

7. Logic

Logic is the process of reasoning correctly and drawing the correct conclusions from the facts. Being logical also involves providing valid explanations for your conclusions. Instead of taking ideas for granted, make sure solid evidence supports them. To determine whether your reasoning is logical, ask yourself:

- Do I have evidence for this statement?
- Is there any evidence that contradicts this statement?

> **logic** The process of reasoning correctly and drawing the correct conclusions from the facts.

- Is this really true, or am I just taking it for granted?
- Is there any other possible conclusion?
- Do any of my ideas contradict one another?

Illogical: Women cry more often than men. They are obviously more emotional.

Why It's Illogical: Crying doesn't prove that women are more emotional. It proves that they show emotions differently.

Logical: Women cry more often than men. They display emotions differently than men do.

Illogical: All of our students are above average.

Why It's Illogical: It is statistically impossible for a majority of people to be above average when compared to each other.

Logical: All of our students have special talent in a certain area.

Critical thinking is important but not always easy. It is a learning process, requiring time and practice. Following specific guidelines, such as the seven standards described above, is an excellent way to become a more effective critical thinker. Do you follow these seven standards of critical thinking in your thought, speech, and writing? Can you recognize when one or more of these standards is missing? Resolve to work hard to overcome the thinking pitfalls that are particularly challenging for you. Try your hand at correcting flawed thinking in **Activity 34** on pages 253–254.

BECOMING A BETTER DECISION MAKER

Important decisions can affect your life for years to come. For this reason, intelligent decision making is one of the most important benefits of effective critical thinking.

A **decision** is a reasoned choice among several options, or possible courses of action. We make minor decisions all day long—what to wear, what to eat, what route to take to school—without thinking much about the process. When it comes to major decisions, however, we need to rely on a step-by-step decision-making process.

decision A reasoned choice among several options, or possible courses of action.

Why Good Decisions Matter

We all face many important decisions over the course of our lives—academic decisions, career decisions, relationship decisions, and other personal decisions. Although it's easy to feel like we don't have to make a decision until we are faced with a problem, no positive change happens without making decisions. To turn our dreams into reality, we have to take concerted action, and this action requires making decisions.

ACTIVITY 34: Developing Your Critical Thinking

A   Below are seven statements, one for each of the seven standards of critical thinking. Each statement fails to meet the standard in some way. Explain what is wrong with each statement, then rewrite each one to correct the flaw.

1. Clarity

Unclear: All are invited to partake in refreshments in the parking lot after the festivities of the football game have reached their conclusion.

Why It's Unclear: _____

Clear: _____

2. Precision

Imprecise: Internet companies are out to scam people.

Why It's Imprecise: _____

Precise: _____

3. Accuracy

Inaccurate: Drug testing doesn't work.

Why It's Inaccurate: _____

Accurate: _____

4. Relevance

Irrelevant: Steve is not well liked; that's why he's flunking all his classes.

Why It's Irrelevant: _____

Relevant: _____

continued...

5. Depth

Shallow: Our government only passes good laws.

Why It's Shallow: _____

Deep: _____

6. Breadth

Narrow: The painting looks like chickens ran across it. No one could like such a thing.

Why It's Narrow: _____

Broad: _____

7. Logic

Illogical: Jane, who lives in a rundown neighborhood, steals from her friends. All people who live in rundown areas steal from others.

Why It's Illogical: _____

Logical: _____

B Few people follow all seven of these critical thinking standards all the time. What flaws do you see most often in your thinking? In others' thinking? Explain.

_____

_____

_____

C Politicians are sometimes accused of ignoring the standards of critical thinking—especially breadth and depth—in their speeches and campaign statements. Why might a politician deliberately do this?

_____

_____

_____

Decisions are important opportunities to take control of your life. When you make a decision, you are intervening in the flow of your life. You are creating a new future for yourself. For example, let's say that you decide to move to a new city instead of remaining in your hometown. By making this important decision, you are creating an entirely new set of circumstances for yourself. You are creating a future that will be entirely different from the future that you would otherwise have.

Handling Mistakes

When we look back at decisions we have made in the past, we can see that some brought us closer to our goals, while some sidetracked us. Some decisions were consistent with our values, and some were not. Some boosted our self-esteem, and some lowered it. The more aware we become of which decisions were right for us and which were not, the better equipped we will be to make good decisions in the future.

Because no one can accurately predict the future, everyone makes mistakes. A **mistake** is anything you did in the past that you now wish you had done differently. At the time, given the limited information you had, your decision seemed like the best possible one. It is only later, after you live the consequences, that you label your action (or inaction) a mistake. Mistakes can actually be valuable tools for you to learn, and can help you on the path to success as long as you view them in a healthy light. People who fear mistakes have trouble making decisions for fear of doing the wrong thing. Perhaps this means staying in a dead-end job for fear of new responsibilities or avoiding social situations for fear of suffering rejection. Instead of fearing mistakes, accept them as part of being human and view them as learning experiences.

mistake Anything you did in the past that you now wish you had done differently.

Steps in the Decision-Making Process

People often make important decisions on impulse or based on inaccurate information or wishful thinking. The best way to make important decisions, however, is to follow a **decision-making process,** a logical series of steps to identify and evaluate possibilities and to arrive at a good choice. A good decision-making process has seven logical steps:

Step 1: Define the decision you need to make.

Step 2: List all possible options.

Step 3: Gather information on the consequences of each option.

Step 4: Assess the consequences of each option relative to your values and goals.

Step 5: Choose one of the possible options.

Step 6: Act.

Step 7: Evaluate your progress, changing course if necessary.

decision-making process A logical series of steps to identify and evaluate options and to arrive at a good choice.

Wanted: Problem Solvers

As the job market becomes more competitive, particularly for college graduates, companies are looking for candidates with more than work experience and technical expertise. According to *Forbes* magazine, a survey by CareerBuilder identified the ten most in-demand skills for top jobs of 2013, with the following being at the top of the list: (1) critical thinking, (2) complex problem solving, and (3) judgment and decision making. Much of what you will do on the job involves seeking solutions, weighting alternatives, conferring with others, evaluating your decisions and determining if the same course of action makes sense the next time.

A national survey of business and nonprofit leaders conducted by the Association of American Colleges and Universities (AAC&U) found that nearly all employers surveyed (93 percent) say that "a demonstrated capacity to think critically, communicate clearly, and solve complex problems is more important than a candidate's undergraduate major."

And once you're hired, continuing to develop these skills will contribute to your advancement and earning potential. The majority of Fortune 500 companies include problem solving, critical thinking, and decision-making as core competencies for leadership excellence.

What's Your Opinion?

What are some examples you could give a potential employer of how you've used your problem-solving and decision-making skills in school and how that relates to future performance on the job? To learn more about problem-solving decision making, go to one of the following sites:

http://www.studygs.net/creative.htm
https://psychology.about.co/od/problemsolving
http://www.skillsyouneed.com/ips/decision-making.html

Let's look at each step carefully, considering how to recognize and overcome errors that can creep into the process. Once you have thoroughly explored each step, you will try your hand at making a hypothetical decision in **Activity 35** on pages 257–259.

Step 1: Define the Decision

The first step in the decision-making process is to define what needs to be decided and why. This sounds obvious, but sometimes you need to go below the surface to find out exactly what question or problem you're facing. This is a good time to be creative in your thinking, perhaps turning what seems to be a problem into an opportunity. For example, deciding how to deal with an increased workload may seem like a problem, but showing your boss that you can work under pressure could be an opportunity for a pay raise or a promotion.

framing effect The decision-making bias that results from the way a decision, question, or problem is worded.

As you define what you need to decide, be aware that the way a decision, question, or problem is worded biases the way you decide it. This psychological process is known as the **framing effect.** As an example, imagine that you have been offered a new job but aren't sure whether you

ACTIVITY 35: Using the Decision-Making Process

A **Define the Decision.** Consider the following scenario. You have taken a new job downtown that will require a lengthy commute from your apartment in the suburbs. Your car is more than ten years old and has been in the shop several times during the past year. Now it needs a transmission overhaul, too. Your new job starts this coming Monday. What do you need to decide? Write down several different ways of defining the decision you have to make, then put a check mark next to the one that best expresses the decision facing you.

_____

_____

_____

_____

_____

_____

B **List Options.** Two options immediately come to mind: buy a new car or get the old car repaired. Are there any other options? Generate four more.

1. *Buy a new car.*

2. *Get the old car repaired.*

3. _____

4. _____

5. _____

6. _____

continued...

C Gather Information. Assemble information on each option you thought of in B above. Consider all the relevant factors—time, money, safety, convenience, lifestyle, and so on. Consulting people with experience is a good way to gather information about the possible consequences of a decision. For this decision, whom could you consult?

_____

_____

_____

D Assess. Now that you know more about each option, assess how well each one fits with your values and goals.

1. PROS: _Will give me sense of safety and security; promotes my value of independence_

   CONS: _Will sidetrack my savings goals for a few years_

2. PROS: _Will help me save for future and conserve resources_

   CONS: _Car may require future repairs, damaging my financial security_

3. PROS: _____

   CONS: _____

4. PROS: _____

   CONS: _____

5. PROS: _____

   CONS: _____

6. PROS: _____

   CONS: _____

E **Choose.** Which option is the most attractive, given the information you have right now?

_____

_____

Now that you have made your decision, actively discard the other options.
Focus on the positive aspects of your decision. Sign here to indicate your commitment to your decision:

_____

(If you feel uncomfortable with your decision, go back over steps A–E.)

F **Take Action. Get started!** What are three things you could do right away—today—to implement your decision?

1. _____

2. _____

3. _____

G **Evaluate.** Monitor how well the decision is working for you. If you decide that the decision you made is not ideal, what are five things you could do to make it better?

1. _____

   _____

2. _____

   _____

3. _____

   _____

4. _____

   _____

5. _____

   _____

should accept it. Think how the following different ways of framing the decision might affect the choice you make:

- Should I accept this new job?
- Should I settle for this new job?
- Should I reject this new job?
- Should I continue my job search?
- Should I remain unemployed?

Sometimes we unconsciously frame a decision in a certain way because we already know how we really want to decide. When you are faced with a decision, take care to frame the decision in different ways so that you don't exclude any possible options.

success *secret*
Consider every possible option.

Step 2: List All Possible Options
Step 2 is to generate options. Write down every idea, even if it seems silly to you. Even a silly idea might lead to a good option once your creative juices get flowing. Don't be satisfied with one or two options; brainstorm until you have a wide range of possible courses of action from which to choose. Also, consult other people—they can often suggest options you might not have thought of, especially if they have different experiences and points of view.

As you make your list, analyze your expectations about the situation—they may limit your options. For example, people usually choose the very first option that comes to mind, even if it isn't the best one. They also tend to block out information that might make them change their minds. You can avoid this pitfall by generating as many options as possible, seeking the advice of people who have ideas that are different from yours, and allowing yourself plenty of time to generate many options.

Step 3: Gather Information
The more information you can gather about your decision, the easier it will be to generate options and then evaluate them. This is most obvious in a financial decision, such as buying car insurance, where you'll need to gather information on your needs and options. You also need to gather information when making important personal decisions. For example, if you are trying to decide between two different majors at school, you'll want to consider the cost, length, and difficulty of the two programs; the career opportunities in the two fields; and how well your values, interests, and abilities fit with each one.

The Internet can be a wonderful resource for gathering facts and information. Friends or coworkers who have experience in the area you are researching can also be a valuable resource. An informed decision will go a long way toward helping you accomplish your goals.

Step 4: Assess the Consequences

Step 4 is to look into the future and try to gauge the possible outcomes of each course of action. What will the positive consequences of a certain option be? What will the negative consequences be? One good way to organize this information is to make a list of pros and cons for each option you are considering. For example, let's say you are deciding whether to return to school for a degree. The pros of going back to school might include intellectual stimulation and greater career mobility, while the cons might include less free time and more stress.

As you organize your pros and cons, use your values and goals as standards to judge each course of action. Does the option harmonize with your core values? Does it get you closer to your goals? Is it what you believe, deep down, you should do? Try this approach to organizing your options in **Personal Journal 6.4** on page 262. Committing this information to paper is a good way of safeguarding the decision-making process from interference by forgetfulness, old habits, and changing moods. The process of writing also helps you generate ideas.

As you consider the pros and cons of each option, remember that you will always be faced with some uncertainty. You can never fully predict all the consequences of every option. **Uncertainty** means not knowing what the consequences of a decision will be for yourself and others. Uncertainty about the future can lead to paralyzing indecision. However, uncertainty is an unavoidable part of decision making. Doing research can help you predict many of the consequences of your decisions, but you can never be entirely sure what the future will bring.

uncertainty Not knowing what the consequences of a decision will be for yourself and others.

Step 5: Choose One Option

It's the moment of truth. You have acceptance letters from two colleges. Your mouse cursor is hovering over the send button to e-mail your decision to your boss. Feelings of hesitation and self-questioning are normal at a time like this. Sometimes it's hard to figure out which option is the best one. In this situation, you experience conflict. In a decision-making context, *conflict* occurs when no option is significantly more attractive than the others. When we are in conflict, we might be tempted to make no decision at all, holding out for some imaginary solution that will have no negative consequences. We can help ourselves deal with the inherent conflict of decision making by focusing on one central value or goal.

Once you've made your choice, remember that you've done everything in your power to choose the right course. Whether or not the outcome is favorable, you can be confident that your decision was a good one.

Personal Journal 6.4

Pros and Cons

Think of a major decision you are now facing or are likely to face in the near future. Choose two possible courses of action and write down which goal(s) and value(s) each option would support and which it would go against.

PROS		
Action	Goal(s) it would support	Value(s) it would support
Option 1.		
Option 2.		

CONS		
Action	Goal(s) it would contradict	Value(s) it would contradict
Option 1.		
Option 2.		

Based on this information, which option would you choose?

Step 6: Act
A decision only has value if you act on it. This is why a choice is sometimes described as a "course of action." Without action, a decision is an empty gesture.

Try to avoid the pitfall of coming to a mental conclusion to solve a problem, then resting on the feeling of commitment rather than the act of commitment. Indecision creates a kind of mental tension. This tension begins to ease as soon as we make a choice. Taking action on that choice, however, is even more satisfying and will help you become a better decision maker.

After making any kind of significant decision, it is common to feel regret. **Regret** is the feeling of wishing you had decided something differently. You are less likely to suffer from regret if you make decisive, informed choices. If you take action—even the wrong action—you will suffer fewer pangs of regret than if you simply do nothing at all. Don't let fear of regret scare you away from making a decision.

Abraham Lincoln made this phrase famous: "Never change horses midstream." In other words, once you have made a choice, commit to it. If you feel like going back on your decision, make sure you are acting on an impartial evaluation of the situation rather than on an impulse based on fear or regret.

Step 7: Evaluate Your Progress
To make decisions effectively, you need to learn from experience. Therefore, evaluating your progress is an important part of the decision-making process. Evaluate how well the decision is working for you, remembering that every major decision leads to other decisions down the road. Keeping a journal of your progress can be helpful. As you monitor your results, ask yourself:

- Did I overlook any information that would be helpful in the future?
- Would another approach to the decision have worked better?
- Did I allow myself adequate time to generate options?
- What can I learn from the experience to help me make a better decision the next time around?

success *secret*
The results of your decisions can teach you a great deal.

Often, decisions that seem like disasters provide the best lessons of all. They can help you learn more about yourself and your thinking style.

It's Up to You
Using the decision-making process helps you build self-determination and critical thinking skills. As you develop the ability to gather reliable information, to think of creative options, and to make choices based on your goals and values, you will feel more and more in control of your life. If you avoid making decisions, on the other hand, your life will start to pass you by. Physical and mental self-discipline will help you overcome indecision and do what you need to do to reach your goals.

Learning to make good decisions takes time and practice. Once you have mastered the ability to make decisions confidently and accept the consequences without self-blame, you will be well on your way to success.

Self Check

1. Define critical thinking. (p. 244)
2. What are some of the benefits of being a critical thinker? (p. 244)
3. What is regret? (p. 263)

Chapter 6 Review and Activities

Key Terms

self-discipline (p. 222)

persistence (p. 223)

self-determination (p. 224)

responsibility (p. 224)

impulse (p. 227)

consequences (p. 229)

habit (p. 235)

critical thinking (p. 244)

precision (p. 249)

accuracy (p. 249)

logic (p. 251)

decision (p. 252)

mistake (p. 255)

decision-making process (p. 255)

framing effect (p. 256)

uncertainty (p. 261)

regret (p. 263)

Summary by Learning Objectives

- **Define self-discipline and cite its benefits.** Self-discipline is the process of teaching ourselves to do what is necessary to achieve our goals. Self-discipline strengthens our ability to control our destiny, persist in the face of setbacks, weigh the long-term consequences of our actions, make positive changes, break bad habits, think critically, and make effective decisions.

- **Explain how to control impulses.** We can control impulses in three steps: 1. stop; 2. think about the pleasant short-term consequences and the unpleasant long-term consequences of the action; and 3. decide whether the pleasant short-term consequences are worth the negative long-term ones.

- **Describe the process of replacing bad habits with good ones.** Changing our bad habits involves three major steps: 1. wanting to change; 2. understanding the bad habit; and 3. replacing the bad habit with a new, healthy habit.

- **Define critical thinking and list its seven standards.** Critical thinking is active, reflective thinking that involves both thinking skills and the self-discipline to apply those skills. The seven standards for excellent critical thinking are clarity, precision, accuracy, relevance, depth, breadth, and logic.

- **List the steps in the decision-making process.** A good decision-making process follows a logical series of steps to identify and evaluate possibilities and make the best decision. The process involves seven steps: 1. defining the decision that needs to be made; 2. listing all possible options; 3. gathering information on the consequences of each option; 4. assessing the consequences of each option relative to your values and goals; 5. choosing one option; 6. acting on the decision; and 7. evaluating your progress.

Review and Activities

Review Questions

1. What is the difference between persistence and self-determination?

2. Why do some people resist change?

3. What three stages do people go through before they begin to take action to break a habit?

4. How can positive self-talk help you change a bad habit?

5. Describe the framing effect and how it might affect the decision-making process.

6. Why do people sometimes regret the decisions they make?

Critical Thinking

7. **Adapting to Change**   Imagine that you are chronically late to work, and one day your boss announces that employees who come late will be fired. This forces you to begin arriving on time. Now imagine that you are chronically late, but you decide of your own free will to begin arriving on time. In both cases, you need to make the same behavioral change: arriving on time for work. Would this change be easier for you in the first or in the second scenario? Why? What does this tell you about your self-discipline?

8. **Self-Discipline**   Parents help their children develop self-discipline by setting clear, reasonable limits, or guidelines, for acceptable and unacceptable behavior. For example, parents of toddlers often set limits such as "share toys with playmates" and "do not bite." Why would a child who is given no limits have difficulty developing self-discipline later in life? Why would a child who is given too many limits also have difficulty developing self-discipline?

Application

9. **Habit Survey**   Interview three people who have changed a bad habit into a healthy habit. How did they achieve their success? How long did it take? Did they ever have a relapse? If so, what did they learn from each relapse? What behaviors from these interviews would you like to adopt and use in your own life?

10. **Decision Making**   Describe one or two major decisions you have made in your life. How did you go about making your decision? What were your challenges? What were the consequences? What did you learn to help you in making future decisions?

Internet Activities

11. **Critical Thinking Quiz**   Visit http://www.cof.orst.edu/cof/teach/for442/quizzes/q1003.htm to take a fun and challenging quiz to test your ability to think critically and creatively. You will receive your personal score, as well as discover the rationales for the correct answers.

12. **Habits of Mind**   Visit http://www.habitsofmind.org/content/managing-impulsivity to read an online article about habits of mind, specifically, managing impulsivity. Think about how some of your own impulsive behaviors have hurt you in the past. Determine steps you can take to develop your self-discipline, delay gratification, and more effectively manage impulsivity.

Real-Life Success Story

"Should I Make a Change?"

Review your answer to the question in the Real-Life Success Story on page 220. Think about how you would you answer the question now that you have learned more about self-discipline and the process of change.

Complete the Story   Write a note to Jeannette describing the factors that could be holding her back from making her desired change. Then give her advice on overcoming her fear of change and using self-discipline to reach her goal.

"How Can I Succeed?"

Running Late

Elijah Wells, a salesman, had gone back to college to earn his business degree and get a better paying job. Elijah always did the first half of his assignments, but he could never seem to complete them. He often felt too discouraged to go to class, especially on test days. Elijah blamed his difficulties on his instructors' impossibly high standards. He was taken aback when his advisor suggested that his real problem was himself—he was making himself fail because he was afraid of succeeding.

Running Scared

It sounded crazy at first, but Elijah began to realize that his self-defeating behavior really did come from a fear of success. Deep down, he thought he wasn't college material. How could he hold his own with the other, younger students? What if his friends deserted him once he got a degree and a promotion? Instead of focusing on success, he was letting fear lead him straight to failure.

What Do You Think? Why would someone fear success?

Self-Motivation

7 Chapter

introduction

Motivation drives us to reach our goals and realize our full potential. In Section 7.1 you'll explore the different types of motivation and learn why internal motivation is the most lasting form of motivation. You'll also learn how your needs and wants drive your behavior. In Section 7.2 you'll work on overcoming the fears that can drain your motivation and make you afraid to take risks. You'll also learn to use visualization to boost your motivation and self-expectancy.

learning objectives

After you complete this chapter, you should be able to:

- Contrast intrinsic motivation with extrinsic motivation.

- Describe how to distinguish needs from wants.

- Explain why needs motivate our behavior.

- Cite ways to overcome fear of failure.

- Cite ways to overcome fear of success.

- Describe visualization and how it can boost motivation.

Understanding Motivation

THE POWER OF MOTIVATION

motivation The force that moves you to action.

Everything we do is the result of motivation. **Motivation** is the inner force that compels behavior; that moves us to action, giving us energy, direction, and persistence. Motivation moves us toward the goals we have set. Even in the face of mistakes, discouragement, and setbacks, our positive inner drive keeps us moving ahead.

To be successful, you must depend on yourself for motivation. Instead of waiting for something or someone to jump-start you into action, you need to actively look for ways to motivate yourself. When you are self-motivated, you can rely on your own strength and drive to take you where you want to go.

High achievers have high self-motivation; the power to move them to action comes from inside themselves. Sometimes just a little more motivation than usual can lead to incredible results. Think about the difference between simple boiling water and powerful steam. When water is heated to 211 degrees Fahrenheit, it is simply boiling water. Yet when the temperature reaches 212 degrees, only one degree higher, the water becomes steam, which is powerful enough to launch a Navy jet from an aircraft carrier at a speed of 120 miles an hour in only five seconds.

success *secret*
Look for ways to motivate yourself.

Positive and Negative Motivation

We may be driven toward a situation or away from it, depending on how we feel inside. When we are driven toward success, we experience positive motivation. When we are driven away from failure, we experience negative motivation. These two forces are shown in Figure 7.1.

positive motivation The drive to do something because it will move you toward a goal.

Positive motivation is the drive to do something we want to do because it will move us toward a goal or because we associate it with positive thoughts and feelings. We might be positively motivated to work hard on learning a skill or writing a term paper, for example, because it gives us a feeling of accomplishment or because we have a natural curiosity about the topic. Positive motivation boosts our feelings of optimism and self-esteem.

negative motivation The drive to do something in order to avoid negative consequences.

Negative motivation, by contrast, is the drive to do something we have to do in order to avoid punishment or other negative consequences. If we are negatively motivated, we might work hard on a term paper because we are afraid of getting a low grade or disappointing the teacher.

Negative motivation isn't necessarily bad. When our positive motivation is low, it can help us do the things we need to do. Let's say you are afraid of being called on in a certain class. You're tired and can't summon the positive motivation to study. However, the fear of being unprepared or giving the wrong answer might motivate you to study extra hard.

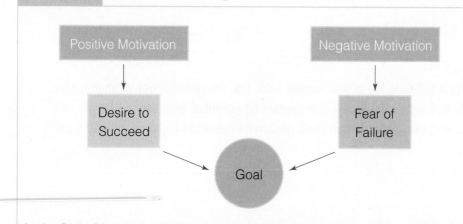

FIGURE 7.1 Positive and Negative Motivation

Positive Motivation → Desire to Succeed → Goal

Negative Motivation → Fear of Failure → Goal

In the Right Direction   Positive motivation harnesses the power of positive thoughts and feelings to move you closer to your goal. *Why do you think negative motivation is associated with low self-esteem?*

When we are positively motivated, we engage in activities that bring us closer to our goals and that give us a sense of pride and accomplishment. When we are negatively motivated, we are driven by unpleasant thoughts and feelings, such as fear, worry, and self-doubt.

We've seen that whatever we spend the most energy thinking about is what will come to pass, whether it is something we fear or something we desire. Positive motivation makes us feel that we are achieving success, rather than simply avoiding failure. If you are experiencing negative motivation, try to consciously switch your thoughts from what you need to avoid to what you want to achieve. Instead of worrying about giving the wrong answer in class, for example, you can choose to focus on why you are in school, what you are gaining from this class, and how you are moving closer to your goals. Work on changing negatives into positives in **Personal Journal 7.1** on page 272.

success *secret*
Positive motivation brings you closer to your goals.

Sources of Motivation

Motivation can come from two sources: outside and inside. Motivation that comes from outside is known as **extrinsic motivation.** *Extrinsic* means external. Motivation that comes from inside is known as **intrinsic motivation.** *Intrinsic* means internal. Intrinsic motivation is the source of all true motivation.

Intrinsic and extrinsic motivation are very different. Intrinsic motivation is positive motivation that fuels your interests and passions. It drives you to do things that you enjoy and that allow you to grow as a person, such as:

extrinsic motivation
Motivation that comes from outside.

intrinsic motivation
Motivation that comes from inside.

- seeking excellence and independence
- feeling good about yourself
- understanding your world
- staying true to your inner values
- determining the course of your life

Personal Journal 7.1

Generating Positive Motivation

Imagine that you are searching for a full-time job in your career field. The job search involves many steps, including perfecting your résumé, gathering references, and contacting potential employers. Will you be negatively motivated or positively motivated? Transform each negative motivation listed below into a positive motivation.

Example

I have to get this job to avoid defaulting on my student loans.

<u>Getting this job will be a big step toward reaching my financial goals.</u>

- -

I have to work hard on my résumé, or else I won't get any interviews.

_____

I'm gathering references because no one will hire me without them.

_____

I'm applying for lots of jobs because I don't want to feel like I missed an opportunity.

_____

I need to practice interview techniques so I don't bungle it on the big day.

_____

I have to follow up on the interview, or else they'll think I don't want the job.

_____

Extrinsic motivation, on the other hand, is more like a quick fix. You do things not because you really want to, but because they are a means to an end, such as:

- looking good
- fitting in socially
- pleasing others
- earning a material reward

- feeling superior to others
- avoiding trouble or punishment

Extrinsic motivation represents positive motivation when it moves you toward a desired goal such as financial independence, professional achievement, or social acceptance. It represents negative motivation, however, when it is based on gaining status, fame and power or when it is based on fear and avoidance. Extrinsic motivation can provide encouragement or inspiration to act, but it only lasts for a while and is a poor substitute for more lasting and satisfying intrinsic goals. Lasting motivation only exists when you feel it inside. You must really want something for yourself to be motivated to attain it.

Intrinsic and Extrinsic Goals

People tend to have different goals depending on what kind of motivation they have. Those who have intrinsic motivation aim for *intrinsic goals,* such as building relationships, giving to others, growing as individuals, and making the most of their potential. People with extrinsic motivation, by contrast, usually aim for *extrinsic goals,* such as acquiring possessions, wealth, fame, beauty, or a glamorous image. It's not wrong or bad to have extrinsic goals, but most people who have a strong drive for money, fame, or a glamorous image live in fear that these desires will never be fulfilled or that they may not last. Even people who do attain these goals often suffer negative symptoms such as anxiety and depression. No matter how much they have, it never seems like enough. Emphasis on intrinsic goals, such as relationships, community involvement, and health, on the other hand, goes hand in hand with greater well-being.

Often, people who have extrinsic goals are trying to fulfill an emotional need with a material object. Jerry's need for an Italian sports car, for example, stems from his feelings of low self-esteem. He is hoping that a glamorous possession will give him a sense of self-worth.

Where does your motivation come from? What drives you to do what you do? What do your goals look like? Use **Activity 36** on page 274 to assess your intrinsic and extrinsic motivation.

Understanding Incentives

As we have seen, people who are extrinsically motivated are concerned with looking good, avoiding punishment, or earning some kind of reward. A reward offered in order to motivate a person to do something is known as an **incentive.** Have you ever won a contest or received an award, where you were recognized by family, friends, teachers, or peers? If so, you have felt the pull and satisfaction of incentives.

Most schools and companies use incentives to motivate people. Schools hand out rankings, special awards, praise from instructors, and prizes and scholarships. Companies use benefits, bonuses, exotic travel trips, pay raises, and improvements to the work environment.

success *secret*
Aim for inner fulfillment, not outward achievements.

incentive A reward offered in order to motivate a person to do something.

ACTIVITY 36: What Motivates You?

A For each item, circle the letter (a, b, or c) of the statement that describes your most likely reaction to the situation described.

1. You have been offered a new position in a company where you have worked for some time. The first thought that likely comes to mind is:

   a. I wonder if the new work will be interesting.

   b. What if I can't live up to the new responsibility?

   c. Will I make more money at this position?

2. You have a school-age daughter. On parents' night, the teacher tells you that your daughter is doing poorly and doesn't seem involved in the work. You are likely to:

   a. Talk it over with your daughter to understand further what the problem is.

   b. Scold her and hope she does better.

   c. Make sure she does the assignments because she should be working harder.

3. You had a job interview several weeks ago. In the mail you receive a form letter which states that the position has been filled. It is likely that you might think:

   a. Somehow they didn't see my qualifications as matching their needs.

   b. I'm probably not good enough for the job.

   c. It's not what you know, but who you know.

4. You are a plant supervisor and have been charged with the task of allotting coffee breaks to three workers who cannot all break at once. You would likely handle this by:

   a. Telling the three workers the situation and having them work with you on the schedule.

   b. Finding out from someone in authority what to do, or doing what was done in the past.

   c. Simply assigning times that each can break.

5. A close (same-sex) friend of yours has been moody lately. On a few occasions, this person has become very angry with you over "nothing." You might:

   a. Share your observations with him or her and try to find out what is going on.

   b. Ignore it because there's not much you can do about it anyway.

   c. Tell your friend that you're willing to spend time together only if he or she makes more effort at self-control.

6. You have just received the results of a test you took, and you have discovered that you did very poorly. Your initial reaction will probably be to:

   a. Feel disappointed and wonder how you did so poorly.

   b. Feel sad and blame yourself for not being able to do anything right.

   c. Feel angry because that stupid test doesn't show anything.

7. You have been invited to a large party where you know very few people. As you look forward to the evening, you would likely expect that:

   a. You'll try to fit in with whatever is happening in order to have a good time and not look bad.

   b. You'll probably feel somewhat isolated and unnoticed.

   c. You'll find some people to whom you can relate.

8. You are asked to plan a picnic for yourself and your fellow employees. Your style for approaching this project could most likely be characterized as:

   a. Taking charge: You would make most of the major decisions yourself.

   b. Following precedent: You're not really up to the task, so you'd do it the way it's been done before.

   c. Seeking participation: You would get input from others before you make the final plans.

9. Recently a position opened up at your workplace that could have meant a promotion for you. However, a person you work with was offered the job rather than you. In evaluating the situation, you're likely to think:

   a. The other person probably "did the right things" politically to get the job.

   b. You didn't really expect the job; you frequently get passed over.

   c. You should probably take a look at factors in your own performance that led you to be passed over.

10. You are embarking on a new career. The most important consideration is likely to be:

    a. Whether there are good possibilities for advancement.

    b. Whether you can do the work without getting in over your head.

    c. How interested you are in that kind of work.

11. A woman who works for you has generally done an adequate job. However, for the past two weeks her work has not been up to par, and she appears to be less actively interested in her work. Your reaction will probably be to:

    a. Tell her that her work is below what is expected and that she should start working harder.

    b. Hesitate; it's hard to know what to do to get her straightened out.

    c. Ask her about the problem and let her know you are available to help work it out.

12. Your company has promoted you to a position in another city. As you think about the move, you would probably:

    a. Feel excited about the higher status and salary that is involved.

    b. Feel stressed and anxious about the upcoming changes.

    c. Feel interested in the new challenge and a little nervous at the same time.

Source: Adapted from Edward L. Deci and Richard M. Ryan, "The General Causality Orientations Scale: Self-Determination in Personality," *Journal of Research in Personality* 19 (1985); 109-134.

continued...

B **Scoring:** First, go back to number 7. Beginning with this item and continuing through number 12, change each A you circled to a C; change each C to an A. Now add up the total number of A's, B's, and C's you selected, and use the information below to interpret your results.

A's _____   B's _____   C's _____

Mostly A's: You are high in intrinsic motivation. You tend to choose situations that stimulate your internal motivation and provide you with opportunities to improve yourself. You probably show initiative, select activities that are interesting and challenging, and take responsibility for your own behavior.

Mostly B's: You lack motivation because you believe that success and achievement are matters of luck or fate, not of effort on your part. You probably feel that you are unable to make a difference or cope with demands or changes, and you may often feel anxious and ineffective.

Mostly C's: You are high in extrinsic motivation. You tend to be motivated by factors such as rewards, deadlines, structures, and the directives of others. In fact, you may be more attuned to what others demand than to what you want for yourself. You probably place extreme importance on wealth, fame, image, and other outward factors.

C According to the questionnaire, what motivates you? Do you agree or disagree? Explain.

_____

_____

_____

_____

_____

D Why would someone who is intrinsically motivated be more likely to seek interesting and challenging activities than someone who is extrinsically motivated?

_____

_____

_____

_____

_____

Why Incentives Fail   There is nothing inherently wrong with incentives. However, incentives are usually only effective if they reinforce motivation that comes from inside. Let's say that your boss offers you a cash bonus if you improve your job performance by a certain amount. Initially, the offer of money might inspire you to work harder. Unless you are truly interested in being a better employee, however, your motivation is likely to fizzle out fairly quickly. The bonus will only motivate you if you are motivated to improve yourself.

Relying solely on extrinsic rewards as motivation can also be self-defeating, because we can confuse the reward with the goal. For example, a child who is bribed into doing schoolwork by the promise of praise, gold stars, or money may develop the belief that these rewards, not the learning that leads to them, are goals in themselves. An addiction to rewards may discourage us from trying new things for fear of losing other people's approval.

An even bigger problem with incentives is that they usually represent someone else's attempts to control our behavior. Think about the parents who promised their teenage son a large allowance in exchange for earning better grades. This reward was really an attempt to get him to do what they wanted him to do. The reward did nothing to increase his interest in learning.

NEEDS AND MOTIVATION

We've seen that achieving extrinsic goals such as wealth, fame, or image is less satisfying than achieving intrinsic goals such as relationships and self-determination. But why? According to many psychologists, it's because intrinsic achievements, such as relationships and self-determination, meet fundamental human needs. A **need** represents something we must have to survive and thrive.

All of us have both physical and psychological needs. We need not only clothing and a roof over our heads, for example, but also a sense that we are secure and loved by others. We need not only food to sustain our body but also self-esteem to sustain our spirit.

Needs motivate much of our conscious behavior. We work to build social and romantic relationships, for example, because we need acceptance and love from others. We strive to reach our goals because we need to experience self-esteem and a sense of competence.

Needs motivate much of our unconscious behavior as well. For example, we all have a natural tendency to imitate the behaviors, postures, and mannerisms of the people around us. We do this unconsciously to create a climate of empathy and mutual acceptance.

need Something you must have in order to survive and thrive.

Needs and Wants

How can we tell needs from wants? A need represents something we must have in order to function. A **want,** on the other hand, represents something we can survive and thrive without.

want Something you can survive and thrive without.

Wants often take the form of material goods beyond the basics necessary for survival. We all need healthful food, suitable clothing, and secure shelter, for example, but we don't really need gourmet coffee, designer labels, or a four-car garage. Wants like these are perfectly normal, but they are unlikely to provide long-lasting satisfaction. Material extras can be fun, but they don't fulfill our needs. If you are having trouble deciding whether something is a want or a need, ask yourself:

- Will I be satisfied after I get this, or will I want something more?
- Am I hoping that this will boost my self-esteem?
- Am I hoping that this will take away a painful feeling, such as loneliness, sadness, rejection, loss, or emptiness?

If something does not truly satisfy you physically or psychologically, it is probably a want, not a need.

A Hierarchy of Needs

How many essential human needs are there? Two? Fifty? Three hundred? According to psychologist Abraham Maslow, human needs fall into five categories. Maslow's **hierarchy of needs,** shown in Figure 7.2, is a diagram of these five central human needs arranged from the most basic (at the bottom) to the most complex (at the top). The five levels of needs are:

- physical needs
- security needs
- social needs
- esteem needs
- self-actualization needs

Maslow's model assumes that we must meet our basic needs before we can turn our attention to the more complex ones. In other words, we seek to fulfill higher, more complex psychological needs, such as the need for esteem, only after our more basic survival needs have been met. Let's look at each level of the hierarchy of needs.

Physical Needs

Physical needs are the basic needs that support our biological health and survival. Physical needs, the most basic and important of all human needs, include:

- fresh air
- clean water
- nutritious food
- shelter from the elements
- sanitary living conditions
- proper clothing
- basic medical care
- sexual intimacy

Think for a moment about how much of your life is devoted to satisfying your physical needs. You work to pay for food, shelter, clothing, and

hierarchy of needs
A diagram of the five central human needs arranged from the most basic to the most complex.

FIGURE 7.2   Maslow's Hierarchy of Needs

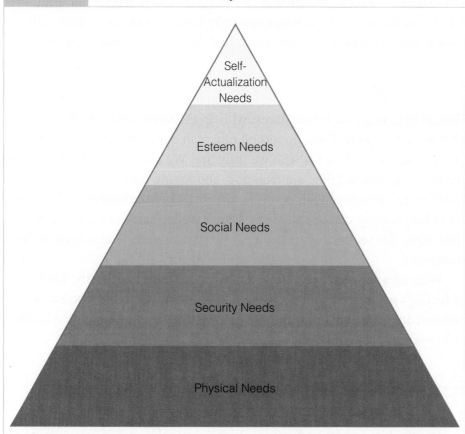

Needs as Motivators   Needs motivate much of our behavior. If we are hungry, we seek food; if we are lonely, we seek companionship; if we are bored, we seek stimulation. *When might someone ignore a lower level need in order to fulfill a higher level need?*

medical care. You do housework and laundry to keep your surroundings clean and sanitary. You go to the doctor and dentist to keep healthy. The more time, money, and energy you must spend to meet your physical needs, the less time, money, and energy you have to spend on meeting higher level needs, such as education or social acceptance. If you have to hold down two jobs to pay the bills, you will be less motivated to pursue an advanced education or devote yourself to serving the community.

success *secret*
Satisfying basic survival
needs requires hard
work.

Security Needs

Once our physical needs are met, security and safety become our next logical concerns. Our needs for safety and security include:

- freedom from physical harm
- a stable environment
- confidence that we can depend on others
- protection from abuse
- freedom from fear, anxiety, and chaos
- structure, order, law, and limits

Before we can seek the fulfillment of higher personal needs, such as self-esteem and social acceptance, we must first have a basic sense of safety and security. Those who constantly worry about their safety will have trouble experiencing happiness, fulfillment, or a sense of belonging.

Social Needs

Human beings are social creatures, with an essential need for others. We all have a need to feel that important others in our lives acknowledge, appreciate, and love us for who we truly are. We also have a need to reciprocate by acknowledging, appreciating, and loving others. This need for fulfilling relationships with others is known as **belongingness.** The need for belongingness can be satisfied through the intimacy of romance or friendship, the security of family ties, or the camaraderie at school or the workplace.

Without a sense of belonging, a person can fall victim to the kinds of feelings associated with depression and low self-esteem: loneliness, unwantedness, or unworthiness. No matter how secure we are physically and psychologically, we always need others.

Esteem Needs

To be happy and successful, people need to feel that they are valuable and worthwhile and that others see them as valuable and worthwhile, too. Esteem from others and self-esteem are closely related. We all need to feel

internet action

STAYING MOTIVATED WITH E-LEARNING

Over the past five years, the number of college students enrolled in an online course has nearly doubled, increasing from 23 percent to 45 percent. As technology options continue to grow exponentially, e-learning will someday soon be considered the "traditional" mode of learning. The greatest challenge students face is motivation. Without physical classrooms and face-to-face interactions with fellow classmates, students can often feel isolated and disconnected. They can easily lose interest in the material and become distracted and unmotivated. Students lacking in motivation will most likely not successfully complete their programs.

It is critical that online students find ways to stay motivated. Being able to share ideas and discuss opinions with others through online study groups, chat rooms, forums, and virtual meetings will help you feel connected. Practicing good time management skills and setting goals for yourself will help you stay on track and keep you from falling behind and getting discouraged. Look for innovative ways to enhance your learning by reading additional articles and viewing videos online. Your success with e-learning is what you make it! It can be very rewarding, fulfilling, and fun!

Think About It

What do you like most about online learning? How do you stay motivated in your classes and ensure you complete your work? To learn more about motivation and e-learning, go to http://www.educationcorner.com/online-education-motivation.html or conduct your own online search using the keywords "online learning," "motivation," and "e-learning."

Applying Psychology

Six Types of Achievement Motivation

1. The first type of achievement motivation is *Status with the Experts*—in other words, gaining recognition as a leader in your field. 2. The second type of achievement motivation is *Acquisitiveness*—which is the desire to acquire something tangible such as a fixed sum of money, a sports car, or a boat. Many people live for the things they love, and they also hate to lose those things. 3. The third type of achievement motivation is *Achievement via Independence*, which is the desire to achieve on your own skills and merits. This could involve going through demanding academic training to become a surgeon, scientist, or any other profession where you are sought after for your ability. 4. The fourth type of achievement motivation is *Status with Peers*. This is different from Status with the Experts because, to put it bluntly, your peers may not be the experts. Many of us are motivated by how we are regarded by our friends or our fellow employees at work. 5. The fifth type of achievement motivation is *Competitiveness,* something we all know about. NBC founder David Sarnoff said, "Competition brings out the best in products and, often, the worst in people." How important is winning at all costs to you? 6. The sixth type of achievement motivation is *Concern for Excellence*. Concern for excellence means that you are motivated every day to be the best you can possibly be in whatever you do. Of the six motivation types, only two—Achievement via Independence and Concern for Excellence—are true intrinsic motivations.

The majority of history's greatest achievers were common men and women with a desire to express something within themselves to solve a problem. Many earned financial security and prestige, but that was only a by-product of their efforts, not a primary motivation. Which of the above motivate you the most? Why?

important, useful, successful, and respected, and we all need for others to recognize our talents and potential.

Low self-esteem can crush our motivation to achieve goals and grow as individuals. To be psychologically healthy, we need to be able to pat ourselves on the back now and then—to celebrate achievements and keep ourselves motivated and to offset those disappointing times when things don't go so well.

Competence   The ability to reach our goals and cope with the challenges of life is key to self-esteem. Because of this, we all have a deep need to feel a sense of competence in the important areas of our lives. **Competence** is the ability to do something well. Being competent means knowing how to do a job well and being able to perform it effectively. We take basic satisfaction in knowing that we have done something well, from making an omelet to writing a book. Once we achieve a goal or build a skill, we are rewarded with the good feeling of knowing that we can accomplish new goals and build new skills. Our self-esteem continues to grow as we set new goals and strive to attain them.

competence The ability to do something well.

Self-Actualization Needs

Self-actualization is the highest level of the hierarchy of needs. Self-actualization means reaching one's full potential and achieving long-term

self-actualization
Reaching your full potential and achieving long-term personal growth.

autonomy Freedom of choice, independence, and the chance to exercise independent judgment.

personal growth. The need for **self-actualization** is the need for personal fulfillment—in other words, for success.

Like success, self-actualization is a journey, not a destination. At no point can we sit back and say to ourselves, "There! I've done everything I need to become self-actualized." We are at our best when we're in a state of constant growth—open to new ideas and quick to make use of new knowledge, even knowledge gained from our mistakes.

Autonomy   We all need autonomy to achieve self-actualization. **Autonomy** means freedom of choice, independence, and the chance to exercise independent judgment. It means having control over our lives, choosing our own activities, and determining our own values.

Autonomy has a powerful effect on our motivation and performance. When we lack autonomy, we feel like powerless participants in a game controlled by others. Our motivation fades quickly. When we have autonomy, however, we are motivated to reach success at both school and work. Students who are free to choose their own educational path, for example, are much more motivated than students who are controlled by their parents. Employees who are given control over their own work are much more motivated than employees who are micromanaged by their supervisors. Have you ever had a job where your supervisor hovered over your shoulder, worried that you might make a mistake? Being controlled in this way robs you of your autonomy and dampens your motivation.

It's time to take a look at your needs. Use **Activity 37** to evaluate how well the three higher level needs are being satisfied in your daily life.

Meeting Your Needs   Imagine that you drew up a list of the things you want most in your life. What would be on the list? Chances are, the things you want the most are the things you need. Let's say you want a successful career and a nurturing relationship. The longing for professional success is related to the need for esteem and self-actualization. The desire for a loving life partner comes from the need for love, acceptance, and belonging. Deep down, we all want and need the same basic things—to feel good about ourselves, have a sense of purpose, be physically and financially secure, grow intellectually, enjoy physical and emotional intimacy with others, and receive compassion and recognition. Think carefully about your wants and needs. This will help you focus on the things that will bring you true success and happiness.

Self Check

1. What is intrinsic motivation? (p. 271)
2. What is the difference between needs and wants? (p. 277)
3. Name the different levels of the hierarchy of needs. (p. 278)

ACTIVITY 37: Are Your Needs Being Met?

A Read each statement below and indicate whether you Disagree, Disagree Slightly, Agree Slightly, or Agree.

	Disagree	Disagree Slightly	Agree Slightly	Agree
1. I get along well with other people.				
2. People are friendly toward me.				
3. People in my life care about me.				
4. I like the people I work and go to school with.				
5. I have satisfying close relationships.				
6. I feel a sense of achievement at school and work.				
7. People I know tell me I am good at what I do.				
8. At work and school, I am learning interesting new skills.				
9. Most days, I feel a sense of accomplishment from what I do and who I am.				
10. I frequently have the opportunity to show how capable I am.				
11. I decide for myself how to live my life.				
12. I don't feel pressured to do, say, or think things that aren't "me."				
13. I rarely am forced to do what other people tell me to do.				
14. I feel free to express my ideas and opinions.				
15. I feel like I can pretty much be myself.				

Source: Adapted from Edward L. Deci and Richard M. Ryan, "Basic Need Satisfaction in Life Scale." *Self-Determination Theory: An Approach to Human Motivation and Personality*, May 2002. University of Rochester.

B **Scoring:** Give yourself one point for every Disagree, two points for every Disagree Slightly, three points for every Agree Slightly, and four points for every Agree. Add up the number of points you assigned to statements 1–5. These statements refer to the need for belongingness. If your total is 15 or lower, this need is not being fully satisfied in your life.

Belongingness total: _____

Add up the number of points you assigned to statements 6–10. These statements refer to the need for competence. If your total is 15 or lower, this need is not being fully satisfied in your life.

Competence total: _____

Add up the number of points you assigned to statements 11–15. These statements refer to the need for autonomy. If your total is 15 or lower, this need is not being fully satisfied in your life.

Autonomy total: _____

continued...

C Which of these needs are being satisfied in your life and which are not? What circumstances in your life do you think account for this?

_____

_____

_____

_____

_____

_____

_____

_____

_____

_____

_____

_____

_____

_____

_____

MOTIVATION AND EMOTION

Motivation and emotion are closely related. In fact, both words come from the same Latin verb meaning *to move*. We move toward things that we associate with pleasant feelings, such as joy, love, and excitement, and we move away from things that we associate with unpleasant feelings, such as fear, sadness, and guilt.

In particular, two strong emotions that are opposites of one another are part of motivation: fear and desire. **Fear** is an unpleasant feeling of anxiety caused by the anticipation of danger. Fear is one of the most powerful emotions that can affect motivation. Fear makes you panic, often needlessly, and it can defeat goals.

The opposite emotion, desire, is like a strong, positive magnet. **Desire** is a conscious drive to attain a satisfying goal. It attracts and encourages plans and effort. Desire is the emotional state between where you are and where you want to be. To attain success, you need to have desire. You need to want to change for the better.

Fear and desire lead to opposite destinies. Fear looks to the past. Desire looks to the future. Fear remembers past pain, disappointment, failure, and unpleasantness and reminds us that these experiences can be repeated. Desire triggers memories of pleasure and success and excites the need to create new successful experiences. The fearful person says, "I have to," "I can't," "I see risk," and "I wish." The person with desire says, "I want to," "I can," "I see opportunity," and "I will."

fear An unpleasant feeling of anxiety caused by the anticipation of danger.

desire A conscious drive to attain a satisfying goal.

The Importance of Desire

Success is not only for the privileged; you don't have to be born rich, talented, or strong. Success depends on desire, focus, and persistence. The secret of success is to make the extra effort, try another approach, and concentrate on the desired outcome. Out of desire comes the energy and will to succeed. To be effective, however, desire has to be accompanied by self-discipline. You might desire to fly to the moon—you might even imagine yourself on the moon—but in reality, you will never even get near the launching pad without self-discipline.

Most basketball fans will never forget the singular play of Michael Jordan, who led the NBA Chicago Bulls to a spectacular run of world titles. Many consider him to be the greatest professional basketball player who has ever played the game. Few younger fans today know that he was cut from his high school basketball team as not being talented enough. What if he had thrown in the towel at that early age and given up on the sport he loved? His early rejection motivated him to practice more and increased his determination to succeed. After a three-season career at the

success *secret*
Desire and self-discipline keep you going along the tough road to your goals.

What Motivates Employees?

According to recent Gallup surveys, 70 percent of U.S. workers are either "not engaged" or are "actively disengaged" in their jobs. This means managers must understand how to continually foster an environment of motivated and productive employees. As you learned earlier in this chapter, extrinsic rewards such as pay and benefits are not as powerful as intrinsic rewards. Recognition for a job well done, even a simple "thank you" or pat on the back, will do far more to engage employees than a pay raise or bonus.

Leaders and managers who develop a strong team environment of open communication, recognition, feedback, coaching, and autonomy will gain higher productivity and engagement. People want to feel valued by their bosses, their company, and their peers. They want to be part of something "bigger" than themselves. As employees are treated with respect and encouraged to share their opinions, they are intrinsically motivated to give more to their job and their company.

What's Your Opinion?

Think about your current place of work or a previous job you have held. What motivates or motivated you to do a good job? What did your boss or company do to make you feel valued? What motivates you when you think about working in your ideal job or for a great company? To learn more about motivation on the job, go to http://humanresources.about.com/od/glossarye/g/employee-motivation.htm or conduct an online search using the keywords "employee motivation."

University of North Carolina at Chapel Hill, where he was a member of the Tar Heels' national championship team in 1982, Jordan joined the NBA's Chicago Bulls in 1984. In 1991, he won his first NBA championship, and followed that achievement with titles in 1992 and 1993, securing a "three-peat." After a brief try at professional baseball, Jordan rejoined the Bulls in 1995 and led them to three additional championships in 1996, 1997, and 1998, as well as an NBA-record 72 regular-season wins in the 1995–1996 season.

What does Michael Jordan have to say about the early disappointment that motivated him to play in the NBA? He says: "I have missed more than 9,000 shots in my career. I have lost almost 300 games. On 26 occasions I have been entrusted to take the game winning shot, and I missed. I have failed over and over and over again in my life. And that is why I succeed."

Like Michael Jordan, Oprah Winfrey overcame rejection with self-discipline and perseverance to become one of the wealthiest and most powerful women in broadcasting and media. Here's what Oprah has to say: "If you concentrate on what you don't have, you will never, ever have enough. Lots of people want to ride with you in the limo, but what you want is someone who will take the bus with you when the limo breaks down. I don't think of myself as a poor, deprived, ghetto girl who made good. I think of myself as somebody who from an early age knew I was responsible for myself, and I had to make good. I still have my feet on the ground, I just wear better shoes."

OVERCOMING FEAR OF FAILURE

The only limits to what you can achieve are the limits you put on yourself. Low self-expectancy and lack of commitment can severely limit your ability to achieve your goals. So can one of the most powerful fears—the fear of failure.

In some cases, fear of failure can generate a kind of negative motivation that works in your favor. This happens when you give your best effort to avoid failure. If you haven't been studying and recently failed several tests, you might be anxious about passing the course; this fear could motivate you to get your study habits back on track. However, most of the time, fear of failure drains your energy and motivation. Fear of failure diminishes your motivation by focusing your attention on the negative possibilities in taking action or making a change.

success *secret*
Fear of failure drains positive motivation.

Fear of failure is often based on irrational beliefs about the terrible consequences that will result if you do (or don't do) certain things. For example, fear of failure may be based on fear of the unknown, of rejection, of disapproval or humiliation, or of looking stupid or awkward. Underneath many of these fears is often an even deeper fear: the fear of being inadequate.

Accept Your Fear

To overcome fear of failure, you first need to accept your fear. Realize that everyone fears failure. Even highly successful people fear failure. Successful people, however, are able to accept their fear and go on anyway.

Consider the following story. A famous actor once suffered a nervous breakdown before he went on stage. He was ordered to rest and repair his damaged nervous system. He was afraid and had lost all confidence in himself. After a while, his doctor suggested that he perform before a small group in his town. When the actor said he was terrified of failing, the doctor answered that he was using fear as an excuse, and fear was not a good reason to quit. He told the actor that successful people admit fear and go on in spite of it. The actor accepted his fear and went on to perform in front of the little group. His performance was a great success, and afterward he realized that he had admitted his fear but had not let it stop him. After that night, he pushed himself to perform in front of larger audiences all over the world, knowing that he could overcome the fear and not let it end his acting career. He knew the fear might always be there, but being frightened would never make him give up again.

Expand Your Comfort Zone

Once you've accepted your fear, you can work on expanding your comfort zone. Your **comfort zone** is the place in your mind where you feel safe and know you can succeed.

comfort zone The place in your mind where you feel safe and know you can succeed.

Most goals require that you move a bit outside your comfort zone. To go after a goal is to move into new areas and to try new things, and doing this can be quite stressful. Since you don't want to become so stressed that you give up your goal, the best course of action is to move outside your comfort zone bit by bit—taking slow, small steps that are challenging but not uncomfortable. Think of the comfort zone as a circle surrounding you, as in Figure 7.3. Each time you accept a new challenge, you expand the circle, gaining more and more freedom of movement.

Rethink Failure

failure An unwanted outcome.

Another way to overcome fear of failure is to rethink what failure means. **Failure** is simply an unwanted outcome. Failure is an event, not a destiny. In fact, failure is a tool for you to use. It is feedback that lets you know where you need to work to improve. View failure as a learning experience that requires a target correction. Failure is a detour, not a dead-end. Ask yourself, which is more painful in the long run: failing or missing out on opportunity after opportunity to pursue your dreams? Picture yourself 20 years in the future. How will you feel when you look back on this time and remember the risks you didn't take? Will you be filled with thoughts of what might have been?

FIGURE 7.3   Expanding the Comfort Zone

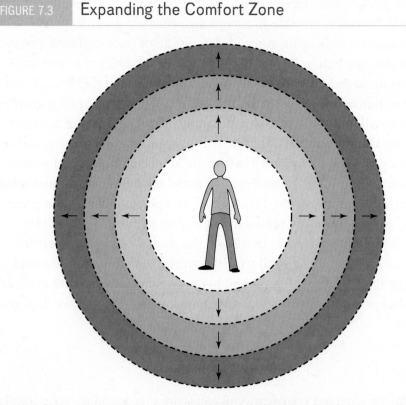

Step by Step   Every time you try something new, you expand your comfort zone. *Why is it better to expand your comfort zone with small steps than with giant leaps?*

Failure Is Part of Success

Failure is a part of life. Every time we do something new, we risk failure. For example, when you learned to drive a car, you didn't know if you would be successful until you tried. Sometimes it takes a lot of trying to achieve success, but when we finally do, we feel confident. We learn that we can succeed at something new.

Actor Jim Carrey was heckled in his first try at comedy and didn't try again for two years. He says, "I have no idea what motivated me to try again. I just felt like giving it a shot. Failure isn't the end unless you give up."

Often, setbacks and hardships strengthen us. Earl Nightingale, a well-known motivational speaker, tells the story of a trip he took to the Great Barrier Reef. He noticed that the coral growing on the sheltered side of the reef, where the sea was peaceful and quiet, looked pale and lifeless. The coral that was constantly beaten by the powerful waves, however, looked healthy and vibrant. Earl asked the guide why this was so. "It is very simple," came the reply. "The coral on the lagoon side dies rapidly with no challenge for growth and survival, while the coral facing the open sea thrives and multiplies because it is challenged and tested every day." So it is with all living things on earth. If we never challenge ourselves, we never have the opportunity to succeed. We can choose to stay where we are, or we can use the failures and setbacks in our lives to strengthen ourselves and help us make progress toward our goals.

Strive to focus on your past successes and forget past failures. Learn from your mistakes, and then erase them from memory. It doesn't matter how many times you have failed in the past. It only matters that you are willing to try again. Use **Activity 38** to assess your view of failure and how you might expand your comfort zone.

OVERCOMING FEAR OF SUCCESS

It is not just fear of failure that can hold us back. It is also fear of success. Low self-esteem is the major reason we fear success and the risks involved in reaching success. If you cannot see your potential and what you can do, you are defeated from the start. You make the excuse, "It is not worth it to succeed." What you are really saying is, "I am not worth the effort." Successful people, however, see themselves as worthy of success. They know they are worth the effort to succeed. This sense of self-worth keeps the hope of achievement alive.

Fear of success defeats any goals you set and causes you to resist change. Consider Joyce's example. Joyce wanted to go to community college to earn an associate degree. She set the goal and made lists of tasks to make it happen, but three years later, she is still "thinking about it." Joyce wants an education, but deep down she's afraid that getting it will change the way friends or members of her family, who have not attended college, relate to her. They may view a college-educated Joyce as different, maybe even conceited.

ACTIVITY 38: Expanding Your Comfort Zone

A What five things would you want to do or try if you could be absolutely, positively sure there was no possibility of failure? (Select things that you really, truly want to do for yourself, not to impress someone else.)

Example

Run for president of the student council

Audition for an a capella singing group

1. _____

2. _____

3. _____

4. _____

5. _____

B In the real world, failure—an unwanted outcome—is always a possibility. Given this fact, how likely are you to try these five things in your real life? Explain.

_____

_____

_____

_____

C If you tried and failed at any of these things, would you try again? Why or why not?

_____

_____

_____

D Imagine that you try and fail at one or more of these things and then give up. Picture yourself 20 years in the future. How do you feel as you look back and remember that you let the fear of failure stop you from pursuing what you wanted in life?

_____

_____

_____

_____

_____

_____

E Select one of the five things you want to do or try. Formulate a series of three increasingly challenging goals that could help you expand your comfort zone in this area.

Goal #1

_____

_____

Goal #2

_____

_____

Goal #3

_____

_____

Fighting Your Fears

To find ways around the fear of success, you need to examine the thoughts and feelings that might be holding you back and discover ways to overcome them.

"Even if I succeed, I still won't be happy." If you fear that success will leave you unfulfilled, it might be time to reexamine your vision of success. Are you hoping that money, power, or the approval of other people will make you a happy person? Remember that success and happiness come from intrinsic goals, such as close relationships, healthy self-esteem, and a commitment to your goals and values. Also work on different sides of yourself so that your happiness is not dependent on accomplishing a single goal.

success *secret*

Having unrealistic expectations of yourself can drain your motivation.

"I won't be able to live up to the expectations." People sometimes do have unrealistic expectations of those who are successful. Ask yourself, however, if your unrealistic expectations of yourself might be undermining your motivation. Do you feel that you'll be a failure unless you climb from achievement to achievement? Let other people have their expectations—you are only responsible for doing what matters to you.

success *secret*

Give yourself permission to make mistakes.

"The minute I achieve success, I'll probably blow it." Success is not an accident, nor is it a possession that can be taken away. Are you secretly worried that you're not good enough and that someone will "find you out"? This fear can dampen your motivation and discourage you from taking risks. Give yourself permission to try new things, be creative, and make mistakes.

"Once I get what I want, I won't be motivated to do anything." Remember that success is a process, not an end in itself. Each achievement builds on past achievements and lays the groundwork for future achievements. Set several goals for yourself in several different areas of your life, so that you will always have something to look forward to.

success *secret*

Use your success to inspire others.

"The more successful you are, the more people dislike you." It's natural to fear that people will be envious of your achievements. Why not turn that fear around, however, and imagine how your success might inspire others? There are many ways to use your success to the benefit of others, such as mentoring, tutoring, teaching, and writing. Look at your attitudes, too—many of us secretly envy people who are successful and therefore dislike them. Turn this envy around, giving others credit, recognition, and support. Then expect this treatment in return.

"Everyone will think I'm stuck up." It is possible that people will find something to criticize. Remember, however, that the person who is most critical of you is you. If you are worried about how the changes you are making will affect the important people in your life, give them permission to give you honest, open, candid feedback if they see you acting differently or deviating from your values. Build a personal support network of people who appreciate and love you for who you are, not what you accomplish.

"I don't want to step all over people to get ahead."

True success does not require exploiting others. You can, and should, succeed by acting in harmony with your values and with respect for others. Trust that it is possible to achieve your own dreams without robbing other people of the chance to achieve theirs.

When you fear success, even the biggest achievements can be sources of anxiety. If you are promoted at work, for example, you might start worrying about letting your boss down, or alienating your coworkers, or making a wrong decision. Even though you've reached an important goal, you can't enjoy it. Use **Personal Journal 7.2** to imagine the positive and negative feelings you might have in situations of success.

VISUALIZATION

We have seen how fear—both fear of failure and fear of success—can make us stumble on the path toward achieving our goals. Although it is helpful to accept our fears and rethink what failure means, we must also visualize ourselves being successful. When this happens, our motivation will become the fuel for action. **Visualization** is the process of creating detailed mental pictures of behaviors you wish to carry out. Visualization, like positive self-talk, harnesses the power of the subconscious mind. When you visualize, you see things in your mind's eye by organizing and processing information through pictures and symbols. You imagine yourself behaving in certain ways, helping that behavior to become real.

With visualization, you focus on the image of what you want until you achieve what you have been visualizing. You might imagine yourself getting a new job, passing a test, or improving your memory and learning ability. If you want to get in shape, you could picture yourself enjoying life as a fit and healthy person. This helps motivate you to exercise and eat healthfully.

Many studies have measured the effects of visualization on athletic performance. In one study, one group of basketball players physically practiced free throws while another group "mentally" practiced free throws by using visualization. Both groups had the same rate of improvement. Combining both physical and mental practice of a sport—or any other skill—helps improve performance even more.

Visualization is so powerful that doctors sometimes have their patients use it as part of their treatment for diseases such as cancer and AIDS. These patients are encouraged to imagine their bodies fighting the disease.

visualization The process of creating detailed mental pictures of the behaviors you wish to carry out.

success *secret*
Use visualization to harness the power of the subconscious mind.

Personal Journal 7.2

Confronting Fear of Success

Write down three positive feelings and three negative feelings that you might experience in each of the following situations.

Your instructor recognizes you in front of your classmates for outstanding work on a research project. You are asked to present your paper to the class on Monday.

POSITIVE FEELINGS	NEGATIVE FEELINGS

You and two friends take an advanced course. You are the only student who receives an A.

POSITIVE FEELINGS	NEGATIVE FEELINGS

You submit several humorous articles to a local newspaper. The editor likes your writing and offers you a small weekly column.

POSITIVE FEELINGS	NEGATIVE FEELINGS

What could you say to yourself in these situations to reduce your negative feelings?

One patient visualized a knight, which represented his body, slaying a dragon, which represented his cancer. The number of cancer cells in his body decreased dramatically.

Visualization and Success

In his book *The Seven Habits of Highly Effective People,* Stephen Covey says that visualization is the ability to see success, feel success, and experience success before actually completing an activity.

All successful people can picture or visualize each experience they want, each goal they want to achieve, and each habit they want to change. They embed the picture in their subconscious minds and imprint it in their brains. They use self-discipline to tell themselves over and over with words, pictures, ideas, and emotions that they are achieving each important personal goal now. Successful athletes such as tennis champion Serena Williams and golf champion Inbee Park can picture the winning shots in advance. They can feel themselves holding their victory trophies. They can visualize what they want to achieve, prepare themselves in their minds, and then make it happen.

Visualization is not about wishful thinking; it is about positive thinking. When you find yourself saying "I can't" or "I won't be able to," visualize yourself succeeding instead. Take a few deep breaths to help you relax. Then, visualize yourself succeeding in the situation. Repeat the scene over and over again, step by step, until you truly believe that you will succeed.

For example, let's say that you don't understand something that you are studying, but you feel uncomfortable asking questions in class. Right now, phrase your question and visualize yourself raising your hand. See the instructor call on you and visualize yourself confidently saying, "Could you please explain more about . . ." or "Could you please go over. . . ." The key is to visualize your self-confidence. When you have the opportunity in class to ask your question, you will have had the experience—if only in your mind—of asking it with confidence. You won't be afraid of stumbling, because you will know exactly what to say. Every day that you visualize your new, positive self, you are that much closer to achieving that goal and all goals in your future.

Through visualization, you can prepare yourself for any kind of challenge—speaking before a group, performing on the playing field, or communicating to the boss. If you perform below what you feel you are capable of, you can tell yourself "Next time I'll do better" and then replay the situation in your imagination the way you want it to take place next time.

The Power of Imagination

Only your imagination limits what you can do with yourself. Unlike other animals, humans can create their own success by using their imaginations, by forming a mental image of what they want and of their possibilities.

success *secret*
Visualize yourself succeeding, and you will succeed.

imagination The creative power of the mind.

Every invention we enjoy in our everyday lives was first just an image in someone's mind. **Imagination** is the creative power of the mind. French emperor Napoleon once said, "Imagination rules the world." A century later, physicist Albert Einstein corrected him by stating, "Imagination is the world." The world you picture in your mind is the world you live in. Your imagination can shape your destiny. Use your imagination to see yourself as the person you want to become.

Steps to Visualization

Visualize your desired goals when you are relaxed. This may be early in the morning when you wake up, before you go to sleep at night, or any other time you feel at ease. Choose a comfortable sitting or reclining position. Close your eyes and pick one central image or situation to focus on. Take the game of basketball, for example. Imagine your only job is to concentrate on one free throw. Discipline yourself to think only of that shot and eliminate everything else from your mind. There is no room for negatives, only the one positive task at hand. Visualize the outcome you want. Picture yourself making the perfect shot.

The key to visualization is focusing on one image at a time. Don't immediately visualize the outcome; think about each step you need to take to achieve that outcome. If you feel any uncertainty or anxiety during one of the steps, stop for a moment. Relax, take a deep breath, and go back to the previous step, before you felt anxiety, and proceed until you are comfortable with each thought and can visualize each step of your goal.

Let's say you have to give a speech in front of your class but have a fear of public speaking. Your first step would be to imagine yourself walking to the front of the class and standing behind the podium. Next, you would visualize your audience. If this thought sparks some anxiety, pause and take a deep breath. Go back to the first step—walking to the front of the class—and then proceed with the next image until you are completely comfortable with it. Then move to the next image—beginning your speech—and each step thereafter until you visualize the end of your speech and hear the applause of the audience. Use **Activity 39** to help you visualize success.

Focus on the Positive   Remember that self-talk has a powerful effect on your subconscious mind. As you visualize, notice and dispute negative thoughts with positive affirmations. Don't focus on doubts; think about the self-image of the person that you would like to become. If you keep experiencing anxiety and find yourself repeatedly going back over the same steps, don't be discouraged. Eventually, you will create a clear picture of yourself as you will be when you achieve your goal. Tell yourself over and over again that you are winning each personal victory now. For example, to achieve the positive self-image

success *secret*
Visualize yourself as the person you want to be.

success *secret*
Use positive self-talk again and again.

you want, visualize yourself as the person you want to be. It is important to do this every day. Visualize yourself making the changes you want to make—right now. Visualize yourself becoming the person you want to be—right now.

Visualization and Positive Thinking   People respond to our thoughts, feelings, and behavior and react accordingly. If you have a positive outlook, you are more likely to attract positive results. You are also more likely to attract positive people who can help you reach your goals. Visualization helps you stay positive by allowing you to create a mental image of yourself achieving your goals. It helps you to stay motivated as you focus on accomplishing your objective—success.

Self Check

1. Why is desire important for success? (p. 285)
2. Define failure. (p. 288)
3. How does visualization work? (p. 293)

ACTIVITY 39: Visualizing Success

A Describe a situation in which you found it difficult to speak up for yourself or your beliefs. Perhaps you didn't voice an opinion in class, or didn't defend yourself against a destructive criticism, or weren't assertive with a salesperson.

_____

_____

B Now use visualization to practice speaking up for yourself. Visualize the same situation or a similar one. This time, however, you speak up for yourself in a polite but assertive way. On the lines below, map out all aspects of the scene, including the setting (time and place), the people present, the action that occurs (including the words spoken), and how you feel during the new, positive scene.

Setting: _____

People: _____

Action: _____

_____

_____

Feelings: _____

_____

C Eyes closed, visualize this situation in full detail at least three times. Do you feel more confident in your ability to speak up for yourself the next time you are in a similar situation? Explain.

_____

_____

_____

_____

_____

continued...

D Now use visualization to enter the future. Picture yourself ten years from now. You have accomplished several of your long-term goals and become the person you want to be. How and where do you picture yourself?

_____

_____

_____

_____

What goals have you accomplished?

_____

_____

What important relationships have you nurtured?

_____

_____

What have you done for others that you feel most happy about?

_____

_____

E Does this positive vision of your future self boost your motivation to achieve your goals? Explain.

_____

_____

_____

_____

Key Terms

motivation (p. 270)

positive motivation (p. 270)

negative motivation (p. 270)

extrinsic motivation (p. 271)

intrinsic motivation (p. 271)

incentive (p. 273)

need (p. 277)

want (p. 277)

hierarchy of needs (p. 278)

belongingness (p. 280)

competence (p. 281)

self-actualization (p. 281)

autonomy (p. 282)

fear (p. 285)

desire (p. 285)

comfort zone (p. 287)

failure (p. 288)

visualization (p. 293)

imagination (p. 296)

Summary by Learning Objectives

- **Contrast intrinsic motivation with extrinsic motivation.** Intrinsic motivation comes from inside. It drives you to do things that you enjoy and feel good about. Intrinsic motivation is associated with goals such as building relationships, giving to others, and growing as a person. Extrinsic motivation comes from outside. It drives you to do things that make you look good to other people. Extrinsic motivation is associated with goals such as attaining wealth, fame, or beauty.

- **Describe how to distinguish needs from wants.** A need represents something we must have to survive and thrive, while a want represents something we can do without. If something does not satisfy us physically or psychologically, it is probably a want, not a need.

- **Explain why needs motivate our behavior.** The quest to fulfill our needs drives much of our conscious and unconscious behavior. For example, the need for belongingness drives us to spend time building family bonds, friendships, and romantic relationships. If we do not fulfill our basic needs, we grow ill and die. If we do not fulfill our higher needs, we fail to make the most of our potential.

- **Cite ways to overcome fear of failure.** When you fear failure, you fear making changes and taking risks. You therefore need to accept your fears and then take small steps to expand your comfort zone.

- **Cite ways to overcome fear of success.** Fear of success stems from low self-esteem. You can overcome this fear by disputing the self-destructive thoughts and feelings that are causing you to fear success.

- **Describe visualization and how it can boost motivation.** Visualization allows you to create detailed mental images of behaviors you want to carry out. When you see yourself accomplishing your goals, step by step, you become more motivated to take action and gain confidence in your ability to succeed.

Review and Activities

Review Questions

1. Contrast positive motivation with negative motivation.

2. Why is intrinsic motivation healthier than extrinsic motivation?

3. Sketch and label the hierarchy of needs.

4. Define belongingness, competence, and autonomy.

5. Why would a person fear success?

6. Explain the benefits of visualization.

Critical Thinking

7. **Extrinsic and Intrinsic Motivation**   Every year, hundreds of thousands of people compete to be selected for reality television shows such as Survivor, American Idol, America's Got Talent, Top Model, Top Chef, Amazing Race, and Project Runway. In exchange for being filmed and performing under stressful circumstances, participants have the opportunity to win prize money and achieve fame. Why do you think so many people want to appear on TV shows like these? Do you think that reality show contestants are intrinsically motivated, extrinsically motivated, or both? Explain.

8. **Confronting Fear**   Describe a situation in your life where fear held you back from taking a risk or pursuing something important to you. What caused your fear? Did you experience any fear of success or failure? How did you handle it then? What do you do differently now to overcome your fears?

Application

9. **Needs Journal**   Review Maslow's Hierarchy of Needs and create a chart for yourself with a row for each of the five needs. Think about the activities you do each week and what motivates you to satisfy your needs in each category. For example, you are probably motivated by physical needs to eat meals and go grocery shopping; and you are probably motivated by social needs to interact with friends and family. Write down your top motivators for each need. You may find that an important activity, like attending school, for example, motivates you on multiple levels, such as social, esteem, and self-actualization.

10. **Visualization**   Ask a close friend or family member if there is anything that might be holding him/her back from achieving a goal. Help him/her identify the obstacles, challenges, or fears. Now ask him/her to visualize, in vivid detail, the goal being attained. Discuss the positive images, feelings and self-talk, and map out a plan for action.

Review and Activities

Internet Activities

11. **Self-Motivation**   Visit http://www.mindtools.com/pages/article/newLDR_57.htm to take a short quiz to determine how self-motivated you are. You will receive an overall score, and then a separate score in four areas considered necessary to build the strongest levels of self-motivation.

12. **Hierarchy of Needs**   Visit http://similarminds.com/cgi-bin/maslow.pl to take a quiz to help you identify the fulfillment level of your needs based on Maslow's hierarchy. You will receive a percentage score for each of the five categories, along with a brief description of how you can better address your needs.

Real-Life Success Story

"How Can I Succeed?"

Look back at your response to the question in the Real-Life Success Story on page 268. Think about how you would answer the question now that you have completed the chapter.

Complete the Story   Taking the role of Elijah's advisor, explain how fear of success is related to low self-esteem. Then give him suggestions for using positive self-talk to help him cope with his self-doubt.

"Will I Ever Be Able to Enjoy Some 'Free' Time?"

Joining the Crowd

Anna Costas is on the way up in her career as a sales rep for an Internet business. One Friday, her coworkers asked her to join them for a night out. Anna needed to prepare for a client presentation on Monday, but she decided to go, thinking: "I'll just pull it together over the weekend. Plus, it's Friday and I need a break." She arranged for a babysitter and joined the group at the restaurant. The rest of the weekend went by in a blur of soccer games, grocery shopping, house cleaning, and laundry.

Working Overtime

Suddenly, it was Monday morning. Running late after getting the kids off to school, Anna had to rush straight to the conference room to deliver her presentation. When she got back to her office, she found an urgent e-mail informing her of a change in her company's advertising rates. "Oh no! This changes everything!" she thought. Anna had made some major errors and gave inaccurate information during the presentation. Now she would need to schedule another meeting, putting her a week behind.

What Do You Think?   How could better time management have kept Anna out of this situation?

Managing Your Resources

8 Chapter

> " Many people take no care of their money till they come nearly to the end of it, and others do just the same with their time. "
>
> Johann Wolfgang von Goethe, Author

introduction

Time and money are valuable—but limited—resources. In order to reach your personal goals, you need to manage your time and money efficiently. In Section 8.1 you'll examine how to make the most of your time. By learning to plan ahead, you'll be able to accomplish more and focus on your priorities. In Section 8.2 you'll learn how to make money work for you. You'll examine your spending habits, learn to make a budget, and develop a plan to align your finances with your goals and values.

learning objectives

After you complete this chapter, you should be able to:

- Outline the three steps in time management and in money management.

- Describe the three categories of time and the three categories of expenses.

- Explain how to make a to-do list and a schedule.

- Define procrastination and explain its causes.

- Describe the criteria for an effective budget.

- Cite ways to reduce excess spending.

Time Management

TAKING CONTROL OF YOUR TIME

time management
The planned, efficient use of time.

We all juggle many responsibilities—school, work, family, social life, leisure activities. How do we find time to do it all? The answer is time management. **Time management** is the planned, effective, and efficient use of time. Time management isn't just about schedules and lists; it's about making the most of your life. Since time never takes a break, time management really means priority management in the time we have available.

Throughout this book, you have been taking a close look at the priorities that are important to you. Time management helps you structure your time and your life around those priorities. When you manage your time well, you can make progress on your long-term goals while still making room for relaxation, friendships, hobbies, and the other activities that are important to you.

Our most precious resources, time and health, usually are taken for granted until they are depleted. As with health, time is the raw material of life. We can bide our time, but we can't save it for another day. We can waste and kill time, but we are also mortally wounding our opportunities. Time is the ultimate equal opportunity employer. Each human being, while alive, has exactly 168 hours a week to spend. Think about it! Scientists can't invent more minutes. Super rich people can't buy more hours. Queen Elizabeth I of England—the richest, most powerful woman on earth of her era—whispered these final words on her deathbed: "All of my possessions for another moment of time!" We worry about things we want to do but can't, instead of doing the things we can do but don't. It is not the experience of today that causes us the greatest stress. It is the regret for something we did or didn't do yesterday, and the apprehension of what tomorrow may bring.

success *secret*
Plan ahead to spend your time doing what you value.

Steps to Time Management

How do you view time—as a never-ending series of deadlines, or as a series of opportunities? No matter who you are or what you do, you need to work toward your goals one day at a time. To use time most effectively and efficiently, you'll need to look at it as a *resource* that allows you to achieve what is most important to you. A resource is something that is ready for your use and can be drawn upon as needed.

Basic time management doesn't have to be complicated. Managing your time involves three basic steps: figuring out where your time goes, determining where you want it to go, and creating a plan to make that happen:

- **Step 1:** Analyze how you use your time.
- **Step 2:** Prioritize your activities.
- **Step 3:** Create a plan for your time.

Let's go step by step.

Step 1: Analyze How You Use Your Time

The first step in managing your time is to take a good look at how you spend your time. Do you know where your time really goes? When you pay attention to how you spend the hours of your day, you may be surprised by what you find.

We perform dozens of activities each day, from getting dressed to checking e-mail. One practical way to analyze your time is to assign each of your activities to one of three different categories of time:

- **Committed time**—*Committed time* is the time you devote to school, work, family, volunteering, and other activities that relate to your short-term and long-term goals. These activities usually take up a fixed amount of time in your schedule.
- **Maintenance time**—*Maintenance time* is the time you spend maintaining, or taking care of, yourself and your surroundings. You need to spend time each week sleeping and tending to your health and fitness, as well as doing chores such as cleaning your home or apartment, maintaining your car, and caring for your pets. Maintenance time is a bit more flexible than committed time.
- **Discretionary time**—*Discretionary time* is time that you can use to do whatever you wish. You might hang out with friends, pursue a hobby, surf the Web, or read a book during your discretionary time. Discretionary time is the most flexible type of time.

How much does each type of time take up in a 168-hour week? Take the example of Letisha, who works full-time and goes to school in the evening to earn her MBA. Letisha works eight hours a day Monday through Friday, volunteers four hours a week, and has three hours of class per week. This adds up to 47 hours of committed time, leaving her 121 hours to do whatever she wants. Or does it? Letisha takes the train to and from work and drives to school, which takes up another two hours a day. She also has to buy textbooks and supplies, do homework, and read articles that relate to her job.

This adds another 38 hours to her committed time, leaving her with 83 hours. Add eight hours of sleep a night, two hours a day for cooking, eating, dressing, and chores, an hour to walk her dog, and she's left with only six hours of discretionary time per week.

Are you like Letisha, with too much to do and not enough time to do it? To measure the demands on your time, complete **Activity 40** on page 308. To get accurate results, you'll need to do this exercise over the span of a week, carefully monitoring how you use your time on each day. Don't guess—make sure to note how you actually spend each hour of the day.

Step 2: Prioritize Your Activities

Once you've figured out how you actually spend your time, you are ready for step 2, prioritizing your activities. Time, like all resources, is limited. You therefore need to figure out which of your activities deserve the biggest share. You do this by *prioritizing*—arranging your tasks and activities in order of importance.

ACTIVITY 40: Time-Demand Survey

A Use the chart below to record the length of time (rounded to the nearest quarter hour) you spend on each activity over the course of a week.

Committed Time	Hours
1. Class attendance	
2. Study (homework, library time, etc.)	
3. Commuting to and from school/work	
4. Job/internship	
5. Volunteering/extracurricular activities	
6. Family responsibilities	
7. Religious activities	
8. (Other—specify)	
Maintenance Time	**Hours**
9. Eating (meals and snacks)	
10. Housekeeping (laundry, grocery shopping, cooking, cleaning, etc.)	
11. Personal hygiene/grooming	
12. Car maintenance/repair	
13. Physical exercise	
14. Sleep	
15. Pet care	
16. (Other—specify)	
Discretionary Time	**Hours**
17. Social activities (building/maintaining friendships, group activities/events, etc.)	
18. Leisure activities pursued alone (hobbies, reading, television, etc.)	
19. (Other—specify)	
20. (Other—specify)	
Total	

B Add up the total number of hours on your chart. A week contains 168 hours. If your total is greater than 168, you are overcommitted. If your total is less than 168, you are letting hours get away from you. Are you overcommitted or undercommitted? If so, by how much?

_____

_____

C Add up how many hours you spent on each time category. Then divide each total by 168. The result represents the percentage of your total weekly hours that you spent on that category.

Total committed time: _____   Percent of total: _____

Total maintenance time: _____   Percent of total: _____

Total discretionary time: _____   Percent of total: _____

Sketch a pie chart of your time using the percentages you calculated above. Label each pie slice with the relevant category. The slices on the pie chart below represent 10 percent increments.

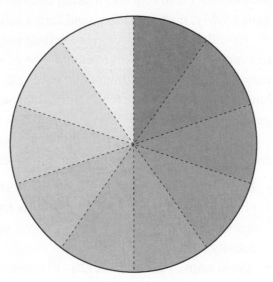

D Are you satisfied with the way you spend your time? Explain.

_____

_____

_____

_____

Take a look at your work, school, family, and social obligations and activities. Which ones are most relevant to your goals and values? Refer back to the values you selected in Chapter 2 and the goals you set for yourself in Chapter 3. Is there anything you would like to spend more time doing? For example, do you have next to no time to keep up with current events, exercise, or read for pleasure? Is there anything you feel you spend too much time doing? If you are committed to completing your degree, for example, could you eliminate some of the time you spend on housework? On shopping or television? Generally, it is discretionary time that can be cut first if you have too much to do and too little time. This makes more time for activities that are directly relevant to your goals. However, don't eliminate fun and relaxation from your life in order to get more done. If you don't allow time to recharge, your energy and enthusiasm will suffer.

Don't Forget Sleep   If you are like most people, your magic solution to getting everything done is to cut back on sleep. Unfortunately, this is both inefficient and unhealthful. Depriving yourself of sleep makes you less productive during the day, so you have to work harder and longer to get the same amount done. This cuts into your sleep time even more. When you're tired, you just don't make good use of time. You have trouble thinking creatively and making decisions. You're also likely to work more slowly, make mistakes, and forget information.

How do you know if you are getting enough sleep? Most researchers recommend at least seven to eight hours of sleep a night; some people may need nine or more hours to feel rested. If you tend to get drowsy after lunch, while reading, or while riding in a bus or car, you are probably not getting enough sleep.

Another cause of sleep deprivation is poor-quality sleep. Here are several ways to improve the quality of your sleep:

- **Exercise.** You'll get to sleep faster and stay asleep better if you are physically tired. For best results, allow five or six hours between your workout time and bedtime. This allows your body temperature and activity level to return to normal.
- **Avoid naps.** Taking short (20–30 minutes) naps during the day can make you more alert, but it can make it harder to get to sleep at bedtime.
- **Say no to caffeine.** Avoid caffeine, especially in the afternoon and evening. Caffeinated beverages and foods, like cola and chocolate, can affect your body for up to 12 hours.
- **Don't work in bed.** Use your bed primarily for sleep. If you study, work, or watch TV in bed, you may begin to associate your sleep space with alertness instead of rest.
- **Choose a bedtime.** Stick to the same bedtime every night, even on weekends (if possible). Your body's internal clock will benefit from maintaining a regular schedule.
- **Relax.** Establish a relaxing bedtime ritual to calm your nerves and tell your body that it's time to head for bed. You might try a cup of herbal

tea or a glass of warm milk at bedtime; milk contains an amino acid with a mild sedative effect.

Important or Urgent? As you prioritize, it also helps to analyze your activities for their urgency and importance. Something is urgent if it calls for immediate action, but it is important only if it relates to one or more of your goals. Your end-of-semester project may be your most important task, but since it's not due for another two months, it's not urgent. The ringing telephone is urgent, but the call might or might not be important. Aim to spend most of your time on things that are both urgent and important. One convenient way to separate essential activities from nonessential activities is to use a chart like the one in **Personal Journal 8.1.** This chart contains

Personal Journal 8.1

Prioritizing Your Life

Imagine that you want to complete the following tasks over the coming week. Decide how important and/or urgent each of these items is to you, then enter each one in the relevant box below.

do grocery shopping · see a movie · file old papers and bills · do laundry · start looking for a summer job · drop off the dry cleaning · study for Friday's exam · return a call from my best friend · fix a flat tire on the car · pay an overdue credit card bill

	Urgent	Not Urgent
Important		
Not Important		

four sections for the four different kinds of activities: important and urgent; important but not urgent; urgent but not important; and not important and not urgent.

Getting More from Your Time

Do you ever feel like you spend much of your day dealing with trivial details that don't amount to much? If so, consider the *80/20 rule* (the Pareto Principle). This rule states that the relationship between input and output, or effort and results, is not balanced. For example, most people spend 80 percent of their time on activities that produce 20 percent of their progress, and 20 percent of their time on activities that produce 80 percent of their progress. In other words, we get 80 percent of our work done during 20 percent of our working hours. This also means that we spend 80 percent of our time on activities that aren't relevant to our goals.

To avoid falling into this trap, plan to spend 80 percent of your time and energy on your top priorities and the remaining 20 percent on your lower priorities. This way, you'll achieve more results in the same amount of time. Activities that should be low priority for everyone include:

- time spent with people who don't make you feel good about yourself
- distractions, like reading every Facebook post, tweet, or instagram or watching whatever is on television
- tasks you don't enjoy or do very well and that you could eliminate, delegate, or even hire someone else to do
- tasks that save a little bit of money but consume large amounts of time, such as washing your car yourself or clipping coupons for food you don't buy
- activities that you feel you "should" be doing but that don't really matter to you, such as certain household chores
- activities that are urgent but have no long-term importance

Think about the 80/20 rule as you complete **Activity 41.** Which activities don't really matter to you? Which do you do only because you think you should? By cutting these unwelcome activities, you can make room for more important ones.

Step 3: Create a Plan for Your Time

Now you should have a better handle on your time and a better idea of how you can use it to your advantage. You're ready for the third and most important step in managing time: making an overall plan for how you will use your time. The most efficient way to do this is to draw up a to-do list and a schedule.

to-do list A personal checklist of tasks and activities that need to be completed over the course of a certain period, such as a week.

Make a To-Do List

A **to-do list** is a personal checklist of tasks and activities you need to complete over the course of a certain period, such as a week. When you group all of your activities together, you can easily see which are most urgent and important. You can also see which ones can be tackled at the same time. If you need to pay several bills, for

ACTIVITY 41: Examining Your Priorities

A Review the time-demand chart you completed in Activity 40. Select two or three specific areas of your life on which you want to spend less time. On the lines below, write down each of these areas. Then list specific things in those areas that you are willing to eliminate, or changes you could make to reduce the amount of time you need to spend in these areas. Remember that small, achievable changes are better than large ones that will never happen. (It may be helpful to look back at Activity 30 on pages 233–234.)

Example	
Housekeeping	*Put laundry away as soon as it is washed.*
	Learn to live with a little more clutter.
	Vacuum biweekly instead of weekly.
1. _____	_____
	_____
	_____
2. _____	_____
	_____
	_____
3. _____	_____
	_____
	_____

B Why did you select these specific activities to cut?

_____

_____

_____

_____

continued...

C Now select two or three areas on which you want to spend *more* time. On the lines below, write down each of these areas. Then list specific things in those areas that you would do if you could find the time.

Example	
Eating	*Prepare more healthful meals.*
	Bring lunch instead of eating fast food.
	Eat with family once a week.
1. _____	_____
	_____
	_____
2. _____	_____
	_____
	_____
3. _____	_____
	_____
	_____

D Why did you select these specific activities to add?

_____

_____

E Describe one or two new activities you can begin this week and one or two old activities you can eliminate. Make sure that the time you cut and the time you add are about equal.

_____

_____

_____

example, handling them all at one sitting will help you finish them faster and reduce interruptions. Perhaps you could go to the post office, dry cleaner, shopping mall, and market all in one trip.

Refer to your to-do list throughout each day and make every effort to stick to it. As you complete each task, put a large check mark next to it. Get in the habit of rewarding yourself with something you enjoy when you complete a big task. This will be a good incentive for you to finish your projects on schedule.

There are several advantages to using to-do lists, which you will discover as you begin to make a habit of using them:

- Recording your tasks on paper keeps you from worrying about forgetting a task or getting sidetracked.
- Keeping a list helps you separate things that matter from things that don't matter (remember the 80/20 rule).
- Putting your tasks down in writing motivates you to get started and complete your assignments on time.
- Checking off a finished task gives you a sense of productivity and achievement. A check mark also serves as a visual reminder that you are ready to go on to the next task.

To-do lists are not about "staying busy." They are about using your time for things that have long-term importance to you.

Make a Schedule

Once your to-do list is complete, you can create a **schedule,** a chart showing dates and times when tasks must be completed. Using a schedule to organize your time offers several advantages. First, by scheduling your time in advance, you can build in leisure time and still complete the items on your to-do list. Daily, weekly, and even monthly planning helps you pace yourself. Second, planning helps you avoid wasted time. Each time you finish a task without knowing what you should be doing next, you lose time. Third, a schedule prevents you from setting yourself up for failure by trying to do more than can be done in a day or a week. Fourth, writing all your activities and "do-by" dates on a schedule provides a graphical reminder of what you have coming up over the following week.

To make an effective schedule, you'll need a realistic idea of how long each task on your to-do list will take. It's easy to underestimate how long a job will take, especially if it depends on the contribution of others. If you don't know how long something will take, ask someone who has done it before.

Your schedule can be in any format as long as it works for you. Many people use their smart phones or tablets for their daily and weekly schedules, as well as a monthly or yearly wall calendar to keep up with their long-term goals. Whatever format you choose, make a point to look over your schedule daily to prepare for projects or events. If you have an oral presentation due in a few weeks, for example, record the due date on your calendar and then schedule research time, writing time, and so on. Don't wait until the last minute. **Activity 42** on pages 316–317 will help you make a to-do list and a schedule. Don't worry about making it perfect; use the exercise as a way to get started.

schedule A chart showing dates and times when tasks must be completed.

success *secret*
Make sure you know how long each task will take.

success *secret*
Look over your schedule daily.

ACTIVITY 42: Time-Management Practice

A In the Task column of the to-do list below, write down all the tasks and activities you must do in the next week. Omit the obvious things that you do every day, such as eating, going to work, and sleeping. Do, however, include tasks such as grocery shopping. In the Do-By Date column, give each task or activity a do-by date.

To-Do List for the Week of _____ , 20 ____		
Task	Do-By Date	Importance

B Now prioritize your tasks and activities. In the Importance column above, assign a number between 1 and 3 to each task listed, with 1 representing very important, 2 representing important, and 3 representing somewhat important.

C Use your to-do list to make a schedule for the coming week. First schedule the tasks you rated as very important. Draw a star next to these. (You may wish to break up any larger tasks into smaller ones, assigning a separate do-by date to each.) Then schedule the tasks you rated as important and, if there is still time, schedule the tasks you rated as somewhat important. Use this schedule over the coming week.

Schedule for the Week of _____ , 20 ____	
Day	Activities
Monday	
Tuesday	
Wednesday	
Thursday	
Friday	
Saturday	
Sunday	

D Did this schedule help you organize your time? Explain.

_____

_____

_____

Identify Your Prime Time As you schedule your tasks, it is helpful to plan your most important and demanding tasks for your prime time. This is your high-energy time—the hours of the day in which your mental and physical capacity is at its peak. Everyone functions best at a different time of day. Most people are at their peak in the morning hours, while a few people feel their best in the late evening. **Personal Journal 8.2** can help you determine your prime time.

TACKLING PROCRASTINATION

procrastination The habit of putting off tasks until the last minute.

One of the biggest plusses of time management is that it helps you overcome procrastination. **Procrastination** is the habit of putting off tasks until the last minute. Procrastination can have minor consequences, such as having to pay a late fine for an overdue library book, or major consequences, such as failing a course or losing a job. It's normal to

Personal Journal 8.2

What's Your Prime Time?
Answer each question by circling Yes or No.

1. Do you like to get an early start to your day, even on weekends?	Yes	No
2. Do you prefer to schedule your classes in the morning?	Yes	No
3. Do you feel sluggish in the morning until you have been up for an hour or so?	Yes	No
4. Do you try to schedule your classes later in the day so you can sleep in?	Yes	No
5. Do you have little trouble staying up past midnight?	Yes	No
6. Do you start to feel tired around 5 PM, but feel recharged after 8 PM?	Yes	No
7. Do you find it difficult to fall asleep if you go to bed before 10 PM?	Yes	No
8. Are you at your best around 8 or 9 AM?	Yes	No
9. Do you usually feel alert when you wake up in the morning?	Yes	No

If you answered Yes to questions 3, 4, 5, and 6, you are probably a night person. If you answered Yes to questions 1, 2, 7, 8, and 9, you are probably a morning person. Use this information to fine-tune your schedule and make yourself more productive.

procrastinate from time to time. When procrastination becomes a habit, however, it can erode your self-determination and self-expectancy. The more you procrastinate, the harder it is to stop.

Procrastination has an enormous effect on success. Consider the key difference between A students and C students. Is it intelligence? Knowledge? Study skills? According to researchers, the real difference between A students and B or C students is that A students get started early. They buy their books on time, come to class prepared, and get started quickly on assignments. They don't procrastinate.

Why We Procrastinate

Everyone procrastinates sometimes on unpleasant tasks, but why do some people seem to procrastinate so often? Many people use procrastination in order to avoid taking charge of their lives. They tell themselves, "I only had 15 minutes to study for that test—getting a C wasn't too bad!" This is known as *self-handicapping*—creating obstacles to your success in order to have an easy excuse for doing poorly. By putting obstacles in their own path, self-handicappers make themselves immune to failure. They can point to their "handicap"—lack of time, lack of sleep, forgetting to study, having a cold—as the real culprit.

Other people procrastinate because they are perfectionists. They want so badly to do something perfectly that they consider themselves failures if they do merely a good job. So they procrastinate and then fly into a panic at the last minute.

Still other people believe that they should wait to start a project until they are "in the mood." Unfortunately, the more they procrastinate, the less likely they are to be in the mood. What was originally a small hassle, such as paying a bill, builds up until it becomes an overwhelming project—paying late fees, dealing with creditors, and so on. You can find out if you have the habit of procrastination by completing **Activity 43** on pages 320–321.

Get Started! The best way to stop procrastinating is to do something—anything—toward your goal. Divide your project into small steps and complete just one step. For example, tell yourself that you will spend just 15 minutes making an outline for that essay, or cleaning the kitchen counters, or choosing a layout for your résumé. When you divide a project into small segments, you will find that it is much less overwhelming. You may even find that you are enjoying the work despite yourself.

Also, get in the habit of planning ahead. Don't delay working on a project; start early. You may want to start with an easy task and then work your way up to the harder ones, or you might prefer to jump right into the hard tasks in order to get them out of the way. Taking action helps keep you motivated and helps to prevent procrastination. Remember this simple truth: The sooner you begin a project, the sooner you'll finish it. You'll also have more time for other activities, which you can enjoy without the stress of the unfinished project hanging over you.

ACTIVITY 43: Do You Procrastinate?

A Read the statements below and indicate the extent to which each one is true for you by making a check mark in the appropriate column.

	Disagree Totally	Disagree Slightly	Agree Slightly	Agree Totally
1. I invent reasons to avoid acting on a problem.				
2. It takes pressure to get me going on difficult projects.				
3. I accumulate piles of mail, newspapers, unpaid bills, broken items, or clothing to be mended.				
4. If I don't want to do a certain project, I put it out of sight so I won't be reminded of it.				
5. I sometimes hope that if I delay long enough, a problem will just go away by itself.				
6. I start studying for tests too late to do as well as I know I could.				
7. I often turn in assignments late because I need extra time to make them perfect.				
8. I start new tasks before I finish old ones.				
9. When working in groups, I try to get other people to finish what I don't.				
10. If I am uninterested in something, I just can't make myself do it.				
11. When I'm working or studying, I often find myself daydreaming.				
12. If I have work to do but my room is a mess, I start cleaning the room instead of working.				

B **Scoring:** Assign yourself one point for every Disagree Totally, two points for every Disagree Slightly, three points for every Agree Slightly, and four points for every Agree Totally.

What is your total? _____

0–20   You are not a chronic procrastinator and probably have only an occasional problem.

21–30   You have a moderate problem with procrastination. Work on planning ahead and getting started before projects reach the crisis stage.

31–40   You procrastinate often and cause needless stress for yourself. You will benefit greatly from breaking the procrastination habit.

41–48   You are a master procrastinator. Free yourself from this habit by confronting the fears behind it.

C Describe the tasks you tend to put off. Why do you think you procrastinate on these?

_____

_____

_____

_____

_____

_____

D What is one action you could take today to catch up on something you've been putting off?

_____

_____

_____

_____

_____

_____

_____

E-MAIL EFFICIENCY AND EFFECTIVENESS

E-mail was supposed to save us time and increase our communication efficiency, yet without effective e-mail management, it can become a hindrance to our productivity. The average office worker spends about thirteen hours per week—the equivalent of twenty-eight days per year, reading, sending, and managing e-mail. And for each incoming e-mail message, it takes people more than a minute to get back to what they were doing before they were interrupted. In addition to being a disruption in our workflow, e-mail overload can make us feel overwhelmed, anxiety-ridden and stressed. To more effectively manage your e-mail communication, consider the following tips:

- Immediately delete e-mails from senders you don't know. If it's important, the person will find a way to reach you.
- Use a spam filter and remove yourself from junk e-mail lists.
- Follow the "Two Minute Rule" (from David Allen's "Getting Things Done"). If an e-mail takes less than two minutes to read and respond, do so now! Otherwise, save it for later. If it will take more than two minutes to read and respond, schedule specific times to respond.
- Utilize your e-mail provider programs for highlighting, flagging, and filing e-mails.
- Create a simple filing system and strive for an inbox with nothing in it.
- Download the latest apps, like CloudMagic onto your smartphone to manage your e-mail on the go.

Think About It

What are some other ways to reduce time spent handing e-mail? What strategies have worked for you? Compare strategies with your classmates. For more resources for effective e-mail management go to http://mindtools.com/pages/article/managing-email.htm or http://blogs.hbr.org/2012/02/stop-email-overload.

A System That Works   To avoid procrastination and make the best use of your time, you'll need to research and experiment with different time-management tools and strategies to find the one that best suits your personality. If you like to be spontaneous, for example, don't try to make yourself follow a rigid schedule. Instead, create a schedule that fits you and that helps you stay focused on what you want and value. Set aside specific times to do things that make you feel good, whether that is vacuuming your bedroom or spending time with family. This will help you create the life you want.

Self Check

1. What are the three categories of time? (p. 307)
2. What are the benefits of making a to-do list? (p. 315)
3. What is procrastination? (p. 318)

MONEY MATTERS

Managing money, like managing time, is a skill. In fact, money management is one of the most important skills you will ever learn. **Money management** is the intelligent use of money to achieve your goals. Learning about money will help you enjoy greater control over your life and increase your confidence about the future.

In school, we all learn English, math, history, and science, but few of us are taught how to function in a money-based society. Many young adults enter the working world with only a vague idea of how much money they will need to pay for the necessities of daily life. We learn as we spend, often gaining unhealthy spending habits and accruing credit card debt. If you manage your money wisely, you can avoid these financial setbacks and make sure that you have the financial freedom to pursue your dreams.

money management
The intelligent use of money to achieve your goals.

Wealth and Well-Being

So what is money exactly? Money is simply a convenient medium of exchange that we use to pay for goods and services. It is not a guarantee of happiness. In fact, once our basic needs are met, more riches can't bring us more contentment. The wealthy are not necessarily happy, and the poor are not necessarily unhappy.

Think about the people, activities, and things that bring you pleasure and contentment. Do they require money? Or do you find pleasure in taking walks on the beach, reading a good book, spending time with your friends and family? Remember that although money does allow for certain luxuries, it does not eliminate life's challenges.

Your Money and You

We all have feelings about money. Unfortunately, people who have strong feelings about money often have trouble handling it rationally. Some people, for example, view money as a security blanket and are afraid to spend a single penny. Others equate it with personal worth and devote themselves to acquiring expensive possessions. Still others fear money and do their best to avoid thinking about it at all. People who avoid thinking about money tend to live for today, spending their paychecks as they come and devoting little thought to financial plans and goals. What is your attitude toward money? Enter your thoughts in **Personal Journal 8.3.**

success *secret*
Money helps us meet our basic needs, but it doesn't buy happiness.

Early Lessons About Money   Our attitudes toward money are strongly influenced by the example our parents set for us. How was money used in your home when you were growing up? Was it a source of stress and arguments? Did your parents juggle credit cards? Were bills always paid late or at the last minute? Was money used as a bribe or reward for doing well in school? Did you understand where your family's money came from and how it was saved and spent? Did you have an allowance and a budget of your own? You may have inherited irrational and self-defeating thoughts and feelings about money. If this is the case,

Personal Journal 8.3

How Do You See Money?

To me, money is _____

_____

My financial goals are _____

_____

If I had a $100 bill in my wallet, I _____

_____

When I think about paying bills, I feel _____

One thing I don't understand about money is _____

To me, planning for retirement is _____

I worry about having enough money for _____

Money helps me enjoy _____

_____

I don't need money to enjoy _____

_____

it's important to face them head-on and dispute them with the ABCDE method you learned in Chapter 5.

Money Is a Tool   The most useful attitude toward money is a practical one. Look at money as a tool. We need this tool to take care of our basic needs for food, shelter, clothing, and medical care. We also need it to achieve important goals. Many important steps in life—getting an education, buying a car, renting or owning a home, raising children, starting a business, traveling, retiring—all require money. In a capitalist society, money is also a powerful tool for expressing our values. We can buy products from companies that follow business practices we support, and we can refuse to buy products from companies that follow business practices we oppose. We can also support charities, such as schools, environmental groups, and human service organizations, that do work we value.

success *secret*
Look at money as a tool to achieve your goals, not as a goal in itself.

MANAGING YOUR FINANCES

When playing a game like Monopoly, it's easy to manage your **finances**—your monetary resources. It's not difficult to make strategic decisions when your money, property, and options are spread out right there in front of you.

finances Monetary resources.

In real life, managing money is more complex. Credit cards allow you to spend money that you don't have. Taxes, insurance, and other bills seem to arrive all at once. Debit cards that withdraw money directly from your bank account can be accessed at ATMs, supermarkets, gas stations, and other stores—how can anyone keep up with their checkbooks with so much action?

success *secret*
Financial planning helps you achieve peace of mind.

While it can be difficult to track your finances down to the penny, you need to know how much money you have and how you want to use it, now and in the future. Many Americans are as little as one paycheck away from homelessness—even multimillion-dollar professional athletes seem to go into debt in the blink of an eye. Having a financial strategy will help you take care of your needs and pursue your dreams without being sidetracked by worry. This does not mean that you can't ever have fun with money, but it does mean that you can make sure you have enough of it to pay the bills and save for the future.

success *secret*
The basic recipe for financial fitness is to spend less than you earn.

The basic recipe for financial fitness is simple: spend less than you earn. This sounds obvious enough, but it requires planning and self-discipline. To manage your money well, follow these three steps:

- **Step 1:** Analyze how you use your money.
- **Step 2:** Prioritize your expenses.
- **Step 3:** Create a plan for your money.

Recognize these steps? They are the same ones you learned for managing your time: analyze, prioritize, and plan.

Step 1: Analyze How You Use Your Money

The first step in improving your money-management skills is to figure out how you handle your money. Do you know where it all goes? One practical way to analyze your spending is to assign each of your expenses to one of three different categories:

- **Fixed committed expenses**—*Fixed committed expenses* are necessary expenses that are the same from month to month, such as rent, car payments, and loan payments.
- **Variable committed expenses**—*Variable committed expenses* are necessary expenses that vary from month to month, such as food and laundry bills, school tuition and books, insurance premiums, auto repairs and registration, vacation expenses, and gifts for birthdays and holidays.
- **Discretionary expenses**—*Discretionary expenses* are lifestyle expenses that are rewarding but not strictly necessary. Common discretionary expenses include entertainment, meals out, movies, magazines, cable television service, and snacks.

Fixed and variable expenses are most people's biggest obligations, but discretionary expenses can add up surprisingly fast. Do you eat out? Do you go to sports events or movies? Do you hunt for bargains, even on things you don't need? There is nothing wrong with discretionary spending, but by the time you're done spending money on things you want, you may not have enough to pay for what you need.

For this reason, one of the most important money-management skills is the ability to distinguish between committed expenses and discretionary expenses. Every time you make a purchase, ask yourself: Is this a necessary expense or a lifestyle expense? Food is a necessary expense, but what about fancy imported jam when the store brand will do? What about cappuccino at a café instead of coffee at home?

The best way to get a handle on your spending is to keep a log of your expenses. This shows you how you deal with money on a day-by-day basis and reveals any negative spending habits.

Some people discover that they spend astounding amounts on small things. Hoyen, for example, kept an expense log and figured out that he spends $148.85 each month on his morning coffee break. Jenna calculated that she lays out $615.00 on birthday presents every year.

Making an expense log requires some diligent work, but it is the best way to get a handle on your money. Use **Activity 44** to create an expense log.

Step 2: Prioritize Your Expenses

Step 2 is to prioritize, to figure out which expenses are important and which are not. Use your values and goals as standards to decide how you will use your money. Do you want to travel abroad? Buy a house or car? Contribute to a cause you find important? You may be passionately

ACTIVITY 44: Expense Log

A For one week, write down exactly how you spend your money. Carry a small notebook and record the date, type of expense, and amount of every purchase you make. Make sure to include small purchases, such as vending-machine purchases. After the week is done, transfer your information to the chart below and assign each expense to a category: fixed committed, variable committed, or discretionary.

Date	Expense	Cost	Category
Example			
Aug. 26	Dry cleaning	$12.34	Variable committed
Aug. 26	Cappuccino	$2.55	Discretionary
Date	Expense	Cost	Category
Total			

continued...

B Add up how much you spent in each of the three categories. Then divide the expenses in each category by the grand total of all your expenses for the week. This is the percentage of your total that you spent in that category.

Total fixed committed expenses: _____   Percent of total: _____

Total variable committed expenses: _____   Percent of total: _____

Total discretionary expenses: _____   Percent of total: _____

Sketch a pie chart of your expenses using the percentages you calculated above. Label each pie slice with the relevant spending category. The slices on the pie chart below represent 10 percent increments.

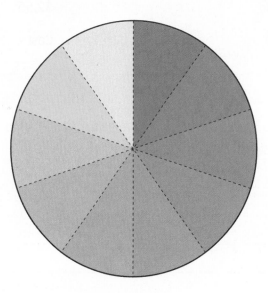

C Are you satisfied with the way you spend your money? Explain.

_____

_____

_____

_____

_____

_____

dedicated to world peace, but if your closet is bursting with shoes or sports equipment, you may be spending your money on the wrong things. You'll need to do some financial planning to make sure that your spending is in line with your values and goals.

As you plan, also think about how much money you will need to devote to the basics such as housing, transportation, food, and health care. Do you want your own place, or would you be willing to live with a roommate? Do you need a car, or could you carpool or use public transportation? Are you planning to eat out once a week, twice a week, or every day? As shown in Figure 8.1, most Americans spend over three-fourths of their income on housing, transportation, food, and health care. After paying for insurance, entertainment, and other expenses such as education, there is often very little left for other things.

Don't Forget Savings Make sure to work savings into your financial plan, too. Most Americans save less than a penny for every ten dollars they earn. Most financial experts, however, recommend saving at least 10 percent of your annual income. Having money set aside allows you to handle unexpected expenses and provides you with peace of mind.

Saving money also helps you reach your goals. Before you make a spending plan, you need to think about how much you will need to set aside in order to achieve your most valued life goals. Obviously, many intrinsic goals, such as building relationships and contributing time to the community, don't cost a cent, but some intrinsic goals do require at least some money. Furthering your education, for example, will probably

success *secret*
Don't spend money on things that don't really matter to you.

success *secret*
Aim to save 10 percent of your income.

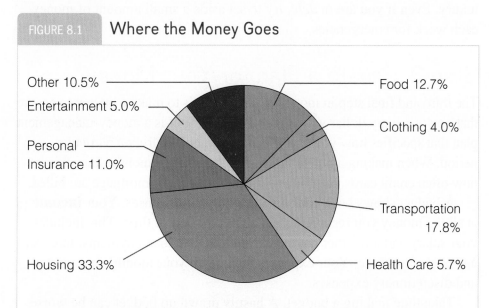

FIGURE 8.1   Where the Money Goes

Other 10.5%
Entertainment 5.0%
Personal Insurance 11.0%
Housing 33.3%

Food 12.7%
Clothing 4.0%
Transportation 17.8%
Health Care 5.7%

Spending by Category   Housing and transportation are Americans' biggest expenses. If you live in an area that lacks affordable housing, you may have to set aside 40 percent of your income to pay the rent or mortgage. *Why do you think that Americans' transportation costs are so high?*

Source: Bureau of Labor Statistics, 2006.

require money. Raising a child will require money. Donating to charitable causes will require money. Try to see savings as a basic necessity, not a luxury. Even if you are in *debt,* try to set aside a small amount of money each week for emergencies.

Step 3: Create a Plan for Your Money

budget A money-management plan that specifies how you will spend your money during a particular period.

income All the money you receive during a fixed period of time.

The third and final step in money management is to make a budget to ensure that you use every dollar with a purpose. A **budget** is a money-management plan that specifies how you will spend your money during a particular period. When making a budget, most people look at a month, since this is how often credit cards, telephone services, and rent or mortgage are billed.

A budget shows both your income and your expenses. Your **income** is all the money you receive during a fixed period of time. This includes your salary and any other payments, such as tips, loan payments, interest, and even allowance. Your expenses include all your monthly committed and discretionary expenses.

Take time making a budget. A hastily drawn up budget can be worse than no budget at all—it can lure you into thinking you have far fewer expenses than you really do. An effective budget meets these criteria:

- It is realistic and accurate, taking into account all the expenses you will face over the month.
- It is balanced, with expenses equal to or less than income.

- It centers around your goals and values.
- It provides for savings.
- It can be modified if necessary.

Keep these guidelines in mind while using **Activity 45** on page 332 to make a practice budget.

STRETCHING YOUR RESOURCES

As we've seen, the basic recipe for financial fitness is to spend less than you earn. This is true whether you are the CEO of a Fortune 500 business or a starving student. If, like many people, you spend more than you earn, you have only three realistic possibilities: earn more, spend less, or both. It's usually not easy to get a raise, find a higher paying job, or take a second (or third) job. Cutting costs, however, is within everyone's reach.

When people try to reduce their expenses, they often become discouraged before they even start. Who wants to eat macaroni and cheese every night or wear the same clothes every day? Cost cutting, however, doesn't have to mean sacrificing every luxury. Approach the cost-cutting task like an analyst examining the finances of a stranger. What areas are money drains? Where can cuts be made? Generate as many creative ideas as you can.

success *secret*
Resist the temptation to overspend.

Applying **Psychology**

The "Mind" of Spending or Saving

Why do some people find it difficult to resist the lure of advertising and therefore succumb to shopping sprees, while others prefer to build their savings accounts? Are you a frugal saver or a compulsive shopaholic? Common sense tells us that we probably develop our financial habits from our parents and early conditioning. Yet, you will find spenders and savers within the same family—those who grew up in poverty, yet created great wealth, and those who squandered their family fortune. Are some people actually "born to shop"?

New research is showing that brain chemistry plays a significant role in our financial habits. According to a study published in the Journal of Consumer Research, an area in the brain called the *insula* is stimulated when people experience unpleasant things. People with more insula activity in their brains are less likely to be big spenders. It could be thought of as our emotional "braking system" for our buying behavior. At the opposite end of the spectrum, the *nucleus accumbens*—identified as the reward center of the brain—"lights up" when people think about something pleasant and serves as the "gas pedal" for our buying behavior. If the *nucleus accumbens* drives impulse purchases, the *insula* is what triggers buyer's remorse. To what extent consumer marketers will utilize advances in neurological scanning to find the "magic buying button" remains to be seen!

Critical Thinking   *What are your thoughts about this new research? Consider and discuss the implications for futuristic consumer marketing technologies.*

ACTIVITY 45: Budget Worksheet

A Use this chart to plan your income and expenses for an average month. To figure out your monthly variable committed expenses, calculate your annual total and then divide by 12. For example, if your car insurance costs $900 per year, then you need to set aside $75 per month for this expense. Record your projected (planned) amounts in the second column, then check your projections by recording the actual amounts in the third column.

INCOME

Item	Projected Amount	Actual Amount
Wages		
Gifts/allowance		
Loans		
(Other—specify) _____		
TOTAL MONTHLY INCOME		

EXPENSES

Item	Projected Amount	Actual Amount
Savings/Emergency Fund		
Emergency fund		
Savings for goal (specify) _____		
Savings for goal (specify) _____		
Total Savings		
Fixed Committed Expenses		
Housing (rent or mortgage payment)		
Car payments		
Child care/child support		
Credit card payments		
Student loan payments		
Phone		
Home insurance		
Car insurance		

Health insurance _____

(Other—specify) _____

(Other—specify) _____

Total Fixed Committed Expenses

Variable Committed Expenses

Food (groceries, lunches) _____

Utilities (electricity, water) _____

Pet expenses _____

Car repair _____

Car registration _____

Dental care _____

Clothing _____

Laundry _____

Dry cleaning _____

Transportation (gas, bus fare, taxi fare) _____

Personal care items _____

Hair cut/style _____

Household repairs and supplies _____

Health care (doctor's visits, medication) _____

Tuition _____

(Other—specify) _____

(Other—specify) _____

Total Variable Committed Expenses

Discretionary Expenses

Eating out _____

Entertainment (movies, plays, outings) _____

Cable TV _____

continued...

Books and educational materials

Magazines and newspapers

Internet service

Health club dues

Vacation fund

Sports

Home improvement (furniture, décor)

Gifts

Charitable contributions

(Other—specify) _____

(Other—specify) _____

Total Discretionary Expenses

TOTAL MONTHLY EXPENSES

B Are your budgeted expenses less than your income, equal to your income, or more than your income? If they are more than your income, how do you plan to make up the difference?

_____

_____

C Did you set aside money for savings? If so, how much and for what? If not, why not?

_____

_____

D How do the projected amounts in your budget compare to the actual amounts? Explain.

_____

_____

_____

Spend, Spend, Spend

Not so long ago, limiting spending was easy. You made a weekly trip to the bank to deposit your paycheck and withdraw enough cash for the upcoming week. No more cash, no more spending.

Today it is easy to spend, spend, and spend some more. Almost every student has access to one or more credit cards and the buying power that goes along with them. We have constant access to cash through ATM machines located everywhere from gas stations and malls to nightclubs. Most ATM cards now function as *debit cards,* making cash unnecessary. But overspending puts you into debt and keeps you from reaching your goals. The average American household has a stack of credit cards and over $8,000 in credit card debt. This is one reason why more and more individuals are filing for bankruptcy.

Drop the Shopping Habit

Many people overspend because they engage in impulse buying and recreational shopping. As mentioned in Chapter 6, **impulse buying** means spending money because you see something and suddenly want it, not because you planned to buy it beforehand. Grocery stores make impulse buying easy by placing appealing items, such as candy and magazines, right next to checkout stands. Even online retailers such as amazon.com cash in on impulse buying by making personalized suggestions for products that shoppers might like to add to their carts.

Recreational shopping means using shopping, especially in malls, as a form of entertainment. Recreational shopping is common in our society; in fact, people now spend more time in malls than anywhere else except home, work, and school. The easiest way to avoid recreational shopping is simply to stop using shopping as a hobby. Plan outings that are low-cost or free, such as hiking, playing sports, or making dinner at a friend's house. Avoid malls, which are specially designed to engage you in an endless loop of shopping.

To avoid impulse buying and recreational shopping, remind yourself again and again to shop only for things that you really need and have planned to buy. Do you really need that fireproof wallet or electronic spatula? Before you buy, ask yourself the following questions:

- Do I really need this item?
- Is there something else I need more?
- What other bills do I have to pay?
- Have I allowed for this item in my budget?
- Is this item worth the time I spent to earn the money to pay for it?
- Do I own something similar already?
- Can I borrow a similar item instead?
- Is there something else less expensive that would be just as good?
- Is this the best time to buy?

impulse buying
Spending money on the spur of the moment, without planning.

success *secret*
Shopping is an expensive hobby.

- Have I comparison shopped for price and quality?
- Do I want to put in the energy required to use, maintain, clean, store, repair, and dispose of this item?
- Am I buying this in an attempt to satisfy a psychological need?

Stopping to ask yourself these questions before you buy can help you limit your spending and become more self-aware. You can also become more self-aware by looking at your past spending mistakes, which you can do in **Personal Journal 8.4.**

credit A sum of money you can use before having to pay back the lender.

Using Credit Wisely

Another important way to take control of your finances is to use credit wisely. **Credit** is a sum of money a person can use before having to pay

Personal Journal 8.4

Look Before You Leap

Think of four purchases you have made over the past year or two that you now wish you hadn't. These might be products, such as clothing or housewares, or services, such as entertainment or travel. For ideas, look around your living space or review past credit card statements. On the chart below, describe each purchase, the reason for the purchase at the time, and why you think you shouldn't have spent the money.

Purchase	Why You Made Purchase	Why You Wish You Hadn't

What could you do the next time you are tempted to make a similar purchase?

back the lender. When you use credit, you are really taking out a loan. Credit transactions can be as simple as using a credit card to buy gas or as complex as taking out a $200,000 mortgage to buy a house.

Credit is useful because it allows you to receive a product or service now and pay for it over time. If you buy a car on credit, for example, you can pay a fixed installment every month until the car is paid for. This makes budgeting easy. Using credit cards is safer than carrying cash and easier than writing checks, and a credit card bill provides a useful record of your purchases.

The Perils of Credit   Unfortunately, credit cards make it easy to accumulate debt. It's easy to lose track of how much you are spending and to engage in impulse buying. Practically every large chain store now offers a credit card, and it is common for consumers to have five or even ten credit cards in their wallets.

It's hard to keep track of credit card bills, especially when each bill is due on a different date. Late fees are steep, often running $29.00 or more. In addition, if you don't pay off your credit card bill every month, you will owe not only the amount of your purchases, but also *finance charges*. Finance charges add up amazingly quickly. Let's say you charge a $2,000 vacation on your credit card. If you only pay the minimum monthly payment, it will take you 11 years to pay off that vacation. Along the way, you'll also pay nearly $2,000 in finance charges, doubling the cost of your vacation. Are you one of the millions who overuse credit? Ask yourself whether you would use credit:

- to pay overdue bills, especially on other credit cards
- to buy an item that costs $5.00 or less
- to pay for a vacation
- to pay for a large purchase you hadn't saved for
- even if you could pay cash

If you answered yes to these questions, you are relying on credit cards to pay for things that you can't really afford.

If you are already in debt, spend as little as you can and devote every penny (after savings) to paying off the debt. If you have multiple credit cards, consolidate your debt to the one with the smallest interest rate. You can also call your creditors or consult a consumer credit counseling service to work out a payment arrangement.

Your Credit Record   The way you use credit affects your financial situation not only today, but also in the future. That's because your credit situation goes into an electronic file, known as a credit record, that employers, landlords, and others can access at any time. A **credit record** is a log of the financial habits of a person who buys on credit.

Several corporations, known as credit bureaus, are in the business of selling the information on your credit record. When you apply for a new

credit record A log of the financial habits of a person who buys on credit.

credit card or a loan at a bank, the bank will ask one or more of these companies for a report on how much you've borrowed, how much you've paid back, and whether you've had problems paying on time.

Having a good credit record is essential if you want to buy a house, lease or buy a car, or rent an apartment. Some employers even check potential employees' credit records. To establish good credit, pay all bills promptly, avoid large debts, and do not bounce checks. To improve a bad credit record, open a small line of credit, such as a credit account at a local store, and make regular payments. This shows potential lenders, employers, and landlords that you are trustworthy.

Keep It in Perspective

Economist John Maynard Keynes once said, "The importance of money flows from it being a link between the present and the future." When you are in debt, you spend most of your time scrambling to make up for the past rather than planning for the future. If you don't keep track of what you spend, you can waste a lot of money without even realizing it. You work hard for your money, and you should use it for the things that mean the most to you. Spending and saving wisely gives you the freedom to plan for the future.

Self Check

1. What is a budget? (p. 330)
2. What is impulse buying? (p. 335)
3. What are the pros and cons of using credit? (p. 337)

Key Terms

time management (p. 306)

to-do list (p. 312)

schedule (p. 315)

procrastination (p. 318)

money management (p. 323)

finances (p. 325)

budget (p. 330)

income (p. 330)

impulse buying (p. 335)

credit (p. 336)

credit record (p. 337)

Summary by Learning Objectives

- **Outline the three steps in time management and in money management.** The three steps in time management are: 1. analyze how you use your time; 2. prioritize your activities; and 3. create a plan (to-do list and schedule) for your time. The three steps in money management are: 1. analyze how you use your money; 2. prioritize your expenses; and 3. create a plan (budget) for your money.

- **Describe the three categories of time and the three categories of expenses.** The three categories of time are: 1. committed time, the time you devote to goal-related activities; 2. maintenance time, the time you spend taking care of yourself; and 3. discretionary time, the time you use to do whatever you wish. The three categories of expenses are: 1. fixed committed expenses, necessary expenses that are the same each month; 2. variable committed expenses, necessary expenses that vary from month to month; and 3. discretionary expenses, lifestyle expenses that are not strictly necessary.

- **Explain how to make a to-do list and a schedule.** To make a to-do list, write down all the tasks and activities you need to complete over the course of a certain period, such as a week. As you accomplish each one, check it off the list. Make a schedule by noting tasks and activities and do-by dates.

- **Define procrastination and explain its causes.** Procrastination is the habit of putting off tasks until the last minute. Procrastination can stem from self-handicapping, perfectionism, or a lack of self-motivation.

- **Describe the criteria for an effective budget.** An effective budget meets the following criteria: it is realistic and accurate, taking into account all the expenses you will face over the month; it is balanced, with expenses equal to or less than income; it centers around your goals and values; it provides for savings; and it can be modified if necessary.

- **Cite ways to reduce excess spending.** Ways to reduce excess spending include using credit wisely; checking impulse buying by stopping to analyze each purchase; and choosing recreational activities other than shopping.

Review and Activities

Review Questions

1. What is the difference between committed time and discretionary time?
2. List three benefits of using a to-do list.
3. Why is it important to prioritize your tasks and activities?
4. How do emotions affect people's relationship with money?
5. Why is it important to analyze your spending habits?
6. What are the pros and cons of credit?

Critical Thinking

7. **Time Management**   Making to-do lists and schedules saves time, but it also takes time. Do you create to-do lists for yourself? If so, how are they working for you? Are they saving you time? If you aren't using to-do lists for yourself, how do you get things done? Think about the pros and cons of using to-do lists and schedules.

8. **Voluntary Simplicity**   Voluntary simplicity is an approach to living that focuses on frugal consumption, ecological awareness, and personal and relationship growth rather than on material wealth and showy accomplishments. People who believe in voluntary simplicity often change their lifestyles to work (and earn) less, want less, and spend less. Does this approach to life and spending appeal to you? Why or why not? In what ways would this lifestyle be challenging for you? What might you miss from the "material world"? What might you gain from living this way?

Application

9. **Money Management Mentors**   Identify two or three people you know who are financially "successful." Set up some time to interview them on their approach to managing money. How closely do they track their spending? What percentage of their income do they save? What tips can they offer you for adhering to a budget? Summarize your findings. How might you be able to adopt any of their habits into your own life? Consider asking if any of these people would be willing to meet with you again to review your progress, and perhaps offer you some ongoing "money mentoring."

10. **Busting Procrastination**   Make a list of important tasks you've been putting off, or projects you have yet to complete. You could include tasks such as simply doing laundry, sending out your rèsumè, following up on a job interview, or paying a monthly bill. Choose the task you're resisting the most, first. Either today or tomorrow, set aside fifteen minutes to work on this task. Assemble whatever materials you need and set a timer for fifteen minutes. When the timer goes off, stop. How much did you get done? Was the task easier than you thought? Are you motivated to continue working? Did you find you wanted to move on to your next task immediately? Continue this habit on a daily basis, perhaps extending your timer for thirty minutes. You will be surprised how much you actually accomplish in a week's time!

Internet Activities

11. **Managing College Life**   College life for students, no matter what age or educational pursuit, can be quite challenging to manage. Besides taking classes, both on-campus and on-line, students may also be working in part-time or full-time jobs while juggling social activities, family obligations, fitness goals, and financial management. Fortunately, there are a multitude of Apps available to help students manage a full range of activities from organizing lecture notes, outlines and projects, and keeping track of assignments to tracking spending, meeting savings goals, and managing social life. Go online and search for apps that work for you and your own situation. To get you started, visit the following sites:

    http://mashable.com/2013/08/08/apps-for-college

    http://buzzfeed.com/regajha/apps-every-college-student-should-download-right-now

12. **Managing Student Loan Debt**   It has become increasingly difficult to keep up with the very loans students took out to ensure their future success. The student loan debt has increased by 300 percent over the past eight years, with over 37 million Americans in debt because of their education. What precautions should you take when applying for, and repaying, student loans? How can you safeguard your future? Conduct an online search for current information about student loan debt, and resources to help manage it. You can start with the following sites:

    https://businessinsider.com/how-to-pay-student-loans-faster-2014-5

    http://projectonstudentdebt.org/recent_grads.vp.html

Real-Life Success Story	**"Will I Ever Be Able to Enjoy Some 'Free' Time?"**

Look back at your response to the question in the Real-Life Success Story on page 304. Think about how you would answer the question now that you have completed the chapter.

Complete the Story   Write a short note to Anna. In it, suggest that she use a to-do list and schedule and explain how doing this could help her stay on track at work and still make time for fun.

"How Do I Stand Up for Myself?"

Climbing the Ladder

Joe was on his way. He had completed his associate degree in accounting and been accepted for transfer to a four-year university. Before continuing his studies, he decided to take a six-month internship at one of the best-known accounting firms in the country. The internship only paid minimum wage, but Joe was excited about getting real-world experience and solid professional references.

Suffering in Silence

It wasn't long before Joe ran into problems. His supervisor, Mr. Douridas, was never around to answer questions, but he almost always found time to criticize Joe's work. Joe double- and triple-checked his figures, but Mr. Douridas always found something to nitpick. Joe suspected that his boss didn't realize the effect of his harsh words, and he wished he could say something to improve the situation—but what? He asked for advice from his coworkers, but they recommended that he keep his mouth shut. Joe became so discouraged that he considered quitting rather than face work one more day.

What Do You Think? How could Joe handle his conflict with his supervisor?

Communication and Relationships

> " The most important single ingredient in the formula of success is knowing how to get along with people. "
>
> Theodore Roosevelt, Politician

introduction

Over the course of this book you've looked at all sides of yourself and considered what you want out of life. In this final chapter you'll learn about making connections with others. In Section 9.1 you'll focus on interpersonal communication. You'll explore the communication process, learn how to become an effective speaker and an active listener, and examine how you can use your communication skills to resolve conflicts with others. In Section 9.2 you'll explore the nature of relationships, learning how they form and develop and what skills you can use to strengthen them.

learning objectives

After you complete this chapter, you should be able to:

- Describe the six elements of communication.

- Summarize the forms and functions of nonverbal communication.

- List several skills necessary for effective speaking and active listening.

- Explain the relationship between stereotypes, prejudice, and empathy.

- Define intimacy and explain how to develop it in a relationship.

- Cite the characteristics of satisfying intimate relationships.

- Explain how to handle conflict effectively.

A LOOK AT COMMUNICATION

communication
The process of giving or exchanging messages.

What exactly is communication? **Communication** is the process of giving or exchanging messages. A *message* is an expression of thought or feeling. Messages can take the form of words, but they can also take the form of sounds, gestures, actions, or facial expressions. A raised eyebrow, a sigh, or a scream, for example, is a message. Messages can even be conveyed through music, dance, visual art, acting, or any other expressive form.

People communicate for many reasons: to convey facts and ideas, share feelings, give orders, persuade, entertain, and even deceive. The most important function of communication, however, is to create and maintain bonds between people. You get to know people through communication, whether in person, by phone, or via a number of online social media platforms. You also maintain your existing relationships through communication. When people avoid talking to each other or feel they have nothing left to say, it is a sure sign that their relationship is in trouble.

People with excellent communication skills enjoy the happiest relationships. They have stronger friendships, romantic relationships, and family relationships, and they get along better with coworkers. Having excellent communication skills also makes you a sought-after employee. Employers are always searching for candidates who have excellent communication skills, as well as skills that depend on good communication, such as teamwork skills, leadership skills, and people skills.

Interpersonal Communication

interpersonal communication One-on-one, usually face-to-face communication.

There are four basic communication skills: writing, reading, speaking, and listening. In this chapter we'll focus on speaking and listening, which are the skills most often used in interpersonal communication. **Interpersonal communication** is one-on-one, usually face-to-face communication. Interpersonal communication is usually spontaneous and informal. This makes it very different from other forms of communication such as written communication, public speaking, and mass (media) communication.

success *secret*
Good communicators are self-aware.

Every time you interact with another person, you engage in interpersonal communication. Even if you don't use words, your body language says a great deal about what you are thinking and feeling. In fact, your body language sends messages even if you aren't aware of it.

Most of us spend a large part of our day talking and hearing other people talk. This doesn't mean that we are great communicators, however. Communicating well requires many skills—self-awareness, cultural awareness, honesty, respect and compassion for others, and openness to other points of view. Take a moment to assess how much you know about communication by completing **Activity 46.**

ACTIVITY 46: How Much Do You Know About Communication?

A Read the following statements about communication and indicate whether each one is True or False by checking the appropriate box.

	True	False
1. Making eye contact with a speaker shows that you are interested in what he or she is saying.		
2. Facial expressions can help you get your message across.		
3. Time and place have a large effect on communication.		
4. Showing respect for others is part of good communication.		
5. Leaning slightly toward a person who is speaking shows that you are interested in what he or she is saying.		
6. Communicating well is a skill that can be learned.		
7. Observing body language is part of listening.		
8. It's important to be able to disagree without getting angry or abusive.		
9. Being silent is one way of encouraging someone to continue speaking.		
10. If someone is telling you about a personal problem, giving advice can make him or her feel that you're not really listening.		
11. A speaker's body language can reveal whether he or she is lying or covering something up.		
12. When someone is struggling for words, it's important not to interrupt to "help."		
13. Part of good listening is trying to understand the other person's point of view.		
14. Emotional self-awareness helps prevent a breakdown in communication.		
15. Listening is a psychological process.		
16. The medium in which a message is conveyed influences the way it is interpreted.		
17. Wordless signals such as body language can convey up to 90 percent of a message.		
18. People are sometimes unaware of the message their body language is sending.		
19. Each person uses body language differently.		
20. Good communicators take responsibility for their own feelings.		

continued...

B **Scoring:** All of these statements about communication are true. The more times you checked True, the more you know about good communication. How many times did you check True? _____

Are you surprised that all of these statements about communication are true? Explain.

_____

_____

_____

_____

_____

C Why would showing respect for others be a part of good communication?

_____

_____

_____

_____

_____

D Do you consider yourself a good communicator? Why or why not?

_____

_____

_____

_____

_____

Elements of Communication

Communication is a process, a back-and-forth exchange of thoughts and feelings. This process is more complex than most of us realize. Every exchange has six different elements: sender, message, channel, receiver, feedback, and context. Let's examine each one. (See Figure 9.1.)

Sender   The *sender* is the person who translates a thought or feeling into a message and then sends this message to another person. The sender could be a writer, a speaker, or a person who sends a nonverbal (wordless) message with physical movement.

Message   The *message* is the sender's expression of a thought or feeling. It can be written, spoken, or nonverbal. Let's say that you and a friend are at a party, and you're ready to leave. You could send this message in several ways: by saying words such as "let's go," by sending a brief text on your smart phone, by gesturing toward the exit, or even by pushing your friend out the door.

Channel   The **channel** is the medium in which a message is delivered. The channel has a large effect on the way the message comes across. Let's say your boss leaves you a voicemail asking you to come to her

channel The medium in which a message is delivered.

FIGURE 9.1   Elements of Communication

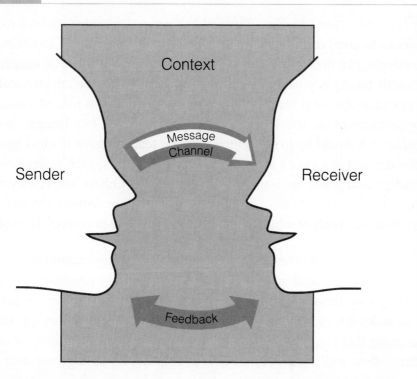

Sending and Receiving   Every communication requires a sender, a message, a channel, a receiver, feedback, and a context. *Which channels of communication make it impossible for the receiver to provide feedback immediately?*

office to discuss a project. Think of how differently this message would come across if she drafted it in a formal memo or hired a singing telegram to surprise you with it at your home.

context The time and place of communication.

Context

Context is the time and place of communication. Context, like channel, has a large effect on the communication process. Let's say you are in your instructor's office discussing a possible grade change. How would the conversation be different if it took place at a crowded party, at a funeral reception, or in class with all your fellow students listening? Would you say the same things? Would you get the same responses? Being aware of context can help you choose the right words and predict the other person's reactions.

Communication Breakdown

success *secret*
Good communication requires effort.

The goal of communication is to have the receiver interpret the message the way the sender intended. This goal sounds simple enough, but it isn't always easy to achieve. The communication process is complex, and misunderstandings can arise easily. Have you ever heard a "yes" when the other person was trying to say "no"? Have you ever made a harmless comment and had someone take it the wrong way?

Each of us has different experiences, goals, expectations, ideas, perceptions, feelings, and moods, and these can create barriers to good communication. Communication breaks down when physical, emotional, or cultural barriers get in the way of understanding.

Physical Barriers

Physical barriers are the most obvious roadblocks to good communication. Background noise or poor acoustics, for example, can make it difficult for you to hear a speaker. You may have trouble taking in what you are hearing or reading if you are physically uncomfortable or if the speaker is using an unpleasant tone of voice. The appearance of the speaker can be a physical barrier, too. Imagine how difficult it would be to concentrate if your teacher came to class one day dressed in a clown suit. Some physical barriers, such as deafening background noise, are impossible to overcome. Others, such as trying to have two conversations at once, can be changed or reduced through self-awareness. Analyze what is bothering you and try to correct the problem.

success *secret*
Emotional awareness helps you communicate well.

Emotional Barriers

Communication is a psychological process as well as a physical one. Barriers, therefore, can be emotional as well as physical. Emotions such as sadness, excitement, boredom, or anxiety can make it hard to pay attention to what someone else is saying. Imagine learning that you have just won the lottery or lost a friend in a car accident—how well would you be able to concentrate during your next class?

Receiver

The *receiver* is the person who takes in, or receives, the sender's message. The way the receiver interprets the message depends on his or her personality, past experiences, interest level, emotional state, and knowledge of the subject. The relationship between the sender and the receiver also affects the way the receiver interprets the message. For example, you probably wouldn't think twice if your boss instructed you to drop what you were doing and work on her expense report. However, how would you react if your roommate ordered you to drop what you were doing and finish her math homework?

Feedback   *Feedback* is the receiver's response to a message. Senders rely on feedback to figure out how the receiver is interpreting their message. Feedback can take many forms—agreement, disagreement, questions, confusion, anger, delight. It can consist of words ("I see"), expressions ("uh huh"), or actions (nodding, smiling, running away).

Conflicting emotions can take a toll on communication, too. Our words are expressions of our thoughts, so confused thoughts will produce confused (and confusing) messages. If you have conflicting feelings about a person, for example, you won't be able to convey a clear message. You might find yourself stammering, hesitating, or saying something you don't really mean.

Speakers and listeners bring their emotions to every conversation, which can lead to misunderstandings on both sides. If you are extremely angry at your best friend, for example, you may find it difficult to choose the right words or construct coherent sentences. You may interpret her words in a distorted way or engage in *selective listening,* choosing what you want to hear and ignoring the rest. People often use selective listening to block out the part of the message that is threatening their self-esteem.

Overcoming emotional barriers requires emotional awareness. When you recognize and accept what you are feeling, you become aware of how your emotions affect your ability to communicate.

Language and Cultural Barriers   For two people to communicate, they should ideally speak the same language. But just because people share a common language doesn't mean they share a common cultural background. It can be difficult to communicate with people from different cultural groups or geographic areas who use words and concepts that are unfamiliar to you. Each culture also has its own conventions about verbal and nonverbal communication, many of which can be baffling to outsiders. In Bulgaria, for example, nodding your head up and down means "no" and shaking your head side to side means "yes." The thumbs-up gesture is positive in most of the world, but in Australia it is an insult.

Cultural *taboos,* or prohibitions, can make it particularly difficult to get a message across. Let's say you ask your new British acquaintance what he does for a living in an attempt to show interest and get to know him better. Unfortunately, in England this question is considered rude because it is interpreted as a question about a person's income. You can avoid such misunderstandings by developing *cultural awareness,* the ability to recognize the ways cultures differ and how these differences affect cross-cultural interactions. Since we function in a global village, it is important for us to learn about communication norms in countries we plan to visit, as well as in individuals from other cultures with whom we interact on a daily basis. Being culturally aware also means being aware of how your culture influences your behavior.

Now it's time to apply what you've learned about communication to real-world situations. In **Activity 47** you'll observe the elements of communication in action.

NONVERBAL COMMUNICATION

Think of how many ways you can express how you feel without saying a single word. You can use gestures, facial expressions, body movements, even sounds. Think about the last time you were bored with a lecture. Did you keep glancing at your watch? Did you yawn? Sigh?

These wordless signals, or cues, are examples of nonverbal communication. **Nonverbal communication** is the process of giving or exchanging information without words. It is "speaking" without words. Did you know that you can even communicate nonverbally in a telephone conversation? A smile affects the tone of your voice.

Nonverbal cues can reveal more about us than the words we speak. They help us get an idea of the person we are talking to—who they are, what they think, what they feel. If someone has crossed arms, he or she may feel defensive. Hands on hips may show aggressiveness. A person who looks down or away from you may feel self-conscious or guilty. Eyes can show surprise or anger.

The most important nonverbal message is self-confidence. A smile, good eye contact, upright posture, and a firm handshake all project your self-assurance. A smile is the universal language that opens doors. It is the light in your window that tells others there is a caring and sharing person inside. When you put out your hand to shake another's, you show that you value that person. This tradition began in ancient times as a double-handed clasp to show that a weapon was not concealed. Anyone who would not shake hands was looked at with suspicion. Think about handshakes you have received from others. Which do you react positively to? A firm handshake (not a tight grip, not a limp hand) conveys the impression of a confident person.

Functions of Nonverbal Communication

Nonverbal communication has many functions. We use it to maintain human bonds, convey facts and ideas, share feelings, give orders, persuade, entertain, or even deceive other people. The most frequent functions of nonverbal communication fall into three categories: managing conversations, providing feedback, and clarifying verbal messages.

Managing Conversations
Managing conversations means starting conversations, helping them flow smoothly, and ending them. People use gestures and facial expressions to signal that they have

nonverbal communication

The process of giving or exchanging messages without words.

success *secret*

Nonverbal signals often tell more than words.

ACTIVITY 47: Analyzing Communication

A Observe a conversation between two people you've never met. Note all six elements of communication: the identity or role of the sender, the content of the message, the channel of the message, the identity or role of the receiver, the content of the feedback, and the context of the conversation.

Sender: _____

Message: _____

Channel: _____

Receiver: _____

Feedback: _____

Context: _____

Could you figure out the relationship between the sender and the receiver? If so, how? If not, why not? (Consider both verbal and nonverbal information.)

_____

_____

_____

_____

_____

Did any physical, emotional, or cultural barriers affect the conversation? Explain.

_____

_____

_____

_____

_____

continued...

B Now describe the same elements for a conversation in which you were involved.

Sender: _____

Message: _____

Channel: _____

Receiver: _____

Feedback: _____

Context: _____

What was the relationship between you and the other person, and how do you think it influenced the conversation? For example, how did it affect the words you chose, your tone of voice, and so on?

_____

_____

_____

_____

_____

Did any physical, emotional, or cultural barriers affect the conversation? Explain.

_____

_____

_____

_____

_____

_____

something to say or that they want to keep the floor. If you begin talking when someone hasn't finished, for example, he or she might talk louder or make a hand gesture indicating "wait." Nonverbal cues can end conversations, too. If you stand up, fidget, and look at your watch while someone is chatting with you, it's obvious that you're ready for the conversation to end.

Providing Feedback The second function of nonverbal communication is to provide feedback. Nonverbal feedback tells you a lot about what the other person is thinking and feeling. Let's say you are a store manager considering two candidates, Patrick and Dayla, for a sales job. During his interview, Patrick smiles and leans forward attentively as you explain the specifics of the job. This says, "I'm really interested in what you're saying" and "I've got a positive attitude." Dayla, on the other hand, smirks and sits back with her arms folded. This sends the message, "I couldn't care less what you're saying" and "I'm too good for this job." Which candidate would you hire?

Clarifying Messages The third function of communication is to clarify verbal messages. Nonverbal cues such as tone of voice and body language can often convey far more information than words. Let's say your roommate tells you the dishes are dirty. If she says this in an apologetic tone with downcast eyes, you will probably figure that she is repenting for leaving dirty dishes in the sink again. But what if she says the same thing in a hostile tone, pointing an accusing finger at you? This same sentence is now sending an entirely different message.

Nonverbal cues can also be a dead giveaway that a speaker feels something different from what he or she is saying. Your company president might say that there won't be any layoffs this year, but if he is shuffling his feet and avoiding eye contact, you might think he knows something he's not saying.

Forms of Nonverbal Communication

Nonverbal communication is versatile in form as well as function. It can incorporate any or all of the five senses—sight, sound, touch, even smell, and taste. A caress can show love, a whistle can mean "look over here!" and a nod can convey agreement. A person might apply cologne or perfume for a date in order to send the message, "I am desirable." A used car dealer might spray his merchandise with new car smell to convince buyers that the cars are just like new. What would you think if your spouse surprised you with a delicious home-cooked meal? What if he or she poured a cup of salt into your coffee? All of these actions send powerful messages.

The three most common and important forms of nonverbal communication are voice, personal distance, and body language. Voice involves sound, personal distance involves sight, touch, and smell, and body language involves sight.

success *secret*
Nonverbal cues often suggest what a person is thinking and feeling.

success *secret*
Pay attention to nonverbal cues in all five senses.

Voice Your voice is a powerful instrument. You can vary the sound of your voice by speed (fast or slow), pitch (high or low), volume (loud or quiet), and tone (empathetic, sarcastic, whining, etc.). Each of these factors influences your message. Speaking loudly, for example, can make you seem agitated or hostile. Speaking quickly conveys the impression of anxiety, excitement, or urgency. Depending on what tone of voice you use, your message can come across as heartfelt, ironic, angry, or in practically any other way.

Personal Distance *Personal distance* refers to the amount of space between you and the people with whom you are communicating. When talking with a stranger or casual acquaintance, the average North American usually stands at least four feet away from the other person. For conversations with friends, family, and coworkers, most of us maintain a distance of 18 inches to four feet. We reserve the space below 18 inches for our most intimate relationships, such as friends and partners. The amount of physical space you keep between yourself and another person, therefore, can say a lot about your relationship.

body language Facial expressions, posture, and gestures.

Body Language **Body language** refers to facial expressions, posture, and gestures. *Facial expressions* involve movements of the mouth, the eyebrows and forehead, and the eyes. Facial expressions are the main nonverbal cues to a person's emotions. Raised eyebrows, for example, indicate surprise or fear; a furrowed brow signals tension, worry, or deep thought; and a distant stare can suggest boredom. Facial expressions are such a basic part of human psychology that it takes a great deal of effort to suppress or fake them.

Gestures are movements of the arms, hands, legs, and feet. They are used to display emotion, illustrate a point, move a conversation in a certain direction, or even signify membership in a social group (think of secret handshakes used by certain clubs).

Posture, the way we carry ourselves when sitting or standing, also says a lot about who we are. An upright posture is associated with confidence and authority, while a lowered head and slumped shoulders indicate inferior status or emotional burden, as in the phrase "to shoulder a burden." Leaning forward shows eagerness and interest in the other person, whereas leaning back can send the message that something is wrong. Changing our posture can make us change the way we feel about ourselves, too; sitting or standing up straight can give us a boost of self-confidence.

success *secret*
Our voices and bodies are powerful communication tools.

Interpreting Nonverbal Cues

Interpreting nonverbal cues is not always easy. For one thing, almost all nonverbal cues have multiple meanings. Depending on the context, for example, laughter can mean many different things. If you laugh at the punch line of a joke, you are probably saying, "I find that funny." But

Applying **Psychology**

Emotional Intelligence

Because our world is changing so rapidly, particularly in areas of social networking, our IQ, or mental intelligence, is not enough to help us live a successful and fulfilling life. We must learn to develop our EQ—emotional intelligence, which is the ability to understand and discriminate and monitor our own feelings, as well as those of others. Although both IQ and EQ are important in determining our success, researchers believe that IQ counts for roughly 10 percent (at best 25 percent), and the rest involves EQ. Emotional intelligence addresses the following categories of behavior: self-awareness, self-management or regulation, motivation, empathy, and relationship management or interpersonal/social skills. Having a high level of emotional intelligence can also help you manage stress by your ability to adapt to change and demonstrate resiliency in the face of challenges. Many of the leading organizations recognize the value of emotionally intelligent leaders, and are implementing training and coaching programs to raise the EQ level of their workforce.

What's Your Opinion?

Why do you think emotional intelligence is so important? In what situations might your EQ better serve you than your IQ? How will society benefit from people developing their EQs, compared to their IQs? Should EQ be taught and tested in schools?

laughter can also signify nervousness, sarcasm, or ridicule, and it can be a way to relieve stress and to boost the mood of people around you.

Nonverbal signals are also influenced by interlocking cultural, gender, and individual differences, as shown in Figure 9.2.

Each culture has different rules about where, when, and with whom the expression of emotion is allowed. In addition, gestures, touch, personal

FIGURE 9.2   Influences on Nonverbal Communication

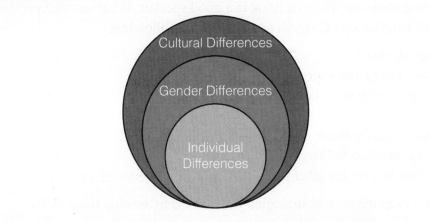

Putting It in Context   Nonverbal signals are used in different ways by different cultural groups, by men and women, and by individuals. *What do you think explains the fact that women use submissive nonverbal signals more often than men do?*

distance, and other nonverbal signals are used in different ways from culture to culture. In Arab cultures, for example, intense and prolonged eye contact is much more frequent than in North American and European cultures, where such eye contact is regarded as intrusive.

Men and women also use nonverbal signals differently, even when they are from the same culture. For example, women smile and make eye contact much more often than men. They also show more submissive nonverbal behaviors, such as lowering their eyes, moving out of other people's path, and allowing other people to interrupt them.

Individuals use nonverbal communication in unique ways, too. Remember the company president who talked about layoffs? You sensed he was lying because he shuffled his feet and avoided eye contact. But when your girlfriend uses the same body language when she tells you she loves you, you know this means she is feeling nervous and vulnerable. That's because you have learned to read her unique body language.

Because of all these influences on nonverbal communication, it's important to interpret nonverbal cues in the light of the verbal message that goes along with them, the cultural background and gender of the sender, and the context of the communication. Perform an experiment in decoding nonverbal communication by completing **Activity 48.**

IMPROVING YOUR COMMUNICATION SKILLS

Communication skills, like all other skills, are developed through learning and practice. Now that you've learned more about the different aspects of communication, you can put this knowledge into practice to improve your communication skills.

Becoming an Effective Speaker

Picture someone who you think is a good speaker. What sets that person apart from others? Chances are, they do the following:

- speak clearly
- use a large and expressive vocabulary
- use positive body language
- tell the truth
- welcome feedback
- pay attention to listeners' nonverbal signals
- show respect for other people's feelings and points of view

Let's examine several strategies you can use to develop these skills.

Build Your Vocabulary
To speak effectively, you need to be able to express what you think and feel in words. English has more than 1,000,000 words, yet the average person can only use 50,000 of them.

ACTIVITY 48: Body Language Log

A Pay attention to the gestures, facial expressions, and postures that a roommate, close friend, or family member often uses. For example, does he or she often roll his or her eyes to signal irritation, or dance to show happiness? List a few of his or her body language habits and what you think they mean.

Body Language	Meaning

B Review your list with the person you observed. Is he or she surprised by any of your observations? Does he or she agree or disagree with the meanings you wrote in the second column? Explain.

continued...

C Now pay attention to the gestures, facial expressions, and postures you often use. Make a list of your body language habits and what they mean. Ask a family member or good friend to help you if you find it difficult to observe yourself objectively.

Body Language	Meaning

D Did any of your observations surprise you? For example, did you become aware of any habits you didn't know you had? Explain.

Building your vocabulary helps you find the right words to express yourself. Since we do much of our thinking in words, expanding your vocabulary also means expanding your tools of thought.

Work on developing your vocabulary by reading widely on the subjects that interest you. Stop when you find an unfamiliar word, guess its meaning from the context, then look the word up in a dictionary to check your guess.

Be Direct and Honest

Effective communicators are honest and sincere, not phony. Being false or manipulative can undermine your credibility, your listener's interest, and his or her trust in you. Honesty, by contrast, creates a positive communication climate. Making eye contact is a good way to create rapport and project honesty. Also make sure to avoid conflicting messages, such as saying that everything is going fine when your body language says otherwise. Have you ever told a white lie to spare a person's feelings, only to have it snowball into a bigger and bigger lie? Avoid this damaging situation by being honest, but tactful, from the start.

Welcome Feedback

Effective speaking also means welcoming feedback, not just talking to hear the sound of your voice. Try to stay open to all kinds of feedback, even if it isn't what you want to hear. Pay special attention to nonverbal feedback, which can help you detect what the other person is feeling. If you see that what you are saying is creating negative feelings, you can try to convey your message in a different way. If you realize you have made a mistake, said something confusing, or hurt a person's feelings, acknowledge the issue and apologize. This helps build trust and prevent conflict.

Show Respect

Respecting others builds trust and goodwill, which are essential for good communication. Make a conscious effort to understand and respect other people's points of view, even if you don't agree with them. This is especially important when you interact with people from other backgrounds and cultures. Approach every conversation as a chance for open, honest communication. This will make the other person feel more at ease, enabling a real exchange of ideas.

Another important way to show respect for others is to take responsibility for your feelings. Do you ever find yourself saying things like, "you make me so mad" or "you're driving me crazy"? Emotional messages like these that begin with the word "you" are known as *"you" statements*. They express a belief about the other person, often blaming him or her for your problems or negative feelings. Instead of beginning with the word "you," try starting with the word "I" or the words "I feel": "I feel angry when you don't say goodbye in the morning." "I get worried when you come home late without calling." Shifting the focus from "you" to "I" shows that you are taking responsibility for your feelings. Adding an explanation of your feelings is a good idea as well, because it helps the other person understand your point of view: "I feel angry when you don't say goodbye in the morning, because I wonder if you still love me." "I get worried when you come home late without calling, because I start imagining that you've been in a car accident." Practice using *"I" statements* in **Personal Journal 9.1.**

Becoming an Active Listener

active listening

Listening with understanding and paying close attention to what is being said.

Communication is a two-way street. When one person is speaking, the other needs to be listening—actively. **Active listening** means listening with understanding and paying close attention to what is being said. Unlike hearing, which is a physical process, active listening is a psychological process. Active listening requires three skills, which make up the acronym EAR—encouraging, attending, and responding.

Personal Journal 9.1

"I" Statements

Change each of the following "you" statements into an "I" statement. Use the format "I feel . . . about . . . because . . ." or "I feel . . . when you . . . because . . . ."

Example

You never do what you promise.

I feel disappointed when you don't keep a promise, because I think that you don't value our relationship.

You always interrupt when I'm talking.

_____

You just have to criticize, don't you?

_____

You're late again, as usual.

_____

You need to help out more around the house.

_____

You get on my nerves when you act so babyish.

_____

How does it feel to begin these statements with the word "I"?

Encouraging   *Encouraging* others means showing a desire to listen. You can do this by using *open questions,* which allow for a broad range of responses. These are more effective at eliciting information than *closed questions,* which ask for a one- or two-word answer. "What careers are you interested in?" is an open question, while "Have you chosen a career yet?" is a closed question.

During a conversation, you can encourage the speaker to continue his or her thoughts in different ways, such as:

- directly asking the person to continue talking ("go on," "you were saying . . .")
- using brief words, sounds, or gestures to let the person know you are listening ("mmm hmm," "really!," "I see," nodding, smiling)
- remaining silent to give the speaker room to continue
- using positive body language such as eye contact and a slightly leaning posture to indicate interest

Resist the urge to interrupt, finish the other person's sentences, or "help" him or her express the message. Use questions infrequently, since questions shift the focus away from the listener and back to you.

Attending   The second component of active listening is paying attention, or **attending**—being focused, alert, and open to receiving information.

Attending can be difficult, especially if you are tired or bored. To boost your interest in the topic of discussion, try to relate it to something in your own experience. Also beware of the habit of planning what you are going to say next while the other person is still talking. Since people think many times faster than they can talk, it's easy to let your mind race ahead of the speaker. If you are buried in your own thoughts, however, you won't be able to pay attention to anyone else. Think of how you feel when you realize that someone isn't really listening to you. Have you ever had a phone conversation with someone who continually puts you on hold in order to take other calls? If you don't pay attention, the other person may feel hurt or annoyed.

attending Being focused, alert, and open to receiving information.

Responding   The third component of active listening is *responding,* or giving constructive feedback. Avoid the temptation to pass judgment or give advice, criticize or minimize the speaker's emotions, or try to change the topic to yourself. We all know what it's like to receive an insensitive response such as, "What's the big deal?" or "That reminds me of the time I . . ."

Instead of dismissing the speaker's concerns with comments like these, use the techniques of paraphrasing and reflecting. **Paraphrasing** is restating the factual content of the message. **Reflecting** is restating the emotional content of the message. Paraphrasing and reflecting show that you have listened and that you accept and value the other person. You can combine paraphrasing and reflecting in a single statement such as, "It sounds like you feel (emotional content of the message) because (factual content of the message)." Try this technique in **Activity 49** on pages 365–366.

paraphrasing Restating the factual content of the message.

reflecting Restating the emotional content of the message.

Listening and Leadership

Even the most enlightened concept of leadership can't work without constructive communication—but how to achieve that? Not by technique alone. We must constantly ask ourselves if we are operating with the old win–lose approach of position power rather than the new win–win approach of relationship power. Is our interest in others only for what they can do for us? Are we in this or that relationship primarily to satisfy *our* needs? Do we give as little as possible in return for a reward we envision?

The best communication techniques in the world won't fool most people for very long. Still, if your understanding of the substance of relationships is solid, learning new techniques for management communications can make a very significant difference. Empowered teams require a new communication style. In a traditional work group, you want compliance. In an empowered team, you want initiative. Directional communication (announcing decisions, issuing orders) inhibits team input. If the team leader or supervisor is still using "boss" language, the team gets the message that they're being told what to do. Managers of empowered teams need to learn to ask open-ended questions and develop the skill of truly listening to the answers.

Listening is a lost art, which must be rediscovered. Few people really listen to others, usually because they're too busy thinking about what they want to say next. In business transactions, clear communication is often colored by power plays, one-upmanship, and attempts to impress rather than to express. In our work, as well as our personal lives, how we listen is at least as important as how we talk. Genuine listening to what others want would allow more sales to be made, more deals to be closed, and greater productivity to be gained. Although it's not always necessary or possible to satisfy those wants, understanding them is the glue of a relationship.

Not paying value by listening is a way of saying, "You're not important to me." The results are reduced productivity (I don't count here, so why should I even try?), employee turnover (Who wants to work in a place where I don't feel valued?), absenteeism (I'm just a cog in the wheel, only noticed when I make a mistake), retaliation (They only listen when the griping gets loud enough), lost sales (They don't seem to understand what I need), and dangling deals (I can't get through to them; it's like talking to a brick wall). Genuine listening can cure a remarkable range of supposedly intractable problems.

Even if you have excellent presentation skills and have an authoritative and persuasive ability to speak to those you lead, make a conscious effort to convert your team meetings into creative dialogue where you ask open-ended questions and solicit feedback and input from all those present. Everyone can be a source of useful ideas. The people closest to the problem usually have the best ideas. Learning flows up as well as down in the

professional **development**)))

Your Cover Letter—The Competitive Edge

Many job seekers wonder if it is still necessary or encouraged to include a cover letter when sending the rèsumè to a prospective employer. In fact, the cover letter is often treated as an afterthought or unimportant attachment by job seekers. This is a mistake and you could be missing out on an opportunity to cut through initial screenings and land an interview. In today's world, even though the job application process is primarily online, the importance of a cover letter is still significant. According to research conducted by a top consulting and search firm, 91 percent of executives polled said that cover letters are valuable when evaluating job candidates.

The cover letter is actually a personal marketing letter for yourself and provides a brief introduction and enticing "rationale" as to why you are the top candidate for the job. Some important tips for creating a successful cover letter include:

- Be brief and concise—Keep it to one, clearly written page, with a few paragraphs.
- Identify yourself—Let the reader know who you are immediately.
- Customize it—Establish reference/connection points with the job and company.
- Connect your qualifications and skills to the job requirements.
- Give examples of why you would be a great addition to the team.
- Make it personal—Create excitement about your interest in the job and company.

Remember . . . if you don't create and submit a cover letter, someone else will be taking the initiative.

What's Your Opinion?
In what ways can the cover letter be just as effective as a rèsumè in landing you a job interview?
For more tips and tools for creating a powerful cover letter, along with examples and sample templates, go to http://jobsearch.about.com/od/coverlettertips/fl/cover-letter-tips-2014.htm.

organization. Nothing is sacred except the governing vision and values. The process of open dialogue improves performance. The more information people can access, the better.

Most importantly, don't view any suggestion or comment from the group as silly or irrelevant. Appearing foolish in front of one's peers is a major embarrassment and stifles any future desires to offer ideas that might be considered "off the wall." The most common mistake in communicating is saying what you want to say, rather than what they need to hear and then listening to what they have to offer. It's rightly been said that you can get more people to vote for you in twenty minutes by showing interest in them, than you can in twenty weeks by showing how interesting you are.

Communication and Self-Esteem
Throughout this section we've looked at why communication matters, how it works, and how you can use it to improve your personal and work relationships. There is one other benefit of good communication: greater self-esteem.

Communication is the way we build connections with other people, showing them who we are and what we feel. When you speak effectively and listen actively, you make a positive impression on others and receive positive feedback in return. This boosts your self-esteem and gives you greater confidence in social situations. When you speak and listen with respect and understanding for others, you also attract friends and partners who show respect and understanding for you.

Developing your communication skills also helps you become more assertive. As you become a more confident communicator, you will feel more comfortable stating your thoughts and feelings, asking for what you want, and saying no without feeling guilty. This will not only make you feel more self-confident, but will also help you reach your goals and build relationships based on honesty and openness.

Self Check

1. What is communication? (p. 344)
2. Name three barriers to good communication. (pp. 348–350)
3. What does EAR stand for? (p. 360)

ACTIVITY 49: Giving Feedback

A Change each of the following ineffective responses to an active listening response that paraphrases and reflects the message.

_____

"I've worked here for five years, and Mr. Havivi still hovers over me while I'm doing the receipts, like he's expecting me to take cash from the till. I can't stand it anymore!"

Ineffective Response: <u>"Don't worry about it, he's just like that."</u>

Active Listening Response: <u>"It sounds like you feel frustrated because you think his hovering</u>

<u>means he doesn't trust you."</u>

_____

"My boyfriend is driving me crazy. He spends all his time playing computer games while I'm out working and wondering how we are going to pay the rent. I don't know what to do!"

Ineffective Response: <u>"Mine is worse. Sometimes you just have to take the good with the bad."</u>

Active Listening Response: _____

_____

_____

"I'm really upset about the grade I got on the math test. I studied all semester, but still only got a C."

Ineffective Response: <u>"At least you didn't get a D."</u>_____

Active Listening Response: _____

_____

_____

_____

continued...

"My dog got hit by a car last night when the sitter let her out by accident. I'm so devastated; I don't think I can come in to work."

Ineffective Response: "Don't take it so hard. It was only a dog. At least it wasn't a person."

Active Listening Response: _____

_____

_____

_____

"I got this great job working for the mayor. I can't believe they chose me when they must have had so many qualified applicants! I'm nervous but excited for my first day of work."

Ineffective Response: "I'm sure you'll be fine. Can you get me a job there, too?"

Active Listening Response: _____

_____

_____

Healthy Relationships

A LOOK AT RELATIONSHIPS

No one reaches success alone. No matter who you are, where you go to school, and what you do for a living, you will always need to deal with other people. The more respect and compassion you have for other people's thoughts, feelings, and needs, the more they will have for yours. Understanding and getting along with other people, therefore, is crucial to your success.

For physical and psychological health, we all need **relationships,** meaningful connections with other human beings. Healthy relationships not only satisfy our need for relatedness but also boost our self-esteem and provide a source of understanding and support. Healthy relationships don't just happen—they require self-awareness, empathy, and good communication. In this section you'll look at the skills you'll need to build and maintain positive relationships with friends, partners, coworkers, acquaintances, peers, and others.

relationship A meaningful connection with another human being.

Group Relationships

Let's look first at groups. A **group** is a set of people (usually three or more) who influence each other and share common goals. We are all members of at least one group, such as a family group, a school or student body, an ethnic group, or a religious group. People need groups for many reasons. Central among these are:

group A set of people (usually three or more) who influence each other.

- Groups satisfy our basic need to belong.
- Group membership can give us prestige and recognition.
- Group members offer us support during difficult times.
- Group members provide us with companionship.
- Group members can encourage us and help us accomplish our goals.
- Group members can share knowledge, skills, feelings, and experiences.
- Membership in groups helps us shape our collective identity.

We choose some, but not all, of our groups. We may choose to join a club, school, or company, but we don't choose our family, our age group, or our ethnic group. Some groups are also more cohesive (functional and united) than others. Very large groups, such as racial groups, are usually less cohesive than smaller groups. Groups that face a great deal of internal conflict, such as some political parties, can become so disunited that they break apart.

Group Norms All groups have norms, or standards, that guide the behavior of their members. These norms may be formal or informal. Most schools and companies have formal norms, or codes of conduct,

success *secret*

Think about how group norms affect your behavior.

that specify things such as what kinds of clothing are and are not acceptable. Within an individual office or classroom, there may also be informal norms about things like taking breaks or raising your hand before speaking. Family groups have norms, too, often based on the status of each person in the group. Most families have norms regarding privacy, appropriate language in the home, and the division of household chores. Some family norms are related to cultural or religious tradition. For example, many families have rules regarding dress, social activities, and religious observances.

Conformity

conformity A change in behavior caused by a desire to follow the norms of a group.

People behave differently in groups than they do when they are alone or with one other person. One common example of this is conformity. **Conformity** is a change in behavior caused by a desire to follow the norms of a group. When we conform, we change some aspect of our real selves in order to gain group acceptance. For example, we may fail to speak up in class if most of our classmates have a different opinion from ours.

Conformity is not always negative. We conform every time we follow common social conventions such as waiting patiently in line or staying quiet during a movie. These social conventions help to keep order and create an atmosphere of fairness and mutual respect.

success *secret*

When you are anxious to conform, you lose your real self.

Unfortunately, people often conform on more important matters, compromising their beliefs or values in order to gain acceptance from others. People with low self-esteem tend to conform more quickly than people with high self-esteem because they are afraid that others will not like them as they really are. At the extreme, conformity can lead to *deindividuation,* a state of reduced inhibition and self-awareness that can lead people to do things they would never do alone, such as rioting or physically attacking another person.

Groupthink   One common type of conformity is groupthink. *Groupthink* is a type of simplistic thinking used by group members who are more concerned with maintaining a clubby atmosphere than with thinking critically. Groupthink often happens when a group has to make a decision quickly or under pressure, or when a group is composed of similar people who don't want to consider diverse points of view.

One of the most famous examples of groupthink is the poor decision to launch the space shuttle *Challenger,* which exploded just after takeoff in 1986. Although many people at NASA warned that a critical part of the shuttle was unsafe, decision makers were more concerned with pushing the launch forward than with looking at all the information. Similar warnings about dangerous parts preceded the explosion of the space shuttle *Columbia* in 2003.

Groupthink doesn't just happen when lives are at stake. Imagine that you're part of a team in charge of improving career counseling at your school. Instead of tackling the tough problems, however, the members of the team are concerned with maintaining a pleasant social atmosphere. No one wants to rock the boat by suggesting a creative idea. People with differing opinions keep quiet and eventually change their minds to go along with the leader's pet idea. In the end your team comes up with an impractical plan that has no chance of success.

To avoid groupthink, group members and leaders need to value diversity and encourage differing opinions. It's unrealistic to expect everyone in a group to agree, but it is realistic to aim for *consensus*—agreement by most (but not all) members of the group.

Diversity

The flip side of conformity is diversity. **Diversity** means variety. It is present everywhere, in every group and in every aspect of humanity. Diversity occurs at the personal level through individual differences in areas such as values, religious beliefs and practices, political attitudes, sexual orientation, and physical and mental disabilities. Diversity occurs at the social level, too, through group differences in areas such as race, culture, national origin, and language.

diversity Variety.

Diversity is a major source of strength for any group—a company, a school, a sports team, a society. However, personal and social differences among people can cause conflict. It's easy to get along with people who are similar to you, especially if they share your values and goals. It can be much harder to remain open-minded toward people who are different from you. Do you interact with people who are different from you? Take an honest inventory in **Personal Journal 9.2** on page 370.

Rejecting Stereotypes and Prejudice

How can you learn to enjoy all the different and unusual things that you come across in life, as well as to enjoy your own sense of being individual and unique? The key is to reject stereotypes and prejudices. A **stereotype** is a set of oversimplified beliefs about the attributes of a group of people. Stereotypes are often about different racial groups, but they can also be about people of a different age, gender, sexual orientation, religion, weight, or appearance from our own. Stereotypes very often lead to **prejudice,** a negative feeling or attitude toward a group and its members. We use stereotypes to make quick conclusions about other people without having to do a lot of thinking. Unfortunately, this prevents us from appreciating individual differences.

stereotype A set of oversimplified beliefs about the attributes of a group and its members.

prejudice A negative feeling or attitude toward a group that results from oversimplified beliefs about that group.

Stereotypes and prejudices are usually based on fear and misunderstanding. An older person, for example, might see television news reports about gangs and decide that all young people are potential delinquents. A teenager might have a fear of growing older and therefore develop a prejudice against the elderly. We may also adopt the stereotypes held by our parents or friends, simply because we have never taken the time to examine them.

Personal Journal 9.2

Understanding Diversity

How diverse is your social world? Fill in the lines below.

People I interact with who are of a different race than mine:

_____

_____

People I interact with who are of a different sexual orientation than mine:

_____

_____

People I interact with who are of a different national origin than mine:

_____

_____

People I interact with who are of a different cultural heritage than mine:

_____

_____

People I interact with who hold religious beliefs different from mine:

_____

_____

People I interact with who have different physical or mental disabilities than I have:

_____

_____

People I interact with who have different political beliefs than mine:

_____

_____

Are you comfortable interacting with people who differ from you? Explain.

People have an unconscious motivation to believe that the groups they belong to are better than other, similar groups. If we are young, or heterosexual, or Christian, or brunette, we will tend to see ourselves as better than people who are older, or homosexual, or Muslim, or blond—no matter how worthy these people may be as individuals.

Discrimination is the act of treating a person or group differently based on a characteristic. It is the actual behavior that results from prejudice. I can be positive *toward* someone (such as hiring an employee simply because of his ethnic background) or *against* someone (not hiring someone simply because of his ethnic background). Both forms of prejudicial treatment are destructive and don't focus on positive merits and contributions.

Positive Stereotypes

What about so-called *positive stereotypes,* such as "African Americans are good at sports" or "Asian Americans are good at math"—those can't be harmful, can they? Yes, they can. Positive stereotypes like these put pressure on members of those groups to fit that stereotype. If they can't or don't want to conform, they often face criticism and develop low self-esteem.

Positive stereotypes may also mask negative feelings about a group. Consider a recent survey of American attitudes toward Chinese Americans. A large majority of the respondents praised Chinese Americans for their strong family ties, said they were honest businesspeople, and admired their commitment to education. However, one quarter of the people surveyed, including many who had articulated very positive attitudes toward Chinese Americans, admitted that they didn't approve of marriage between Asian Americans and Caucasian Americans and that they wouldn't vote for an Asian American presidential candidate. This shows that positive attitudes in one area can accompany negative attitudes in another.

Stereotypes and You

Stereotypes block critical thinking and limit our views of others. They also limit our views of ourselves, our identities, and our own potential. As individuals, we have the right to determine our own identities and challenge the stereotypes that some people might hold about us. What stereotypes might apply to you? Challenge them in **Personal Journal 9.3** on page 372.

Developing Empathy

We can combat stereotypes and prejudice and keep an open mind toward other people by developing empathy. **Empathy** means awareness of and sensitivity to the feelings, thoughts, and experiences of others. It means seeing life through other people's eyes—experiencing their pain, curiosity, hopes, and fears. It means watching a marathon runner at the 20-mile mark and feeling your own legs ache.

You can feel empathy for anyone—whether that person is of a different generation, a citizen of another country, or simply someone with a different point of view. Instead of being quick to criticize or judge others, try

success *secret*
Don't assume that the groups you belong to are better than other groups.

discrimination The act of treating a person or group differently based on a characteristic.

success *secret*
Positive stereotypes often mask negative feelings.

empathy Awareness of and sensitivity to the feelings, thoughts, and experiences of others.

Personal Journal 9.3

Circles of Yourself

Write your name in the center circle below. Then, in each of the four surrounding circles, write the name of a group you identify with.

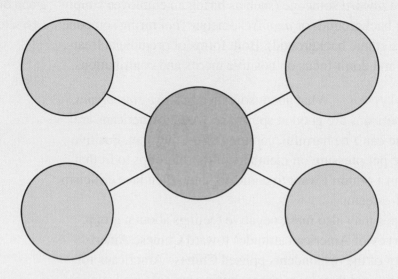

Think of stereotypes that are associated with each of these groups but that don't represent who you are. For each group, write a sentence in the following format:

"I am a(n) . . . , but I am/do NOT . . . . "

Example

I am a <u>vegetarian</u>, but I do NOT <u>eat sticks and twigs.</u>

I am a(n) _____, but I am/do NOT _____

I am a(n) _____, but I am/do NOT _____

I am a(n) _____, but I am/do NOT _____

I am a(n) _____, but I am/do NOT _____

to see the situation through their eyes. How do they feel? What are they afraid of? What concerns them most? Their answers may be surprisingly similar to yours. By seeing through other people's eyes and feeling their emotions, we are able to modify our attitudes, responses, and actions so that we don't hurt other people's feelings.

You will have many roles in your life: student, employee, partner, parent, relative, friend. In each of these roles, it helps to feel empathy for others. For instance, suppose another student in your class isn't learning the course material as quickly as you are. How do you respond? Someone without empathy might say, "Bill's so slow and doesn't get anything. What a loser." However, when you empathize with someone, you can say, "I can understand how Bill could have felt confused by that last lecture. I hope he'll ask the instructor for extra help." If you were having problems, how would you want others to respond?

success *secret*
Be quick to empathize and slow to criticize.

Empathy can help you look beyond yourself for meaning and honesty in your relationships with others and with the world. Concern for others is an essential skill when working in groups, living with a partner or roommate, or simply being a good friend, relative, or member of society. Every so often, perform an empathy checkup on yourself to see where you can improve. Ask yourself:

- *If I were my partner, how would I feel about sharing my life with me?* Would I think I was supportive? Independent? Interesting? Understanding? An equal partner?
- *If I were my child, how would I feel about having a parent like me?* Would I think I was patient? Encouraging? Positive? Supportive? Nonjudgmental?
- *If I were my instructor, how would I feel about having a student like me?* Would I think I showed a lot of effort? A lot of interest? Curiosity? Discipline? Concern for others in class?
- *If I were my boss, how would I feel about having an employee like me?* Would I think I was a good worker? Productive? Reliable? Responsible? Nice to work with?
- *How would I feel if I were an immigrant who had just arrived in America?* Would I feel isolated? Frightened? Unsure of whom to trust? Challenged? Optimistic? Hopeful?
- *How would the world appear to me if I were a child?* Big? Confusing? Exciting? Scary? Hard to understand? Fun?

success *secret*
Perform an empathy checkup on yourself.

Empathy and Self-Awareness

Empathy is founded on awareness of yourself and your relationship with the world. When you see yourself as part of a larger whole, you have respect for the people and things around you. Personal success is founded both on self-respect and on respect for the people and things that surround you. Philosopher Alan Watts, who wrote about ideas from India, China, and Japan, believed that we should not think of ourselves as separate beings trying to control the outside world. Instead, we should see ourselves as part of the world and the people that share it.

Successful people realize that they do not, and cannot, know everything about their world. They realize that their heredity, environment, and personality affect how they perceive the world and how they think. Have you ever heard someone say, "We don't relate" or, "You wouldn't understand"? This translates to, "You don't think as I do" or, "I don't understand why you think the way you do." It is easy to see why there is so much misunderstanding and fighting in the world, within families, and among nations. Everyone sees life through a different lens and marches to a different beat.

Does it trouble you that many people are different from you? Do you ever worry that you seem strange or different to other people? Everyone is different because everyone is unique. We will come across many different people, places, and experiences in our lifetimes. A lot of those people, places, and experiences will seem very strange and unfamiliar to us. Sometimes, we will seem strange and different to other people as well. We can enjoy all the different and unusual things that we come across in life while also enjoying our own sense of being individual and unique. With advances in transportation and technology, the globe is becoming smaller. People from all around the world are being brought together, and events on one continent affect those on all the others. Being conscious of the world around you and understanding your relationship to it will contribute to your overall sense of well-being.

INTERPERSONAL RELATIONSHIPS

Our group relationships are the core of our collective identity. Our interpersonal relationships, by contrast, are the core of our relational identity. Just as interpersonal communication is communication between two people, an **interpersonal relationship** is a relationship between two people. Building healthy interpersonal relationships is essential to a successful personal and professional life. People with healthy interpersonal relationships are happier and suffer less stress and illness than people who have destructive relationships or who suffer loneliness.

Intimacy

We all have a variety of interpersonal relationships—family relationships, romantic relationships, friendships, school and work relationships, and acquaintanceships. The most important of these are our intimate relationships, those characterized by intimacy. **Intimacy** is a sense of closeness, caring, and mutual acceptance that comes from sharing your true inner self. Intimacy doesn't always involve sexuality. Friendships can be highly intimate, for example, and sexual relationships can lack intimacy.

Intimate relationships differ from casual relationships in several major ways. In intimate relationships, people:

- know a great deal of private information about each other
- feel more affection for one another than for most other people
- influence each other's lives often, and in a meaningful way
- think of themselves as a unit, as "us"
- trust one another
- hope and expect that the relationship will be permanent

Although we see many of the same people every day, such as coworkers, fellow students, neighbors, and instructors, we become intimate with very few. In fact, most people have only a few intimate relationships at any one

interpersonal relationship A relationship between two people.

intimacy A sense of closeness, caring, and acceptance that comes from sharing your true inner self.

time. Intimacy takes time to develop. It goes beyond simply knowing the facts about someone's life. We may know a great deal about someone, such as a roommate, but not be intimate with him or her. For intimacy to develop in a relationship, both people must be open about their thoughts and feelings. In healthy, intimate relationships, this openness is combined with mutual respect for one another's goals and boundaries.

Breadth and Depth   Another characteristic of intimate relationships is that they have both breadth and depth. When a relationship has *breadth,* the participants talk about a wide range of topics. When a relationship has *depth,* the participants talk about topics that directly concern their inner self. Successful intimate relationships usually have a great deal of breadth and depth—people discuss many subjects and reveal many of their inner thoughts and feelings. Casual relationships lack depth, although they may have breadth. Take the relationship of coworkers Mandy and Gerardo. The two chat in the lunchroom most days, talking about everything from their weekend plans to their boss's taste in jewelry. However, their conversations steer away from subjects such as their romantic lives and their hopes and dreams for the future. Although the two spend a considerable amount of time together, their relationship has very little intimacy.

Looking at the breadth and depth of your relationships is a good way to assess their level of intimacy. Use the chart in **Activity 50** on pages 376–377 to examine your close relationships.

internet action

MANAGING YOUR ONLINE IDENTITY

With the multitude of communication mechanisms and sites available at our fingertips, it is critical that we exercise some caution and discrimination. Our sharing of personal opinions and activities with "friends" may quickly go viral and global. There may be personal information about you that could cause a dent in your professional image, perhaps jeopardizing an important job or career opportunity. It is easy to be misunderstood or misrepresented when messaging is quick, sometimes emotional, and may include pictures. For instance, on Facebook, it can be especially challenging to control the arrival of tagged photos that you may or may not have sanctioned.

It is important to consider the personal image or "brand" we want to present to world. With hundreds upon hundreds of social networking sites, we should pick and choose which ones will be most beneficial and productive in enhancing our success. Joining specific

online networking sites can certainly boost our exposure to potential job and career opportunities. Consider conducting periodic searches for your name to monitor what information and images of you are currently on the Internet. Familiarize yourself with the latest tools and techniques for creating a positive online identity and marketing yourself effectively.

Think About It

Have you thought about a personal online networking strategy for yourself? In what ways do you think this would be beneficial? Go online and research "building your social network." Here are a couple of links to get you started:

http://careeronestoporg/JobSearch/FormaNetwork/take-your-network-online.aspx

http://executivecareerbrand.com/10-best-ways-to-build-your-personal-brand-online

ACTIVITY 50: Your Close Relationships

A Write down the names of up to six people with whom you have close relationships, and describe their relationship to you (e.g., wife, father, friend). Then describe what important thoughts and feelings you share with one another and what important thoughts and feelings you don't share (or haven't yet shared) with one another.

Name/Relationship	We Share	We Don't Share

B Are you satisfied with the level of intimacy in your relationships? Why or why not?

_____

_____

_____

_____

C Would you like to share more with any of the people on your list? If so, what would you want to share and why? If not, why not?

_____

_____

_____

_____

_____

_____

_____

D Very few people reveal everything of themselves to another person. Are there any private thoughts or feelings that you would never share with anyone? Explain.

_____

_____

_____

_____

_____

_____

_____

_____

Self-Disclosure

self-disclosure
Communicating your real thoughts, desires, and feelings.

How does intimacy develop in a relationship? The primary way to build intimacy is self-disclosure. **Self-disclosure** is communicating your real thoughts, desires, and feelings. When people say that someone is "real" or "genuine," they usually mean that the person is good at self-disclosure. Self-disclosure means letting other people see the real you. By demonstrating emotional openness, you show the other person that you care about the relationship.

Successful people reveal their true selves to others, not just what feels comfortable. Often, we build a wall around us, revealing only what we think others should see. We are too afraid to take the risk of being vulnerable. However, this can prevent us from realizing our full potential, and it can be a barrier to fulfilling relationships. Self-disclosure becomes easier with practice. When you show yourself as you truly are, you gain self-respect and the respect of others. This encourages you to self-disclose even further.

success *secret*
To build intimate relationships, you need to reveal your true self.

How much do other people know about you? According to a model known as the *Johari window,* shown in Figure 9.3, all the information about you falls into one of four categories:

- The *open self* represents the things that you know about yourself and that you have no reason to hide from other people.
- The *hidden self* represents the things that you know about yourself but that you hide from other people.
- The *blind self* represents the things that other people can see about you, but that you cannot see about yourself.
- The *unknown self* represents the things that no one can see about you, such as your unknown talents, abilities, and attitudes, as well as forgotten and repressed experiences and emotions.

This communication model is especially effective in improving understanding between individuals within a team or group or among groups. By disclosing information, individuals build trust among themselves (expanding the open self quadrant vertically). By receiving constructive feedback, they can also learn more about and how to better themselves (expanding the open self quadrant horizontally).

It is healthy to expand your open self. You can do this by self-disclosing and increasing your self-awareness.

Successful Intimate Relationships

success *secret*
Self-awareness is crucial in relationships.

Intimate relationships are such a fundamental part of our lives that we often take them for granted. Yet our identities, our day-to-day lives, and our emotional states are all deeply dependent on these relationships. For this reason, you owe it to yourself to invest time and effort in your relationships.

There is no one-size-fits-all formula for good relationships. However, to be emotionally rewarding, an intimate relationship needs to have all three of the following characteristics:

FIGURE 9.3 The Johari Window

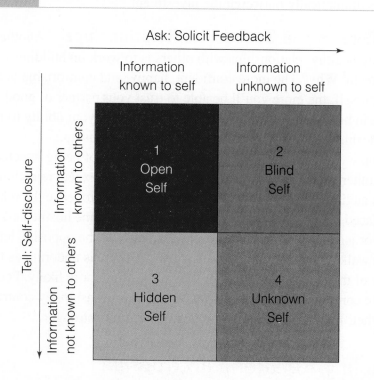

Ask: Solicit Feedback →

	Information known to self	Information unknown to self
Information known to others	1 Open Self	2 Blind Self
Information not known to others	3 Hidden Self	4 Unknown Self

Tell: Self-disclosure ↓

To Disclose or Not to Disclose The Johari window shows how we understand ourselves and how we interact with others. *Which of these four selves do you think contains the most information about you? Explain.*

Source: Joseph Luft, *Group Processes: An Introduction to Group Dynamics* (Palo Alto, CA: National Press, 1970).

- sharing
- sociability
- emotional support

Sharing means self-disclosing as well as having things in common, such as interests and activities. It also means providing instrumental support when it is needed. Being sociable means having fun together and enjoying one another's company. Providing emotional support means caring about the other person's thoughts and feelings, showing appreciation and affection, and providing encouragement. This is the emotional core of a relationship. To provide emotional support to a friend or partner and to increase the amount of support you receive in return, strive to:

- be self-aware and emotionally aware
- show, and truly feel, empathy
- practice active listening
- consider the other person's motivations and needs
- display concern, caring, and genuine interest
- provide encouragement and emotional support
- avoid hurtful behaviors such as dishonesty, selfishness, dependency, attempts at control, and physical or psychological abuse

success *secret*
The more you invest in a relationship, the more you get back.

Being a supportive friend or partner takes effort and commitment, but the rewards dramatically outweigh the investment.

Self-Esteem and Successful Relationships

Another way to ensure healthy relationships with others is to work on building your self-esteem. Why? The more confident, happy, and comfortable you feel with yourself, the more you'll be able to trust your partner or good friend, believe in his or her good intentions, and believe in your ability to maintain a healthy, mutually beneficial long-term relationship.

People with low self-esteem often live in terror of being rejected by the other person in the relationship. People who expect rejection are always anxious that the other person secretly wants to leave the relationship. Faced with such anxieties, people tend to become hostile and withdrawn or jealous and controlling. They can also do the opposite, letting people walk all over them and abuse them. All of this undermines the quality of the relationship, making actual rejection more likely. People who are confident in their ability to sustain a relationship, by contrast, enjoy their relationships more—which makes them stronger.

Handling Relationship Conflict

Every relationship, no matter how harmonious, occasionally faces conflict. **Conflict** is disagreement that occurs when individuals or groups clash over needs, values, emotions, or power. Conflict can take the form of an argument with a friend, a dispute with a coworker, or a quarrel with a spouse. Conflict often occurs when people differ in one of the following areas:

conflict Disagreement that occurs when individuals or groups clash over needs, values, emotions, or power.

- **Needs**—Each of us is constantly striving to meet our needs. Conflicts can arise when our attempts to meet our needs are unsuccessful, and we perceive that someone else is to blame. Conflict can also arise when we ignore or dismiss our own or others' needs.
- **Values**—Serious conflicts can arise when people hold opposing values, especially when people confuse their individual values with absolutes of right and wrong.
- **Emotions**—Conflicts often occur when people differ on an emotionally charged issue such as politics, education, or religion. Conflict can also occur when people ignore or dismiss their own or others' emotions.
- **Power**—Conflicts often happen when people try to exercise power, for example by demanding that other people do things their way. Conflict can also occur when one person or group senses that another person or group is trying to control them.

Irritation, frustration, and anger often accompany conflict. As unpleasant as these emotions can be, however, conflict is a natural and normal part of human interaction. In fact, conflict can actually be healthy. It can lead to growth, innovation, and new ways of thinking. It can provide a chance to discuss important thoughts and feelings. How have you handled conflict in the past? Record your personal experiences in **Personal Journal 9.4.**

Personal Journal 9.4

Dealing with Conflict

Describe three interpersonal or group conflicts that you have been involved in over the last year: one at work, one at school, and one at home. What caused them, and how did you handle them—or not handle them?

Work

Cause:

_____

How You Handled It:

_____

School

Cause:

_____

How You Handled It:

_____

Home

Cause:

_____

How You Handled It:

_____

Are you proud of the way you handled these conflicts? If so, why? If not, what could you do better next time? Remember to use the ABCDE method to work through difficult situations.

Resolving Conflict Effective communication is the key to resolving conflicts. Good communication helps you resolve conflicts in a positive way, while poor communication prevents conflicts from being resolved and often makes them worse. When faced with conflict, it is important to:

- **Move away from confrontation.** Accept that there is a problem, then focus on the facts, not on blame.
- **Listen actively.** Try to understand the other person's point of view. Pay full attention and withhold judgment.
- **State your needs.** Be open about your needs and remember that you and the other person have an equal right to have your needs met.
- **Generate options for resolving the conflict.** Brainstorm possible solutions to the conflict, then discuss how well each one would work.
- **Commit to a solution.** Once you choose a solution, follow through and do what you promised. This shows that you respect the other person's needs and are serious about resolving the conflict.

By employing these strategies with openness and mutual respect, both parties can "win" by having at least some of their needs met. Good conflict resolution can not only solve the problem at hand but can also lead to deeper understanding in the relationship.

> **success** *secret*
> Focus on solutions, not blame.

Respect and Success

Good relationships, like good communication, depend on respect for others as well as yourself. Every human being is unique, with the right to fulfill his or her potential in life. People who are successful in sports, business, education, or any other activity in life accept their uniqueness. They feel comfortable with themselves and are willing to have others know and accept them just as they are. They know that skin color, religion, birthplace, or financial status do not determine a person's worth. People who are positive and empathetic naturally attract friends and supporters. They seldom have to stand alone.

Self Check

1. Define conformity. (p. 368)
2. What is the difference between stereotypes and prejudice? (p. 369)
3. List four sources of conflict. (p. 380)

Key Terms

communication (p. 344)

interpersonal communication (p. 344)

channel (p. 347)

context (p. 348)

nonverbal communication (p. 350)

body language (p. 354)

active listening (p. 360)

attending (p. 361)

paraphrasing (p. 361)

reflecting (p. 361)

relationship (p. 367)

group (p. 367)

conformity (p. 368)

diversity (p. 369)

stereotype (p. 369)

prejudice (p. 369)

discrimination (p. 371)

empathy (p. 371)

interpersonal relationship (p. 374)

intimacy (p. 374)

self-disclosure (p. 378)

conflict (p. 380)

Summary by Learning Objectives

- **Describe the six elements of communication.** The six elements are: 1. sender, the person who sends a message; 2. message, a thought or feeling; 3. channel, the medium; 4. receiver, the person who takes in the message; 5. feedback, the receiver's response; and 6. context, the time and place.

- **Summarize the forms and functions of nonverbal communication.** The most important nonverbal cues are personal distance, voice, and body language. They function to manage conversations, provide feedback, and clarify messages.

- **List several skills necessary for effective speaking and active listening.** Skills necessary for effective speaking include using an expressive vocabulary, being clear and honest, welcoming feedback, and showing respect. Skills necessary for active listening are encouraging, attending, and responding (EAR).

- **Explain the relationship between stereotypes, prejudice, and empathy.** Stereotypes, oversimplified beliefs about a group, often lead to prejudice, a negative feeling toward that group. Empathy helps us overcome stereotypes and prejudice.

- **Define intimacy and explain how to develop it in a relationship.** Intimacy is a sense of closeness, caring, and mutual acceptance that comes from sharing your true inner self. Intimacy is built through self-disclosure.

- **Cite the characteristics of satisfying intimate relationships.** The three core characteristics of satisfying intimate relationships are sharing, being sociable, and providing emotional support.

- **Explain how to handle conflict effectively.** To handle conflict, focus on facts, brainstorm possible solutions, and discuss how well each one meets both your needs. Commit to a solution and follow through on it.

Review and Activities

Review Questions

1. How can emotions cause communication breakdown?

2. What is cultural awareness?

3. Give three examples of nonverbal communication and explain what they mean.

4. Define paraphrasing and reflecting.

5. Why are positive stereotypes harmful?

6. What is self-disclosure, and why is it important?

Critical Thinking

7. **Rapport Building** Rapport is about making a two-way connection with other people and the foundation for any relationship. The ability to build rapport comes naturally to some people, while others really need to work at it. It requires having empathy, using good listening skills, and paying attention to body language. Think about your relationships; how easy was/is it for you to build rapport? How did you do it? What are some ways you can become more effective in building rapport with new people you meet?

8. **Vocabulary Building** People who read extensively and have large vocabularies are generally considered to be more intelligent, and usually have higher career success. What do you think explains this? In what ways could the high-tech world of sound bites and texting have a detrimental impact on vocabulary building? What impact could the pervasive use of the short acronyms from "text language" have on our ability to think, write, and speak intelligently?

Application

9. **Nonverbal Communication** Take 30 minutes out of your day to observe people in a public place, like a mall or park. What do you notice about their nonverbal communication? Make a list of their different facial expressions and gestures and what you think they mean. Now find and watch a short video clip of a professional speaker. Notice the nonverbal gestures while giving a presentation. Write down your observations. How did the gestures enhance the communication of the message?

10. **Relationship Qualities** Ask five women and five men to complete the following two statements: "A true friend _____." and "My ideal romantic partner _____." Ask all of the respondents to explain why they completed the sentences the way they did. Compare your results with a classmate's. Did you receive similar responses? Did women and men answer the questions differently? Prepare your notes for a discussion.

Internet Activities

11. **Multigenerational Communication**   At this point in time, we have four major generations living, working, and interacting with each other. This creates challenges not only in familial relationships but also in our work environments. Even our personal relationships can be impacted by the differences in values, beliefs, and behaviors, which make communication challenging. Conduct some online research to identify the various generations and obtain an understanding of their characteristics. What communication challenges have you experienced in your own life as a result of generational differences? What strategies do you think would be helpful in improving communication and collaboration between the generations? Conduct an online search for information on generational differences. Here are some readings to help you get started:

    http://www.fdu.edu/newspubs/magazine/05ws/generations.htm
    http://www.biz.colostate.edu/mti/tips/pages/interactionamongthegenerations.aspx
    http://www.wmfc.org/uploads/GenerationalDifferencesChart.pdf

12. **Your Communication Style**   Each of us is born with certain personality traits, many of which play a major role in the way we communicate. We are also influenced by our childhood upbringing and experiences, which determine certain communication behaviors. Each of us has developed a communication style that we may choose to enhance or change. As you've learned in this course, there are specific skills you can develop to significantly improve your communications. Visit the following two sites to take two communication assessments, one to determine your style, the other to assess your skills:

    http://newlineideas.com/communication-style-quiz.html
    http://www.helpguide.org/mental/effective_communication_skills.htm. You will receive a score, as well as tips for understanding and enhancing your communications.

Real-Life Success Story

"How Do I Stand Up for Myself?"

Review your answer to the question in the Real-Life Success Story on page 342. Think about how you would answer the question now that you have learned more about respectful communication and managing conflict.

Complete the Story   Taking the place of a helpful coworker, write an e-mail to Joe explaining how he can use assertive communication, "I" statements, and conflict-resolution strategies to improve his relationship with his boss.

Further Reading

Adler, Ronald B., and Neil Towne. *Looking Out, Looking In: An Introduction to Interpersonal Communication.* 12th ed. New York: Holt, Rinehart, and Winston, 2007.

Allen, David. *Getting Things Done: The Art of Stress-Free Productivity.* New York: Penguin, 2002.

Altman, Kerry Paul. *The Wisdom of the Five Messengers: Learning to Follow the Guidance of Feelings.* Baltimore: Sidran, 2007.

Bassham, Gregory, William Irwin, and Henry Nardone. *Critical Thinking: A Student's Introduction.* 3rd ed. New York: McGraw-Hill, 2007.

Buckingham, Marcus, and Donald O. Clifton. *Now, Discover Your Strengths.* Tulsa, OK: Gardners, 2005.

Byrne, Rhonda. *The Secret.* New York: Simon & Schuster, 2006.

Covey, Stephen. *The Seven Habits of Highly Effective People.* New York: Simon & Schuster, 2004.

Davis, Martha, Elizabeth Robbins Eshelman, and Matthew McKay. *Relaxation and Stress Reduction Workbook.* 6th ed. Oakland, CA: New Harbinger, 2008.

Dickson, Amanda. *Wake Up to a Happier Life: Finding Joy in the Work You Do Every Day.* Salt Lake City, UT: Shadow Mountain, 2007.

Ellis, Albert. *How to Stubbornly Refuse to Make Yourself Miserable about Anything.* New York: Kensington, 2006.

Feldman, Robert S. *Understanding Psychology.* 9th ed. New York: McGraw-Hill, 2009.

Fiore, Neil. *The Now Habit.* Chagrin Falls, OH: Findaway World, 2008.

Freston, Kathy, and C. Oz Mehmet. *Wellness: A Practical and Spiritual Guide to Health and Happiness.* New York: Weinstein, 2008.

Gamble, Teri Kwal, and Michael Gamble. *Communication Works.* 9th ed. New York: McGraw-Hill, 2007.

Goleman, Daniel. *Emotional Intelligence.* 10th ed. New York: Bantam, 2005.

Hanna, Sharon L. *Person to Person.* 5th ed. Englewood Cliffs, NJ: Prentice Hall, 2007.

Herman, Kenneth. *Secrets from the Sofa: A Psychologist's Guide to Achieving Personal Peace.* Bloomington, IN: iUniverse, 2007.

Jakes, T. D., and Phil McGraw. *Reposition Yourself: Living Life Without Limits.* New York: Simon & Schuster, 2007.

Jeffers, Susan J. *Feel the Fear and Do It Anyway.* 20th ed. New York: Random House, 2006.

Lawrence, Judy. *The Budget Kit: The Common Cents Money Management Workbook.* 5th ed. New York: Kaplan Publishing, 2007.

Miller, Dan. *No More Mondays: Fire Yourself—And Other Revolutionary Ways to Discover Your True Calling at Work.* New York: Doubleday, 2008.

Morgenstern, Julie. *Time Management from the Inside Out.* 2nd ed. New York: Henry Holt & Company, 2004.

Orman, Suze. *9 Steps to Financial Freedom.* Rev. ed. New York: Crown, 2006.

Pausch, Randy, and Jeffrey Zaslow. *The Last Lecture.* New York: Hyperion, 2008.

Seligman, Martin. *Learned Optimism.* New York: Knopf, 2006.

Shriver, Maria. *Just Who Will You Be? Big Question. Little Book. Answer Within.* New York: Hyperion, 2008.

Thaler, Richard H., and Cass R. Sunstein. *Nudge: Improving Decisions about Health, Wealth, and Happiness.* New Haven, CT: Yale University Press, 2008.

Tolle, Eckhart. *A New Earth: Awakening to Your Life's Purpose.* New York: Penguin, 2008.

————. *The Power of Now: A Guide to Spiritual Enlightenment.* Novato, CA: New World Library, 2004.

Waddington, Tad. *Lasting Contribution: How to Think, Plan, and Act to Accomplish Meaningful Work.* Beverly Hills, CA: Agate, 2007.

Waitley, Denis. *Empires of the Mind.* New York: Quill, 1996.

————. *The Joy of Working.* Rev. ed. New York: Random House, 1995.

————. *The New Dynamics of Goal Setting.* London: Nicholas Brealey, 1997.

————. *The New Dynamics of Winning.* New York: Quill, 1995.

————. *The Psychology of Winning.* New York: Berkley Books, 1992.

————. *Seeds of Greatness.* New York: Simon & Schuster, 1988.

————. *The Winner's Edge.* New York: Berkley Books, 1994.

Willett, Walter C., P. J. Skerrett, and Edward L. Giovannucci. *Eat, Drink, and Be Healthy: The Harvard Medical School Guide to Healthy Eating.* New York: Free Press, 2005.

Ziglar, Zig. *Over the Top.* Nashville, TN: Thomas Nelson, 2007.

————. *See You at the Top.* 25th ed. New York: Pelican, 2000.

Ziglar, Zig, Jim Savage, Krish Dhanam, Bryan Flanagan. *Top Performance: How to Develop Excellence in Yourself and Others.* Grand Rapids, MI: Baker, 2004.

Glossary

ABC model   A model of human behavior in which an activating event (**A**) triggers an irrational belief (**B**), which then triggers negative behavioral consequences (**C**).

ABCDE method   An approach to coping with negative thoughts and feelings by disputing (**D**) the irrational beliefs that trigger them and exchanging them (**E**) for more positive ones.

accomplishment   Anything completed through effort, skill, or persistence.

accuracy   Factual truth.

activating event   In the ABC model, a negative event that triggers an irrational, self-destructive belief.

active listening   Listening with understanding and paying close attention to what is being said.

adapting   Being flexible to change.

aerobic exercise   Sustained, rhythmic physical activity that causes a temporary increase in heart and breathing rate.

affirmation   A positive self-statement that helps a person think of himself or herself in a positive, caring, and accepting way.

aggression   Behavior intended to harm or injure a person or object.

all-or-nothing thinking   A cognitive distortion in which people view issues as black and white, with no shades of gray in between.

anaerobic exercise   High-intensity exercise that strengthens muscles and involves short bursts of intense exertion.

anger   A strong feeling of displeasure, resentment, or hostility.

antibodies   Proteins produced by the immune system to fight disease.

anxiety   A generalized feeling of worry and nervousness that does not have any specific cause.

assertiveness   Standing up for one's rights without threatening the self-esteem of the other person.

attending   An active listening skill that involves being focused, alert, and open to receiving information.

attitude   A belief or opinion that predisposes people to act in a certain way.

autonomic nervous system (ANS)   The part of the nervous system that monitors and controls most involuntary functions, including heartbeat and sweating.

autonomy   Freedom of choice, independence, and the chance to exercise independent judgment.

avoidance   An unwillingness to face uncomfortable situations or psychological realities.

behavior   Anything that people think, feel, or do.

belongingness   Fulfilling relationships with others.

biofeedback   A treatment technique that uses electronic instruments to measure and display information about a patient's bodily processes (such as heartbeat) in order to help the patient gain greater control over them.

blind self   In the Johari window, information that other people can see about a person, but that the person cannot see about him- or herself.

body image   How a person thinks and feels about his or her body and appearance.

body language   Facial expressions, posture, and gestures.

breadth   1. In critical thinking, the degree to which a statement considers other arguments and points of view. 2. In relationships, the number of topics one discusses with another person.

budget   A money management plan that specifies how a person will spend his or her money during a particular period.

catastrophizing   Dramatically exaggerating the negative consequences of any minor event.

channel   The medium in which a message is delivered.

clinical psychologist   A psychologist who diagnoses and treats individuals with emotional disturbances.

closed question   A question worded in a way that elicits only a one- or two-word answer.

cognition   Mental processing of information in any form.

cognitive distortion   A self-critical, illogical pattern of thought.

cognitive therapy   A technique of psychotherapy based on the idea that the way we think affects how we feel.

collective identity   The sum of the social roles an individual plays and the social groups to which he or she belongs.

collectivism   A philosophy that values group goals over individual goals and defines a

person's identity more through group identifications than through personal attributes.

comfort zone   The place in the mind where a person feels safe and knows that he or she can succeed.

committed time   Time devoted to school, work, family, volunteering, and other activities that relate to short-term and long-term goals.

communication   The process of giving or exchanging messages.

competence   The ability to do something well.

complaint   The sharing of distress, discomfort, or worry with another person.

conditional positive regard   Love and acceptance of a person, particularly a child, on the condition that he or she behave in a certain way.

conflict   1. Disagreement that occurs when individuals or groups clash over needs, values, emotions, or power. 2. Indecision that occurs when no option is significantly more attractive than the others.

conformity   A change in behavior caused by a desire to follow the norms of a group.

conscious mind   The part of the brain that controls the mental processes of which one is aware.

consciousness   Awareness of the sensations, thoughts, and feelings one is experiencing at a given moment.

consensus   Agreement by most, but not all, members of a group.

consequences   In the ABC model, negative feelings and behaviors that result from irrational beliefs.

constructive criticism Criticism that focuses on specific behavior and that usually mentions positive points and offers suggestions for improvement.

context The time and place of communication.

coping Facing up to unpleasant or threatening situations.

coping skills Behaviors that help a person deal with stress and other unpleasant situations.

cortisol A steroid hormone that regulates metabolism and blood pressure and that is released into the bloodstream during times of stress.

credit A sum of money a person can use before having to pay back the lender.

credit record A log of the financial habits of a person who buys on credit.

critical thinking Active, self-reflective thinking.

criticism Any remark that contains a judgment, evaluation, or statement of fault.

cultural awareness Ability to recognize the ways in which cultures differ and how these differences affect cross-cultural interactions.

culture The behaviors, ideas, attitudes, and traditions shared by a large social group and transmitted from one generation to the next.

debit card A plastic bank card that can be used both as an ATM card and as a credit card.

debt 1. Money owed to a lender. 2. The state of owing money to a lender.

decision A reasoned choice among several options, or possible courses of action.

decision-making process A logical series of steps to identify and evaluate options and arrive at a good choice.

deindividuation A state of reduced inhibition and self-awareness that can lead group members to do things they would never do alone.

denial The unhealthy practice of reducing anxiety by ridding the mind of painful thoughts and feelings.

depression An illness characterized by profound feelings of sadness, hopelessness, and helplessness.

depth 1. In critical thinking, the degree to which a statement digs below the surface to consider the substance of the issue. 2. In relationships, the importance and self-relevance of the topics one discusses with another person.

desire A conscious drive to attain a satisfying goal.

despair An unpleasant feeling of hopelessness and defeat.

destructive criticism Criticism that addresses a person's attitude or some other aspect of him- or herself instead of focusing on specific behavior.

discretionary expenses Lifestyle expenses that are rewarding but not strictly necessary.

discretionary time Time that can be used however one wishes.

discrimination The act of treating a person or group differently based on a characteristic.

disgust   A negative feeling of aversion or repulsion toward someone or something.

dispute   To confront irrational beliefs with the reality of the situation.

distress   Stress caused by negative events that produces negative physical and emotional effects.

diversity   Variety.

downward comparison   A type of social comparison that involves comparing oneself to people who are less successful in a certain area.

dream   An aspiration, hope, or vision of the future that gives one's life direction.

80/20 rule   The theory that the relationship between input and output, or effort and results, is not balanced.

embarrassment   An unpleasant feeling that occurs when a person believes that others have found a flaw in him or her.

emotion   A subjective feeling that is accompanied by physical and behavioral changes.

emotional awareness   The process of recognizing, identifying, and accepting one's emotions.

emotional reasoning   A cognitive distortion in which people believe that whatever they feel is true must really be true.

emotional support   The giving of trust, empathy, care, love, concern, and unconditional approval.

empathy   Awareness of and sensitivity to the feelings, thoughts, and experiences of others.

encouraging   An active listening skill that involves showing a desire to listen.

endorphins   Proteins in the brain that act as natural painkillers.

escape response   A behavior used to avoid dealing with a problem.

esteem   1. (v.) To appreciate the value or worth of a person or thing. 2. (n.) Appreciation and high regard.

ethics   The principles one uses to define acceptable behavior and decide what is right and wrong.

eustress   Stress caused by positive events that provides a surge of energy.

external obstacle   A barrier caused by factors in the outside world, such as a person or an event.

extrinsic   External.

extrinsic goals   Goals related to looking good to others, earning a reward, or avoiding negative consequences.

extrinsic motivation   Motivation that comes from outside.

facial expressions   A type of body language involving movements of the mouth, the eyebrows and forehead, and the eyes.

failure   An unwanted outcome.

fear   An unpleasant feeling of anxiety caused by the anticipation of danger.

feedback   In communication, the receiver's response to the sender's message.

filtering   A cognitive distortion in which people block positive inputs and focus on negative ones.

finance charges   Fees that are charged by lenders, usually based on the amount of money owed.

finances   Monetary resources.

fixed committed expenses   Necessary expenses that are the same from month to month.

framing effect   The decision-making bias that results from the way a decision, question, or problem is worded.

gender   The set of characteristics used to define male and female.

gender bias   When someone is treated differently or unfairly due to one's gender.

gender role   Society's expectations of how males and females should think, feel, and act.

gestures   A type of body language involving movements of the arms, hands, legs, and feet.

goal   An outcome that a person wants to achieve and toward which he or she directs focused effort.

group   A set of people (usually three or more) who influence each other.

groupthink   A type of simplistic thinking used by group members when they are more concerned with maintaining a clubby atmosphere than with thinking critically.

guilt   A negative feeling that occurs when a person believes that his or her actions have harmed someone else.

habit   A behavior that has become automatic through repetition.

happiness   A state of well-being that comes from having a positive evaluation of one's life.

hassles   Small, stress-causing annoyances of everyday life.

helpless thinking   A cognitive distortion in which people believe that their lives are not under their control.

hidden self   In the Johari window, information that a person knows about him- or herself but that he or she hides from other people.

hierarchy of needs   A diagram of the five central human needs arranged from the most basic to the most complex.

"I" statement   A statement about a problem that begins with the word *I* and that communicates feelings without blaming the other person for the problem.

ideal self   The person one wants to be or feels he or she ought to be.

identity   How a person chooses to define him- or herself to the world.

imagination   The creative power of the mind.

important   Relating to one's personal or work goals.

impulse   A sudden wish or feeling that can lead to unplanned and unwise actions.

impulse buying   Spending money on the spur of the moment, without planning.

incentive   A reward offered in order to motivate a person to do something.

income   All the money a person receives during a fixed period of time.

individual identity   The physical and psychological characteristics that distinguish an individual.

individualism   A philosophy that values individual goals over group goals and defines identity more through personal attributes than through group identifications.

inner critic   The critical voice that bombards people with constant negative self-talk.

instrumental support   The giving of resources such as money, labor, time, advice, and information.

intelligence   A set of abilities that enables a person to solve certain types of real-world problems.

interests   Personal preferences for specific topics or activities.

internal obstacle   A barrier caused by factors within oneself, such as perfectionism or low motivation.

interpersonal communication   One-on-one, usually face-to-face communication.

interpersonal relationship   A relationship between two people.

intimacy   A sense of closeness, caring, and mutual acceptance that comes from sharing one's true inner self.

intrinsic   Internal.

intrinsic goals   Goals related to things that a person enjoys and that will help him or her grow as a person.

intrinsic motivation   Motivation that comes from inside.

irrational belief   A distorted, self-destructive idea or assumption that interferes with one's thinking.

job-specific skill   The ability to do a specific task or job.

Johari window   A model of self-awareness and self-disclosure that shows the proportion of information about a person that he or she is aware of and that other people are aware of.

joy   A feeling of happiness one experiences following achievement of a goal.

judgmentalism   The habit of condemning people or things because they are not the way one thinks they should be.

knowledge   An understanding of facts or principles in a particular subject area.

label   A simplistic statement that people use to define who they are.

life coach   A professional motivator who helps clients identify their goals and make the changes necessary to lead a more rewarding life.

logic   The process of reasoning correctly and drawing the correct conclusions from the facts.

logos   Science, study; one of the two Greek roots of the word psychology.

loneliness   Sadness about being alone.

long-term consequences   The distant, often unpredictable results of an action.

long-term goal   A goal one plans to achieve in the more distant future.

love   A feeling of affection, devotion, or attachment toward someone.

magical thinking Believing that one's thoughts control events.

maintenance time Time devoted to maintaining, or taking care of, oneself and one's surroundings.

meditation The practice of calming and emptying the mind by focusing on one particular element, such as a sound, a word, an image, or one's breathing.

message An expression of thought or feeling; the content of communication.

mind reading A cognitive distortion in which people think bad thoughts about themselves and therefore assume that everyone else is doing the same.

mistake Anything a person did in the past that he or she now wishes he or she had done differently.

money A convenient medium of exchange used to pay for goods and services.

money management The intelligent use of money to achieve one's goals.

motivation The force that moves a person to action.

need Something a person must have in order to survive and thrive.

negative escape response An escape response that makes a person feel better temporarily but that eventually makes the problem worse.

negative motivation The drive to do something in order to avoid negative consequences.

negative thinking Focusing on the flaws and problems in oneself, other people, and the world.

nervous system A system of nerve cells that regulates behavior by transmitting messages back and forth between the brain and the other parts of the body.

neurons Cells in the nervous system that transmit messages via chemical and electric signals.

nonverbal communication The process of giving or exchanging messages without words.

norms Standards or rules that define appropriate and inappropriate behavior in specific social positions and settings.

obstacle Any barrier that prevents a person from achieving his or her goals.

open question A question worded in a way that allows a broad range of responses.

open self In the Johari window, information that a person knows about him- or herself and that he or she has no reason to hide from other people.

optimism The tendency to expect the best possible outcome.

overgeneralizing Drawing broad negative conclusions based on limited evidence.

paraphrasing An active listening skill that involves restating the factual content of a speaker's message.

parasympathetic nervous system The part of the autonomic nervous system that calms the body after a stressful emergency situation.

passive-aggression Indirect, disguised aggression toward others.

perfectionism The belief that a person is only worthwhile if he or she is perfect.

persistence   The ability to go on despite opposition, setbacks, and occasional doubts.

personal digital assistant (PDA)   A small wireless electronic device that provides basic record-keeping tools, such as a to-do list and schedule.

personality   The relatively stable pattern of behavior that distinguishes one person from all other people.

personalizing   Assuming that everything has to do with oneself somehow.

pessimism   The tendency to expect the worst possible outcome.

positive escape response   An escape response that makes a person feel better and does not make the problem worse.

positive motivation   A drive to do something because it will help accomplish a goal.

positive stereotype   Positive but oversimplified beliefs about the attributes of a group and its members.

positive thinking   Focusing on what is good about oneself, other people, and the world.

possible selves   The person or persons we might realistically become in the future.

posture   A type of body language that involves the way a person carries him- or herself when sitting or standing.

precision   Exactness.

prejudice   A negative feeling or attitude toward a group that is based on oversimplified beliefs about that group.

pride   A positive feeling that occurs when a person achieves a personal success.

prioritize   To arrange in order of importance.

private self-consciousness   The tendency to be aware of the private, inward aspects of oneself.

probing   Asking for specifics from a person who has given a general or vague criticism.

procrastination   The habit of putting off tasks until the last minute.

progressive muscle relaxation   A stress-relief technique that involves tensing and relaxing muscle groups in sequence in order to reduce tension.

psyche   Mind; one of the two Greek roots of the word psychology.

psychologist   A person who studies human behavior with the goal of describing, predicting, explaining, and (in some cases) changing it.

psychology   The scientific study of human behavior.

public self-consciousness   The tendency to be aware of the aspects of oneself that are on display in social situations.

rational emotive behavior therapy (REBT)   An approach to coping with problems that focuses on uncovering people's irrational beliefs and transforming them into rational, helpful ones.

receiver   In communication, the person who takes in, or receives, a message.

recreational shopping   The use of shopping, especially in malls, as a form of entertainment.

reflecting   An active listening skill that involves restating the emotional content of a speaker's message.

regret   The feeling of wishing one had decided something differently.

relational identity   How an individual identifies him- or herself in relation to important others.

relationship   A meaningful connection with another human being.

resource   Something that is ready for use and can be drawn upon as needed.

responding   An active listening skill that involves giving constructive feedback.

responsibility   The ability to make independent, proactive decisions and to accept the consequences of them.

role model   A person who has the qualities one would like to have.

sadness   A somber emotion of sorrow over a loss.

schedule   A chart showing dates and times by which tasks must be completed.

selective listening   The process of choosing what one wants to hear and ignoring the rest.

self   The sense of being a unique, conscious being.

self-acceptance   Recognition and acceptance of what is true about oneself.

self-actualization   Reaching one's full potential and achieving long-term personal growth.

self-awareness   The process of paying attention to oneself.

self-blame   A cognitive distortion in which people blame everything on themselves, regardless of the real cause.

self-consciousness   The tendency to frequently think about and observe oneself.

self-defeating attitude   A negative attitude about oneself that leads to failure.

self-determination   Determining the path one's life travels.

self-direction   The ability to set a well-defined goal and work toward it.

self-discipline   The process of teaching oneself to do what is necessary to reach important goals, without becoming sidetracked by bad habits.

self-disclosure   Communicating one's real thoughts, desires, and feelings.

self-esteem   Confidence in and respect for oneself.

self-expectancy   A person's belief that he or she is able to achieve what he or she wants in life.

self-handicapping   Creating obstacles to one's own success in order to have a handy excuse for doing poorly.

self-honesty   The ability to see one's own strengths and weaknesses clearly.

self-hypnosis   The practice of entering a state of reduced consciousness in order to make the subconscious mind receptive to positive messages.

self-image   All the beliefs a person has about him- or herself.

self-presentation   Altering one's behavior to make a good impression on others.

self-talk   What people say or think to themselves about themselves.

sender   In communication, the person who translates a thought or feeling into a message and then sends that message to another person.

sex   The biological category of male or female.

shame   A negative feeling that occurs following a personal failure.

short-term consequences   The immediate, often predictable results of an action.

short-term goal   A goal with a specific plan of action to accomplish now or in the near future.

shyness   Anxiety in social situations that comes from worrying about what others will think of oneself.

skill   The ability to do something specific as a result of learning and practice.

social comparison   The practice of comparing one's traits and accomplishments with those of others.

social role   A set of norms that defines how people are supposed to behave in a given social position or setting.

social support   Words and actions from other people that help a person feel valued, cared for, and connected to a community.

stereotype   A set of oversimplified beliefs about the attributes of a group and its members.

stress   A physical and psychological reaction to the demands of life.

stressor   Any cause of stress, such as a problem, challenge, or change.

subconscious mind   The part of the brain that controls the mental processes of which one is not actively aware.

success   Lifetime fulfillment that comes from creating a sense of meaning in one's work and personal life.

sympathetic nervous system   The part of the autonomic nervous system that prepares the body for stressful emergency situations.

t'ai chi   An ancient Chinese martial art that increases balance and concentration through gentle, flowing movements and deep breathing exercises.

taboo   A cultural prohibition on saying, touching, or doing a certain thing.

time management   The planned, efficient use of time.

to-do list   A personal checklist of tasks and activities that need to be completed over the course of a certain period, such as a week.

trait   A disposition to behave in a certain way, regardless of the situation.

transferable skill   An ability that can be used in a variety of tasks and jobs.

trigger   A person or situation that provokes anger.

uncertainty   Not knowing what the consequences of a decision will be for oneself and others.

unconditional positive regard   Love and acceptance of a person, particularly a child, regardless of his or her particular behavior.

unknown self   In the Johari window, information that no one can see about a person, such as his or her unknown talents, abilities, and attitudes, as well as forgotten and repressed experiences and emotions.

uplifts   Small, positive moments and activities of everyday life that help relieve stress.

upward comparison   A type of social comparison that involves comparing oneself to people who are more successful in a certain area.

urgent   Calling for immediate action.

values   The beliefs and principles that one chooses to live by.

variable committed expenses   Necessary expenses that vary from month to month.

vicious cycle   A chain of events in which one negative event causes another negative event.

visualization   The process of creating detailed mental pictures of the behaviors one wishes to carry out.

want   Something a person can survive and thrive without.

worry   Distress and anxiety caused by contemplating worst-case scenarios.

yoga   A spiritual and physical practice that involves stretches, breathing exercises, relaxation, and sometimes meditation.

"you" statement   A statement about a problem that begins with the word *you* and accuses the other person of causing the problem.

Credits

Photo Credits

Chapter 1
Opener: Exactostock/Superstock/RF; p. 41: Exactostock/Superstock/RF.

Chapter 2
Opener: © Digital Vision/RF; p. 54: Purestock/SuperStock/RF; p. 87: © Digital Vision/RF.

Chapter 3
Opener: © Brand X/Jupiter Images/Getty Images/RF; p. 106: E. Audras/PhotoAlto/RF; p. 124: © Brand X/Jupiter Images/Getty Images/RF.

Chapter 4
Opener: ColorBlind Images/Blend Images LLC/RF; p. 150: © Chris Ryan/age fotostock/RF; p. 157: © Lars A. Niki/RF; p. 177: ColorBlind Images/Blend Images LLC/RF.

Chapter 5
Opener: Les and Dave Jacobs/Blend Images/RF; p. 181: © Digital Vision/Getty Images/RF; p. 219: Les and Dave Jacobs/Blend Images/RF.

Chapter 6
Opener: Comstock/Getty Images/RF; p. 229: © Digital Vision/Getty Images/RF; p. 267: Comstock/Getty Images/RF.

Chapter 7
Opener: © Stockbyte/Getty Images/RF; p. 285: © Steve Lipofsky/Corbis; p. 302: © Stockbyte/Getty Images/RF.

Chapter 8
Opener: © Royalty-Free/CORBIS; p. 331: © Getty Images/Blend Images/RF; p. 341: © Royalty-Free/CORBIS.

Chapter 9
Opener: Getty Images/Image Source/RF; p. 355: Monkey Business Images/Cutcaster/RF; p. 385: Getty Images/Image Source/RF.

Text Credits

Chapter 1
Ralph Waldo Emerson, Philosopher. Adapted from Dr. Auke Tellegen's Multidimensional Personality Questionnaire.

Chapter 2
Adapted from A. Fenigstein, M. F. Scheier, and A. H. Buss, "Public and Private Self-Consciousness: Assessment and Theory," Journal of Consulting and Clinical Psychology 43 (1975): 522–527. Viktor Frankl, Man's Search for Meaning. Boston, MA: Beacon Press, 2006.

Chapter 3
Redford Williams, M.D., a Duke University internist. Nathaniel Branden, Taking Responsibility: Self-Reliance and the Accountable Life. New York, NY: Simon and Schuster, 1997.

Chapter 4
Edward Deci, Why we do what we do: the dynamics of personal autonomy. New York, NY: Putnam's Sons, 1995. Adapted from the Web site www.truth-for-healthy-living.org. Copyright © 1997–2013 Richard Terry Lovelace, MSW, Ph.D. (www.truth-for-healthy-living.org). Reprinted by permission of the author. Originally published in SELF magazine and then by John Wiley & Sons, Inc., in Stress Master.

Chapter 5
Saul Bellow, Novelist. Thomas Hardy, Novelist.

Chapter 6

Henry Ford, automaker. James Baldwin, Novelist. James Michener, Chesapeake. New York, NY: Random House, 1978. Jay Leno, Leading With My Chin. New York, NY: Harper Collins. 1996. JK Rowling, "The Fringe Benefits of Failure, and the Importance of Imagination," Harvard Magazine Inc., June 5, 2008. JK Rowling, "The Fringe Benefits of Failure, and the Importance of Imagination," Harvard Magazine Inc., June 5, 2008. Mark Twain, Novelist. Mark Twain, Novelist.

Chapter 7

Maya Angelou, Novelist. Michael Jordan, Athlete. Michael Jordan, Athlete. Oprah Winfrey. Jim Carrey, Actor.

Chapter 8

Johann Wolfgang von Goethe, Novelist. Queen Elizabeth I of England (1533–1603). Bureau of Labor Statistics, 2006.

Chapter 9

Theodore Roosevelt, Politician.

Openness, 60
Opportunity, goals and, 90, 101, 104
Optimism, 16, 180–185
Overgeneralizing, 208

P

Paraphrasing, 361
Parasympathetic nervous system, 107
Pareto Principle, 312
Park, Inbee, 295
Passive-aggression, 118
Perceiving, 20
Perceptions, 24
Perfectionism, 100
Persistence, 16, 222–224
Personal distance, 354
Personal fulfillment, 4.
    See also Success
Personality
   defined, 59
   traits of, 59–64
   types of, 78, 80
Personalizing, 209
Pessimism, 182–183
Physical barriers to
    communication, 348
Physical needs, 278–279
Physical self, 153, 157
Pitch discrimination, 65
Positive attitude, 182.
    See also Attitude
Positive emotions, 21–22
Positive escape response, 107
Positive motivation, 270–271, 272
Positive regard, 138–139
Positive relationships, 8
Positive self-image, 25.
    See also Self-image
Positive self-talk, 163, 239, 243
Positive stereotypes, 371
Positive thinking, 179–219
   attitude and, 181–183, 194, 201–203
   changing negative thoughts, 211–216
   defined, 180
   distorted thoughts and, 203, 208–211
   failure avoidance, 183–184
   habits and, 185–186, 189–191,
      194, 235, 238–243
   health and, 194–200

importance of, 8, 180–181
   learned helplessness, 184–185
   optimism and, 16, 180–185
   power of, 182
   visualization and, 297
Possible selves, 158, 160
Posture, 354
Pound, Ezra, 180–181
Power
   attitude and, 201–202
   conflict and, 380
   of imagination, 295–296
   of motivation, 270–277
   of positive thinking, 182
   of self-esteem, 128
Precision, 249
Prejudices, 369, 371
Pride, 21
Prime time, 318
Prioritization
   of expenses, 326–330
   of time, 307, 310, 311, 313–314
      (*See also* Time management)
Private self-consciousness, 46
Probing, 169
Problem solving, 20, 256. *See also*
    Decision-making process
Procrastination, 318–322. *See also*
    Time management
Progressive muscle relaxation, 110
Psyche, 17
Psychology
   defined, 17
   goals of, 18–19
   human behavior and, 17–19
   reasons to study, 17–18
   of spending, 331
   understanding, 17–23
Public self-consciousness, 46
Purpose, importance of, 49–51

Q

Questions, 361

R

Rational emotive behavior therapy
    (REBT), 209
Reading, 344, 359
Reality check, 112

Reasoning
   defined, 20
   emotional, 209
Receiver, 348–349
Recognizing, 20
Recreation, to reduce stress, 112
Recreational shopping, 335
Reflecting, 361
Regret, 263
Relational identity, 32
Relationships
   casual, 374–375
   conflict in, 380–382
   conformity, 368–369
   defined, 367
   diversity, 369, 370
   empathy, 244, 371–374
   group, 367–368
   intimacy, 374–375
   positive, 8
   respect and, 382
   self-disclosure, 378
   stereotypes/prejudices, 369, 371
   stress and, 112
   success of, 378–380
Relaxation, stress and, 110
Relevance, 250
Remembering, 20
Resilience, anger and, 121
Resistance, to change, 101, 231–232
Respect, 359–360, 382
Responding, 361
Responsibility, 224–225
Resume, 363
Rewards, used to motivate, 273–277
Role models, 10, 11–13
Roosevelt, Theodore, 343
Rowling, JK, 224
Ryan, Richard M., 275, 283

S

Sadness, 22
Santos, Bill, 2
Sarnoff, David, 281
Savings, 329–330. *See also* Money
    management
Schedule, 315
Scheier, M. F., 47
Schwartz, Daylle Deanna, 143
Security needs, 279–280

ingredients of, 4, 7–8
inner self, 24
psychology of, 17–23
respect and, 382
role models, 10, 11–13
social world, 30, 32–33, 37–38
work and, 71
Support, social, 139–140, 141–142
Sympathetic nervous system, 107

T

Taboos, 349
Taking Responsibility: Self Reliance and the Accountable Life, 225
Talents, measurement of, 64–68
Target, 229
Technology, stress and, 106
Therapy, cognitive, 208
Thinking style, 185
Thinking/thoughts
  all-or-nothing, 208
  creative, 16
  critical, 244–252
  distorted, 203, 208–211
  feelings, and actions, 20–21
  helpless, 208
  negative, 182–183, 194–196, 211–216
  positive (*See* Positive thinking)
Thomèe, Sara, 106
Timbre discrimination, 65
Time management, 306–322
  defined, 306
  procrastination, 318–322
  steps to, 112, 306–318

To-do list, 312, 315
Tolerance, 55
Tonal memory, 65
Traditions, 33
Traits, personality, 59–64
Transferable skills, 69, 71, 75
Triggers, of anger, 119, 120
Trust, success and, 16
Twain, Mark, 239
Tweezers dexterity, 65
Twitter, 143

U

Uncertainty, 261
Unconditional positive regard, 138–139
Unknown self, 378
Uplifts, 106
Upward comparison, 158

V

Values
  conflict and, 380
  culture and, 33
  defined, 52
  self-awareness and, 52, 54–58
  work and, 55, 58
Variable committed expenses, 326
Vega, Suzanne, 222
Verbal/linguistic intelligence, 67
Vicious cycle, 202–203
Visualization, 20, 293, 295–299
Visual/spatial intelligence, 67

Vocabulary building, 356, 359
Vocation, success and, 16
Voice, 354
Voltaire, 224

W

Wal-Mart, 229
Wants, 277–278
Watts, Alan, 373
Wealth, 55, 323. *See also* Money management
Well-being, money and, 323
Wells, Elijah, 268, 302
Wheel of life, 27–29
Williams, Redford, 116
Williams, Serena, 295
Winfrey, Oprah, 286
Wisdom, success and, 17
Women
  body image, 157
  gender identity and, 37–38
  nonverbal communication and, 356
Work
  happiness and, 71
  myths about, 78
  personality types and, 78, 80
  positive thinking at, 190
  rewards received from, 71
  self-awareness and, 71, 78, 80
  stress and (*See* Stress)
  values and, 55, 58
Work ethic, 16
Worry, 190–194
Worthiness, 136